Chinese Foreign Policy

Chinese Foreign Policy

The Maoist Era and its Aftermath

JOSEPH CAMILLERI

University of Washington Press
Seattle

Published in the United States of America by the University of Washington Press, 1980, by arrangement with Martin Robertson & Company Ltd., Oxford, England

Library of Congress Catalog Card Number 80–50686
ISBN 0-295-95776-X

Filmset by Vantage Photosetting Co. Ltd.
Southampton and London
Printed and bound by Richard Clay (The Chaucer Press) Ltd.
Bungay, Suffolk

I have long aspired to reach for the clouds,
Again I come from afar
To climb Chingkangshan, our old haunt.
Past scenes are transformed,
Orioles sing, swallows swirl,
Streams purl everywhere
And the road mounts skyward.
Once Huangyangchieh is passed
No other perilous place calls for a glance.

Wind and thunder are stirring,
Flags and banners are flying
Wherever men live.
Thirty-eight years are fled
With a mere snap of the fingers.
We can clasp the moon in the Ninth Heaven
And seize turtles deep down in the Five Seas:
We'll return amid triumphant song and laughter.
Nothing is hard in this world
If you dare to scale the heights.

MAO TSE-TUNG
('Chingkangshan Revisited')*

* Poem written in 1965 and published for the first time in the January 1976 issue
of the journal *Shikan (Poetry)*

Contents

Preface

With the gradual but steady consolidation of communist rule since the October Revolution of 1949, Chinese policies at home and abroad have come to play an increasingly important role in international relations. For more than a quarter of a century, China's impact on the world was to a very large extent associated with, indeed personified by, the theoretical and practical genius of Mao Zedong. As Chairman of the Chinese Communist Party, founder of the People's Republic, spiritual leader of the nation, and undisputed interpreter within China of Marxist–Leninist doctrine, Mao Zedong exerted almost to the very last days of his life the most profound influence over the domestic and external affairs of his country. It is well to remember, however, that Mao's power was never so absolute as to enable him to shape at will the structure of the communist political system. Indeed, it took several years of institutional consolidation after the victory of 1949 before Mao felt confident enough to hasten the process of collectivization and embark on the Great Leap Forward. Despite the success of the mass mobilizations and political campaigns, the failure of the economy to make the long and rapid strides Mao had expected and the emergence of an entrenched bureaucracy severely eroded Mao's authority and self-confidence. Several more years were to elapse before he could orchestrate the wide-ranging counter-attack on the bureaucratization of party and government that was to be the Cultural Revolution. But even then the social and political ferment unleashed by the Red Guard campaigns could not achieve all the objectives Mao had set himself. Periods of intense ideological struggle and political instability could not be indefinitely maintained and were almost invariably followed by periods of consolidation, institutionalization and centralized planning. To some extent this dialectical development reflected Mao's own philosophical and psychological predisposition as well as the sharp fluctuations in the efficacy of his powerbase and leadership role.

In any case, Chinese policies and the vast economic and social changes unleashed by the Communist revolution cannot be explained purely in terms of the perceptions and organizational skills of a few leaders, however decisive their contribution may have been. Maoism as a movement owed a great deal of its political success to un unerring ability to express clearly but imaginatively not only the material but the emotional and cultural needs and aspirations of a large cross-section of Chinese society. Perhaps the most important legacy of

Mao Zedong thought was its coherent but potent vision of a new social order and its commitment to restore China to her rightful place in the world. In this wider sense, Mao's departure from the centre stage of Chinese politics, coming only a few months after the death of Zhou Enlai, China's most accomplished administrator, spelt the end of an era. With the emergence of new leaders, who do not necessarily share the political and economic priorities of the Maoist model and who are faced with a rapidly changing internal and external environment, it is now possible to assess perhaps a little more objectively the evolution of Chinese foreign policy since 1949.

For purposes of analysis, this study of China's role in the world system divides the period under consideration into three phases: the revolutionary phase (1949–1968); the transitional phase (1969–1973); and the post-revolutionary phase (1973–). Needless to say the dividing line between these three periods is somewhat arbitrary since there are considerable elements of continuity between them just as there are considerable elements of change within each of them. Nevertheless, by defining the distinguishing characteristics of each phase, such a division does help to clarify the changing direction of Chinese foreign policy and places in clearer context the developments of the last few years.

China's conduct in the post-Liberation period was most notable for the way in which the traditional Sino-centric view of the world was blended with a new internationalist outlook. We may legitimately speak of a *revolutionary phase* in so far as Chinese statements and actions during these years consistently challenged the existing world order, the hierarchical structure of the international system, the institutionalized inequality between rich and poor, the tendency towards the bureaucratization of society. The commitment to national self-reliance, the attempt to establish the relevance of China's revolutionary experience for other Third World countries and the conviction that colonialism and neo-colonialism were in rapid decline attested to the Maoist rejection of the status quo. On the other hand, the period also witnessed several compromises with the realities of power and numerous retreats in the light of China's limited military and economic capabilities. Nevertheless, the radical thrust of Chinese domestic and foreign policies, which was partly an expression of her weakness, was never entirely stifled and was evident in her dealings with great and small powers alike. China's tendency during this phase to identify US imperialism as the principal threat to her security and the main obstacle to liberation struggles the world over underlined the convergence of national interests and ideological principles.

However, with the steady deterioration in Sino–Soviet relations, the redefinition of American strategic interests in the wake of the Vietnamese débâcle and increasing internal fatigue resulting from the traumatic events of the Cultural Revolution, the Chinese leadership began to reassess the style and content of its programme. The reappraisal of past policies was to have far-reaching implications for China's external relations. During this *transitional phase*, Peking sought and acquired a new and unprecedented level of international respectability. The twin concepts of 'international disorder' and the 'three worlds' were developed, seemingly under Mao's guidance and inspiration, with a view to enhancing China's diplomatic position without altogether tarnishing her revolutionary reputation. By highlighting the dangers of superpower collusion, Peking was able to put to advantage its continuing dispute with Moscow and the growing strains within both alliance systems, while at the same time improving its own relations with the United States and the developed capitalist world generally.

The new trends in Chinese foreign policy became much clearer with the gradual unfolding of the domestic power struggle which, in fact, preceded Mao's death. The re-emergence of Deng Xiaoping as one of China's most powerful political figures and the subsequent fall of leading radicals and their supporters from positions of influence ushered in a period of intense diplomatic activity and rapidly expanding cooperation with the United States, Japan and Western Europe. During this *post-revolutionary* phase, the attempt to create a new united front to counter alleged Soviet expansionism and the decision to embark on a vast programme of economic modernization with the help of foreign capital and technology were the central concerns giving shape and direction to China's external conduct. Both objectives, which required active cooperation with the West and its anti-communist allies, were far removed from the earlier revolutionary thrust with its emphasis on the worldwide struggle against capitalism and western imperialism.

In order to give added focus to the main themes, this study has chosen to concentrate largely on China's relations with the superpowers, since it is the United States and the Soviet Union which, in different periods, have been perceived by China as posing the most formidable obstacles to the achievement of her interests and objectives. Considerable attention has also been given to the Third World, since relations with the underdeveloped countries of Asia, Africa and Latin America have provided one of the most accurate barometers of China's great power diplomacy and revolutionary commitment. However, in order to analyse the varied and complex issues implicit in the recent evolution of Chinese foreign policy, it was thought useful to examine a little more closely the shifting balance of power in Asia, with particular emphasis on Peking's relations with Japan and Southeast Asia. Clearly, no single survey, however comprehensive or detailed, could hope to do justice to such a large slice of contemporary history. In this sense, the present book offers no more than a partial and preliminary assessment of what is one of the most significant but as yet unfinished political experiments of the twentieth century.

The book has adopted the *pinyin* method of romanization of Chinese words and names, following the new practice of Chinese publications. However, the original spelling in all citations has been kept.

This study would not have been conceived, much less completed, had it not been for the intellectual and moral insights gained from others too numerous to be named individually. Mention must be made, however, of the rewarding period of study I spent in the Department of International Relations at the London School of Economics, where contact with several scholars and, especially, the personal encouragement of Geoffrey Goodwin proved invaluable. I also owe an important though diffuse debt to La Trobe University where I have been teaching for the last seven years; to the Department of Politics for its general support, to the secretarial staff for their wholehearted cooperation, to the libraries for their unfailing assistance, and, of course, to the Social Sciences Research Committee for its generous financial assistance without which this study would not have been possible. I am also deeply indebted to my two research assistants, Noel Murray and Larry Marshall, for their painstaking and methodical work. Finally, may I express my sincere gratitude to my wife whose abundant patience and enthusiasm played such an important part in the realization of this project.

JOSEPH CAMILLERI

August 1979

Romanization of Chinese Names

In keeping with the decision of China's State Council in 1978, this book uses the Chinese phonetic alphabet which standardizes the romanization of Chinese names of persons and places.

In accordance with the new practice, the traditional spelling for 'China' and historical places and persons such as Sun Yat-sen and Confucius has been retained. The main departure from the new convention is the retention of the old spelling for 'Peking' (in preference to 'Beijing').

By way of example, the following are names of significant persons and places according to the Chinese phonetic alphabet. The old spelling is given in parentheses for reference.

Mao Zedong (Mao Tse-tung)
Zhou Enlai (Chou En-lai)
Liu Shaoqi (Liu Shao-chi)
Zhu De (Chu Teh)
Lin Biao (Lin Piao)
Hua Guofeng (Hua Kuo-feng)
Deng Xiaoping (Teng Hsiao-ping)
Li Xiannian (Li Hsien-nien)
Wu De (Wu Teh)
Yu Qiuli (Yu Chiu-li)
Chen Xilian (Chen Hsi-lien)
Geng Biao (Keng Piao)
Ye Jianjing (Yeh Chien-ying)
Wang Dongxing (Wang Tung-hsing)
Nie Rongzhen (Nieh Jung-shen)

Tianjin (Tientsin)
Fuzhou (Foochow)
Guangdong (Kwangtung)
Guangzhou (Kwangchow)
Daqing (Taching)
Nanjing (Nanking)
Dazhai (Tachai)
Xinjiang (Sinkiang)
Xiamen (Amoy)
Yanan (Yenan)
Shandong (Shantung)
Qingdao (Tsingtao)
Taibei (Taipei)

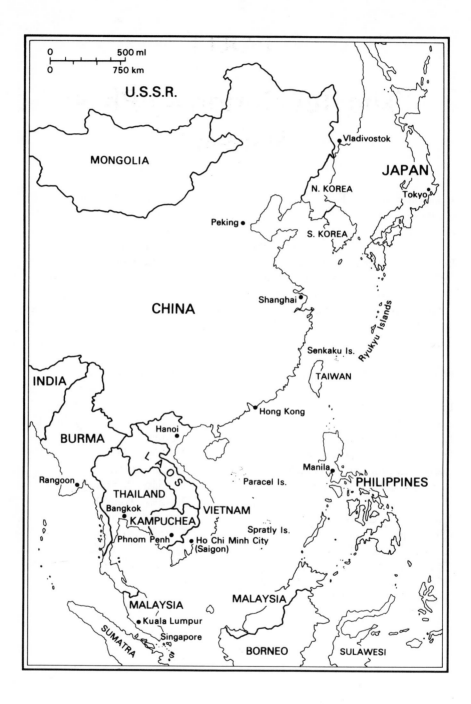

PART I

The Revolutionary Phase
1949–68

CHAPTER 1

Perception and Motivation

For the greater part of the twentieth century China has tended to act as a dissatisfied power, anxious to modify the structure of the international system and her own role within it. The sources of this dissatisfaction are to be found primarily in China's recent history, for it is precisely this historical experience that explains the practical and emotional appeal of communist ideology and its success in blending the universal prescriptions of Marxism–Leninism with China's national aspirations. The Maoist rejection of the status quo may best be understood as the simultaneous response to China's domestic situation on the one hand and to her external environment on the other.

The widespread discontent experienced by modern China is largely attributable to the continuing memory of the humiliation she suffered at the hands of foreign powers throughout the nineteenth and a good part of the twentieth century. Central to the 'opening of China' by the West was the opium trade and the wars that it precipitated in 1840–42 and 1856–60. Threatened by the superior military power of the western countries, China was forced to accede to a series of 'unequal treaties', in which she agreed to indemnify Britain, France, Japan and other foreign powers for large amounts of money and to open almost all important Chinese ports to them. Apart from extra-territoriality and the most favoured nation principle, the treaties of Nanjing, Tianjin and Peking provided the West with various privileges, including control over the rate and collection of trade tariffs, residential and travel rights and the cession of many Chinese territories including Hong Kong, Kowloon, Taiwan and the vast Amur and Ussuri river basins. By the end of the nineteenth century, much of China had been divided into competing spheres of influence between Britain, Russia, Japan, France and Germany.[1] Within these spheres of interest the foreign power had complete jurisdiction, free to build railways, establish military bases and exploit natural resources.

Western penetration was not limited, however, to those areas that formed the traditional core of the Chinese empire, but extended to almost every important tributary state. The territories alienated from Chinese sovereignty or suzerainty by the imperialist powers included Bhutan, Sakhalin, Indochina, Siam, Burma, Sikhim, Malaya, Korea and Nepal.[2] The resulting feeling of humiliation and resentment cultivated in the minds of Chinese people found frequent expression in the writings of Sun Yat-sen, the founding father of Republican China:

3

We are the poorest and the weakest country in the world, occupying the lowest position in world affairs; people of other countries are the carving knife and the serving dish while we are the fish and the meat.[3]

The same burning aspiration to rid the country of the foreigner and to restore China to the dominant position she had occupied under the imperial Middle Kingdom was to dominate Mao's conception of China's destiny:

All these wars of aggression, together with political, economic and cultural aggression and oppression, have caused the Chinese to hate imperialism, made them stop and think, 'What is all this about?' and compelled them to bring their revolutionary spirit into full play and become united through struggle.[4]

It is true that by the time the Communists had defeated their opponents in October 1949, the 'unequal treaty' system had been dealt a decisive blow, but China still saw herself as a recent semi-colony that had only just emancipated herself and had yet to secure her proper place in the world.

In reality, until western penetration China's external environment had remained inextricably tied to her internal order. In the words of John Fairbank, '. . . when the barbarians were not submissive abroad, rebels might more easily arise within'.[5] Accordingly, successive dynasties accepted and fostered the perception of China as the Middle Kingdom, the only great empire on earth, the only civilization, the centre of the world. The mystical influence of the Emperor or Son of Heaven extended not only throughout China proper but outward beyond her borders bestowing order and peace on all mankind. As intermediary between heaven and earth, the source of all law and the fount of all authority, the Emperor enjoyed the mandate to rule all men. This theoretical universality of imperial rule posed considerable problems for China's foreign relations. All non-Chinese states and peoples were expected in theory to accept the supremacy of the Son of Heaven, but theory could not always be easily squared with fact. Although the Manchus, Mongols, Uighur Turks, Tibetans and others were included in the Chinese world order, their cultures were fundamentally different from those of China. Their largely pastoral–nomadic economies and their predominantly tribal political organization were not susceptible of sinicization. Similarly to the south, geographical barriers and the cultural independence of Southeast Asian societies prevented the inclusion of these peoples into the Confucian state, created and held together primarily through the universal acceptance of social practices and principles. These adjacent tribes or states were therefore considered barbarian in so far as they were not part of the Heavenly Kingdom, but in so far as they accepted the supreme position of the Chinese Emperor, observed certain ceremonies and presented tribute, they were given a place in the all-embracing Chinese political and moral order.

The tributary system thus became the keystone of imperial Chinese diplomacy. Those barbarians who wished to participate in the benefits of Chinese civilization were expected to present tribute memorials of various sorts on appropriate statutory occasions as well as symbolic tributes of local products and to perform the appropriate ceremonies of the imperial court, notably the Kotow, the three kneelings and nine prostrations. In return non-Chinese rulers were given imperial gifts, a patent of appointment and an official seal for use in correspondence, a noble rank in the imperial hierarchy and certain privileges of trade at the frontier and the capital.[6] The Confucian world order consisted then of a loosely connected system of tributary states in which China occupied the dominant position. This network of tributary relations between the Middle Kingdom and its vassals was the only framework of foreign relations known to traditional China.

The Sino-centric perception of the world, which theoretically owed its origins to the universal pre-eminence of the Son of Heaven, may be said to have found practical expression in a hierarchical system operating in concentric circles of decreasing efficacy. The point to note is that the cultural subordination of all local authorities and non-Chinese regimes in the East Asian area remained the overarching organizational principle of the Chinese imperial edifice. The need to maintain Chinese superiority often in the face of military weakness necessitated such strategies as cessation of contact, cultural absorption of the foreigner, offering of material and other inducements, divide and rule tactics, and, in extreme cases, acceptance of barbarian rulers at the apex of the Chinese Empire. But whatever the attempted solution to the problem of imperial authority, the principle of Chinese superiority was never abandoned. It is precisely this principle that sharply differentiated the Chinese world order from the European balance of power system based on the notion of legally equal sovereign states.

In spite of the many fluctuations in imperial fortunes, at no point in its history was the monolithic prestige of the Chinese empire effectively challenged by any rival state. It is not surprising, therefore, that traditional China should have remained immune to western norms of international diplomacy even after European economic, political, cultural and technological penetration had effectively transformed the Chinese state into a tributary of the West. But the Chinese perception of world order could not indefinitely defy the facts of China's internal and external environment. However deeply ingrained, the Sino-centric view of the universe could not withstand the onslaught of western imperialism and the accompanying disintegration of the Chinese political order. By the turn of the century the concept of a Chinese universal kingship had irrevocably collapsed.

The sharp and revolutionary break in the Chinese image of world order first became apparent in the 1890s with the gradual acceptance of the western multi-state system and the hesitant but futile efforts to transform the empire into a constitutional monarchy. This trend was subsequently confirmed with the growth of Chinese nationalism and the willingness of the Nationalist government to engage in international transactions in accordance with the principle of national sovereignty. But the recognition that China no longer occupied the central position in the international order, and that this order was based on concepts entirely different from those that had formed the basis of the traditional Chinese cosmology, did not mean that Chinese society or its leaders accepted this situation with enthusiasm or equanimity.

It was the function of Maoist ideology to express and articulate China's profound sense of humiliation, bitterness and dissatisfaction, and to adjust the Chinese view of the world so that China might once again play a pivotal role in the affairs of the world. By replacing the Confucian ideology with the twin western doctrines of nationalism and communism, and by assimilating them to Chinese ways so as to limit the full force of western influence, Chinese Marxism was to provide the basis for realizing the almost unlimited potential of China's human and material resources.

In spite of its many internal differences on strategy and tactics, the Chinese Communist leadership was at one in expressing the disproportion between China's power potential and her actual influence and status on the international stage. In his speech to the First Plenary Session of the Chinese People's Political Consultative Conference in September 1949, Mao made abundantly clear his view of China's vocation as a great power and civilization:

> Our nation will never again be an insulted nation. We have stood up. Our revolution has gained the sympathy and acclamation of the broad masses throughout the world. . . . The era in which the Chinese were regarded as uncivilized is now over.[7]

The emphasis on economic reconstruction, the mobilization of national resources in the military field and in nuclear technology and above all the ideological commitment to the 'People's Revolution' were all designed to bring about the realization of China's potential. But the Maoist attempt to develop China's power and assert her independence was to incur the antagonism of both superpowers. Within months of the Communist victory, China was to be subjected to a carefully orchestrated policy of diplomatic isolation and eventually surrounded by a semi-circle of hostile American bases stretching from Japan to Thailand.

Opposition to Prevailing Equilibrium

Because of the profound disenchantment with the dominant structures and patterns of international interaction, the Chinese challenge to the prevailing equilibrium, at least during the period that stretched from Liberation to the Cultural Revolution, was both radical and wide-ranging. By adopting the precepts of an internationalist ideology while at the same time refusing to accept as ultimate any truth that had its origins outside China, Maoism transformed the Marxist–Leninist world view into an instrument peculiarly suited to China's traditional perceptions and current needs. The unique blend of nationalism and internationalism, which formed the basis of Mao's thought, became a theoretical and practical tool enabling China to question the hegemonic ambitions of the two superpowers and the bipolar model of inter-state relations that emerged soon after the conclusion of World War II.

It is worth noting that, both before and after Liberation, the Chinese Communist leadership sought to relate China's domestic revolution to the international situation.[8] Throughout the protracted struggle against the Kuomintang, Mao constantly referred to events outside China and to the policies of other powers for they represented obstacles or opportunities that the revolutionary movement could not overlook when charting its own course. Indeed, one of the main functions of the Chinese revolution, viewed by the Maoist leadership largely in terms of 'the contradiction between imperialism and the Chinese nation',[9] was China's emancipation from her semi-colonial and semi-feudal status. Mao, in fact, saw the massive impoverishment of the Chinese peasantry as 'the result of the collusion of foreign imperialism and domestic feudalism'.[10] These two evils had to be eradicated simultaneously if China was to be restored to a prosperous and self-respecting society. Never again would China allow her domestic affairs to be governed by the decisions of a foreign power.

It is true that in the period immediately after Liberation, Mao and his colleagues sought to maintain close relations with the Soviet Union and to avoid open disagreement with Soviet leaders even though significant differences had already emerged between the two sides. However, there is reason to believe that the new Sino–Soviet relationship was not simply an ideological alliance but a marriage of convenience in which Peking intended to retain a considerable degree of independence. On the other hand, it is equally true that in the immediate aftermath of the Communist victory it was the United States that was considered by the Maoist leadership to be the major stumbling block to the realization of Chinese objectives and aspirations.

The Communist leaders could not easily forget the very considerable military and economic assistance that the United States had supplied to the Kuomintang. In his vehement attack on the US White Paper *United States Relations with China* published by the US State Department on 5 August 1949, Mao accused the United States of a host of military activities designed to help Chiang Kai-shek win the civil war. Apart from supplying money, munitions and advisers, the United States was accused of participating directly in the war, of stationing its troops in major Chinese cities, of taking aerial photographs of China's strategic areas, and of controlling all of China's air space.[11] If the United States refrained from despatching large forces to support the Nationalists, it was not because of any objection in principle but mainly on grounds of expediency, for fear of domestic and international opposition.[12]

A characteristic feature of the Maoist denunciation of American policy, which was to be consistently maintained throughout the years of Sino–American friction, was the sharp distinction drawn between the actions of the US government and the attitudes of the American public, between the 'public opinion of Wall Street' and the 'public opinion of the American people'.[13] Indeed, during the latter years of the civil war Mao had made every attempt to persuade the Americans to adopt an even-handed position between the Communists and the Kuomintang. He welcomed American participation in the war against Japan, and described cooperation between the United States and the Chinese Communist Party as 'beneficial and satisfactory to all concerned'.[14] Mao's advice, however, was rejected by the Roosevelt administration, which adopted instead a policy of unilateral support for Chiang Kai-shek. After the defeat of the Nationalist forces, Mao was still willing to entertain the possibility that some time in the future the ties between the two nations could develop 'to the point of the "closest friendship" ',[15] but for the moment serious obstacles existed as a result of the ties, the propaganda and the 'many filthy tricks' perpetrated by 'the Chinese and US reactionaries'.[16]

According to Mao, the Chinese people's democratic revolution, because of its obvious anti-imperialist character, was bound to incur the hostility of the imperialists. The United States, now the most formidable of the remaining imperialist powers following the defeat of fascist Germany, Italy and Japan, was represented as the greatest threat to world peace, and the American participation in the Chinese civil war as 'an important component of the US imperialist policy of worldwide aggression since World War II'.[17] In due course, the analysis of US imperialism was to be extended and refined to take account of the expanding economic and strategic objectives of American monopoly capital.[18] Imperialist oppression and exploitation, spearheaded by the United States, was advanced as 'the main reason for the retarded economic development of many Asian, African and Latin American countries' and 'a clean sweep of colonialist economic relationships' was claimed to be the only way to 'build independent and prosperous national economies'.[19]

But China's unfavourable external environment and the dominance of the United States within the international system were not regarded as permanent. In a major address to the eleventh enlarged session of the Supreme State Conference in February 1957, Mao painted an optimistic picture of China's future domestic and international situation.[20] Even as early as 1947, Mao was confidently predicting the end of the era of imperialism. While acknowledging the long-term potential of the masses of the people in the imperialist countries themselves, the Chinese believed that the most potent source of revolution would remain for the foreseeable future in the colonies and semi-colonies, and especially in those parts of the Third World where US imperialism was seeking to maintain its control through armed intervention and the establishment of military bases. The American policy of containment and the western system of military alliances represented in Mao's view a facade of strength that would eventually crumble under the impact of the worldwide anti-imperialist struggle. Irreconcilable domestic and international contradictions would ultimately disintegrate the 'superficial and transient' power of the United States.[21] The struggle against American imperialism was, at least for the time being, to be waged outside United States borders by all nations striving to liberate themselves from the grip of American economic and military power. World capitalism was to be eroded by action at its periphery rather than by a devastating blow at its centre.

As with the struggle against the Kuomintang, so with the fight against imperialism the Chinese Communist leadership envisaged a merger of the forces of socialism and nationalism. The fusion of the forces of anti-imperialism, anti-neo-colonialism and anti-capitalism was to become the distinctive element in Mao's conception of 'people's war'. Applying the Chinese experience to the international situation, China's leaders elevated the struggle against colonialism and neo-colonialism in the Third World to a much higher level of historical significance than had been contemplated by either Lenin or Stalin. Convinced of the revolutionary potential of peasant mobilization, Mao envisaged a growing confrontation in different parts of the world between the United States and national liberation movements.[22] Although the possibility of a total nuclear war was never excluded, China regarded as much more likely a series of protracted struggles, especially in the newly independent states of Asia and Africa, as well as in Latin America, that would increasingly over-extend and finally sap the strength of the United States.

According to the Chinese the process of liberation had been gaining momentum throughout the post-1945 period. The mood of revolutionary optimism reached its height in Lin Biao's celebrated statement of September 1965:

> Since World War II and the succeeding years of revolutionary upsurge, there has been a great rise in the level of political consciousness and the degree of organization of the people in all countries, and their capacity for mutual support and aid has greatly increased.[23]

Great emphasis was placed by Lin Biao on the mutually reinforcing character of these struggles and on the increasing commitment that the United States felt obliged to make in an effort to suppress or contain them.[24] His analysis was in keeping with previous official Chinese interpretations of the contemporary world situation which pointed to four 'fundamental contradictions', namely those between the socialist and imperialist camps, between the proletariat and the bourgeoisie in capitalist countries, between the oppressed nations and imperialism, and among the imperialist countries themselves.[25] But all four contradictions were said to be concentrated in Asia, Africa and Latin America, for these were the 'storm centre of world revolution'.[26] China had always considered the Third World, propelled by rising nationalist and economic aspirations, to be the scene of the most profound political changes. Lin Biao's subsequent characterization of the Third World nations as 'the rural areas of the world', which would progressively encircle 'the cities of the world', that is, North America and Western Europe, simply provided a more emphatic formulation of an already well-established analysis.

Needless to say, the focal position ascribed by Lin Biao to the anti-imperialist movement of Asia, Africa and Latin America constituted an exceedingly optimistic assessment of the revolutionary potential of these societies. While grudgingly admitting that American military and economic power had also grown since World War II, he preferred to stress the vulnerability of the American position by pointing to the dispersion of American resources and the increasing distance between the military conflicts in which the United States was involved and its supply lines.[27]

Not surprisingly, the refusal of Soviet leaders to accept the Chinese appraisal of the revolutionary potential of the Third World and Khrushchev's determination to pursue the policy of 'peaceful coexistence' with the United States became a major factor in the Sino–Soviet split. Although Peking was willing to accept the notion of peaceful coexistence as a norm in interstate relations, it was totally opposed to any suggestion of downgrading the importance it attached to the anti-imperialist struggle. State-to-state relations were not to be confused with the requirements of the class struggle and the overthrow of colonial oppression.[28] The decisive role attributed to the revolutionary struggles of the oppressed people and nations of the Third World and the consequent estrangement from Moscow eventually compelled Peking to redefine its formulation of the four major contradictions in the world so as to take account of its revised assessment of Soviet policies. Far from performing the leading role within the socialist camp, the Soviet Union had now assumed an imperialist character, making it an enemy of socialism and of the oppressed nations, a party to inter-imperialist rivalries and the victim of internal contradictions between the proletariat and the bourgeoisie.[29] By the mid-1960s, China was strenuously trying to portray herself as the great champion of national liberation struggles and the arch opponent of 'aggression and oppression by US imperialism and Soviet revisionism'.[30]

At this point, the question arises: was Chinese foreign policy during the 1950s and 1960s based on a realistic understanding of the nature of American and Soviet power and of the implications of the 'balance of terror'? This is a large and complex question to which we shall need to return. For the moment suffice it to say that China's revolutionary commitment was predicated on psychological as much as on strategic considerations. When confronted with the formidable obstacles facing the enterprise of undermining the dominance of the two superpowers, Mao and his associates tended to point to China's own experience and to the overwhelming odds that had to be overcome before the final victory of October 1949. The key to the Communist success, which was preceded by 'hundreds of struggles, great and small, military and political, economic and cultural, with bloodshed and without bloodshed . . .',[31] lay in the persistence, patience and ingenuity with which the Chinese Communist leaders were able to exploit the enemy's internal divisions and the skill with which they used their limited resources to attack the enemy at his most vulnerable points. Even when the fortunes of the struggle had reached their lowest ebb, the Maoist outlook remained confident that the balance of forces both at home and abroad would ultimately swing in favour of the revolutionary cause.

By the mid-1950s, Mao was arguing that the international situation had reached a new turning point. At the Moscow meeting of representatives of Communist and Workers' Parties of socialist countries in November 1957, he argued that there were now two winds in the world, the East wind and the West wind, and that 'the East wind [was] prevailing over the West wind'.[32] But on what grounds could this rather surprising conclusion be justified? Mao defended his thesis by pointing to the numerical superiority of the anti-imperialist camp. Moreover, despite external appearances of wealth and power, the West was considered to be in a state of decay. Though economically advanced, it was politically 'corrupt and backward'.[33] In the words of one observer, Mao was to give the Marxist analysis of the capitalist West 'an individual and characteristic dialectical twist', enabling him to argue that the increasing aggressiveness of imperialism was a direct consequence of the growing strength of the socialist world.[34]

This favourable, yet threatening, situation called for a determined and uncompromising response from the socialist world and particularly from Moscow. As it became more and more obvious that the Soviet leadership would not accept this challenge, Chinese foreign policy was inevitably driven towards a policy of economic and military self-reliance. Paralleling this shift and the deterioration in Sino-Soviet relations was the introduction of a new element in Chinese analysis of the international situation which stressed the domestic economic and political crises now confronting the two superpowers and the debilitating effect of their imperialist rivalries.[35] Clearly, the Maoist support for liberation struggles was an integral part of China's policies towards the two superpowers and an instrument for preventing the United States and the Soviet Union from freezing the international status quo to the detriment of Chinese interests. By depicting herself as the champion of revolutionary causes, China could make use of her enhanced international prestige in the Third World to embarrass the Soviet Union and gain additional leverage in her relations with the United States.

China's decision to reject the bipolar equilibrium, to oppose both Soviet and American hegemony, is no doubt largely explicable in terms of her historical experience, geopolitical position and ideological outlook. At the same time, such an explanation would remain incomplete if it did not give adequate attention to Mao's own personal self-assertive style and to his emphasis on dialectical analysis and confrontation politics. Whereas other communist leaders were often led to advocate acceptance of established norms, avoidance of conflict in the face of a powerful enemy and dependence on foreign models of development, Mao steadfastly stressed the themes of criticism and self-criticism, struggle and uninterrupted revolution, independence and self-reliance. Mao's most innovative reaction against tradition has been accurately described in terms of the need to liberate 'in disciplined politicized fashion the aggressive emotions which were denied legitimate expression in the political culture of dependency'.[36] Perhaps Mao's most important contribution was his capacity to bring together thought and action, theory and practice, in the political task of liberation.

Underlying Ideology

Given the importance attached by Mao to the revolutionary struggle against Chiang Kai-shek's government, it would be useful to examine, however briefly, the doctrinal and strategic considerations that determined the behaviour of the Chinese Communist Party (CCP) from the 1920s to the 1940s. Mao repeatedly underlined the need to treat Marxist–Leninist doctrine not as dogma but as a guide to action. His primary concern was always the concrete application of Marxism to the specific conditions currently prevailing in China.[37] On three occasions, in 1924, 1935 and 1945, the attitude to be adopted towards the bourgeoisie posed a major doctrinal issue for the Chinese Communist leadership. At stake was the practical problem of alliances.

In answer to the question: 'Who are our enemies? Who are our friends?'[38] Mao Zedong's analysis led him to distinguish five categories:

(a) the landlord class and the comprador class (comprising capitalists and merchants and regarded as the vassals of the international bourgeoisie);

(b) the middle bourgeoisie (internally divided, with some of its members opting for revolution, and others for the counter-revolution);

(c) the petty bourgeoisie (consisting of three groups: (i) those who had satisfied their own needs; (ii) those who had satisfied their basic needs, but who regarded foreigners as exploiters, while doubting the success of the anti-imperialist movement; (iii) those whose living condition was constantly deteriorating);

(d) the semi-proletariat (made up of peasants, farm labourers and craftsmen most of whom were inspired by a revolutionary zeal to change the status quo);

(e) the proletariat (comprising some two million workers, sailors, miners, factory workers, who were firmly dedicated to the revolutionary cause).

Summing up the conclusions to be derived from this analysis, Mao stated:

> . . . our enemies are all those in league with imperialism – the warlords, the bureaucrats, the comprador class, the big landlord class and the reactionary section of the intelligentsia attached to them. The leading force in our revolution is the industrial proletariat. Our closest friends are the entire semi-proletariat and petty bourgeoisie. As for the vacillating middle bourgeoisie, their right-wing may become our enemy and their left-wing may become our friend – but we must be constantly on our guard and not let them create confusion within our ranks.[39]

In other words, western capitalism had created within China two main categories of people, a small minority prepared to do the bidding of the foreigner and a large majority consisting of the working class, the peasantry, the urban lower middle class, the nationalist middle class, and the intellectuals coming from these classes. It was the task of this majority group to act as 'the gravediggers of imperialism'.[40]

The significance of this analysis of Chinese society for revolutionary movements in the post-1945 period is to be found in the Maoist reliance on the rural 'semi-proletariat', which subsequently led to the theory of the establishment of rural revolutionary base areas and the encirclement of cities from the countryside. Once the Communist leadership gained power in China, Peking began to advance the claim, on the basis of China's prolonged and varied experience in fighting colonialism and the decisive victory of her revolution, that the Maoist liberation strategy had validity beyond China's borders and was of universal practical importance for the contemporary struggle of all the oppressed peoples and nations of the world.[41]

Given that Asia, Africa and Latin America comprised predominantly colonized, peasant-based societies, China concluded that they were likely to be the scene of prolonged liberation struggles. In Maoist terms, there were two main possibilities for revolution open to the underdeveloped world: either the traditional national democratic revolution led by the national bourgeoisie and committed to the elimination of foreign control and to the abolition of the feudal structure of society, or the new national democratic revolution led by the proletariat, and the Marxist–Leninist revolutionary party, as a transitional step towards a fully fledged socialist revolution.[42] If Chinese statements often tended to blur the distinction between the two revolutionary strategies, it was largely in order to highlight their common inspiration and common enemy, namely the elimination of feudalism and the defeat of imperialism. In this sense, a large number of Third World countries, including Korea, Vietnam, Cuba, Indonesia, Algeria and Angola, could be considered as having experienced wars of national liberation, since they were all committed to the expulsion of the colonial authority and the establishment of national independence.

Lin Biao's article of September 1965, written to commemorate the twentieth anniversary of the Chinese triumph over Japan, argued that, though the classes leading these people's wars might vary, the victories in these people's wars had by their very nature 'weakened and pinned down the forces of imperialism'.[43] Vietnam was cited as the most convincing current example of a victim of aggression defeating US imperialism.[44] But Lin Biao was very careful to stress that no national liberation movement could depend for its success solely or even primarily on external support.[45] It is precisely this aspect of Maoist doctrine that enabled Chinese foreign policy to combine a certain degree of revolutionary romanticism with a considerable measure of political pragmatism and to encourage resistance against oppression while at the same time avoiding any specific commitments. Following an interview with Mao Zedong, Edgar Snow reported in 1965 the Chairman's affirmation that there were no Chinese forces in North Vietnam or anywhere else in Southeast Asia. China had no troops outside her own frontiers. China gave support for revolutionary movements but not by sending troops.[46]

What then was to be the real nature and extent of Chinese support for other national liberation struggles? Apart from the supply of military equipment, training and propaganda facilities as well as financial assistance, the most important form of aid was to be the moral and psychological encouragement provided by Chinese foreign policy and the very example of China's revolutionary experience. The Maoist strategy, with its emphasis on communist leadership, the correct implementation of a united front policy, reliance on the peasantry and the establishment of rural bases, the strategy and tactics of protracted armed struggle and the policy of self-reliance,[47] had resulted in the Communist victory of 1949 and provided the invincible optimism so necessary to the triumph of all revolutionary struggles. Perhaps the clearest expression of the scope and limits of China's role in other people's wars was given by the Chinese Foreign Minister, Chen Yi:

> The question of world revolution is one for the countries concerned. If countries are not ripe for revolution, then China cannot do anything about it. However, China will support revolutions against imperialism and oppression. . . . We are Marxists. We must support them! We don't care if we hurt the feelings of the United States, or even of Mr Khrushchev. We can't exchange this for our friendship with the oppressed people, but it must be noted, Chinese troops will not cross our borders to advance revolutions.[48]

A careful reading of the Maoist philosophy suggests that the success of the revolution depends much more on the zeal of the revolutionary than on the superiority of his weapons. In other words, no matter how advanced the military technology of the adversary, the outcome of war is ultimately determined 'by the political consciousness of the men, by their courage and spirit of sacrifice'.[49] The Maoist conviction has been that if the revolutionary holds fast to his long-term objective and does not confuse temporary retreat with surrender, he will be able to wage a protracted struggle for as long as is necessary, engaging in a major military confrontation only when conditions are favourable to him. Having accepted change as the law of history, the revolutionary knows that no setback, however serious or prolonged, can be permanent. Nor is the acceptance of change a passive act. Like a mountain to be moved, resistance against oppression defines the purpose of the revolutionary and bestows meaning on history.[50]

War, however, is not viewed as an end in itself or as a direct consequence of the revolutionary's ideology. Rather, it is 'the product of imperialism and the system of exploitation of man by man'.[51] Reference has already been made to the way in which China's leaders sought to apply their revolutionary experience to the liberation struggles of Asia, Africa and Latin America. There were nevertheless frequent shifts of emphasis in attitudes to the Third World, usually in response to Peking's fluctuating relationship with the two superpowers. Prior to 1958, the Chinese had sought to project a more moderate image and, in an effort to avoid provoking the Russians, tended to de-emphasize their own revolutionary model. By the late 1950s, the Chinese, having perceived the beginnings of a new revolutionary upsurge throughout the Third World, became increasingly vehement in their attacks on US imperialism. From August 1963 to May 1970, Mao made eight separate statements calling upon the people of the world to unite in the struggle against imperialism. His May 1970 statement described US imperialism as 'a huge monster . . . now in the throes of its death-bed struggle', and reaffirmed the thesis that 'the people of a small country can defeat aggression by a big country', provided they rise up and take their destiny in their own hands.[52] During the Cultural Revolution of 1966–68 the Peking press portrayed Mao Zedong thought as a major new contribution to Marxism–Leninism involving the elaboration of both the principles and the organization necessary for the effective transition to communism.[53]

The Cultural Revolution, although arising primarily from China's internal situation, was also inspired by foreign policy considerations. In 1964–65, the escalation of the war in Southeast Asia, as reflected in the bombing of North Vietnam and the implied threat to China, led to a tense debate within China as well as between China and the Soviet Union. Fearing the possibility of an American nuclear attack, many political and military elements within the Chinese power structure, led by such men as the former Chief of Staff Marshal Lo Ruiqing, were calling for a rapprochement with Moscow and for greater moderation in Mao's radical domestic reforms as well as in his polarizing policies in the Third World. It is probably at this point that Mao, assisted by his more radical associates, decided on some drastic surgery both of the Communist leadership and of the whole body politic in order to create a popular revolutionary movement that would be consistent with and give permanence to his dynamic and ambitious vision of a transformed domestic and world order.

Although the Cultural Revolution was certainly a traumatic experience for both China and the outside world, it did not represent a radical departure from the existing Chinese Communist outlook. Since 1949, Peking had always perceived the world as engaged in a protracted and bitter struggle. Central to the Chinese understanding of the existing system of states was the expectation of a profound shift in the global balance of power as well as of radical structural change within domestic society. Conscious of the dialectical development of international forces, Chinese leaders were extremely attentive to the contradictions inherent in a constantly changing international situation.

In an effort to influence the socioeconomic forces at work outside China's borders, Chinese foreign policy, while taking account of the importance of conventional diplomacy, attempted to make use of other tools, both overt and covert. Even in its official propaganda, Peking often made explicit its intention to influence the social forces, economic conditions or political trends prevailing in various countries at any given time for the specific purpose of removing those ruling elites variously described as 'imperialist', 'neo-colonialist', 'reactionary' or 'counter-revolutionary'. In order to advance this rather ambitious undertaking, China repeatedly advocated a 'united front' strategy in order to bring together all actual or potential supporters of the revolutionary struggle, whether they belonged to 'national' or 'class' forces, and to mobilize their joint resources, preferably under communist leadership. Mao had made use of this strategy when he joined with the Nationalist forces, in spite of Kuomintang provocations, in order to oppose Japanese aggression. He was to rely on exactly the same strategy in the last phase of the Chinese revolution when the Communists were able to gain the support not only of the peasantry but of the intelligentsia and other social strata disadvantaged and embittered by the corruption, nepotism, misgovernment and inefficiency of the Kuomintang.

Transposing this domestic strategy to the international plane, Chinese foreign policy sought to portray the 'forces of Marxism–Leninism' as the core of a worldwide united front against 'imperialism, reaction and modern revisionism'. Just as the Chinese Communist Party had been the determining factor in the domestic united front during China's revolution, so revolutionary China would now participate and play a leading role in the 'broadest possible united front' against US imperialism. The concept was given its most forthright exposition by Mao himself in January 1964:

> The people 'of the countries of the socialist camp should unite, the people of the countries of Asia, Africa and Latin America should unite, the people of the continents of the world should unite, all peace-loving countries and all countries that are subject to US aggression and control, interference and bullying should unite and form the broadest possible united front to oppose the US imperialist policies of aggression and war and to safeguard world peace.[54]

The shifts in China's foreign policy from Liberation to the Cultural Revolution may thus be interpreted not in terms of the oscillation between acceptance and rejection of the united front principle, but rather in terms of the changing definitions of the united front. To this extent, the contrast between the relative restraint displayed at the 1955 Bandung Conference and the militancy of the Red Guard campaigns of 1967 may be understood in terms of the changing realities of China's external environment at least as much as of her internal situation.

Power Realities

While fully recognizing China's ideological perception of the international system and her revolutionary motivation, the fact remains that Chinese foreign policy, whether or not it liked the prevailing international order, could neither dominate nor escape from it. Whatever the aspirations of her leaders, China could not but act as a state in a system of sovereign states. Moreover, China's capacity to act on the international stage was strictly governed by the nature of her domestic base and the measure of her national power. China's international conduct was bound to reflect the socioeconomic needs of an underdeveloped country in the process of rapid economic and political change. On the other hand, it is equally true to say that China's revolutionary tactics were peculiarly suited not only to her Marxist–Leninist ideology but to the natural tendency of a dissatisfied power to challenge the existing international political order. In other words, China's ideologically motivated behaviour in the 1950s and 1960s can be shown to have been consistent with both revolutionary orthodoxy and considerations of power, security and prestige.[55]

As we have already seen, China's Sino-centric view of the world prevailed long before the European state system had come into existence and paid little attention to formal state boundaries. The essence of this view was that power and authority emanated from the centre of the Chinese empire and that they radiated outwards, declining with distance and accessibility. This partial model has been analysed in some detail by John K. Fairbank[56] who postulates a series of concentric zones, overlapping in some areas, but largely distinct, each possessing a different relationship with the core of the Chinese state. A similar analysis is offered by Norton Ginsburg who examines this relationship in terms of the distance between the zone and the centre and the fluctuation in the degree of power and authority enjoyed by the centre.[57] This spatial framework may be outlined as follows:

Zone 1 (Core)
    China proper (eighteen provinces) where control has been continuous from Han times, extending from the Great Wall in the North to Indochina in the South, and from the western plateaux to the East China Sea.
Zone 2 (Sinic Zone)
    area including the remaining 60 per cent of modern China and comprising Tibet, Manchuria, Outer Mongolia, the offshore islands, as well as several tributary states, such as Korea and Annam.
Zone 3 (Inner Asian Zone)
    area covering most other tributary states along the Chinese border, such as the Ryukyu Islands, Burma, Cambodia, Laos, the Himalayan States, Malaya, part of Borneo and, for a brief period, Japan.
Zone 4 (Outer Asian Zone)
    area covering the rest of the countries in Asia, including India, Pakistan, Ceylon, Indonesia, New Guinea and the Philippines.
Zone 5 (Great Beyond)
    area covering countries in Europe, America and Africa, regarded as 'barbaric'.

There is no reason to believe that this cultural, geographic and strategic view of the outside world had altogether disappeared with the advent of China's Communist leadership. The model may be said to have retained considerable relevance for Chinese foreign policy in so far as that policy has to contend with certain inescapable political and geographical realities. On the other hand, the course of modern history had produced significant ideological and territorial changes in the political map of the world which made it impossible for China to return to her traditional system of foreign relations. The Maoist perception of world order therefore, differed, significantly from the traditional model, but at the same time retained the fundamental principle of a radius of influence emanating from the centre and reaching outwards, though gradually declining as a result of ideological and geographical distance. While the traditional model was based on an entirely different philosophical system, and while it identified security with a policy of the status quo rather than the ideology of change, nevertheless its hierarchical conception had left its mark on Chinese perceptions and was most evident in Communist China's determination to remove all alien influence from her periphery. In this sense, the Maoist model of world order, which prevailed during the first phase of Communist China's foreign policy, may also be represented by a number of concentric zones:

Zone 1—the area incorporated by the modern Chinese state, with only a few boundaries still in dispute (principally those with India and the Soviet Union). Taiwan may be regarded as an integral part of this zone, since the continuing dispute relates to the legitimacy of the Nationalist government rather than to China's territorial integrity.

Zone 2—this area, considered by China as essential to her security and other national interests, covered mainly the border areas, more specifically North Korea, Outer Mongolia, Burma and Indochina. It was not so much a direct sphere of influence as a buffer zone, in which China's minimal objective was to prevent the military presence of other great powers.

Zone 3—often designated as the 'intermediate zone', this area comprised the remaining parts of East, South and Southeast Asia, as well as the Middle East, black Africa and Latin America. Although all these countries did not necessarily adhere to the same policies as China, they were regarded as forming an integral part of the Third World and as sharing China's commitment to economic development and national independence.

Zone 4—this region, sometimes also included in the 'intermediate zone', covered those industrialized states that, though possessing radically different social systems, nonetheless shared China's opposition to the hegemonic ambitions of one or other of the two superpowers.

Zone 5—the area consisting mainly of those great powers representing China's major actual or potential enemies.

This division of the world into zones is of course no more than a vast generalization of the manner in which the Chinese perceived their complex relationship with the rest of the world. But it does highlight certain important characteristics of the Chinese view of their place in the international system. Of particular significance is the concept of the 'intermediate zone', which basically corresponded with the area known as the Third World, and which constituted a potential 'third force', seeking to place limitations on the political, economic and military domination of one or other of the two superpowers. If China decided immediately after Liberation to lean to the Soviet side, it was largely because at the height of the cold war there was little possibility of a middle road between the two great power blocs.

The Chinese attitude to the Third World, therefore, was not simply the product of revolutionary zeal, it was also the outcome of the Chinese assessment of the policies of the two superpowers. If friendship, support, and influence could not be found within the two global alliance systems, they would have to be sought in the Third World. The opening to the Afro–Asian bloc had in fact begun in the mid-1950s. Shortly after the Sino–Indian agreement of April 1954, both countries expressed their adherence to the Panch Sila or Five Principles; these included mutual respect for each other's territorial integrity and sovereignty, non-aggression, non-interference in each other's internal affairs, equality and mutual benefit and peaceful coexistence. In April 1955, Peking confirmed the new spirit of accommodation by its participation at the Bandung Conference of twenty-nine Asian and African nations. In a major speech at the conference, Zhou Enlai outlined China's wish to seek common ground in spite of existing differences.[58] In a subsequent speech, before the Political Committee of the Conference, he gave further assurances of China's intentions and reiterated her desire to recognize 'the equality of all nations, large and small'.[59]

It will be readily seen that, in this period at least, China's interest in the Third World was expressed not in terms of the export of, or even support for, revolution, but of solidarity among countries striving to achieve complete independence. The fluctuating importance attached by Chinese foreign policy to the distinct but related themes of peaceful coexistence and armed struggle indicates the inherent flexibility of the Maoist conception of the intermediate zone, even during the height of revolutionary fervour. In reality, the zone was not a fixed geographical base but a shifting and fluid 'ideological and political battleground' in which China sought to isolate her main enemy while joining forces with all nations or movements willing, for whatever motive or reason, to make common cause with her.

Possibly one of the most significant developments in the evolution of the intermediate zone concept was its extension and redefinition in the mid-1960s, as a result of which it was made to encompass certain Western European and other countries critical of American policies. In an interview given to a group of Japanese socialists in August 1964, Mao Zedong indicated that Europe was beginning to challenge American dominance.[60] An even more explicit statement with respect to France's position in the de Gaulle era was given by Mao in an interview with Edgar Snow. As a result of the intensified Franco–American conflict, France was said to be 'in the Third World but not of it'.[61] In fact, the Sino–French negotiations leading up to the establishment of full diplomatic relations in January 1964 became the occasion for the official reformulation of the intermediate zone and its division into two parts, one part consisting of 'the independent countries and those striving for independence in

Asia, Africa and Latin America', and the other part consisting 'of the whole of Western Europe, subjected to US control, interference and bullying'.[62] In February 1964, Mao was reported to have said:

> France, Germany, Italy, Britain, and, if she can cease to be America's agent, Japan and ourselves – that is the Third Force.[63]

Clearly Maoist foreign policy was now contemplating the possibility of a third force whose purpose would be to undermine the global control of international relations exercised by the United States and the Soviet Union.

China's concern to reduce the dominance of the superpowers was also reflected in her attitude to the United Nations, which she attempted to portray, until her admission to the organization, as the instrument of Soviet and American interests. Interpreting her exclusion from the international body as a demonstration of American hegemony, she refused to enter the United Nations except in circumstances that would weaken the prevailing duopoly in international decision-making. According to the Chinese Foreign Minister, Chen Yi, the United Nations had to be freed from 'the control of the United States and other big powers'.[64] Should basic reforms not be forthcoming, Chen Yi envisaged the establishment of a 'revolutionary United Nations' whose function would presumably have been to apply Mao's revolutionary strategy to the international arena.

Chinese acceptance of the Maoist radical vision stemmed in part from the expectation that its ideological impact on international politics would be far greater than that warranted by China's limited military and economic capabilities. Throughout the 1950s and 1960s, the Chinese did not possess a significant nuclear arsenal. Nor could their navy and airforce be regarded as a match for American or Soviet naval and aerial power. Although Chinese ground forces were substantial, they could not be used to liberate Taiwan or remove the United States from the Asian rimlands. Because of the weakness of her economic base, China could not project her military power far beyond her borders to assist an ally or client state. Throughout the greater part of the Vietnam war, China was in no position to compete with the Soviet Union as the supplier to North Vietnam of sophisticated military hardware. As for the use of aid and trade as instruments of diplomacy, they could provide China with only limited leverage given the underdeveloped state of her own economy.

China's revolutionary objectives had therefore to contend with the formidable obstacles posed by the economic and strategic superiority of the United States and the Soviet Union. Could Mao's military strategy and tactics developed for guerrilla and mobile warfare with conventional weapons successfully contend with the military might of these two giants? Would they be applicable in the event of an all-out nuclear war even for the defence of the Chinese mainland? Could the Maoist revolutionary strategy be implemented when confronted with the politics of the atomic age? More fundamentally, how could China overcome the dilemma of opposing the existing international system and yet have to live within it?

Some observers argued that with the passage of time Peking could be persuaded to accept rather than subvert the prevailing international order. According to John Fairbank, Chinese behaviour would assume such motivation once certain basic needs had been satisfied. Foremost among these were the search for greater prestige in the world to redress the humiliation of the last century; the need for international recognition to reinforce domestic legitimacy; the attempt to secure certain kinds of economic and, especially, technological exchanges; and the desire to become part of the international framework of bargaining and diplomacy. It was precisely this kind of analysis which led Fairbank to advocate the termination of American efforts to achieve the diplomatic and economic isolation of China.[65]

However, in the 1950s and 1960s China preferred not to be drawn into any balance of power arrangement whether in the form of a global strategic alliance or an Asian regional system. This refusal derived to a considerable extent from China's determination to preserve both her revolutionary ideology and her identity as a world power, but also from the rigidity of America's cold war policies. During the Cultural Revolution the Chinese appeared anxious to maintain a radical posture on a whole range of foreign policy issues even at the risk of antagonizing their principal neighbours. Although they found themselves in direct opposition to both superpowers, they appeared reluctant to play off one against the other. Even as late as April 1969, the new Party Constitution adopted at the Ninth Congress reaffirmed the twin struggle against 'imperialism headed by the United States' and against 'modern revisionism headed by the Soviet renegade clique'. However, there was now growing evidence that the militant phase in Chinese foreign policy was rapidly coming to an end. China's external conduct could not but reflect the subtle interaction between ideological motivation and national interest in the rapidly changing context of domestic and international politics.

Foreign Policy Objectives

In one very important respect, Communist China behaved throughout the 1950s and 1960s exactly like any other traditional nation-state. She never lost sight of the primary goal of preserving her national unity and independence and removing any foreign presence from what she considered to be China's rightful territory. This fundamental consideration explains both China's attitude to the Taiwan question and her refusal to accept permanent subordination to the Soviet Union.

The search for territorial integrity, however, should not be confused with territorial expansionism. Even in the recovery of what she regarded as lost territories, China was inclined to pursue very low-risk policies. She was extremely cautious in engaging her troops outside her boundaries, making use of them only in cases where Chinese security appeared to be seriously threatened or where the continued survival of a communist buffer state was at stake, as for example during the Korean war. The strategic and operational premises that governed the deployment of Chinese troops were generally predicated on considerations of defence rather than offence.

Other students of Chinese foreign policy have advanced a rather different interpretation, arguing that China's Communist leadership was motivated by an ideology that found expression in a ruthless exertion of power over other nations and identified with the most violent currents of traditional, xenophobic nationalism.[66] The condemnatory quality of much western academic analysis was supported by Indian charges of Chinese expansionism during the Sino–Indian boundary dispute as well as Russian accusations that China was seeking to conquer territories that had belonged or had been loosely linked to her in the very distant past. On closer examination, however, the validity of these charges appears open to serious doubt.

In order to reach a proper understanding of the problem of China's territorial boundaries, one must set it in its historical context. Several references have already been made to the carving up of Chinese territory and to the near dissolution of China's national identity which took place in the nineteenth century. The territorial acquisitions of Russia, Japan and Britain at the expense of China, and the latter's loss of all her spheres of influence, especially in Indochina, explain the determination of the Communist leadership to consolidate China's territorial integrity and to bring Manchuria, Inner Mongolia, Xinjiang, and Tibet under central Chinese control. But in carrying out the policy, the Chinese moved with considerable caution and moderation.

On the question of disputed boundaries, Zhou Enlai outlined China's conciliatory attitude at some length at the Bandung Conference:

> We have common borders with four countries. With some of these countries we have not yet finally fixed our border line and we are ready to do so . . . But before doing so, we are willing to maintain the present situation by acknowledging that those parts of our border are parts which are undetermined. We are ready to restrain our government and people from crossing even one step across our border. . . .[67]

The signing of a border agreement with Burma in 1960 was, in fact, the culmination of a prolonged diplomatic effort by the Chinese to ensure a cooperative relationship with their southern neighbours. The border settlement, which was much more favourable to Burmese than to Chinese claims, was regarded by Peking as laying the foundation for similar settlements with other countries, notably Nepal, Afghanistan and Pakistan. Even in the case of their dispute with India, the Chinese, while refusing to accept the boundaries set by Britain and insisting that the entire border should be renegotiated, maintained that both sides should respect the status quo and refrain from any military action.

But while showing extreme care in the use of military force, China was equally determined to develop to the full her potential as a military power. She refused to accept any limitation on her drive towards equality with the superpowers in nuclear capability, in the belief that such equality was essential to her security. Apart from its purely military value, the acquisition of a nuclear deterrent was intended to improve China's diplomatic position vis-à-vis the United States and the Soviet Union and to reduce her vulnerability to external pressure. Confronted with the hostility of the two superpowers and aware of the risks of nuclear war, China became more convinced than ever of the almost complete coincidence between her own interests as a state and those of world revolution.

In addition to territorial consolidation and the acquisiton of a nuclear deterrent, China sought to demonstrate her independence by establishing closer relations with European governments, particularly those that were increasingly critical of Soviet or American policies. In accordance with this strategy, Peking made efforts to improve its relations with Western Europe both before and after the Cultural Revolution. Significantly, China had kept open the channels of trade with nearly all advanced industrialized countries even when they were still unwilling to accord her diplomatic recognition. Similarly, the Chinese leadership endeavoured to develop closer links with at least some of the Eastern European countries as a means of reducing the degree of Soviet control over the communist world, while at the same time widening China's room for manoeuvre

A different but somewhat more practical application of the notion of the intermediate zone involved China's endeavour to secure a sphere of influence around the perimeter of her boundaries. There is no evidence, however, to indicate that, in this context, the establishment of spheres of influence was equated with the creation of communist regimes. Peking was quite prepared to promote non-aligned, non-communist governments willing to develop friendly relations with China, and to regard this a more manageable, less risky and more productive exercise. This attitude governed China's relations with the neutralist governments of Nepal, Burma, Laos, Cambodia and Indonesia, except during the brief interlude of the Cultural Revolution, although even during this period China's intransigence stemmed as much from the belief that such a policy had considerable native support in the country concerned as from her own revolutionary enthusiasm.

Although it is in her relations with Southeast Asia that China displayed some of the most striking fluctuations between moods of intransigence and policies of caution and moderation, the same tension between the radical orientation of the Maoist vision and short-term power considerations tended to colour the whole of Chinese foreign policy. When confronted, however, with the intransigence of Washington's cold war policies, China was inclined to harden her own position. Given increasing Soviet and American hostility, Maoist China felt compelled to oppose all superpower arms control agreements and to resist any limitation on her nuclear aspirations. Accordingly, the Chinese rejected the 1963 Partial Test Ban Treaty, declined to participate in the Geneva

Disarmament Conference, refused to become a party to the Non-Proliferation Treaty when it opened for signature in July 1968, and even argued that proliferation, especially among socialist or anti-imperialist states, might be a valuable development helping to restrict Soviet and American interventionism. While not questioning the radicalizing effect on foreign policy of such domestic upheavals as the Great Leap Forward and the Cultural Revolution, it can nevertheless be argued that the periodic fluctuations between radicalism and moderation were determined not so much by turning points in domestic politics as by changes in the international political situation.

The dichotomy between intransigence and moderation was perhaps nowhere better illustrated than in the Chinese attitude to the use of armed force. On the one hand, one found the uncompromising radicalism of Lin Biao and his attack on 'Khrushchev revisionists' for exaggerating the danger of a nuclear conflict growing out of a liberation struggle. The benefits of revolutionary warfare were far greater than the costs. War was 'a great school' that could 'temper the people and push history forward'.[68] In any case, the pressures militating against all-out war were very great, and the wars of national liberation that had occurred since World War II, far from leading to world war, had contributed to the defence of world peace.[69] Eager to highlight the alleged Soviet betrayal of the revolutionary cause, the Chinese insisted that peace could be gained only by resisting the attacks of imperialists and colonialists. The monstrous evil of war would be ultimately eliminated, but only by opposing war with war. Peace would be the result not of compromise but of struggle.

On the other hand, while stressing the virtues of revolutionary war, Maoist China was equally at pains to emphasize her credentials as a peace-loving nation, which she claimed to have demonstrated not only by her support for the struggles of the world's peace forces, but also by her steadfast refusal to launch wars of expansion or to export revolution as a substitute for the indigenous liberation struggles of other countries. In spite of China's perceived contribution to peace, the risk nevertheless remained that one of the great powers, in particular the United States, might launch a sudden attack against her. For its part, Chinese diplomacy would do all in its power to avoid a military confrontation with the United States, but would never bow to US nuclear blackmail. While anxious not to provoke a thermonuclear exchange, China would not be intimidated by the American propaganda of nuclear terror. Joining with all other 'peace-loving countries', China would mobilize on the most extensive scale to resist American designs for aggression and war.[70]

The Sino–Soviet disagreement on nuclear strategy centred, in reality, not on the desirability but on the likelihood of nuclear war. Both sides recognized the destructiveness of nuclear weapons but, whereas the Russians ascribed to them a major role in international politics, the Chinese tended to downgrade their importance and to argue that a nuclear war would not jeopardize the eventual triumph of communism but rather spell the end of capitalism.[71] Although China would consistently try to prevent the launching of imperialist wars because of the enormous sacrifices they would impose upon the people of various countries, even in the eventuality of such a war those sacrifices would not be in vain.[72]

Paradoxically enough, by playing down the likely adverse consequences of a nuclear exchange, China was hoping to curb not only the effectiveness of nuclear blackmail but the very probability of nuclear war. It is precisely in this context that Mao spoke of the atomic bomb as a 'paper tiger'. In accordance with his general revolutionary philosophy, he argued that the outcome of war would be decided by the masses and not by the weapons that were used. If revolutionaries were to act only in the belief that their fire-power was superior to that of the enemy, no revolution would ever take place. While armed with sophisticated nuclear weaponry, there were serious limits to the capacity of imperialist forces to wage war since such military adventures were unlikely to have the support of the masses in the aggressor nations.

Given that reactionary regimes were by their very nature oppressive, they would sooner or later lose the active or even tacit support of the people, who would ultimately join the side of the revolution and bring about the downfall of the existing order. According to the Chinese analysis, the revolutionary had to distinguish between the apparent power of the opponent, which was to be *tactically* respected, and his essential weakness, which was to be *strategically* exploited. In November 1957, referring to an earlier interview with American journalist Anna Louise Strong, Mao restated his conception of the 'paper tiger':

> I said that all the reputedly powerful reactionaries were merely paper tigers. The reason was that they were divorced from the people. You see, wasn't Hitler a paper tiger? Wasn't Hitler overthrown? I also said that the tsar was a paper tiger, the Chinese emperor was a paper tiger, Japanese imperialism was a paper tiger. You see they were all down and out. US imperialism has not yet fallen and it has the atom bomb. I believe it will also fall. It is also a paper tiger. ... In order to struggle against the enemy, we have formed the concept over a long period, namely that strategically we should slight all enemies, but tactically we should take full account of all enemies.[73]

It should not be inferred from the above analysis that Mao was advocating mass destruction through war. Rather the argument was that the revolutionary must be prepared to resort to violent struggle in order to overthrow the status quo. It was never suggested that such a struggle need involve the use of nuclear weapons. The Maoist contention was simply that the revolutionary should not allow himself to be intimidated by the nuclear threats of imperialist or revisionist forces. In any case, Chinese leaders stressed on several occasions that they would never be the first to use nuclear weapons, that their nuclear arsenal was intended for self-defence, and that they favoured complete and general nuclear disarmament.[74]

It is because large-scale war was ruled out as a feasible means of defeating imperialism that discussion of war in China was based almost exclusively on the notion of a defensive strategy. It is for precisely the same reason that China concentrated her energies on supporting liberation struggles and on fanning the flames of local conflicts likely to embarrass either of the superpowers or to get the United States bogged down in a protracted and unpopular war against a coloured people. This strategy, aimed at overcommitting and neutralizing the resources of the great powers, was particularly suited to China's limited means. The question confronting the Chinese leadership was whether such a strategy would ultimately exhaust the United States and whether China could effectively pursue this strategy in the face of both Soviet and American opposition. In effect, two questions were involved here: Could China effectively break the bipolar structure of the international system without first raising herself to the status of a superpower? Conversely, was the growth of China's power a necessary and sufficient condition for the achievement of her ideological and national objectives?

The far-reaching implications of these questions were, to some extent, obscured for the best part of two decades by the scope and intensity of the Sino–American conflict, which may be described as the distinctive feature of this first phase in Communist China's external relations. Her opposition to American policies, which in part derived from and at the same time strengthened her revolutionary aspirations, also helps to explain both the Sino–Soviet alliance and the subsequent rift between the two communist powers. It was only with the intensification of the Sino–Soviet dispute and the failure of American intervention in Vietnam that Chinese leaders began to reassess some of the major premises that had governed their diplomacy since 1949. The emergence of the Soviet Union as China's main enemy and the increasing difficulty in reconciling national interest and ideological commitment, partly as a result of far-reaching changes in the political and economic functioning of the Chinese state, eventually produced a decisive shift in the conduct of China's foreign policy.

CHAPTER 2

The Sino–American Confrontation

Mao's experience during the revolutionary struggle had predisposed him to regard 'US imperialism' as the principal obstacle to Chinese aspirations and objectives. The past record of American alignment with Chiang Kai-shek's forces, in spite of Mao's repeated efforts to secure America's support for the CCP or at least its neutrality in the civil war, could not be easily forgotten. In a major speech to the UN Security Council delivered soon after China's intervention in the Korean war, the Chinese delegate portrayed American attitudes towards Communist China as a direct continuation of the interventionist policy of the 1940s.[1]

While there may be some dispute as to the precise magnitude of American military and economic assistance to the Nationalists, there can be little doubt that the United States played a very considerable role in the Chinese civil war. Secretary of State Dean Acheson gave a rather candid outline of the dimensions of US participation in July 1949:

> Since V-J Day, the United States Government has authorized aid to Nationalist China in the form of grants and credits totalling approximately 2 billion dollars. . . . In addition . . . the United States Government has sold the Chinese Government large quantities of military and civilian war surplus property with a total procurement cost of over 1 billion dollars. . . .[2]

Having failed in its efforts to stabilize the corrupt and incompetent Nationalist regime, American diplomacy found considerable difficulty in adjusting to the new strategic and political realities resulting from the Communist triumph. Indeed, Acheson described the Maoist victory as an attempt at foreign domination 'masked behind the facade of a vast crusading movement'.[3] In these circumstances, it was argued, the United States would be able to maintain its 'historic policy of friendship with China' only if the Chinese people came 'to recognize that the Communist regime serves not their interests but those of Soviet Russia'.[4] It would appear that from the outset American policy-makers were determined to thwart Communist China's claim to legitimacy and to prevent the Chinese civil war from reaching its natural and logical conclusion.

The hostility of the People's Republic of China towards the United States was the product of many factors, but none was to prove more important than the American decision to recognize and support an alternative Chinese regime that made no secret of its intention to reconquer the mainland. With the passage of time and the gradual elaboration of the US policy of containment, Peking came to regard the American diplomatic recognition of Taiwan and the strategic relationship with the Nationalist government as part of a more general attitude designed to contain the legitimate expansion of Chinese influence in Asia. China was particularly antagonized by Washington's determination to promote and protect not simply neutral but firmly anti-communist regimes throughout the Asian rimlands, not only in Taiwan and South Korea, but in Japan, the Philippines, Thailand and Indochina. The net result of American strategy was to convince Chinese leaders of Washington's resolve to be the leader of a powerful coalition of anti-Chinese forces throughout the Asian continent.

While making use of the domino theory to justify the military encirclement of the Chinese mainland, the United States was also able to exploit its supremacy in the United Nations to ensure China's diplomatic isolation. This twin policy was clearly spelt out to British Prime Minister Attlee during his visit to Washington in December 1950. Apart from mobilizing the resources of the United Nations to exert maximum political and economic pressure on Peking, the American President also envisaged

> . . . the possibility of some military action which would harass the Chinese Communists and of efforts which could be made to stimulate anti-communist resistance within China itself, including the exploitation of nationalist capabilities.[5]

Some five months earlier, the United States had already rejected the Indian proposal that the People's Republic of China be admitted to the UN Security Council and that the United States, the Soviet Union and China, with the help of other countries, begin discussions to end the Korean war and reach a permanent solution of the Korean problem. In January 1951 the US Senate passed a resolution calling on the United Nations to declare Communist China an aggressor in Korea and to refuse to admit the Communist Chinese government as the representative of China.

The Chinese reaction to the perceived hostility of American intentions was both direct and predictable. In his Report to the People's Political Consultative Conference of September 1950, Zhou Enlai warned against the exclusion of 'nearly 500 million Chinese people from the UN'.[6] But while accusing the United States of manipulation and obstruction at the United Nations and while reaffirming Taiwan to be an inseparable part of China, Peking was careful not to allow the Sino–American conflict to escalate into total confrontation. An important characteristic of China's conduct, even at the height of hostility between the two countries, was the anxiety not to provoke an American attack on Chinese territory.

Chinese fears, it should be noted, were aroused not only by American actions in Asia but also by the inflammatory statements of several American leaders.

Truman himself set the stage for future threats when on 30 November 1950, he answered a question on the possible use of the atomic bomb in Korea by saying that there had always been 'active consideration of its use'.[7] Soon after the conclusion of the Korean war, the militant right-wing of American politics was to initiate a bitter and malicious campaign for war against mainland China. Although numerically not large, the war party included the powerful China lobby, the extreme wing of the Republican Party, a host of admirals and retired generals and legions of cold warriors who had come to believe their own propaganda about the red menace and were now intent on destroying it. In defence of 'the forward positions of freedom in Asia', Dulles warned the Chinese that the United States, far from being a 'paper tiger', was ready to use against them 'new and powerful weapons of precision, which can utterly destroy military targets without endangering civilian centers'.[8] In March 1955, military advisers were urging the President to respond to the outbreak of hostilities in the Taiwan Strait between China and Chiang Kei-shek's forces by destroying Peking's military potential. Some voices even advocated the use of the atomic bomb as the only means of dealing with China's aggressive fanaticism.

Throughout the 1950s and the greater part of the 1960s American foreign policy was predicated on the premise that Communist China was an aggressive, unpredictable, irrational power. According to Secretary of State Dulles, the only way to make Peking's behaviour conform with established norms was to pursue a policy of threat and brinkmanship:

> I believe that promises of the Communists are never dependable merely because they are promises. They are only dependable if there are unpleasant consequences in case the Communists break their promises.[9]

The same understanding of Chinese motivation was to underlie almost every important American policy statement during this period. In December 1963, Assistant Secretary of State for Far Eastern Affairs Roger Hilsman explained:

> First and foremost, the Chinese Communist leaders have shown themselves to be dangerously overconfident and wedded to outdated theories, but pragmatic when their existence is threatened . . . A second major fact about Communist China's leaders is their parochialism: they have seen extraordinarily little of the outside world, and their world view is further constricted by their ideology.[10]

American diplomacy had become so obsessed with the allegedly expansionary and subversive tendencies in Chinese foreign policy as to lose sight of its own imperialist thrust into Asia. America's misconception of the true nature and consequences of its actions was thus subtly but unmistakably projected on to Chinese perceptions and behaviour. Having failed to recognize its own will to power and the irrationality of its self-imposed role as policeman of the world, American foreign policy defined its objectives as rational and defensive and those of its opponents as misguided and provocative.[11]

The Taiwan Dispute

In analysing China's grievances against American policies, reference has already been made to the importance of the Taiwan dispute and to the conflict between Peking's concern for territorial integrity and the legitimation of Communist rule on the one hand and Washington's insistence on maintaining a rigid dividing line between the communist bloc and the 'free world' on the other. Much of the Chinese resentment against the United States grew, in fact, as a direct result of the apparent shift in American policy. Immediately after the success of the Communist revolution in October 1949, the Maoist leadership was led to believe that the United States would not interfere in China's domestic situation and that Taiwan would be considered China's internal affair. In January 1950, President Truman stated:

> The United States has no predatory designs on Formosa or on any other Chinese territory. The United States has no desire to obtain special rights or privileges or to establish military bases on *Formosa at this time.* Nor does it have any intention of utilizing its armed forces to interfere in the *present* situation. The United States Government will not pursue a course which will lead to involvement in the civil conflict in China.[12] [italics added]

Although the above statement may have been reassuring to Peking, a close reading suggests that even at this early stage Washington was leaving its future options open by qualifying its statement of intent with the phrases 'at this time' and 'in the present situation . Moreover, the American President made it clear that, although no military aid or advice would be provided to Chiang Kai-shek's forces on Taiwan, the existing programme of economic assistance would be continued.

While leaving in doubt the legal status of Taiwan, Dean Acheson reiterated on the same day the determination of the United States not to become militarily involved in any way on the island.[13] In a major speech to the National Press Club on 12 January 1950, the American Secretary of State repeated that respect for China's territorial integrity constituted the cardinal principle of United States policy towards Asia.[14] But when pressed to clarify its position regarding the eventual return of Formosa to the Republic of China, the State Department contented itself with the legally ambiguous statement that Formosa had been administered since 1945 by China and that the surrender of Japanese forces on Formosa had been made to Generalissimo Chiang Kai-shek.[15] By June 1950, the United States was ready to reverse its non-intervention policy and its pledge to respect China's integrity. In May Senator Tom Connally, Chairman of the Senate Foreign Relations Committee, had already pointed in the course of an interview, to the powerful domestic and external pressures seeking a redefinition of the American defence perimeter in the Western Pacific.[16] The outbreak of hostilities in Korea provided the advocates of a hard-line policy towards Peking with the necessary pretext for a radical shift in American foreign policy. Accordingly, on 27 June 1950 Truman declared that the occupation of Formosa by Communist forces would constitute a threat to the security of the Pacific area. The restoration of Formosa to China was now made conditional on China's adherence to a series of United States requirements:

> The determination of the future status of Formosa must await the restoration of security in the Pacific, a peace settlement with Japan, or consideration by the United Nations. . . .[17]

The Chinese response to these American initiatives was swift and consistent with China's previously stated position. Zhou Enlai described the intervention of the Seventh Fleet in China's unfinished civil war as 'aggression against the territory of China, and a total violation of the United Nations Charter' and the entry of the United States in the Korean war as 'a premeditated move . . . designed to create a pretext for the United States to invade Taiwan, Korea, Vietnam and the Philippines'.[18] It is significant that even at the height of the Korean war the most vehement Chinese denunciations of American policy were made in relation to 'the unlawful and criminal act of armed aggression against the territory of China, Taiwan'. In his impassioned speech to the UN Security Council in November 1950, the Chinese delegate devoted most of his time to a blistering attack on the duplicity of American statements and actions with respect to Taiwan. He reminded the meeting that the Cairo Declaration of 1 December 1943, jointly signed by the British, American and Chinese governments, and the subsequent Potsdam Declaration had explicitly stipulated that all territories stolen from China by the Japanese, including Formosa, should be restored to the Republic of China. No one after 1945 had 'ever questioned the fact that Taiwan [was] an inseparable part of Chinese territory, *de jure* or *de facto*'.[19] The Chinese representative went on to reject categorically any suggestion that the civil war in Korea provided 'a justification or pretext for United States aggression against Taiwan'.

In China's view, American actions in both Korea and Taiwan were part of a much larger design aimed at containing and dominating China:

> After war broke out in Korea in June 1950 Truman changed the policy and adopted a policy of aggression towards China. While sending troops to Korea the US at the same time despatched the Seventh Fleet to the Taiwan Straits and exercised military control over Taiwan. Beginning from that time the United States started new aggression against China.[20]

Taiwan was deemed central to the American Pacific strategy because control of the island would enable the United States 'to dominate with air power every Asiatic port from Vladivostok to Singapore'. This analysis of the situation reinforced China's determination to liberate Taiwan, but at the same time emphasized her relative impotence. By the early 1950s China's very considerable involvement in the Korean war had made an additional military engagement against Chiang Kai-shek's forces an extremely risky undertaking.

Conscious of China's strategic inferiority, the United States proceeded to take advantage of this fact and to strengthen its military relationship with

Taiwan. In February 1951 the two governments signed a Mutual Defense Assistance Agreement in which the United States undertook to provide the Nationalists with 'military material for the defense of Taiwan against possible attack'. Although Washington insisted that such aid could only be used for defensive purposes, it soon became obvious that the United States would no longer attempt to restrict the Nationalist forces if they chose to launch military operations against the Chinese Communist mainland. In his State of the Union Message of February 1953, President Eisenhower announced that the Seventh Fleet would no longer be employed to shield Communist China, thereby formalizing the 'unleashing' of Chiang Kai-shek.[21]

With the tacit approval if not active encouragement of the United States, the Nationalists had obtained effective control of several groups of offshore islands – notably the Dachens, some two hundred miles south of Shanghai, the Mazus off the port of Fuzhou, and Jinmen off the port of Xiamen – and were using them as a base from which to maintain a harassing blockade of China's central coast. As a result of American military assistance, the organization and equipment of the Nationalist armed forces were significantly upgraded during 1954. By this time, the United States had already succeeded in giving shape to the Southeast Asian Treaty Organization (SEATO) in order to counter alleged communist expansion in Indochina, and was now being pressed by President Syngman Rhee and others to form a parallel Northeast Asia treaty organization comprising the United States, Japan, South Korea and Taiwan. Although the proposal was probably never seriously considered by Washington, it did appreciably increase the atmosphere of crisis in Sino–American relations and accentuated Chinese fears of an impending Nationalist attack.

Given its limited range of options, Peking decided to apply some pressure on the United States, and on 3 September 1954 began to subject Jinmen to heavy shelling. Not only were the Chinese anxious to prevent the Nationalists from strengthening their foothold in Taiwan and the offshore island, but they were obviously concerned to probe the precise extent of American support for Chiang Kai-shek – a policy that had already strained Washington's relations with neutrals and even allies. Perhaps contrary to Chinese expectations, the United States responded by strengthening its commitment to Taiwan, and in December signed a mutual defence agreement which, though it did not explicitly cover the offshore islands, undoubtedly encouraged Chiang Kai-shek to believe that he had gained a guarantee for the defence of the Jinmen and Mazus in exchange for the evacuation of the more vulnerable Dachens. In any case, in late January 1955 the so-called Formosa resolution was passed by both houses of Congress in order to plug the loophole left by the defence pact. The resolution gave the President the wide-ranging authority to defend Formosa and the Pescadores against armed attack, including

> . . . the securing and protection of such related positions and territories of that area now in friendly hands and the taking of such other measure as he judges to be required or appropriate in assuring the defense of Formosa and the Pescadores.[22]

Dulles had thus succeeded in his twin strategy of keeping tensions high and extending the US defence perimeter to include the Jinmen and Mazu Islands. The Mutual Defense treaty between the United States and the Nationalist regime in Taiwan and the subsequent congressional resolution, taken in conjunction with the other bilateral and multilateral treaties already concluded by the United States in East and Southeast Asia, thus set the seal on the Western Pacific security system.

Confronted with such overwhelming military power and Chiang Kai-shek's continuing fortification of the offshore islands, the Chinese leadership concluded that no significant strategic gains were likely to be made with respect to Taiwan in the immediate future. Accordingly, they concentrated on reinforcing their own bases opposite Taiwan and proceeded to explore the possibility of a diplomatic breakthrough. In response to the Dulles demand for an immediate cease-fire in the Taiwan Strait area, Zhou Enlai issued a statement in April 1955 in which he outlined, in keeping with the spirit of moderation he displayed throughout the Bandung Conference, the Chinese government's willingness 'to sit down and enter into negotiations with the United States'.[23] The tone was now distinctly more restrained than previous Chinese statements. As recently as December 1954, a leading editorial article in the *People's Daily* had branded the 'US–Chiang Kai-shek treaty' as a 'criminal act' and an 'alliance for aggressive war'.[24]

On the other hand, although Chinese diplomacy was now formally committed to the relaxation and elimination of tension in the Taiwan area, the overriding Chinese objective remained the total withdrawal of the American military presence from Taiwan. Ambassador Wang made the Chinese position abundantly clear at the Sino–American ambassadorial talks that began in Geneva in August 1955. China rejected the American notion of defending Taiwan and reserved its own right to liberate the territory.[25] The objective was not negotiable, only the means. In January 1956, Zhou Enlai went so far as to suggest that it might be possible to liberate Taiwan 'by peace means'.[26] The new conciliatory character of Chinese diplomacy was especially noticeable in the invitations extended to the 'Taiwan authorities' to enter in discussions with the People's Republic regarding the 'specific steps and conditions for the peaceful liberation of Taiwan'.[27]

In spite of China's placatory gestures, the Geneva talks remained deadlocked, for the positions of the two sides were essentially non-negotiable. Far from allowing China to liberate Taiwan, the United States continued to provide military support for Chiang's harassment of the mainland. From the heavily fortified islands the Nationalists intensified their shelling of mainland ports and disruption of China's coastal shipping, and carried out almost daily air strikes from Taiwan itself with the aid of American supplied planes and equipment.[28] In May 1957, the United States and Taibei signed an additional agreement providing for the deployment on Taiwan of Matador missiles, surface-to-surface missiles with a range of about 600 miles and capable of carrying either nuclear or conventional warheads.[29] Quite understandably, Peking now became increasingly alarmed at the prospect of a Nationalist thrust, for not only had Chiang's forces been considerably strengthened by the greatly expanded programme of American military aid, but the Nationalist incentive to attack was probably heightened by China's known intentions to acquire a nuclear deterrent in the near future. If Chiang Kai-shek was ever to invade the mainland, the early months of 1958 may have offered the last possible chance.

It was probably in order to forestall this possibility that the Maoist leadership decided once again to renew and intensify its shelling of Jinmen in August 1958. China's military initiative immediately prompted Dulles to issue, with the President's approval, an eight-point statement in which he reminded the Chinese that the United States was bound by treaty to help defend Taiwan from armed attack and that the President was authorized by the Joint Resolution of the Congress to secure and protect such related positions as Jinmen and Mazu. Washington had become so entangled with Chiang Kai-shek's political and military manoeuvrings that the offshore islands, once remote outposts, were now considered of vital strategic interest to the United States.[30] Indeed, Mao repeatedly characterized these islands as a 'noose' and 'trap' into which US imperialism had fallen. The only way out of the trap would be for the Americans to withdraw.[31]

American and Nationalist disengagement was undoubtedly the desired outcome but, as Allen Whiting has argued, not necessarily the specific objective of the Chinese bombardment of Jinmen. It is quite possible that Mao had not anticipated the severity of the American response, for as he himself admitted: 'I did not calculate that the world would become so disturbed and turbulent.'[32] But there is no reason to believe that he expected the 1958 crisis to bring about a drastic revision of the status quo in China's favour. Rather the intention appears to have been to increase international tensions in order, on the one hand, to mobilize domestic energies and resources and on the other, to convey to the United States the seriousness of China's long-term commitment to the liberation of Taiwan. The Maoist strategy was to apply maximum pressure on the United States through a combination of propaganda and intermittent shooting without permitting the pressure to develop into a major confrontation.[33] Precisely the same tactic was to be utilized in 1962, when in response to the seemingly provocative gestures of the Nationalist government the People's Republic heavily reinforced its troops opposite Taiwan and launched one of its most violent denunciations of US imperialism and the 'Chiang Kai-shek gang'.[34]

For all the apparent fluctuations between intransigence and moderation, China's attitude to the Taiwan problem throughout the 1950s and 1960s remained remarkably constant. Time and again Zhou Enlai was to return to the two points of principle that he regarded as prerequisites for a Sino–American rapprochement:

(1) all disputes between China and the US, including the dispute between the two countries in the Taiwan region, should be settled through peaceful negotiations, without resorting to the use or threat of force; and
(2) the US must agree to withdraw its armed forces from Taiwan and the Taiwan Straits. As to the specific steps on when and how to withdraw, they are matters for subsequent discussion.[35]

So long as the United States refused to consider, even in principle, the possibility of disengagement, there could be no progress in relations between the two countries. Though many factors had contributed to the strained relationship, the crisis had arisen 'primarily because the United States [was] forcefully occupying China's province of Taiwan'.[36] For China, the US military presence in Taiwan had become a living symbol of American hostility and the most concrete manifestation of the Western Pacific security system, which the United States had presumably constructed for the purpose of containing Chinese power and influence.

Korea and the Policy of Containment

It has often been argued that the decision to turn Taiwan into a major military base and endow it with a pivotal function in America's defence perimeter was a direct consequence of the Korean war. It is perfectly true that the North Korean attack across the 38th parallel on 25 June 1950 acted as a powerful catalyst for the extension of the US policy of containment to the Asian rimlands. On the other hand, there is considerable evidence that suggests that the United States had already taken significant initiatives to thwart the extension of communist influence in Asia well before the outbreak of hostilities in Korea. In 1946–47 the United States was urging France to establish a non-communist nationalist counterforce to the Vietminh in Indochina. By mid-1949, the Truman administration had begun to depict Bao Dai as a staunch patriot, capable of successfully opposing Ho Chi Minh and worthy of American support. In February 1950, the United States extended recognition to the Bao Dai government even though it was widely regarded in Asia and elsewhere as a puppet regime with a little or no authority to act as the representative of the Vietnamese people. American efforts to contain communism in Asia led Dean Acheson to announce in May that the United States would grant military and economic aid to restore security and develop 'genuine nationalism' in Indochina.[37] The outbreak of war in Korea merely served to accelerate this policy and to justify the rapid expansion of American military assistance to the French war effort in Indochina.[38]

But of even greater and more immediate concern to China must have been the evolving strategic relationship between the United States and Japan. Within twelve months of the formal Japanese surrender, the United States as the occupying power had moved towards the abandonment of the reparations programme and was beginning to implement a series of increasingly less restrictive economic guidelines. In a major policy pronouncement on 12 May 1949, the United States announced its unilateral decision to terminate all reparation payments for the duration of the occupation and to permit Japan to resume full-scale production in the following war-related industries: iron and steel, light metals, metal-working machinery, shipbuilding, oil-refining and storage, synthetic oil and synthetic rubber. Beginning in 1948 the United States began to consider rearming Japan. According to one official American publication:

> By 1950, as the apprehension of an attack by the Soviet Union increased, the original policy of the United States in regard to the continued demilitarization of Japan was almost completely reversed.[39]

By the fall of 1949, the State Department had agreed to the necessity of maintaining American military forces in Japan for its external and internal defence for an indefinite number of years following the conclusion of a peace treaty.

The rearmament of Japan, manifested in plans for 'police' and 'self-defence' forces, and arrangements for a Japanese peace treaty that would exclude the legitimate interests of the two wartime allies, Russia and China, thus preceded the Korean war and reinforced Peking's assessment of the US role in Korea as part of a larger strategy of offensive design. In China's view, Japan had become 'the headquarters of the United States for its aggression against Korea and Taiwan'.[40]

It has been argued by some observers that China's fear of a rearmed Japan became a self-fulfilling prophecy, that Washington's increased concern for the Northeast Asian region and its intensified military activity in relation to Japan followed rather than preceded the beginning of the Korean war.[41] As for America's direct intervention in the Korean conflict, the official explanation has always depicted it as the unavoidable response to a blatant, unprovoked and unexpected act of aggression. In his memoirs, President Truman justified United States policy in the following terms:

> Communism was acting in Korea just as Hitler, Mussolini, and the Japanese had acted ten, fifteen, twenty years earlier ... If the Communists were permitted to force their way into the Republic of Korea without opposition from the free world, no small nation would have the courage to resist threat and aggression by stronger Communist neighbours.[42]

It is difficult, however, to reconcile this interpretation of events with the position formally announced by Dean Acheson in January 1950 excluding Korea as well as Taiwan from the United States defence perimeter.

In the ensuing six months, intelligence reports repeatedly pointed to increased signs of North Korean military activity. As late as May 1950, in the course of an interview, Senator Tom Connally, Chairman of the Senate Foreign Relations Committee, conveyed the distinct impression that the administration was resigned to the loss of the Republic of Korea.[43] On 9 June 1950 Ambassador Muccio submitted a statement to Congress in which he stressed North Korea's military superiority and its continuing desire to dominate the south.[44] These warnings, however, were consistently disregarded presumably on the grounds that the Korean peninsula was not of strategic importance in the defence of the United States security system. These puzzling facts, taken in conjunction with the strong pressures for an anti-communist crusade emanating from the Chiang Kai-shek and Syngman Rhee regimes and their supporters among the US military establishment, have prompted several writers to advance the hypothesis that the North Korean attack was deliberately encouraged by the United States through diplomatic inaction and local provocation, or at least welcomed as a pretext for launching a major assault on Asian communism.[45]

Whatever the precise intentions of American policy-makers, there is little doubt as to the manner in which General MacArthur's provocative statements were interpreted by China. The Chinese could hardly have remained insensitive to the General's declaration made as early as 1948 'that 1000 American bombers and large quantities of surplus US military equipment, if utilized efficiently, could destroy the basic military strength of the Chinese Communists'.[46] Nevertheless, in the early stages of US involvement in the Korean war, Peking's response was remarkably low-key. Although the Chinese spoke of 'a prolonged war of attrition', they gave no hint of imminent Chinese assistance to North Korea. Statements emanating from Peking in the month of July emphasized North Korean self-sufficiency and its capacity 'to defeat imperialist aggression' and eventually attain national liberation. Not only were expressions of wholehearted support for the communist cause left unspecified, but the assertion was frequently made that preparations for the liberation of Taiwan constituted the most efficient contribution that China could make to the North Korean struggle.[47]

Washington's decision to intervene in the Korean conflict under the UN umbrella enabled MacArthur to break the North Korean offensive. By 30 September, with the enemy in full retreat, the US–UN forces had actually regained the 38th Parallel. However, MacArthur, not content with a return to the *status quo ante*, now called for North Korea's unconditional surrender. Indeed, MacArthur had already been authorized by the Joint Chiefs of Staff on 27 September 'to proceed north of the 38th Parallel'. On 29 September, the new Secretary of Defense, General Marshall, advised MacArthur that in his march towards the Yalu he should feel 'strategically and tactically unhampered'. Increasingly disturbed by the apparent shift in America's strategic objectives in the Korean war, Zhou Enlai summoned the Indian ambassador to China, K. M. Pannikar, and in the course of the meeting gave a clear warning that China would enter the war if American forces continued north of the 38th Parallel. Chinese fears and anxieties were also reflected in the changing disposition of several People's Liberation Army (PLA) units and the increased troop concentrations in northeast China beginning in late September when entire armies were redeployed in preparation for possible entry into the war.

In spite of Peking's warnings in late September and early October in which 'the war of aggression' against neighbouring Korea was increasingly portrayed as a threat to Chinese security, American policy appeared more committed than ever to the elimination of the opponent. On 2 October, a Russian resolution introduced at the UN calling for a national election under UN supervision as well as a cease-fire was immediately rejected under American pressure. Instead, the international organization was manipulated on 7 October into authorizing its forces in Korea to achieve the unification of the country, if necessary by military means. By mid-October, American leaders could have been in no doubt as to the mounting troop concentrations in Manchuria, China's warnings of intervention or the likelihood of an expanded theatre of conflict. The possibility of Chinese or Russian involvement in the war had, in fact, always preoccupied President Truman and his advisers. It was no doubt this concern that prompted the American leader to ask MacArthur, during their meeting at Wake Island on 15 October, whether there was any chance of 'Chinese or Soviet interference'. In reply, MacArthur claimed 'that there was no evidence from Peking even suggesting that Red Chinese intervention was under serious consideration'.[48] The explanation for this patent and probably deliberate misreading of the situation – Chinese troops were beginning to cross the Yalu River from Manchuria into North Korea the very day that MacArthur and the President were conferring – no doubt lies in MacArthur's long-cherished plans to expand the war into China and thereby strike a devastating blow at the heart of Asian communism. The objectives of the American administration were perhaps less clear but more sophisticated. Truman, the State Department and the Joint Chiefs of Staff were all anxious to avoid a major confrontation in the Far East and to concentrate American strategic power in Europe. The Korean conflict was nevertheless considered useful in demonstrating the American determination to contain and punish the enemy, while at the same time conveying to allies the sense of global crisis and the consequent need for a massive rearmament programme.[49]

On 14 October, Chinese troops crossed into Korea, but every effort was made to limit the range and duration of the thrust. By making a highly visible foray and then suddenly withdrawing, by emphasizing that its forces in Korea were 'volunteers', Peking was obviously signalling to the opponent the limited and essential defensive character of its objectives. Predictably, MacArthur disregarded these warnings, authorized the movement of all UN forces to within thirty to forty miles of the Manchurian border and proceeded to attack the electric plants on the Yalu even though the Chinese were already publicly committed to their defence. Indicative of MacArthur's strategy was his decision to launch a major offensive on 24 November, the very day that the Chinese delegation was due to appear at the United Nations where it was hoped peace talks might begin. Originally, the offensive had been scheduled for 15

November but was later postponed, thus coinciding exactly with the delay of the Chinese delegation's arrival, which had also been initially expected on 15 November. This perfect synchronization of dates may have been fortuitous, but it is difficult to avoid the conclusion that MacArthur's plan was to stifle any attempt at a negotiated settlement. Inevitably, the American initiative incurred China's total condemnation and prompted the Chinese spokesman to describe United States policy as part of a larger plan aimed at engulfing China and the rest of Asia.[50]

By the end of 1950, the United States appeared in no mood to compromise. Powerful forces within the country were demanding that China be branded the aggressor in Korea and sanctions levied against her, while other more extreme voices were openly advocating the use of the atomic bomb as the only means of asserting American supremacy. MacArthur for his part was recommending that the United States should:

(1) blockade the coast of China; (2) destroy through naval gunfire and air bombardment China's industrial capacity to wage war; (3) secure reinforcement from the nationalist garrison on Formosa . . . and (4) release existing restrictions upon the Formosan garrison for diversionary action, possibly leading to counter-invasion against vulnerable areas of the Chinese mainland.[51]

Although these recommendations were never accepted and eventually led to MacArthur's dismissal, the very fact that the United States President had for so long tolerated and even cooperated with the General's adventurous schemes was bound to have a profound impact on the Chinese perception of American objectives. While it is true that Truman frequently reiterated his opposition to the extension of the conflict, it is equally clear that he was intent on punishing 'Chinese aggression'. If such punishment was not allowed to include the bombing of Manchuria or the unleashing of Nationalist troops against the mainland, it was not because of any appreciation of the requirements of Chinese security but rather because of the 'very grave risk of starting a general war'. In defining his war strategy, Truman made abundantly clear his belief that China's actions benefited from the military support of the Soviet Union.[52]

But while Washington was aware of the risks of military escalation, it soon discovered that MacArthur's removal was not in itself sufficient to put an end to the policy of adventurism that he had initiated. Pressures exerted by allies and the United Nations finally persuaded the United States in June 1951 to agree to talks with the enemy, although these were to be restricted exclusively to military matters leading to an armistice. During the course of these negotiations, which lasted for more than two years, the Americans repeatedly under-rated the will and fighting capacity of the opponent, making vain attempts to take advantage of their superior aerial and naval power in the hope of improving their bargaining position at the negotiating table and inflicting massive devastation behind the front lines. By July 1953, UN ground forces had increased to 933,000 but a corresponding increase in Chinese manpower maintained the war in a state of stalemate until the armistice agreement of July 1953. The Korean conflict had been one of the most expensive and destructive wars in history, in which the United States had to limit its objectives for fear of becoming entangled in a losing ground war against China or in a nuclear exchange with the Soviet Union. Within these limitations American foreign policy nevertheless remained firmly committed to Truman's cold war strategy and to the policy of military containment.

The Korean experience taken in conjunction with Washington's military support for Chiang Kai-shek's forces in Taiwan came to be interpreted by Peking as the first in a long series of hostile acts aimed at encircling, isolating and undermining the People's Republic of China. Although unable to develop a single strategic system in the Pacific to correspond with the Atlantic alliance, the separate mutual defence treaties signed with the Philippines, Japan, Australia and New Zealand, South Korea, and Taiwan, and the Manila Pact enabled the United States to extend its containment policy from Europe to Asia. By the mid-1950s, Chinese leaders could be forgiven for believing that China was intended as the prime target of this overwhelming ring of military power. This was certainly the conclusion drawn and constantly reiterated in Chinese statements throughout the period of Sino–American friction.[53]

China: The International Outlaw

The American response to Chinese charges of imperialism was to portray US actions as justifiable efforts to contain Chinese aggression. In other words, United States hostility towards China was portrayed by American policy-makers as the natural reaction of a country committed to the legitimate interest of defending non-communist Asia. During the 1960s, this reaction was reinforced by the increasingly distorted perception of China as a dangerous enemy, the new leader of revolutionary communism and the arch-instigator of subversive activity not only in Southeast Asia but throughout the Third World. According to the official American view, China was seeking to displace the Soviet Union as leader of the international communist movement with the specific intention of injecting a far greater measure of radicalism in the movement's anti-imperialist strategy and of using this development as a stepping stone to the domination of all Asia.

The more moderate phase in Chinese foreign policy, especially evident during the mid-1950s when Chen Yi affirmed that China's policy of peaceful coexistence applied even to the United States,[54] was now dismissed as a temporary aberration in Chinese conduct. Accordingly, the pragmatic approach to diplomatic bargaining adopted by the Chinese representatives at the ambassadorial talks first in Geneva and subsequently in Warsaw met with an intransigent insistence by the United States that China accept the conceptual framework and general principles of the American world view.

Similarly, Washington rejected the Chinese proposal of July 1963 for a disarmament conference of the heads of government of all the countries of the world to discuss the possibility of the complete and total prohibition and destruction of nuclear weapons.[55] Equally unacceptable to the State Department was the Chinese proposal made at the Warsaw talks in November 1964 that China and the United States pledge not to be the first to use nuclear weapons against each other.[56]

The American perception of China as an 'international outlaw' was given frequent expression by senior American policy-makers, notably by Under-Secretary of State George Ball who, in October 1964, questioned China's right to be 'recognized as a member of the society of nations'.[57] In February 1966 William Bundy, Assistant Secretary of State for Far Eastern Affairs, portrayed China as a country seeking 'to subvert and overthrow existing governments'.[58] Such pronouncements were inevitably interpreted by the Chinese as evidence of America's resolve '. . . to remain the enemy of the Chinese people to the very end', and of its intention to shift 'its global strategy from Europe to Asia'.[59] The perceived shift in American strategic thinking was described as preparation 'for a trial of strength with Chinese people'.[60]

But the official American line remained tied to the contention that it was China and not the United States that was harbouring aggressive designs in Asia. Secretary of State Dean Rusk presented the most comprehensive outline of this view in April 1966, stressing the offensive purpose of China's military development and describing her objectives as 'dominance within Asia and leadership of the Communist world revolution employing Maoist tactics'.[61] Mr Rusk went on to indicate what he thought should be the key elements of American policy towards China. Given the authoritative nature of the statement, it may be profitably to examine in some detail the main propositions and their likely interpretation by the Maoist leadership.

The Secretary of State began by reaffirming the strong American resolve to support the various anti-communist regimes on China's periphery. Indeed, American policy was to take the initiative in bolstering all those forces in Asia antagonistic to Chinese objectives. Of particular importance was the need to extend continuing assistance to Chiang Kai-shek's regime and to preserve its membership of the United Nations and its agencies. While seemingly anxious to reassure Peking of Washington's peaceful intentions, the American Secretary of State proceeded to envisage situations, notably the war in Vietnam, that might in fact lead to a Sino–American confrontation. To avoid such an outcome it was necessary for China – presumably not for the United States – to reconsider her role in the international system. Mr Rusk referred to American willingness to engage in political discussions with China, especially on the questions of disarmament and non-proliferation, but was careful to emphasize that such dialogue would be used to change Peking's stand. In any case, the Secretary of State seemed to indicate that no fruitful negotiations could take place until and unless China had abandoned her present policies.

Peking's Response

Enough has already been said to suggest that China's reaction to American policy in the 1950s and 1960s was one of comprehensive opposition coupled with an ingrained suspicion of United States diplomatic gestures and initiatives. Frequently, Chinese leaders would sound warnings against entertaining any 'illusions about American imperialism'.[62] Throughout this period China's primary objective was to frustrate or neutralize American attempts at isolating her and containing the expansion of her influence. In pursuing this goal, Peking evolved a subtly conceived diplomacy alternating between phases of intransigence and moderation.

By the mid-1960s the need to break the 'American nuclear monopoly' had assumed increasing importance, hence the renewed stress on China's nuclear deterrent.[63] Significantly, the nuclear programme initiated in the late 1950s remained unaffected by the turbulent events of the Cultural Revolution. By 1970 China was known to be constructing copies of the TU-16 Badger medium bomber with a range of 1500 miles. In addition, a booster assembly had been developed for the firing of IRBMs with a 2000 miles range. In the period 1964–70 China carried out eleven nuclear test explosions ranging in yield from 20 kilotons in December 1964 to over 3 megatons in October 1970.[64]

Peking's nuclear ambitions were not so much the military expression of an expansionist policy but part of a larger strategy designed to deny the United States the capacity for 'nuclear blackmail'. China's interest in acquiring at least a minimal nuclear deterrent was intended to strengthen the leverage she could command in her relations with both superpowers. Chinese attitudes to arms control and disarmament problems may be said to have derived almost entirely from this fundamental outlook. If the Chinese consistently opposed all Soviet–American attempts to regulate the nuclear arms race, it was largely because they were not themselves willing to accept any limitation on their freedom of action at least until they had effectively broken the nuclear monopoly enjoyed by Moscow and Washington.

The basic Chinese view of the desirability of nuclear proliferation, especially within the socialist camp, was made explicit as early as 1951.[65] In any case, as subsequent statements were to reveal, China did not accept the Soviet position that her security would best be served by Soviet protection. Once the Soviet Union refused to provide her with the necessary assistance for the development of a nuclear capability, Peking interpreted the decision as inspired by the policy of rapprochement between the two countries as 'aimed at depriving the Chinese people of their right to resist the nuclear threats of US imperialism'.[66]

Whatever her long-term nuclear objectives, China, confronted as she was with the enormity of American power and the unreliability of Soviet support, was compelled, at least in the immediate term, to qualify strategic boldness with tactical caution. In the first place, she took great pains to avoid direct military confrontation with the United States. Reference has already been made to

China's moderate stance at the Bandung Conference, to her stated willingness to negotiate with the United States and to the subsequent agreement to hold talks at ambassadorial level (pp. 19, 33). Additional evidence of China's low-risk diplomacy was provided by her repeated offers to conduct ministerial discussions with the United States and the carefully controlled probing of American intentions with respect to Taiwan.

On the other hand, Peking was equally mindful of the need for periodic demonstrations of intransigence and militancy. Apart from its total rejection of the various 'two Chinas' solutions proposed by successive United States administrations, Peking felt it necessary to reiterate its determination to liberate Taiwan. Equally firm was China's denunciation of Kennedy's counter-insurgency strategy, and her confidence in its ultimate defeat.[67] In August 1963, Mao went so far as to intervene in America's internal affairs, by issuing a major statement in support of the Negro struggle against discrimination.[68]

In spite of the self-assertive and seemingly radical tenor of her pronouncements, China nevertheless refrained from taking what she considered to be provocative action. In a major statement on Chinese foreign policy in April 1966, Zhou Enlai reaffirmed his country's resolve not to provoke a war with the United States.[69] Although he also pledged support for countries that were the victims of aggression, he was careful to leave unstated the precise nature and extent of such support. Certainly, nothing was said that suggested the possibility of direct Chinese participation in a local military conflict. The case of Korea had already shown that China would intervene directly only in order to defend essential security interests or to maintain the delicate balance of power along her perimeter should it be seriously threatened by the unilateral initiative of an antagonistic power. As for threats of military retaliation, they were obviously intended to deter an American first strike. Indicative of the defensive character of Chinese strategy was the desire to convert an American attack from the sky into a protracted ground war. Apart from the claim that such a war would 'have no boundaries', Chinese warnings were most notable for their lack of precision and their references to an ill-defined and remote future:

> Should US imperialism dare to attack China either on a limited scale or in full strength, the only result will be the total annihilation of US aggressors. As for a possible sudden attack by US imperialism, the Chinese people are fully prepared, at all times. . . .[70]

The task of reconciling strategic boldness with tactical caution was probably nowhere more difficult or better illustrated than in China's attitude towards American military intervention in Vietnam. On the one hand, the Indochina conflict presented Peking with an excellent opportunity to demonstrate its practical solidarity with a neighbouring revolutionary movement and its commitment to the withdrawal of the US military presence from Southeast Asia. On the other hand, were China to go too far in exploiting these opportunities she might have been instrumental in escalating the conflict into a major Sino–American confrontation.

In Vietnam China found perhaps the most suitable conditions for a major application of her liberation war strategy. The profound peasant discontent in South Vietnam and the friendly neutrality of Cambodia were important factors that enhanced the possibility of a protracted struggle but yet did not require China's direct military intervention. A successful conclusion to this struggle would greatly magnify China's power and prestige in Asia, vindicate her revolutionary strategy and undermine the confidence of America's Asian allies, forcing them to accommodate their interests as best they could with those of China. That big stakes were involved in this conflict was openly acknowledged by Peking in a series of official statements. The Vietnam question was, in fact, described as 'the focal point in the present world-wide struggle between the revolutionary forces of the people and the forces of counter-revolution'.[71] But while seeking to give maximum support to the anti-American forces in the Vietnam struggle, the Chinese avoided provocative actions of their own and even warned North Vietnam against military adventurism, indicating quite clearly that they themselves would not intervene unless the United States attacked China or invaded North Vietnam.

The dichotomy in the Chinese attitude of inciting and assisting the communist revolutionary cause on the one hand, and of defending Chinese security on the other, formed the basis of China's position towards the Vietnam war throughout the 1960s, and especially during the period of escalation in America's military involvement. Promises of 'full support' for the struggle against 'US armed aggression in South Vietnam'[72] were in part inspired by fears for China's own security. Guo Mojo, Chairman of the Chinese Peace Committee, warned that 'the security of China and Vietnam are indivisible'.[73] In response to this perceived threat, China attempted to mobilize worldwide opposition to the American military role in Southeast Asia. In July 1963, ten Chinese mass organizations adopted a joint resolution aimed principally at the socialist camp. With a view to extracting maximum advantage from the conflict with the Soviet Union, they warned Soviet leaders not to 'make a deal with US imperialism at the expense of the interests of the South Vietnamese people'.[74]

But while pledging her own support and seeking the support of others for the Vietnamese struggle, at no stage did China make a firm commitment to intervene militarily on Vietnam's behalf. In replying to the demands of the government of the Democratic Republic of Vietnam in 1964, Chen Yi reiterated China's sympathy for Hanoi's predicament but carefully avoided giving any concrete undertaking.[75] In the months that followed there appeared to be a hardening of the Chinese position. A statement in August 1964 spoke of 'lending a helping hand' and added that '. . . the debt of blood incurred by the US to the Vietnam people must be repaid'.[76] In January 1965, Chinese pronouncements appeared even more ominous with references to the duties incumbent upon the Chinese government and people 'for the defence of peace in this area'.[77] But it was not until August 1965 that China made a statement committing her to 'all-out support and assistance, up to and including the sending . . . of our men to fight shoulder to shoulder with [the Vietnamese people] to drive out the US aggressor'.[78] Even then, however, the conditions under which she would act remained deliberately ambiguous.

As the United States stepped up its escalation of the war, especially through the bombing of North Vietnam, Peking was anxious to convince Washington that these intimidatory tactics would not succeed. Following the American air raids against Hanoi and Haiphong, Chinese leaders emphasized that all those committed to the struggle against US aggression were no longer 'subject to any restrictions', and that in this protracted war the initiative lay as much with the communist side as with its opponents.[79] But within a few days of this seemingly provocative statement, China made it equally clear that in the present circumstances her 'no holds barred' policy was to be taken as advice to the Vietnamese on how to conduct the war rather than as a guide to future Chinese actions. However substantial, outside aid could merely complement but never replace the local struggle.[80]

Broadly speaking, one may characterize the Chinese strategy with regard to Vietnam as an attempt to deter any extension of the conflict that could involve a direct confrontation with the United States, while encouraging the guerrilla campaign and working towards the political disintegration of the South Vietnamese regime until the US retired from the scene outmanoeuvred and psychologically exhausted. In keeping with this strategy, Peking was quite content to cold-shoulder any American peace initiative[81] in the belief that, given time, a protracted struggle would ensure a communist victory at minimum risk to Chinese security.

The above analysis has attempted to demonstrate how China's national interests, dictated principally by the factors of history and geography, combined with the demands of the Maoist ideology to produce in the period up to the Cultural Revolution a highly assertive Chinese foreign policy. The purpose of this self-assertion was to gain for China international recognition of the legitimacy of her government and of her aspirations towards great power status, as well as the capacity to radiate outwards in ever-widening concentric circles the principles of Mao's revolutionary strategy.

It is precisely China's revolutionary vision and the consequent desire for a surgical transformation of the international system that predisposed the Chinese leadership to adopt the posture of 'strategic boldness' in relation to the prevailing bipolar equilibrium. China's commitment to this policy also stemmed from her dissatisfaction with the existing disproportion between her actual influence and her power potential. The disadvantage of her position was perceived at least until the late 1960s as the result of a hostile environment created largely by the United States, although the Soviet role assumed increasing importance, especially after the early 1960s.

But while pursuing a policy based on the rhetoric of self-assertion, Chinese goals were not to be attained through a major military confrontation with either of the superpowers but rather as a result of a carefully conceived and well-orchestrated campaign, operating mainly at the level of propaganda. This form of revolutionary diplomacy was supported and given its very raison d'être by the strategy of people's war. Local military victories over the United States, though peripheral in relation to that country's overwhelming military might, would nonetheless succeed in significantly reducing, if not totally eliminating, the American military presence on the Asian mainland, particularly to the south of China's borders.

The net effect of Communist China's policy was to introduce a new element of polarization into the international system, not along the lines of the existing power rivalry between the two superpowers, but in the context of a revisionist challenge to the existing balance of power. Acting as one of the most dissatisfied powers in the world, China presented herself as the 'champion of the poor, the proud and the oppressed'. Sooner or later such a challenge was bound to incur not only Washington's but Moscow's hostility and shatter the precarious bonds of the Sino–Soviet alliance.

CHAPTER 3

The Sino–Soviet Alliance and its Demise

In analysing China's relations with the Soviet Union no attempt will be made to cover the whole area of this vast subject or to provide a detailed historical survey. The main concern will be to characterize the changing pattern of Chinese attitudes and policies towards the Soviet Union during the 1950s and 1960s in order to shed some additional light on the nature of the Maoist challenge to the international status quo. We have already observed in Chapter 1 how, in the immediate aftermath of the October Revolution, Chinese foreign policy was motivated by a profound sense of dissatisfaction with the prevailing international order. China's new leaders were intent on re-establishing her territorial integrity, regaining her freedom of action and developing a military capability commensurate with her security requirements. But the very pursuit of these objectives brought about a head-on confrontation with the United States, thereby reinforcing China's diplomatic isolation and strategic weakness while accentuating her commitment to revolutionary struggle at home and abroad. Faced with an overwhelmingly hostile environment, Peking came to the logical conclusion that only an alliance with the Soviet Union could provide China with any reasonable prospect of achieving her ideological and foreign policy goals.

The Alliance: Ideal and Actuality

The Sino–Soviet Treaty of Friendship, Alliance and Mutual Assistance of 14 February 1950 pledged the Soviet Union not only to protect Communist China from attack by Japan or any of Japan's allies, but also to act in 'conformity with the principles of equality, mutual benefit and mutual respect for the national sovereignty and territorial integrity and non-interference in the internal affairs' of the People's Republic. Peking appeared ready to follow unreservedly the Soviet lead in foreign policy. To the great surprise of many observers, Mao had made this momentous decision in spite of the strains and stresses that had persistently marked the delicate relationship between Stalin and the Chinese Communist Party during the 1930s and 1940s.[1]

As far back as 1930, mistaken Russian directives had forced the Chinese

Communists to attempt a premature and totally unsuccessful seizure of power. Rather than acknowledge its own misreading of China's internal situation, Moscow obliged Chinese Communist leaders to accept most of the responsibility for failure. By the mid-1930s, Stalin was increasingly pre-occupied with the Japanese and German threats to Russian security, and accordingly support for the Chinese revolution disappeared almost entirely from his list of priorities. Soon after the war, the Soviet leadership again miscalculated the trend of Chinese events and sought to persuade Mao to dissolve his armies and join forces with the Nationalists. As Stalin was to admit later in 1948:

> . . . we invited the Chinese comrades to come to Moscow. . . . We told them bluntly that we considered the devlopment of the uprising in China had no prospects and that the Chinese comrades should seek a *modus vivendi* with Chiang Kai-shek. . . . The Chinese comrades agreed here with the views of the Soviet comrades, but went back to China and acted otherwise. They mustered their forces, organised their armies, and now, as we see, they are beating the Chiang Kai-shek army. Now, in the case of China, we admit we were wrong.[2]

These erroneous and self-interested policies on the part of the Soviet Union could hardly have failed to make a deep and lasting impression on Mao who, in order to win control of the Chinese Communist Party, had to wage a protracted campaign against the Moscow line during the late 1920s and early 1930s. Even at the height of Sino–Soviet friendship, Chinese sources were not reticent to emphasize the very serious differences that had punctuated the early history of relations between the two parties.[3]

The far greater element of cordiality in Sino–Soviet relations immediately after the Communist seizure of power and Moscow's automatic recognition of the People's Republic of China were bound to reduce but not totally eliminate the impact of past disputes and disagreements. Even the treaty establishing a military alliance between the two communist nations had to be preceded by hard and prolonged bargaining. As Mao was to reveal much later in December 1958:

> In 1950 I argued with Stalin in Moscow for two months. We argued about the Treaty of Mutual Assistance and Alliance, about the Chinese Changchun Railway, about the joint-stock companies, about the border question.[4]

Mao was undoubtedly aware, even in this early phase of the Moscow–Peking axis, of the serious contradictions that existed between two socialist countries at markedly different stages of economic and political development. However, the confrontation with Stalin, reminiscent of similar struggles with the Soviet Union during the previous two decades, had now to be subordinated to the higher interests of socialist unity. The Chinese slogan 'lean to one side' was the natural consequence of Mao's class analysis of the international situation and of his commitment to the anti-imperialist struggle.

But Peking's firm alignment with the Soviet Union was not merely the expression of China's ideological preference; it was an obvious necessity for both strategic and economic reasons. The decision of the United States not to recognize the new Chinese government, the outbreak of the Korean war, America's direct intervention in the Taiwan dispute, China's failure to gain admission to the United Nations and the UN embargo of May 1951, all combined to intensify China's isolation from the non-communist world and increase her dependence on the Soviet Union. China's entry into the Korean war resulted in the subordination of economic objectives to the needs of national defence and the growing reliance of the Chinese army on Soviet training and equipment.

A series of agreements accompanying the Sino–Soviet treaty of February 1950 provided for the eventual return of the Chinese Changchun Railway, Port Arthur and Dairen; a Soviet long-term credit to China of $300 million; and the transfer gratis to China of certain ex-Japanese property acquired by the Soviet Union in Manchuria. Notes were also exchanged recognizing the independence of Outer Mongolia, and further agreements were signed on 27 March 1950 for the purpose of establishing joint-stock companies to exploit China's mineral resources as well as a joint-stock civil aviation company. These accords, which were complemented by the Sino–Soviet Trade Agreement of 19 April 1950, were no doubt intended as a concrete demonstration of Soviet goodwill towards the new China. Far from absorbing Chinese border regions into the Russian sphere, Moscow appeared ready to assist in the restoration of China's economic and military power.

Following a Sino–Soviet conference held in Moscow from 18 August to 23 September 1952, it was jointly announced that, while steps were being taken to effect the promised return of the Changchun Railway, Moscow would delay, in response to Peking's request, the withdrawl of Russian troops from Port Arthur until both countries had established treaty relations with Japan. On the occasion of the fifth anniversary celebrations of the Chinese Communist regime and the visit to Peking of a top-level Soviet delegation – including Khrushchev and Bulganin – the two countries issued a Joint Declaration on 12 October 1954 in which they reaffirmed their desire to 'strengthen and broaden their ties of brotherly friendship'.5 The Soviet Union also agreed to the retrocession of Port Arthur, which was effected by 31 May 1955; to the return of its shares in joint Sino–Soviet companies (reportedly relinquished on 1 January 1955); and to the granting of additional long-term credits valued at $130 million. Soviet aid was also to be provided for another fifteen industrial projects, including the construction of two new railroads linking the two countries.

Judging simply on the basis of public declarations of friendship and support, one would have gained throughout the 1950s the distinct impression of a flourishing Russo–Chinese relationship. On the occasion of the seventh anniversary of the Sino–Soviet treaty, a leading member of the Central Committee of the CCP described the friendship between the two countries as 'a powerful guarantee of China's independence and security, and a bastion of peace in the Far East and the world'.[6] In a major speech during his visit to Moscow in November 1957, Mao himself referred in glowing terms to the benefits of the Sino–Soviet alliance:

> This is a great alliance of two great socialist countries. We share the same destiny and the same life-spring with the Soviet Union and the entire socialist camp.[7]

The same references to the vitality of socialist solidarity and cooperation appeared in the communiqué issued at the end of talks held in Peking in July–August 1958 between Mao and Khrushchev.[8] In June 1959 a leading Chinese commentator described Sino–Soviet friendship as 'indestructible'.[9] At the Jubilee banquet to celebrate the tenth anniversary of the founding of the People's Republic of China, both Zhou Enlai and Khrushchev reaffirmed the importance of the friendship between their two countries. In November 1959, Vice-Chairman Dong Biwu was confidently predicting that 'reactionary' attempts to 'undermine Sino–Soviet unity' would 'continue to suffer ignominious defeat'.[10]

In February 1960, Chen Yi was generously praising the nature and quantity of Soviet economic and technical aid and extolling the virtues of the Sino–Soviet alliance, which he described as 'the pillar supporting the mansion of world peace'.[11] Even as late as February 1962, a leading editorial of the *People's Daily* stressed the contribution that the Sino–Soviet treaty had made to 'the common upsurge of the socialist and communist construction in the two countries' and to 'the might of the socialist camp'. This alliance was described as 'the cornerstone of the unity of the socialist camp' and 'a powerful bastion guarding Far Eastern and world peace'.[12] But for all their effusiveness and constancy, these protestations of fraternal friendship and proletarian solidarity could not indefinitely conceal the growing conflict of interests that was ultimately to create an unbridgeable gap between the foreign policies of the two man communist states.

As I have already indicated, China's decision to align herself with the Soviet Union and to accept Moscow's primacy in the international communist movement was motivated by both practical and ideological considerations. In return for her recognition of the Kremlin's authority within the socialist camp, China no doubt expected the Soviet Union to provide her with the support and protection necessary for the achievement of certain minimum national objectives.

The first set of expectations concerned the East–West strategic relationship.[13] The Chinese were particularly anxious that the Soviet Union should achieve nuclear parity with the United States, or at least sufficient military capacity to be able to exert diplomatic and strategic pressure on the West, while at the same time deterring an American nuclear attack. For Mao, the emerging nuclear stalemate, while imposing major inhibitions on the conduct of the imperialist camp, created unprecedented opportunities for the socialist commonwealth to pursue more dynamic and thrustful policies. Apart from enhancing the prospect of defending communist interests in Europe and the Far East, the build-up of Soviet strategic forces promised to provide new avenues of manoeuvrability, particularly in support of the various struggles for national liberation. In China's view, the Soviet bloc had to take advantage of Moscow's military–technological breakthrough of the late 1950s and pursue 'a policy of "brinkmanship" in selected areas under the cover of the Soviet nuclear shield'.[14] Whatever the realism of this attitude, the Maoist leadership obviously expected that Soviet deterrent power would be placed at the service of the entire international communist movement and not simply used as an instrument of Soviet national interests.

A second series of Chinese expectations referred more specifically to China's national objectives, of which probably the most important was the recovery of Taiwan. Closely allied to this demand was the proposition that the Soviet Union should actively press for the removal of American military bases – especially those equipped with nuclear weapons – which formed a semi-circle around China in the Far East, the Western Pacific and Southeast Asia. The major obstacle to the communist liberation of Taiwan was, in fact, the American military presence in the region, most strikingly demonstrated by the Seventh Fleet.[15] In addition, Communist China expected automatic support, at least of a political kind, in the case of a confrontation with any other Asian power. This reading of the implications of the Sino–Soviet alliance was to be most severely tested during the course of the Sino–Indian border dispute.

Finally, Peking no doubt estimated that its alignment with Moscow would provide a valuable and reliable channel of economic and military aid. Soviet assistance, particularly in the form of heavy and sophisticated machinery and equipment, was regarded as crucial to China's industrialization programme. The Soviet Union was also expected to help China develop a modern defence industry and equip her army with tanks, artillery and transport. But quite apart from this conventional assistance, it became increasingly clear that China was also hoping to receive from Moscow atomic weapons and missiles, or at least the technology necessary for their manufacture.

This long list of benefits which China hoped to derive from her alliance with the Soviet Union has been neither detailed nor exhaustive, but it does nevertheless indicate the magnitude of Chinese demands, which Soviet leaders were ultimately unable or unwilling to satisfy. It was Peking's growing realization of this simple but fundamental fact that precipitated the end of the Sino–Soviet axis. As one surveys the course of events, particularly in the light of what both sides subsequently revealed of their secret exchanges, it becomes evident that the gradual escalation of the conflict was the unavoidable consequence of contradictory expectations, which themselves derived from the combined effect of competing national interests and divergent ideological perceptions.

To gain some insight into the considerable and widening disparity between

China's original estimation of the alliance and the subsequent reality, it may be profitable to examine in greater detail the role of the factors to which I have already alluded – economic and military aid, nuclear strategy and the Taiwan dispute – in the evolution of the Sino–Soviet Relationship. In the matter of economic assistance, reference has already been made to the two loans granted by the Soviet Union in 1950 and 1954 respectively, totalling some $430 million of credits. As Soviet sources were to acknowledge at a later date, Sino–Soviet cooperation did not reach its peak until after 1953, when some of the 'disagreeable' strings imposed by Stalin on Soviet aid, notably his insistence on joint-stock companies and mining and industrial concessions, 'were removed on the initiative of the CPSU [Communist Party of the Soviet Union] Central Committee and Comrade N. S. Khrushchev'.[16]

Soviet leaders were subsequently able to claim that Soviet aid had enabled the People's Republic to build whole branches of industry in which China had been previously deficient, namely 'aircraft, motor and tractor-building industries, power-producing, heavy machine-building and precision machine-building industries, instrument-making and radio-engineering and various branches of the chemical industry'.[17] According to Soviet estimates, a very large proportion of China's iron, steel and coal production as well as of her tin and synthetic rubber output derived from factories built and constructed with Soviet assistance. More than 10,000 Soviet specialists had been sent to China for varying terms between 1950 and 1960, while some 10,000 Chinese engineers, technicians and skilled workers, and about 1000 scientists had received training in the USSR between 1951 and 1962. During this same period more than 11,000 students were trained at Soviet higher educational institutions, while between 1954 and 1963 the Soviet Union turned over to China more than 24,000 sets of scientific and technical documents, including 1400 projects of large industrial enterprises.[18]

Although Chinese authorities did not challenge the accuracy of these claims or the beneficial role of Soviet aid for which they expressed their gratitude, they presented a markedly different analysis of the Sino–Soviet economic relationship.[19] Soviet aid to China, it was argued, was rendered mainly in the form of trade and required repayment in the form of goods, gold or convertible foreign exchange. By the end of 1962,

> ... China had furnished the Soviet Union with 2100 million new rubles' worth of grain, edible oils and other foodstuffs. Among the most important items were 5,760,000 tons of soya beans, 2,940,000 tons of rice, 1,090,000 tons of edible oils and 900,000 tons of meat.[20]

During the same period, China also furnished the Soviet Union with significant quantities of mineral products and metals, including tin, mercury, tungsten, and molybdenum, lithium, and beryllium concentrates, many of which, it was claimed, were 'indispensable for the development of the most advanced branches of science and for the manufacture of rockets and nuclear weapons'.[21]

Moreover, there is reason to believe that many of these exports were in repayment not for the financing of industrial projects but for military deliveries amounting to some $2000 million during the period 1950–57. In other words, in order to repay these military loans, China had to commit a substantial proportion of her exports for delivery to the Soviet Union without the expectation of any future return. According to one estimate, in 1956 the value of these repayments may have exceeded by more than four times the capital inflow from Soviet loans that year.[22] Another writer has suggested that, even if China were registering an annual export surplus of 1000 million rubles, as was the case in 1958, and allocating it entirely to debt repayment, some 40 per cent of Chinese exports to the USSR would have remained committed to repayment for nearly a decade.[23]

Not only did these exports represent a significant drain on China's agricultural and industrial surplus, but they made the availability of Soviet credits dependent on the level of China's agricultural production. The failure of Soviet deliveries of projects to meet original plans may thus be explained in terms of the relationships between these two variables. It is unlikely to have been altogether coincidental that the disappointing Chinese harvests of 1954 and 1956 should have been followed by drastic reductions in the supply of Soviet capital goods and considerable delays in the completion of many industrial enterprises.[24] Nor was China's export surplus needed only for purposes of debt repayment; it was also necessary to cover the substantial deficit with the USSR on service account resulting from such items as Soviet technical assistance and transportation costs.

It will be readily seen from what has been said that Sino–Soviet trade during the 1950s conformed to the system of unequal exchange that has generally prevailed in relations between highly industrialized and underdeveloped societies. While the bulk of Soviet exports to China comprised machinery of various kinds, Chinese exports to the Soviet Union, especially in the early and mid-1950s, consisted predominantly of raw materials, foodstuffs and nonferous metals. Complementing this pattern of commodity concentration was the marked dependence of the Chinese economy on Sino–Soviet trade. While more than 50 per cent of China's capital transactions were directed to the Soviet Union, only about 15–20 per cent of Soviet trade was with China. It was no doubt this imbalance in the economic relationship, most dramatically evident in the field of technology, which led Maoist China to a critical reassessment of her economic dependence on the Soviet Union.

By the late 1950s, Chinese political leaders and economic planners were publicly questioning the importance of Sino–Soviet trade for the future of China's industrialization. The gradual loosening of the UN embargo, the emergence of alternative sources of supply and the development of a comprehensive industrial infrastructure thus prepared the ground for the increasingly conscious policy of self-reliance that was to culminate in 1960 in the termination of all Soviet technical and scientific aid to China. At the height of the ideological debate between the two countries in 1964, Peking was to accuse Moscow of

> . . . unscrupulously [withdrawing] the 1390 Soviet experts working in China, [tearing] up 343 contracts and supplementary contracts concerning exports, and [scrapping] 257 projects of scientific and technical cooperation, all within the short space of a month.[25]

Although the abrupt recall of all Soviet specialists undoubtedly created, at least in the short-term, serious economic difficulties for China, much of the evidence would suggest that the Maoist conception of economic development had been questioning for some time the value of Soviet technical and scientific aid and the relevance of the Soviet Union's organizational and economic experience for the special conditions currently prevailing in China.

Nor was Chinese disenchantment with the quantity or quality of Soviet aid confined to the economic sphere, for significant differences between the two countries soon emerged on the question of military assistance. It is true that the Soviet Union did initiate major weapons shipments to China, particularly after the latter's entry into the Korean war, and that these were largely responsible for the modernization of the Chinese army and airforce which, by December 1951, was estimated to comprise a total strength of 2480 aircraft of all types, including 700 MIG-15 fighters and 200 piston light bombers. By 1952 IL-28 jet light bombers were being introduced, and these were followed by a token number of TU-4's B-29 type piston medium bombers.[26]

Most of these military deliveries had been financed by large loans from Moscow, totalling some $2000 million. Although little is known of the terms for settlement, it is generally understood that this large sum had to be repaid with interest. Even as early as June 1957, Long Yun, a senior member of the National Defence Council, was reportedly protesting that China had to bear the entire cost of the anti-imperialist struggle in Korea.[27] The same theme was to form the basis of a much sharper and more direct censure in February 1964 when China claimed that Soviet loans were used 'mostly for the purchase of war material from the Soviet Union, the greater part of which was used up in the war to resist US aggression and aid Korea'.[28]

The process of estrangement in the military relationship between Peking and Moscow probably dates from early 1958, for as late as November 1957 Marshal Zhu De was still praising the Soviet Union for the 'tremendous generous assistance' it had rendered to brother socialist countries, while Defence Minister Marshal Peng Dehuai was depicting the Soviet armed forces as 'the great example for the modernization of the Chinese armed forces'.[29] An army training programme promulgated in January 1958 envisaged the incorporation of 'modern military techniques and military science' as well as 'Soviet advanced experience in this field' and combat training 'under the modern conditions of atom bombs, chemical warfare and guided missiles'.[30] These combat plans were obviously premised on the application of Soviet military techniques and the acquisition of powerful and sophisticated Soviet weapons, and closely related to the defence agreement concluded with the Soviet Union on 15 October 1957.

However, as Peking subsequently revealed, the Soviet Union terminated the defence agreement in June 1959 and refused to provide China with a nuclear capability.[31] But well before the actual abrogation of the agreement, a dramatic change in China's military thinking had already occurred. The new military line, which deprecated reliance on foreign military experts and techniques, notably those of Soviet origin, and elevated men above weapons as the decisive factor in military victory or defeat, was expounded in a succession of statements during 1958 and was no doubt related to the Great Leap Forward (reflected in the slogan 'more, faster, better and more economically') and the Maoist determination to transform the entire nation into a vast militia, organized in communes.[32] An obvious contributing factor to this strategic and ideological shift had been Khrushchev's unresponsiveness to Peking's military demands. Thus, by applying to China's present defence needs the revolutionary principles of defeating a better equipped enemy with inferior weapons and relying on the mobilization of the masses, the Maoist leadership was in a sense making virtue out of necessity.

The rejection of Soviet military tactics and the decision to do without much Soviet support in the field of modern weapons, leading to Soviet cutbacks in aircraft deliveries in 1959 and the subsequent withdrawal of Soviet technicians and military advisers in mid-1960, stemmed largely from the failure of the two countries to agree on the nature and conditions of Soviet military assistance.

It is now generally accepted that the high-level Chinese delegation which visited Moscow in November 1957 had sought nuclear weapons for China. Although the Sino–Soviet defence agreement of October 1957 may have included a nuclear-sharing formula, it is clear that the arrangement was never implemented, probably because of the stringent controls demanded by the Soviet Union. A clue to the Soviet position was provided by a Chinese accusation made in September 1963, indicating that

> ...in 1958 the leadership of the CPSU put forward unreasonable demands designed to bring China under Soviet military control. These unreasonable demands were rightly and firmly rejected by the Chinese Government.[33]

The Russian proposal, probably patterned on the Warsaw Pact integrated defence structure, may have envisaged the creation of a joint land and sea command in the Far East under Soviet leadership. The net effect of the scheme, which would have been to make the installation of nuclear weapons in China conditional on a subordinating their use to ultimate Soviet control, convinced the Chinese leadership of the need to develop a nuclear deterrent by its own unaided efforts.

It is more than likely that China's decision to construct her own weapons was taken at the Enlarged Conference of the Military Affairs Committee in May–July 1958, which also formulated, under Mao's guidance, the new army guidelines based upon the PLA's own revolutionary experience. Accordingly, a statement by Marshal Nie Rongzhen, which appeared in the *People's Daily* on 2 August, asserted that China would develop its own nuclear capability without making 'wholesale use of the existing experiences of other countries'.[34] Mao himself is reported to have said during this period that it was 'entirely possible for some atom bombs and hydrogen bombs to be made in ten years' time',[35] while Foreign Minister Chen Yi had also stated in the course of an interview in May 1958 that China intended to become a nuclear power.[36]

The emerging conflict between the Soviet Union's obvious interest in maintaining its nuclear monopoly within the communist camp and China's nuclear aspirations rapidly intensified and eventually became the subject of a most acrimonious public exchange between the two governments. In Septmber 1963, Chinese leaders castigated the Soviet government not only for unilaterally abrogating the agreement to provide China with nuclear technical data, but for conveying to the United States 'secrets between China and the Soviet Union concerning nuclear weapons'[37] and for blatantly giving 'more and more military aid to the Indian reactionaries'.[38] Undoubtedly, however, it was the Taiwan crisis of August–September 1958 and the Soviet Union's unsatisfactory response which indicated in most dramatic fashion to the Maoist leadership Moscow's unwillingness to provide vigorous and uncompromising support for China's fundamental objectives.

Given that Soviet Defence Minister Malinovsky accompanied Khrushchev during his visit to Peking in July–August 1958,and that the build-up for the projected Chinese shelling of Jinmen had already begun, one can only assume that the Taiwan Strait crisis was a major subject of discussion. It is highly significant, therefore, that the communiqué issued at the end of the visit should have made no specific reference to this critical issue, thereby conveniently allowing Moscow to withold a firm and public expression of support for Peking's position. The recurring emphasis in the document on 'all-round cooperation', far from strengthening China's hand, was simply designed to inhibit China from taking any major initiative without prior consultation with Moscow. If Chinese military operations in 1958 carefully avoided any of the risks involved in taking the offshore islands, it was probably because of Moscow's insistence that no situation should be allowed to develop that might compel the Soviet Union to invoke its nuclear deterrent.

In the ensuing polemics between the two countries, the Kremlin defended its position by recalling Khrushchev's letter to President Eisenhower of 7 September 1958 in which he announced that an attack on the Chinese People's Republic would be regarded as an attack on the Soviet Union and his subsequent warning of 19 September 'that if the aggressor used nuclear weapons, the Soviet Union would use its own nuclear rocket weapons to defend China'.[39] But the Soviet attitude did not harden until the Chinese had themselves offered to negotiate on the dispute, by which time it had become evident that the Americans would not intervene directly. As the Chinese subsequently explained, Soviet leaders expressed their support for China only when the prospect of a superpower crisis had evaported.[40]

Even well before the Sino–Soviet dispute had become public knowledge, Peking made little effort to conceal its profound displeasure with the Soviet Union's apparent indifference to Chinese interests. Accordingly, throughout the latter months of 1958 a series of statements appeared in the Chinese press hurling angry accusations against 'neurotics' frightened by 'the war provocations and military extortions of the American imperialists'.[41] On 1 November, the *People's Daily* issued a veiled but unmistakable denunciation of Soviet leaders for being 'scared out of their wits' and for advising China to 'face sufferings, change [her] ideological habits, and give up [her] struggle'.[42]

By 1959 the Chinese government apparently came to the conclusion that Soviet policy, far from assisting China to recover Taiwan, was moving towards a 'two Chinas' solution.[43] What was now in doubt was not simply the extent of Soviet support for Chinese objectives but the very credibility of the Sino–Soviet alliance. Although in the early period of open polemics both sides still claimed that the military provisions of the treaty remained valid – a Soviet statement in August 1963 reaffirmed that 'China's external security was governed by the might of the Soviet Union',[44] and in May 1964 Zhou Enlai stated that China would fight on the side of the USSR in the event of an imperialist attack against the Soviet Union[45] – by 1965 Chen Yi was casting doubts, obliquely but openly, on the reliability of Soviet nuclear protection.[46] China was now willing to conduct her diplomacy on the assumption that the Soviet nuclear umbrella as well as Soviet support for the Peking claim to Taiwan were irrevocably lost. In the Chinese view, the Soviet Union was unlikely to intervene directly on China's behalf except in the most improbable circumstances, and then only if it could be confidently assured that such intervention would not provoke American retaliation.

With the benefit of hindsight it can be readily seen that the Sino–Soviet conflict grew in intensity in direct proportion to the developing Soviet–American accommodation. In actual fact, one of the principal reasons why Moscow was unwilling to accede to many of China's demands was its desire to promote a climate of détente with Washington. As tension between the Soviet Union and the United States decreased in the late 1950s, the main factor that had cemented the Sino–Soviet alliance began to disappear. Although largely symbolic in nature, the secret discussion at Camp David between Khrushchev and Eisenhower in September 1959 provided a striking demonstration of this relationship, which China was bound to view with alarm and suspicion.

But why was the Soviet Union now seeking ways of reducing tension with the United States and containing the spread of nuclear weapons, while China was attempting to pursue a more revolutionary and explicitly anti-American policy than ever before? The answer to this question and China's increasing realization of its implication may be said to lie at the root of the Sino–Soviet conflict. The Soviet Union was now a highly developed industrialized state, a thermonuclear world power, less and less vulnerable to the economic or military pressures of the West. By contrast, China, the most populous nation in the world, was a predominantly agricultural state still struggling to complete the first stage of industrialization, and a regional power with limited military capacity or diplomatic manoeuvrability. Unlike China, the Soviet Union was now a satisfied power with no territorial claims comparable to Taiwan, extending its control over a large and relatively stable buffer zone in Eastern Euope, its status as a superpower recognized and accepted by the entire world community. For the Soviet Union, the conflict of interests with the United States had assumed the form of a peaceful competition between equals. In China's case, the conflict was far more direct and more complete, for what was at stake was the satisfaction of her national interests and revolutionary objectives, requiring a radical revision of the political map of Asia and the rest of the world. For China, the enormity of the Soviet crime consisted precisely in the willingness of Soviet leaders to do business with China's arch-enemy, the United States, a power intent on frustrating the realization of Chinese aims and aspirations.

Historical Evolution of the Dispute

I have already observed that the Maoist decision to 'lean to one side' taken immediately after the victory of the Chinese Communist revolution was governed by pragmatic as well as ideological considerations (see p. 49). In the prevailing context of international bipolarity and China's domestic weakness there was no other practical option open to Peking. However, the cumulative impact of a long series of events beginning with the Korean war was to bring about a gradual but profound change in China's objective situation, both domestically and externally. Making use of the Soviet nuclear umbrella, Chinese military intervention in Korea was able to thwart the advance of US and allied forces operating under the UN command while at the same time deterring the United States from using its technological superiority to undertake action against industries and communications in Chinese territory. In a sense, China's ability to carry on a major war for nearly three years against a powerful coalition of states greatly enhanced her international prestige and contributed to the internal consolidation of her new government. The death of Stalin in March 1953 and the signing of the Korean armistice four months later combined to give added impetus to China's re-emergence as a major actor on the international stage, on the one hand by bringing undisputed Russian dominance of the world communist movement to an end, and on the other by freeing China's from a military conflict that had always carried the risk of uncontrollable escalation.

It was probably not until 1954 that China had achieved the necessary stability to formulate a coherent and long-term foreign policy. The new initiatives taken by China in 1954 in applying the concept of 'peaceful coexistence' to relations with India, Burma and her other Asian neighbours represented in many respects a significant advance on current Soviet thinking. The spirit of moderation so masterfully displayed by Zhou Enlai at the Bandung Conference, the championing of the five principles of peaceful coexistence and the offer to begin negotiations with the United States on the issue of Taiwan, all testified to the renewed vigour of Chinese diplomacy and to the desire to evolve a more equal, or at least less subservient, relationship with the Soviet Union.

The Hungarian and Polish crises of October–November 1956 were to provide China with her first major opportunity to play a significant and distinctive role in the affairs of the communist world. In Poland, the process of democratization initiated by the Polish government following the Poznan riots of June 1956 had caused increasing alarm to various elements within the Soviet leadership and especially among Khrushchev's 'Stalinist' critics, many of whom were calling for the use of armed force in order to arrest the trend towards liberalization and subdue the Polish Communist Party to Moscow's wishes. Hungary, like Poland, had for some time been in a state of unrest, which culminated in the riots and demonstrations of 23 October. The next day Soviet troops appeared in Budapest and two days later Imre Nagy formed a new government. Although an armistice was proclaimed and Soviet troops subsequently left Hungary, the national uprising had assumed such proportions that the new regime felt compelled to accede to demands for free elections, rights of opposition and withdrawal from the Warsaw Pact. Confronted with the prospect of a major defection from the communist camp, which might eventually threaten the whole Soviet empire in Eastern Europe, the Soviet leadership finally decided on military intervention and the replacement of the Nagy government by a more orthodox and pliant regime.

In analysing China's response to these events, it is instructive to note that, while Peking gave its approval to the Soviet use of force in Hungary, it forcefully withheld its support for Soviet plans to crush Gomulka in Poland. Indeed, it would appear that China insisted upon Soviet intervention in Hungary at a time of disagreement and indecision within the Soviet leadership, arguing that Moscow's failure to act would lead to the victory of counter-revolution and the defeat of the socialist forces in Hungary. By contrast, in the case of Poland, the Chinese rejected a Soviet proposal to have Poland condemned by a meeting of communist parties.

Far from agreeing to the restoration of the Stalinist pattern in Polish affairs, there is evidence to suggest that Maoist China favoured a process of 'controlled democratization' within the Soviet bloc, and that this Chinese view was conveyed to the foreign communist delegates, and in particular to the First Secretary of the Polish United Workers Party, Edward Ochab, who was attending the Eighth Congress of the Chinese Communist Party in September

1956. Ochab took advantage of this occasion to express his enthusiasm for the 'creative' example of the Chinese path to socialism:

> The PZPR/Polish United Workers (Communist) Party is following with great attention the creative work of the Communist Party of China and the bold decision taken by your Central Committee on the immortal principles of Marxism–Leninism with special allowance made for the characteristics of your vast country.[47]

In keeping with its general position of support for greater national autonomy within the socialist family of nations, Peking endorsed and may even have been partly responsible for the drafting of the Soviet declaration of 30 October, which offered to negotiate economic and military relations among the Warsaw Pact signatories, including the stationing of Soviet troops in Eastern Europe.[48] In a separate statement on 1 November, the Chinese leadership strongly endorsed Moscow's admission of error in its relations with the satellites and reaffirmed the view that the 'socialist commonwealth' as a geographical and ideological entity depended for its survival on adherence to the principles of mutuality and respect in inter-party relations. The mistaken violations of these principles by the Soviet Union had brought about the expulsion of Tito's Yugoslavia from the Soviet orbit in 1948 and were now again evident in the Polish–Hungarian situation. On the other hand, the statement was equally adamant that attempts to introduce greater internal independence for the members of the socialist bloc should not be allowed to endanger communist control in Eastern Europe or the primacy of Soviet leadership.[49]

China's implicit endorsement of Soviet military intervention to put down any anti-communist revolts was made explicit in a series of newspaper editorials in early November, which acclaimed Soviet repression of the Hungarian revolt as 'a glorious manifestation of proletarian internationalism' and proof of Moscow's determination 'to support the cause of socialism and peace'.[50] China's two-edged policy, which included support for Gomulka's type of national communism coupled with opposition to 'revisionist' tendencies, found expression in a major ideological declaration issued at the end of December. It was addressed as much to the estrangement between Belgrade and Moscow as to the events in Hungary and Poland. Coming soon after Peking's publication of Kardelj's criticisms of Soviet policy on 7 December, and of Tito's famous Pula speech on 12 December, which had called for the 'democratization of the Communist Bloc', the Chinese statement explicitly acknowledged the existence of 'contradictions' between both socialist countries and communist parties, but added that these were 'not basic... not the result of a fundamental clash of interests between classes but of conflict between right and wrong opinions or of a partial contradiction of interests'.[51] In keeping with its preference for a spirit of compromise, the Chinese analysis recognized the efforts of the Soviet Communist Party to correct Stalin's mistakes and eliminate their consequences, but recommended that these efforts should be 'protected' and entail 'thoroughgoing ideological education' as well as 'an objective and analytical attitude'. Referring to 'all those comrades who made similar mistakes under [Stalin's] influence', Peking advocated moderation and a 'comradely attitude' towards them. The whole statement was intended as a warning against 'big-nation chauvinism'.[52]

The loss of confidence within the international communist movement in the wisdom and credibility of the Soviet leadership had provided Maoist China with a ready-made opportunity to enter the ideological arena and demonstrate a unique capacity, sadly lacking in the Kremlin, to analyse the causes of the crisis of world communism and adapt the principles of Marxism–Leninism to the new situation that had arisen in Eastern Europe. That China was aware of the far-reaching implications of these developments is indicated by Zhou Enlai's decision to interrupt his goodwill tour in January 1957 and proceed to Moscow, Warsaw and Budapest to play the role of doctrinal interpreter and inter-party mediator. The communiqué issued at the end of his discussions in each capital stressed the importance of satisfying the aspirations of communist parties for greater internal autonomy, although he was equally insistent on the need to maintain the unity of the socialist camp under the leadership of the Soviet Union.[53]

The Chinese initiative in European affairs significantly altered the structure of the Sino–Soviet relationship. Maoist China had become a principal actor within the international communist system, whose voice had to be heeded by all communist parties. The Soviet Union was no longer able to exercise an exclusive leadership role in the affairs of the communist bloc. Encouraged by the success of its active intervention in inter-party disputes, Peking now sought to consolidate its ideological position by taking the lead in the campaign against revisionism. Although Moscow was also displeased by the defiant reassertion of Titoist independence at the Yugoslav Communist Congress in April 1957, its attitude was still far less uncompromising than the position expressed in the editorial of the *People's Daily* of 5 May, in which China launched one of her most violent attacks on the Yugoslav leader and his policies.

On the other hand, Moscow could not easily avoid another break with Yugoslavia, since it was hardly possible to tolerate within the communist fold any ideology that could serve as a justification for a 'neutralist' stance. The Soviet leadership was nevertheless anxious to prevent an irrevocable rupture, which would in any case adversely affect Moscow's relations with the entire non-aligned bloc. One may therefore conclude that the Kremlin's progressively more vehement denunciations of the Titoist deviation were more closely related to the pressures exerted by China than to its own assessment of the situation. The Chinese, for their part, were anxious to stiffen as far as possible the Soviet campaign against Yugoslavia, so as to prevent the latter's policy of coexistence with the United States from spreading to other communist countries. In a very real sense, the effort to discredit Yugoslav revisionism was an attempt to forestall the possibility of Soviet–American détente, which would obviously operate to the disadvantage of Chinese interests. Peking's fears in this regard had already been aroused by a number of Khrushchev's statements and initiatives during 1957, apparently designed to achieve a lessening of military tensions with the West. Significantly, at a time when China was anxious to establish control over Taiwan, the Soviet Union was conveying to the United States its readiness to 'recognize the status quo . . . [and] renounce any attempt to alter the existing situation by force'.[54] Soviet diplomacy was also exploring the possibility of a great power summit peace conference that might include India but not China, as well as a series of bilateral negotiations with the United States covering such questions as disarmament, arms control and the development of commercial and cultural ties.

By this time a pronounced leftward shift in Chinese domestic politics, which was to culminate in the Great Leap Forward of 1958, was also contributing to a more militant foreign policy. The failure of the Hundred Flowers experiment to establish a stable framework for intellectual freedom, the increasing dissatisfaction with the Soviet economic model and the growing determination to apply China's revolutionary experience to present needs, thus combined with Chinese misgivings about the nature and direction of détente to strengthen Mao's resolve to gain for China formal recognition of her own equal status in the formulation of policy within the socialist camp. At the Moscow Conference of Communist and Workers' Parties, attended by Mao himself, the stage had therefore been set for Peking to press its own views on the transition from capitalism to socialism and on the wider question of bloc strategy in relations with the West. Prior to the conference, addressing a meeting of the Supreme Soviet on 6 November 1957 in celebration of the fortieth anniversary of the October Revolution, Mao praised Russian accomplishments and Russian assistance to China but was also at pains to stress the unique character of the Chinese revolution and the need for China to pursue her own course. While agreeing in principle with Khrushchev's policy of peaceful coexistence, he insisted on the expansionist aims of US imperialism and its unrelenting interference in the internal affairs of other countries.[55]

In his speech to the representatives of the twelve communist parties meeting in Moscow, Mao introduced the notion of an East Wind and a West Wind, and asserted that the East Wind was prevailing over the West Wind. Although some interpreted the statement to mean that the socialist forces were overwhelmingly superior to the imperialist forces, others gained the distinct impression that by 'East' was meant the underdeveloped countries of Asia, Africa and Latin America, including China, and that the term 'West' denoted the so-called advanced countries, whose industrial and military power concealed corruption and political backwardness. Although obviously aimed at the apparent superiority of the western world, the allusion could also have been intended as an indirect attack on the Soviet Union.

In the official declaration issued at the end of the conference, the twelve parties reaffirmed the policy of peaceful coexistence as 'the dependable pillar of peace and friendship among the peoples'.[56] However, while incorporating the general line of the Khrushchev thesis, the declaration represented a significant concession to the Chinese position. Adherence to peaceful coexistence was counterbalanced by the thesis that 'so long as imperialism exists there will always be soil for aggressive wars', and by the argument that aggressive imperialist forces were responsible for 'continuing the "cold war" and the arms drive'.[57] Equally significant was the advocacy of 'intensified struggle against opportunistic trends in the working-class and communist movement' and the outright condemnation of revisionism 'as right-wing opportunism'.[58]

While it is true that the declaration strongly asserted the possibility of creating, as a result of the decisive switch in the international balance of forces in favour of socialism, 'the necessary conditions for the peaceful realization of the socialist revolution', it was nevertheless acknowledged that 'the forms of the transition to socialism may vary for different countries'. Moreover, although the Chinese delegation finally adhered to the declaration in its entirety, it was subsequently learnt that Peking had vehemently resisted the Soviet thesis of peaceful transition and had in fact submitted on 10 November a separate memorandum,[59] which acknowledged the two roads to socialism but strongly advised against overemphasizing the possibility of peaceful transition. The statement argued that there was still not a single country where this possibility was of any practical significance. The parliamentary form of struggle had to be fully utilized, but its role was limited and had to be complemented with the more crucial task of 'gathering the revolutionary forces'. The battle lines had thus been drawn for the major ideological conflict that was from now on to affect every aspect of the Sino–Soviet relationship.

As already indicated, the year 1958 saw a renewed militancy in Chinese domestic and foreign policy. The intensification of revolutionary pressures on the masses in the name of the Great Leap Forward, and the accompanying vast mobilization of labour in the communes as part of the drive for increased production, were paralleled by an increasingly bitter campaign against Titoism, a much more assertive diplomacy, especially in relation to Middle East affairs and the Taiwan dispute, and a determined refusal to participate in Comecon's plans for economic integration. The Soviet Union, for its part, showed no signs of abandoning its previously stated positions. Although the communiqué issued in Peking at the end of Khrushchev's meeting with Mao Zedong on 3 August explicitly stated that the two countries would 'wage an uncompromising struggle against revisionism – the chief danger in the communist movement',[60] it was made clear that Moscow would not deviate from its commitment to the policy of peaceful coexistence.

The peace theme was expounded with even greater force by Khrushchev during his visit to Peking in October 1959 following his discussions at Camp David. President Eisenhower was now credited with understanding the need to relax international tensions. The catastrophic consequences of war were such that it had to be excluded as a means of resolving international disputes. No doubt the Soviet leader must have had his Chinese hosts partly in mind when he warned 'cold war warriors' against pushing the world towards 'a new world war'.[61] Yet these were precisely the views that China was openly attacking as 'revisionist'.

Closely related to and partly explaining the difference in the Sino–Soviet attitudes to war was the divergent stand on the question of liberation struggles. In China's view, peace would ultimately depend on 'the resolute struggle of the nations of the whole world against imperialism'.[62] Irrespective of the degree of practical support that Peking was willing to offer communist or other revolutionary movements, the very advocacy of a much more forceful policy than was acceptable to Soviet diplomacy meant that Maoist China was challenging the authority of the Soviet Union to formulate strategy and tactics on this issue for the entire socialist commonwealth.

By late 1959 the conflict between the two principal communist states had so widened that the Soviet Union no longer felt obliged to support China in her border dispute with India. Contrary to the accustomed Soviet position, the Tass statement of 9 September emphasized Moscow's neutrality, contenting itself with a bland expression of hope that the two nations would settle their misunderstandings on the basis of their traditional friendship. As if to underline the Soviet Union's indifference to Chinese claims and aspirations, in February 1960 Khrushchev visited India and Indonesia, two countries with which China's relations had markedly deteriorated. Although they were not yet aiming their attacks directly or openly against each other, both Russia and China were already using every incident and forum to justify their respective positions and undermine each other's credibility within the international communist movement.

Alarmed by the possible long-term consequences of the ideological rift for relations both within the communist camp and between East and West, Khrushchev sought to use the Bucharest meeting of the twelve communist parties in June 1960 to reassert Soviet primacy, establish closer integration of the socialist commonwealth and obtain decisive endorsement for his attempts to ease international tensions and initiate a diplomatic dialogue with the United States. Far from resolving the dispute, the conference resulted in a statemate punctuated by charges of revisionism and counter-charges of dogmatism. The Chinese delegate, Peng Zhen, accused Khrushchev of having organized the meeting for the specific purpose of attacking and isolating the Chinese Communist Party. By appearing as the advocate of communist unity and by pledging China's continuing support for the conclusions of the 1957 Moscow declaration, China thus deflected much of the criticism levelled against her.

While compelled to adhere to the thesis that imperialist wars could be prevented or at least contained, Peking had again succeeded in tying the Soviet leadership to the proposition that the aggressive circles in the United States were the main threat to peace and that 'revisionism' was the most dangerous trend within the ranks of world communism. Needless to say, this result, which fell far short of Soviet expectations, merely postponed the eventual showdown for it had already been agreed that the dispute would become the subject of worldwide inter-party discussion in preparation for another conference to be convened in Moscow later in the year.

In the intervening months both sides attempted without success, through a mixture of persuasion and coercion, to modify each other's views. By August–September, Soviet–Chinese relations had deteriorated further following the abrupt withdrawal of a large number of Soviet technicians from China, the return of many Chinese students from Russia and the marked decline of cultural links between the two countries. At the very time that Peking was reaffirming the need for China to pursue a policy of self-reliance, a number of Soviet papers published an article explaining that no country, not even one as large as China, could successfully build socialism in isolation, without the cooperation and assistance of all the other socialist countries.[63]

When the various communist delegations assembled in Moscow in November 1960, it immediately became evident that agreement on a new common statement of principle would prove extremely difficult. While the long document on the strategy of international communism that was finally approved after almost three weeks of argument behind closed doors represented a significant Soviet victory on many points, it remained nevertheless an ambiguous declaration often embodying contradictory positions. Although accepting the Soviet thesis that the present epoch was marked by the growing proponderance of the 'socialist world system' over the forces of imperialism and, consequently, that it was now possible to banish 'world war from the life of society even while capitalism still exists in part of the world', the declaration failed to issue a clear condemnation of the 'fraternal activities' of the Chinese and Albanian parties.[64] Nor was the Soviet view of peaceful coexistence endorsed as the sole acceptable foreign policy line for the communist bloc. Indeed, the document reaffirmed the warlike nature of imperialism and described American imperialist circles as 'the main centre of world reaction' and 'the enemy of the peoples of the world'. The Chinese had withdrawn their open challenge to Marxist–Leninist orthodoxy as defined by the CPSU, yet they had succeeded in making criticism of the Soviet leadership an accepted principle within the socialist commonwealth.

Events after the 1960 declaration amply demonstrated that neither side was willing to abandon the struggle for ascendancy. Khrushchev renewed his attack on the Chinese by using Albania as his main target. All Soviet technicians and economic aid to Albania were withdrawn in April 1961. On 24 August 1961, the CPSU Central Committee sent a letter of violent denunciation to the Albanian Party. On 27 October 1961, on the occasion of the Twenty-Second CPSU Congress, Khrushchev called explicitly for the overthrow of the Albanian party leaders, Hoxha and Shehu.[65] Zhou Enlai, leader of the Chinese delegation at the Congress, responded by laying a wreath on Stalin's tomb, by suddenly leaving for Peking before the conclusion of the Congress and by confidential criticisms of the errors of the CPSU leadership. In the space of these few months, it would seem, the Maoist strategy had shifted from the long-standing attempt to accommodate the dispute within the framework of socialist solidarity to the dismissal of Khrushchev's policies as irrevocably 'revisionist'.[66]

Alarmed by the deterioration in Sino–Soviet relations, many communist parties, especially the North Vietnamese Party, called for yet another international meeting of communist parties to settle the dispute. For a few months, following the North Vietnamese appeal, public polemics between Moscow and Peking subsided. But according to a subsequent Chinese statement it was during the seeming calm of April–May 1962 that the Soviet Union intensified its subversive activities in the Ili region and 'coerced several tens of thousands of Chinese citizens into going into the Soviet Union'.[67] By the end of the summer of 1962, Peking was beginning to reopen its campaign against the Soviet Union, although Khrushchev was continuing with his conciliatory attitude. In meetings with the departing Chinese ambassador, Liu Xiao, on 13–14 October 1962, he asked that Mao forget the past so that Sino–Soviet relations might 'start with a clean page'. The Soviet leader expressed sympathy for the Chinese position with regard to the Sino–Indian border, and on 25 October 1962 a *Pravda* editorial gave clear support to Peking in its conflict with India. Such support was not to be repeated again.

One may speculate about the reasons for the Soviet attempt at conciliation. It may have been related to the approaching Cuban crisis and to the desire for Chinese support, or to the need for a coordinated position with respect to the Vietnam war. Whatever may have been Moscow's calculations, the Soviet diplomatic defeat in Cuba, far from receiving Peking's sympathy, became the target of merciless Chinese attacks. Inevitably, the Soviet Union hardened its own position, returned to a neutral stand vis-à-vis the Sino–Indian border dispute and proceeded to mount further attacks against the CCP through the successive congresses of the Bulgarian, Hungarian, Czechoslovakian and Italian communist parties held in November–December 1962. Tito's state visit to the Soviet Union also provided an opportunity for Khrushchev to deliver a major speech on 12 December denouncing Chinese motives and policies.

Mao's response came in a series of articles dating from mid-November 1962 to March 1963 in which he made more explicit than ever before the nature of China's grievances and her renewed determination to pursue an independent policy. Peking called for the revolt of communist parties against the CPSU leadership, derided the temporary Soviet majority in the international communist movement and elaborated further the 1960 thesis that the real arena of revolutionary struggle against imperialism was to be found in the underdeveloped areas of the world and that the real leader of the struggle was the Chinese Communist Party.

The Cuban crisis, in effect, provided the Chinese with the necessary ammunition to refute and deride Khrushchev's policy of peaceful coexistence.

By exaggerating the dangers of nuclear war, Soviet policy was running the risk of paralysing the will to resist oppression and of restraining revolutionary movements and 'just wars' of liberation instead of encouraging them as the most appropriate instrument for curbing the aggressive designs of imperialism. In a clear reference to Khrushchev's withdrawal of Soviet missiles from Cuba, which the Chinese described as appeasement, the *People's Daily* stated that the danger of world war is increased rather than lessened '. . . if one retreats, bows down or even begs for peace before imperialism at the expense of the revolutionary people'.[68] The primary target of Chinese attacks was the alleged weakness of 'vacillation' of the Soviet leadership.[69] But the most bitter denunciation of Soviet policy with respect to Cuba came in December 1962 when the Chinese accused Moscow of adventurism for using 'nuclear weapons as chips in gambling or as means of intimidation', and of 'capitulationism for becoming scared out of [its] wits by imperialist nuclear blackmail'.[70] Soviet actions were sharply contrasted with China's position, which had 'neither requested the introduction of nuclear weapons into Cuba nor obstructed the withdrawal of "offensive weapons" from that country'.[71]

It would appear that with the end of the Cuban missile crisis the Chinese abandoned all hope of restoring in Soviet foreign policy a firm anti-American line. Accordingly, they began to develop a new approach to the international system, which accepted the fact of bipolarity, categorized both superpowers as enemies of the revolutionary struggle and identified the underdeveloped countries of Africa, Asia and Latin America as China's natural friends and allies. The Soviet alliance was replaced by a redefinition of the united front, which, on the basis of Mao's theory of the intermediate zone, was now said to encompass 'independent countries and those striving for independence in Asia, Africa and Latin America'.[72] China's wish to make this united front as extensive as possible was demonstrated in Mao's interview with the Japanese Socialists in which he alluded to the possibility that even Japan might one day become part of the united front.[73] The new policy was given its most comprehensive formulation in the long programmatic statement of 11 November 1965, entitled 'Refutation of the new leaders of the CPSU on "united action"', in which the Maoist leadership sharpened its attack on the Soviet line and advocated an alliance of all the elements in the developed and underdeveloped world that were both anti-American and anti-Soviet.[74] The alliance, which was designed to establish 'an international united front against US imperialism', was to include 'the upper strata in many nationalist countries' and also those 'monopoly capitalists . . . who desire in varying degrees to oppose the United States'.

The Chinese tactic of the united front was intended to promote Mao's revolutionary strategy on the international stage in the face of Soviet and American opposition. It was conceived as a means of countering the growing rapprochement between the two superpowers, a development that the Chinese could not but view with great apprehension. A Chinese account of the improvement in Soviet–American relations published in February 1966 is worth quoting at some length:

> Accompanied by US Secretary of State Dean Rusk, Humphrey recently conferred in New Delhi with Alexei Kosygin. . . . Such talks were 'always helpful to the common cause of peace', he said. 'Looking ahead for the next several years', he added, 'US–Soviet relations can and should be improved.' Back on 7 December 1965, Rusk said: 'we can take seriously the discussion of peaceful coexistence by the Soviet Union. . . .' Earlier, on 21 October 1965, US Chief delegate to NATO, Harlan Cleveland, went even further. He praised 'the Soviet Union's conversion from ambitious outlaw to responsible citizen of the world community'.[75]

In the light of increased cooperation between Moscow and Washington, Peking sought to present itself as the leader of a third force comprised of the oppressed and dissatisfied nations of the world. China's negative response to the signing of the Moscow Test Ban treaty was meant to enhance her image as the champion of the weak and the proud, that is, of the overwhelming majority of countries who refused 'to kneel down on the ground and obey orders as if they were nuclear slaves'.[76] The Test Ban agreement was regarded as another instance of Soviet–American collusion directed against China's interests. The *People's Daily* described it as 'a big fraud jeopardizing the interests of the peoples of the world and the cause of world peace', 'a US–Soviet alliance' aimed at tying China's hands.[77] By contrast, China's entry into the nuclear club was defended as boosting 'the morale of the revolutionary people the world over'. The successful explosion of China's first atomic bomb was seen as dashing 'the dream of the United States to reduce the Chinese people to slaves of the nuclear overlords' and as 'shaking the US nuclear monopoly to its very foundations'.[78] Indeed, the Chinese tended to argue more and more that their acquisition of nuclear weapons had been made necessary by the Soviet betrayal of revolutionary principles and Moscow's policy of growing cooperation with US imperialism. In this sense, China's nuclear aspirations may be said to have been both a cause and a consequence of the Sino–Soviet dispute.

Role of Ideology

In its origins, the struggle between China and the Soviet Union revolved largely around their bilateral relations and their respective authority in the international communist movement. But after 1958 one could detect a sharp conflict as to what policy the communist bloc should pursue in its relations with the outside world, and as to what weight should be accorded to Chinese and Soviet perceptions and interests in the formulation of such policy. Reference has already been made to the conflict of interests arising from the Soviet Union's reluctance to provide China with a nuclear capability; the Soviet vacillation in supporting the Chinese claim to Taiwan; the Chinese opposition to the reduction of tensions with the United States; the Chinese determination to give wholehearted support to revolutionary armed struggles in underdeveloped areas. But it would be inaccurate to regard these differences simply in terms of the disparity between the strategic or diplomatic positions of the two countries. For inextricably interwoven with considerations of national interest were the conflicting ideological perceptions of the two protagonists.

The importance of the ideological element in the evolution of the Sino–Soviet dispute has been highlighted in a sociometric analysis of the conflict that compares the areas of disagreement before and after 1956.[79]

	Pre-1956		Post-1956	
Issues	No.	%	No.	%
Foreign policy	8	30.7	20	25
Ideology	2	7.7	50	62
Economic	8	30.7	7	9
Geography	8	30.7	3	3

Although the year 1956 may at first sight appear to be an arbitrary dividing line, there is considerable justification for treating the Twentieth Congress of the CPSU held in February 1956 as the first decisive step in the ideological schism, since it was at this meeting that Khrushchev was to launch his famous denunciation of Stalinism and introduce major modifications to some of the most widely accepted tenets of Marxism–Leninism. Indeed, in the ensuing polemical debate several years later, the Chinese were to describe the Twentieth Congress as 'the root from which stems all the evils done by the Khrushchev revisionists'.[80] The concepts of 'peaceful coexistence', 'peaceful competition' and 'peaceful transition' as well as the Soviet Union's alleged alignment with imperialism against socialism, with the United States against China, with reactionary forces against national liberation movements, and with Titoist revisionism against true Marxism–Leninism, were all attributed to the decisions taken at the Twentieth Congress.

Peking's reaction to Khrushchev's violent attack against the Stalin personality cult represented a subtle mixture of measured approval and detached analysis. An authoritative Chinese statement in April 1956 acknowledged that 'the prevalence of the cult of the individual had, for a long time in Soviet life, given rise to many errors in work and had led to ill consequences', and praised the Twentieth Congress for 'courageous self-criticism' and for demonstrating 'the great vitality of Marxism–Leninism'.[81] But in taking account of the abuses of power and arbitrary rule, the Maoist position was also at pains to defend Stalin's 'correct side', for, as chief leader of the party and the state, he had 'creatively applied and developed Marxism–Leninism . . . and proved himself to be an outstanding Marxist–Leninist fighter'.[82] The importance of his role in history was said to derive from his defence of 'Lenin's line on the industrialization of the Soviet state and the collectivization of agriculture'.[83]

Even in this early phase of the ideological debate, it is clear that the Chinese were unwilling to give their complete approval to the process of de-Stalinization initiated· by Khrushchev in February 1956. This reluctance stemmed not so much from China's desire to uphold the Stalinist legend as from her dissatisfaction with Khrushchev's failure to consult Peking before proceeding with his denunciation of the Stalinist period, an initiative that was bound to have a dramatic and lasting impact on relations within the world communist system. As already indicated, the Chinese Communist Party had suffered on more than one occasion as a result of Stalin's errors. Accordingly, a major statement carried by the *People's Daily* in December 1956 freely admitted the serious mistakes that the Soviet leader had made both in domestic and foreign policy. His arbitrary method of work had obstructed the principles of democratic centralism in the life of the party as well as in the organization of the state. At a meeting of party secretaries in January 1957, Mao acknowledged that Stalin had been 'a bad teacher for a lot of people' and that his refusal to tolerate internal party struggle was part of a metaphysical and rigid approach that led him and his followers to adopt mistaken positions.[84]

The Maoist critique of Stalin's estrangement from the masses and his ruthless suppression of counter-revolution was thus widened to encompass the Soviet leader's erroneous attitude towards foreign countries and fraternal parties, in particular his 'tendency toward great-nation chauvinism' and his lack of any 'spirit of equality'. Although most of these criticisms featured frequently in many of Mao's speeches during the late 1950s, perhaps the most comprehensive outline to date of Mao's theoretical evaluation of the Stalinist period is to be found in his comments on Stalin's *Economic Problems of Socialism in the USSR* and in his notes on a popular Soviet textbook on political economy, which had been published in 1955.[85] One of the most significant conclusions to emerge from these writings and remarks, all of which appeared between 1958 and 1962, thus preceding official documents like 'On the question of Stalin',[86] is that, in Mao's view, the seeds of Khrushchev's revisionism were already present in the 'backward experiences' of the Stalinist period. Mao criticized Stalin for his failure to take sufficient account of the revolutionary potential of underdeveloped countries; for underestimating the importance of the anti-colonial struggle as a catalyst for revolution; and for concentrating, when dealing with the problem of socialist transition, on the relations of production, while neglecting the political and ideological superstructure, and particularly the relationship between the superstructure and the economic base.[87]

But perhaps the most fundamental criticism levelled against Stalin was his inability to recognize the persistence of contradictions in a socialist society, from which stemmed his ruthless suppression of inter-party criticism and debate. According to Mao's analysis:

> As long as contradictions exist between the subjective and the objective, between the advanced and the backward, and between the productive forces and the relations of production, the contradiction between materialism and idealism will continue in a socialist or communist society, and will manifest itself in various forms.[88]

This type of contradiction was likely to occur in relations between different sections of the people, between the government and the people, between socialist countries and even between communist parties.[89] By placing Stalin's mistakes in historical perspective and by giving him due credit for his achievements, the Maoist leadership had thus developed a powerful instrument with which to attack the Khrushchev line. On the one hand it endorsed Khrushchev's attack on Stalin in so far as it contributed to a dilution of Soviet authority within the communist bloc, but on the other hand it maintained that contradictions still existed within and between socialist societies, thereby underlining further the legitimacy of ideological differences between socialist countries.

On the question of relations between the socialist and capitalist blocs, Khrushchev asserted at the Twentieth Party Congress, in opposition to the Leninist doctrine of the inevitability of war, that times had changed and that the socialist camp was now so strong that no one would dare attack it. War, therefore, was no longer to be regarded as 'fatally inevitable'. Furthermore, because the peace-loving masses of the world were inspired and sustained by the strength of the Soviet Union, it was now perfectly conceivable that in certain countries socialism could be achieved by the process of 'peaceful transition', perhaps through 'parliamentary means', as opposed to the violent revolution solemnly advocated by Lenin.

Khrushchev's attempt to modify Marxist–Leninist doctrine was far from acceptable to the Chinese leadership. In his Moscow speech in celebration of the fortieth anniversary of the Russian Revolution, Mao was careful to balance his support for the notion of peaceful competition between the socialist and the capitalist countries with a pointed reminder of the interventionist politics of the United States, to which he attributed responsibility for the Taiwan dispute, the Hungarian counter-revolution and the Middle East crisis.[90] While directing most of its fire throughout the late 1950s against Yugoslav revisionism, Peking was in fact seeking to expose the policy of accommodation to which Soviet diplomacy was increasingly attracted. In condemning Tito's Yugoslavia for rejecting the 'division of the world into two antagonistic military–political blocs', for claiming to stand 'outside the two blocs of socialism and imperialism', for arguing that 'the US-dominated United Nations can "bring about greater and greater unification of the world"', and that economic cooperation with imperialist countries can assist 'the socialist road to the development of the world economy', Maoist China was aiming at what she considered to be the initial signs of revisionism in Soviet foreign policy. Gradually, the attacks became progressively more explicit and the identity of their real target was publicly acknowledged. By the mid-1960s, the Chinese opposition to Soviet revisionism had become total and apparently irreversible, at least if one is to judge by such statements as Lin Biao's 'Long live the victory of people's war' and its denunciation of the Khrushchev revisionists for taking 'a gloomy view of war' and failing to support the 'revolutionary wars waged by the oppressed nations and peoples'.

In replying to Chinese charges regarding the abandonment of revolutionary principles, the Soviet Union accused China of dividing the revolutionary movement along geographical and even racial lines, and reminded her that the main counterweight to US imperialism was to be found in Moscow's military might rather than in Peking's empty rhetoric. As the conflict developed in intensity, the Soviet leadership sought to portray China as pursuing aggressive designs liable to produce a third world war.[91] In 1964 Suslov, the leading Soviet ideologue, had already accused the Chinese leadership of wanting 'to preserve the atmosphere of the "cold war" as a suitable background for an adventurist policy'.[92]

In contrast to the seemingly aggressive intransigence of the Chinese, Soviet leaders emphasized the possibilities for the relaxation of tensions within the existing international system. Not only was it now possible to avert a world war, but the Leninist principle of peaceful coexistence of states with different social systems was described as 'the unshakable foundation of the foreign policy of the socialist countries'. In an effort to demonstrate the revolutionary credentials of its diplomacy, Moscow would periodically couch the policy of peaceful coexistence in language designed to highlight its contribution to anti-colonial and revolutionary struggle. It depicted peaceful coexistence as 'the highest form of class struggle', and argued that the most important form of support that communist powers could give to wars of liberation was to prevent the intervention of the major imperialist powers and the internationalization of local conflicts.

But Maoist China was certainly not prepared at this time to entertain such an optimistic view of the likely evolution of relations with the West. China, it should be remembered, was a dissatisfied power for whom revolution was the only available means for removing the American military presence from her immediate periphery. For the Chinese it was rather difficult to conceive of the possibility of 'eliminating war from the life of mankind' so long as socialism had not won the final victory over the forces of reaction. Peaceful competition and disarmament might be useful foreign policy goals, but they could not be imposed on the enemy. Similarly, while it might be tactically advantageous 'to refer to the desire for peaceful transition', in most cases the 'people's revolution' would be needed 'to repulse counter-revolutionary attacks'.[93] Rejecting the Soviet argument that 'the chieftain of US imperialism had become "sensible" or "peace-loving"', Peking accused the 'modern revisionists' of arguing for the coexistence of imperialism and socialism.[94]

By 1964, the Maoist leadership had reached the conclusion that the revisionist disease had corrupted not merely Soviet foreign policy but the entire Soviet approach to the construction of communism. By appealing to 'personal material interests', Khrushchev's policy had created a 'privileged stratum', a new 'aristocracy'. which was now the principal vehicle for the spread of revisionism throughout the socialist system. The net effect of this cancerous growth was 'to reduce the ideal of communism . . . to efforts to stuff one's belly with a plate of goulash', minimize 'proletarian internationalism' and foster 'narrow egoism and nationalism'.[95] Nor did Khrushchev's successors prove at all concerned to reverse the revisionist trend in Soviet policy. On the contrary, in Peking's view, they had formed 'a counter-revolutionary "Holy Alliance"' with 'Japanese militarism in the east, with West German militarism in the west and with the Indian reactionaries in the south'.[96] Soviet efforts to create 'an anti-Chinese ring of encirclement around China' provided the ultimate proof that the Soviet Union had become the objective ally of the United States and the objective enemy of China. The essence of Khrushchev revisionism was now defined as the protection of imperialist rule in the capitalist world and the restoration of capitalism in the socialist world. In November 1965, Peking formally described 'the antagonism between Marxism–Leninism and Khrushchev revisionism', hence between China and the Soviet Union, as constituting 'a difference of fundamental line' and therefore 'irreconcilable'.[97]

With the benefit of hindsight it would appear that the ideological conflict between China and the Soviet Union owed much of its momentum, if not its origin, to the breakdown of international authority created by the process of de-Stalinization. By presiding over the disintegration of the organization and doctrine of the communist movement so painstakingly constructed by Stalin, Khrushchev had, whether consciously or not, encouraged the emergence of polycentric tendencies that carried with them the very real possibility of doctrinal conflict, notably between the two main centres of power within the socialist bloc. Given their different stages of economic development, their different historical traditions and the markedly different character of their respective revolutions, it is hardly surprising that the two leading communist regimes should have evolved rival interpretations of Marxism–Leninism and conflicting analyses of their external environment. Given the Maoist emphasis on self-reliance in determining China's revolutionary strategy and the backward state of her economy, it is only natural that the Chinese leadership should have developed a conception of the twin historical processes of imperialist decline and socialist advance substantially different from that espoused by the Soviet Union. Whereas Peking tended to expect the disintegration of the imperialist system to occur at its periphery through the revolt of the oppressed and exploited classes in the Third World, the Soviet analysis normally identified the decisive anti-imperialist force to be the socialist system itself, and more particularly the military and economic might of the Soviet Union. In sharp contrast to the Chinese perception, Moscow viewed the liberation of colonial, semi-colonial and neo-colonial societies as the consequence of the confrontation between the two systems, rather than as the principal factor contributing to proletarian revolution and the demise of imperialism.

Foreign Policy Differences

Having traced the historical evolution of the Sino–Soviet dispute and characterized its ideological component, it may be profitable to examine some of the specific policy differences that arose between the two countries in order to determine the limits and dimensions of their conflict. In pursuing his ideological duel with the Soviet Union, Mao, as we have already seen, repeatedly emphasized China's commitment to revolutionary struggle and her total opposition to US imperialism. It is not surprising therefore that the Sino–Soviet conflict should have reached its greatest intensity during the 1960s in relation to the Vietnam war, for it is here that the triangular relationship between the United States, the Soviet Union and China received its clearest definition. According to the Chinese interpretation, the Soviet interest in promoting negotiations was part of a larger effort aimed at striking 'a bargain with US imperialism'.[98]

In countering these Chinese accusations, the Soviet Union insisted on the duplicity of Chinese intentions and contrasted Peking's alleged interest in joint action with the USSR and other socialist countries with its obstruction of Soviet aid destined for the Democratic Republic of Vietnam.[99] As for China's advocacy of protracted struggle, Moscow emphasized the self-interested nature of her motives and the strategic advantage that the Chinese hoped to gain from a Soviet–American conflict.[100]

China, for her part, made no secret of her opposition to negotiations so long as American troops had not withdrawn from Vietnam. Throughout the 1960s and early 1970s China looked on Vietnam as a major test of her revolutionary strategy and of her dual confrontation with the two superpowers. In the Chinese perspective, the Indochinese conflict offered a tailor-made opportunity to embarrass the Soviet Union, weaken the United States, and retard the progress of Soviet–American détente. These underlying objectives were clearly reflected in the anti-Soviet propaganda that emanated from Peking during the latter part of the 1960s, when the sincerity and efficacy of Soviet military and diplomatic aid to Hanoi were repeatedly questioned.[101]

Paradoxically, Chinese claims of Soviet appeasement and cowardice towards the United States and insufficient Soviet assistance to the Vietnamese struggle invariably obliged Moscow to demonstrate its revolutionary credentials by increasing military aid, thereby stiffening Vietnamese resistance and enhancing the prospects of precisely the kind of protracted conflict that the Chinese had been advocating. The Indochinese war had thus become a major theatre of the Sino–Soviet dispute and a testing ground of the competing policies of peaceful coexistence and people's war.

Nor was the Chinese attack on Soviet–American collusion and Moscow's desire to contain wars of national liberation confined to the Southeast Asian region. The Chinese applied precisely the same critique to Soviet efforts at mediation between India and Pakistan. The Tashkent Declaration of January

1966, which provided for a cease-fire in the India–Pakistan war, was denounced as a stratagem designed to publicize the Soviet line of peaceful coexistence, while continuing to support the 'Indian reactionaries'.[102] Similar sentiments were expressed vis-à-vis the emerging Soviet relationship with Japan, and its alleged connection with the American policy of accelerating the re-militarization of Japan.

But perhaps the most revealing instance of Sino–Soviet rivalry in the Third World was China's attempt in 1964 to exclude the Soviet Union from participation in the second Afro–Asian conference to be held in Algiers. The Chinese argued that, given its European history and tradition, it would be out of place for the Soviet Union 'to participate in a conference of the heads of Asian and African countries'.[103] At first, Chinese pressures appeared to succeed as the Soviet Union, although adamant about the validity of its case, voluntarily withdrew its application.[104] But this difficult question together with several other divisive issues within the Afro–Asian world finally prevented the conference from taking place. China had failed to get the international forum she wanted for the dissemination of her views, and had left herself vulnerable to the Soviet charge of subordinating 'the interests of the struggle against imperialism' to her ambitious plans 'to achieve hegemony at this forum'. On the other hand, China had at least demonstrated a power of virtual veto over any major decision by the Afro–Asian countries, which did not coincide with her interests.

It remains perhaps to say a word about the border dispute between the two countries. In March 1963, Peking reminded the Soviet Union that, at the time of the inauguration of the Chinese People's Republic, it had been announced that the new government would examine old treaties, especially those concluded by China during the age of European imperialism, and seek to renegotiate those 'unequal' treaties by virtue of which she lost vast territories to the imperialist powers, including Russia. With regard to these outstanding issues, which were a legacy from the past, China had given the undertaking to settle them peacefully through negotiations and, pending a settlement, to maintain the status quo. But Peking now argued that conditions were ripe for such negotiations and proceeded to list a number of treaties, notably the treaties of Aigun (1858), Peking (1860) and Ili (1881), which she claimed Tsarist Russia had imposed on China.

By this time tensions had already developed along the Sino–Soviet frontier, and especially in the Xinjiang Uygur Autonomous Region where, according to the Chinese statement of September 1963, Soviet agencies and personnel had carried out large-scale subversive activities in April and May of 1962 inciting and coercing several tens of thousands of Chinese citizens into settling in the Soviet Union.[105] In reply to these allegations, Moscow accused the Chinese a few weeks later of having 'systematically violated' the Soviet border and attempted to develop some parts of Soviet territory without permission. The Moscow statement went on to stress the dangers of an artificial aggravation of the dispute and issued a clear warning that any further provocative acts by the Chinese would meet a 'most decisive rebuff'. Although China and the Soviet Union subsequently agreed to begin negotiations on border problems in February 1964, they both used the occasion to justify their respective positions and accuse each other of border violations. Moreover, while Moscow was insisting on limiting the talks to specific local issues, such as the ownership of certain islands in the Amur River, Peking was demanding a comprehensive review of the territorial dispute. The inability of the two sides to agree on a negotiating agenda eventually led to the suspension of the talks in May 1964.

In his interview with the Japanese Socialists in July 1964, Mao reopened the border question by claiming that the Soviet Union had occupied 'too many places' after World War II both in Europe and in Asia. Referring to earlier annexations, he stated:

> About a hundred years ago, the area to the east of [Lake] Baikal became Russian territory, and since then Vladivostok, Khabarovsk, Kamchatka, and other areas have been Soviet territory. We have not yet presented our account for this list.[106]

The Chinese claim immediately prompted Moscow to charge Maoist China with expansionist ambitions, and in October 1964 an authoritative article appeared in the Soviet press, defending the 'unequal treaties' and refuting Peking's claim to various parts of Soviet territory extending over a million and a half square kilometres.[107] By this time, the Soviet Union, which had been taking steps to strengthen its military and economic relationship with the Mongolian People's Republic, had succeeded in persuading Ulan Bator to take official note of Chinese irredentism and place the defence of its territory in Soviet hands.

During the Cultural Revolution both sides continued to manoeuvre in the border regions for diplomatic and strategic advantage. In May 1966, Chen Yi resurrected the Maoist attack on Russian annexations in the nineteenth century, and in October Soviet sources accused Chinese troops of firing indiscriminately at Russian ships navigating in the Amur. In response to the alleged actions of organized Chinese 'People's' movements in the Amur and Xinjiang region calling for the return of 'lost territories', the Soviet defence position was subsequently reinforced both in the Far East and the Mongolian People's Republic. By contrast, Peking appeared to make little effort to strengthen the disposition of its forces, preferring to wage a war of words.

Although the border dispute subsequently intensified (a subject to which I shall return in Chapter 6, pp. 152–4), it appeared that both China and the Soviet Union preferred to pursue their conflict either by proxy or through the medium of diplomacy and propaganda. In each case, the display of military power was probably intended as a deterrent or intimidatory tactic rather than as a prelude to a major strategic thrust. Indeed, it can be argued that for China at least the primary function of the territorial dispute was to provide her with a convenient and adjustable signalling mechanism through which she could convey to the

Soviet Union her opposition to the status quo and, in particular, to the unequal relationship to which she had been subjected. In this sense, China's rejection of the 'unequal treaties' closely paralleled her dissent from Moscow's ideological authority and her twin policies of economic self-reliance and military independence. By the mid-1960s Peking had clearly understood that the Maoist objective of undermining the bipolar system of international relations would inevitably arouse the hostility of both superpowers. Soviet power and interests represented at least as great an obstacle to the fulfilment of Chinese objectives and aspirations as American imperialism.

CHAPTER 4

China and the Third World

Largely influenced by the spectacular success of the Chinese revolution, the Maoist leadership came to expect that the movement for liberation and independence would soon sweep the rest of Asia, more or less as Russian leaders some three decades before had assumed that the Bolshevik seizure of power would act as the precursor of a revolutionary tide that would engulf the entire European continent. Addressing a political meeting in Peking in 1951, Zhou Enlai pointed confidently to the rising consciousness of the Asian people and the growth of liberation movements, and described the unity between China and Asia as 'a powerful and matchless force in the Far East'.[1] As early as January 1950, Liu Shaoqi had argued that the road taken by China 'should be followed by all peoples of the colonial and semi-colonial countries so that they may achieve their independence and a people's democracy'.[2]

But during this initial phase of her foreign policy, Communist China, faithful to her decision to 'lean to one side', was always careful to balance any reference to the unique contribution of the Chinese revolutionary experience with repeated affirmations of the central importance of the Russian revolution. As Liu Shaoqi put it, 'without the October Revolution of Russia it would have been impossible for our Party and the Chinese people to attain the victory of today'.[3] Deference to Soviet leadership during the early 1950s reflected not only China's undoubtedly genuine commitment to socialist solidarity but also the very limited influence that she could expect to exert on the stage of world politics. Despite these constraining factors, Chinese diplomacy was nevertheless anxious to project the image of a modern, rapidly developing, cooperative society deserving of legal and political recognition as an important member of the world community. At the same time, Peking was concerned to create the basis for a provisional alliance between the socialist and neutralist camps by demonstrating its support for the process of decolonization, by encouraging the policy of non-alignment and where possible enhancing its radical content and by strengthening the anti-western tendencies underlying the outlook of much of the Afro–Asian world.

In these early years, however, the very considerable demands made by the Korean war on China's relatively meagre resources and the rather high priority she ascribed to her own domestic political and economic needs meant that many of the fine sentiments used to describe the relationship with the emerging Third World operated largely, if not exclusively, at the level of rhetoric and exhortation. In the case of relations with India, presumably a crucial test case of China's attitude towards the group of non-aligned states, the liberation of Tibet proved to be an additional complicating factor. On the other hand, the Indian government had paved the way for a diplomatic dialogue by recognizing the People's Republic in January 1950, thus becoming the second neutral independent Asian state (after Burma) to do so. Although voicing initial objections to the Chinese use of force in Tibet, India eventually acknowledged the legality of the Chinese claim to sovereignty over the territory and yielded its residual rights deriving from the British colonial legacy. Having taken note of Delhi's conciliatory gestures and of its sympathetic efforts to mediate in the Korean conflict, and having abandoned its denunciation of Nehru as a lackey of western imperialism, Peking was by 1954 ready to inaugurate a policy of mutual friendship and peaceful coexistence.

The Spirit of Bandung

The new element of moderation in Chinese foreign policy first became evident at the 1954 Geneva Conference and particularly in the last and crucial phase, which began in mid-July and was marked by extremely hard bargaining between France and the Democratic Republic of Vietnam (DRV). The part played by Zhou Enlai as leader of the Chinese delegation in persuading the DRV to accept less than it had anticipated or was entitled to expect on the basis of its military position is explained primarily in terms of China's strategic objectives in the Southeast Asian region. Throughout the negotiations, Zhou sought to exclude any American military presence from Indochina and to prevent the participation of any Indochinese state in the SEATO alliance. Although the Chinese leader did not succeed in getting the United States to sign the Geneva agreements, he was willing to accept a unilateral declaration by the United States not to disturb the accords, in return for which he offered to apply pressure on the DRV to relinquish its claim to direct influence in Cambodia and Laos. Zhou Enlai's moderating role at the first major international conference attended by the People's Republic served to reinforce China's stature among Third World countries. Although Peking had condoned the truncation of Vietnam, the promise of aid and trade to the DRV combined with the limitations imposed upon the American containment strategy helped to offset any adverse effect on China's revolutionary image and to confirm her status as a major Asian power.

The same conciliatory attitude was to characterize China's role at the Bandung Conference in April 1955. Zhou Enlai in fact outlined seven principles that would govern China's relations with other Afro–Asian countries. These included respect for each other's sovereignty and territorial integrity; abstention from aggression and threats against each other; non-interference in the internal affairs of one another; recognition of the equality of races;

recognition of the equality of all nations, large and small; respect for the rights of all people to choose their own political and economic system; and mutual benefit in economic and cultural relations. All of these principles, which were originally formulated by India and China as the five principles of peaceful coexistence, or Panch Shila, were subsequently incorporated in the final declaration adopted by the conference as basic guidelines for relations among nations. It would be a serious mistake, however, to regard this statement of general principles as a mere rhetorical exercise. For the Chinese, at least, it represented an effective means of containing the expansion of the US military presence in the Asian rimlands, of strengthening the Afro–Asian movement for national independence, and of cementing the bonds between the newly independent states, thereby creating a 'region of peace' free from great power intervention. It is precisely these considerations that prompted China to foster greater cooperation with India, Burma and Indonesia and to establish diplomatic relations with such countries as Afghanistan, Nepal, Egypt, Syria, Yemen and Ceylon, all of which had social systems vastly different from hers. Indeed, Peking was ready to improve relations even with those neighbouring governments that had committed themselves to various forms of military alignment with the United States, as in the case of Pakistan, which was a member state of SEATO and the Baghdad Pact, and of Japan, which was tied to the American nuclear deterrent by the US–Japan Security Treaty of 1951. Clearly, the intention behind all these diplomatic initiatives was to demonstrate China's independence from the Soviet Union as well as her capacity to thwart the American policy of containment. In agreeing to impose strict limits on the degree of support they would offer to revolutionary movements, the Chinese were obviously hoping that Asian governments would in return cooperate with them in exerting maximum political pressure on the United States and other western powers to reduce, if not altogether remove, their military presence in East and Southeast Asia.

As already indicated, the process of diplomatic normalization with Asian states received considerable impetus in April 1954, when China and India reached an agreement on the status of Tibet. It was this treaty that recognized Tibet as an integral part of China and formalized the joint Indian and Chinese adherence to the 'five principles of peaceful coexistence'. Although China also undertook to respect India's special trade interests and Tibet's autonomy and cultural and religious traditions, it soon became apparent that the shift in Chinese foreign policy in favour of peaceful diplomacy was not solely aimed at cultivating India's friendship. A similar approach was to govern relations with Rangoon, especially after the border incident in the Wa state of Burma in 1956, which threatened to undermine the professions of friendship so regularly proclaimed by both sides. The disputed territory included three villages inhabited by the Kachin tribe and claimed by the Chinese because of their strategic value, as well as a small tract badly needed by the Burmese, previously leased from China and carrying Burma's only road linking the Shan and

Kachin states. During his visit to Rangoon at the end of 1956, Zhou Enlai promised his hosts that Chinese policy towards Burma would not follow the pattern of 'big-power chauvinism'. After prolonged and complex negotiations the boundary conflict was settled in January 1960 on terms considered generally favourable to the Burmese. A friendship and mutual non-aggression treaty was also concluded, its most significant provision being the agreement by both nations 'not to carry out acts of aggression against the other and not to take part in any military alliance directed against the other Contracting Party'. In return for certain concessions on the border dispute, China had thus secured Burmese recognition of her broad strategic and political interests in the South and Southeast Asian region.

Equally significant for the future direction of China's Third World policy was to be the rapidly improving relationship with Indonesia. In April 1955, China concluded a dual nationality treaty with Djakarta that acknowledged for the first time the right of overseas Chinese to acquire foreign citizenship. In spite of recurring outbursts of anti-Chinese activity, notably in 1959–60, Peking chose to turn a blind eye to Indonesian provocations and to continue with its programme of economic and diplomatic support. In contrast to the Indian case, Indonesia non-alignment, which had adopted an explicitly anti-imperialist stance especially under Sukarno's leadership in the late 1950s, represented in Chinese eyes a much more acceptable model of peaceful coexistence, since it tended to focus attention on the hegemonic or neo-colonial ambitions of the western powers, thereby reflecting one of the main preoccupations of Chinese diplomacy.

Emphasis on the doctrine of peaceful coexistence was to be equally prominent in the development of Sino–Cambodian relations. Although diplomatic links were not immediately established between the two countries, their respective prime ministers paid visits to each other in 1956. Apart from reaffirming her commitment to the Panch Shila, China agreed to help in Cambodia's national construction through a programme of technical assistance and a gift of materials and goods valued at approximately £8 million. These diplomatic contacts and economic and cultural exchanges were all designed to strengthen Prime Minister Sihanouk's determination to maintain his country's independence, to adhere to a position of neutrality and not to participate in military blocs.[4]

A very similar pattern of diplomatic and economic activity was to evolve in China's relations with Nepal. The Sino–Nepalese agreement signed in September 1956 required each party 'to safeguard the proper interests of nationals of the other in its territory in accordance with the laws of their country of residence' and abrogated all previous treaties and documents between China and Nepal, including those between the 'Tibet region of China' and Nepal. An agreement on economic assistance signed on the same day committed China to supplying Nepal with aid amounting to 60 million Indian rupees over the following three years. It was claimed that no conditions were attached to the agreement and that the money and the materials specified in it would be used in accordance with the wishes of the Nepalese government.[5]

China's sustained efforts to normalize and improve relations with all her Asian neighbours in the mid-1950s would suggest that, in the view of the Chinese leadership, a peaceful international environment and the relaxation of tensions around her borders provided the best avenue for domestic economic development and external security. On the other hand, Chinese support for African and Asian neutralism helped to project an image of China as a country that shared the experiences and aspirations of other Third World countries. In this sense, the rejection of colonialism was the dominant theme linking China's revolutionary strategy and her official diplomacy. Accordingly, a leading statement in 1954 asserted that the

> ... colonial and semi-colonial states have either won national independence or are engaged in the struggle for national independence. Both the Chinese people and the people of these countries have for a long time been subjected to the oppression and exploitation of imperialism and have suffered long enough . . . They share a common interest in the wiping out of colonialism, and there are no basic conflicts of interest among them . . .[6]

By stressing the identity of interests between Communist China and neutralist Asia, Peking was attempting not only to highlight the long-term revolutionary significance of the movement for national independence but also to derive at least short-term advantage from a buffer zone that might safeguard China against military attack.[7]

It is worth noting, however, that, even when the conciliatory phase of Chinese foreign policy was at its peak, Peking was always at pains to differentiate its support for non-alignment from the Titoist version of neutralism. In the first place, the Chinese regarded the reduction of international tensions not as an end in itself but as a means of strengthening the socialist camp and thereby advancing the cause of world revolution. The value of peace lay precisely in the fact that it helped to change the balance of forces and enabled the anti-imperialist camp to wage its struggle from a position of greater strength. The call for peace and peaceful coexistence was supported only so far as it encouraged 'the broad masses to force the imperialist blocs to abandon their diabolical plans of war'.[8]

The Maoist attitude diverged therefore from the Titoist concept of coexistence, which viewed the interests of the newly independent states as separate from those of the communist system, as having a legitimacy of their own and the capacity to create a third force standing apart from both camps while working for mutual conciliation and cooperation. Nor was Yugoslav revisionism merely different from general neutralism. On 26 June 1958, the *People's Daily* accused the Yugoslav leadership of being an agent of American imperialism.[9] Far from practising a genuine policy of peace and neutrality, Titoism was dividing the socialist camp and damaging the interests of the national independence movements. As the *People's Daily* indicated in March 1959, Yugoslavia's hostility towards China and the Soviet Union was living proof of its collusion with the imperialist powers, hence of its betrayal of the anti-colonial struggle.[10]

The increasingly bitter denunciation of Yugoslav revisionism reflected the general radicalization of China's domestic and foreign policies during the late 1950s. Indeed, as we have already seen in Chapter 3 (pp. 61–3), Chinese dissatisfaction with the direction of Soviet policy was also beginning to gather momentum at this time and to cast a shadow on the Moscow–Peking alliance. Khrushchev's willingness to extend large-scale assistance to India, Burma and Indonesia provided perhaps the first indication of the incompatibility of Russian and Chinese interests in the Asian arena. The Soviet Union's decision to recognize Japan in 1956 and the subsequent criticism of China's stand in the dispute with India merely confirmed Chinese suspicions that Soviet policy in Asia was directed as much against China as against the United States.

But the Maoist preoccupation with the dangers of Tito's neutralism and Khrushchev's revisionism stemmed in large measure from the perceived need to oppose American strategic objectives, especially in the Asian rimlands. The refusal of the United States to accept an Indochina solution based on local communist control and strong Chinese influence, which had resulted in massive American support for the French war effort, now prompted Washington to initiate a far-reaching policy designed to neutralize the consequences of the French defeat and the subsequent Geneva agreements. Not only was the United States unwilling to become a party to these accords, but it established the SEATO alliance for the explicit purpose of blocking all further communist gains in Southeast Asia. In keeping with this strategy, the Eisenhower administration set about furnishing the Diem regime in South Vietnam with extensive military and economic assistance, thereby encouraging it to refuse to hold elections in 1956 for the unification of North and South Vietnam as envisaged in the 1954 Geneva settlement. A programme of economic and military intervention was also launched in Laos in order to bolster the rightist and neutralist elements, which were struggling to curb the advance of the Pathet Lao forces. These and other manifestations of American expansionism indicated to the Chinese that the Bandung policy of peaceful coexistence had failed to undermine United States power and influence in South and East Asia. The inability to score any significant successes against the American policy of containment together with the steady deterioration in Sino–Indian relations and the growing estrangement with the Soviet Union combined to modify China's approach to the struggle against imperialism and to inaugurate a more militant phase in her policy towards the new and underdeveloped states of Asia and Africa.

New United Front Strategy

In the Bandung phase of its foreign policy, Peking had attempted to construct a united front consisting largely of non-aligned governments, in the expectation that under China's leadership such a diplomatic coalition would gradually erode American power in Asia and establish the legitimacy of Chinese interests and objectives. Once it became clear that this notion of a 'united front from above' would not yield the desired results, the Maoist leadership was increasingly attracted by the prospect of intensifying the struggle against the main enemy, shifting the emphasis from state to people's diplomacy, and focusing attention on the potential for wars of liberation not only in Asia but throughout the Third World. By ascribing to people's war a far more critical role in the revolutionary transformation of international relations than ever before, Chinese leaders appeared anxious to replace, or at least complement, the 'united front from above' with a 'united front from below', in which the energies of the oppressed masses of colonial or semi-colonial societies would find expression in armed struggle against the imperialist enemy.

The new united front strategy inevitably required China to extend her involvement beyond Asia to include such areas as the Middle East, Africa and Latin America, all far removed from her traditional sphere of influence. In seeking to establish a worldwide presence, Peking was hoping to fashion a foreign policy commensurate with China's power potential as well as with the universal requirements of her revolutionary ideology. Paradoxically, however, the attempt to enlarge the geographical spread of her own contribution to the advancement of world communism, far from enhancing in Chinese eyes the value of socialist unity, resulted in the aggravation of tensions within the Soviet bloc and a renewed determination on China's part to pursue a more radical and independent policy. In this sense, the progressively more assertive application of the Chinese revolutionary model to relations with the Third World both justified and reinforced the Maoist perception of the declining utility of the bloc in promoting Chinese interests and objectives.

The new mood of militancy in Peking's foreign policy closely paralleled its changing analysis of the international situation. By the end of 1957, Mao had already proclaimed that the East wind was prevailing over the West wind. The United States was variously described as a paper tiger trapped in a morass of difficulties, an enemy who had placed a noose around his neck, 'a rotting bone in a graveyard'. While recognizing the obstacles and upheavals standing in the path of a revolutionary movement, Chinese statements throughout 1958 emphasized the theme of ultimate victory through struggle, and predicted the imminent collapse of imperialism.[11] Conscious of the rising tide of revolution, the forces of reaction headed by the United States were unavoidably committed to the suppression of national independence movements. Although outwardly favouring compromise, the United States was constantly striving to extend its military presence throughout the Third World, prepared at any time to engage in armed intervention to defend its strategic and economic interests. Struggle, by both political and violent means, was therefore depicted by the Chinese as the only avenue to success given the aggressive character of imperialism and the growing signs of its vulnerability to a worldwide offensive.

In the Maoist vision, the Third World was no longer equated with a zone of collective peace. It represented an integral part of the anti-imperialist front. The significance of national independence movements was thus reinterpreted to take account of their active struggle against the West. By April 1959 China was ready to place Asia, Africa and Latin America in the 'forefront of the fight against aggression and colonialism'.[12] As the joint China–North Vietnam statement of May 1963 was to affirm, the upsurge of the national-democratic movement in underdeveloped countries had become the main factor responsible for the disintegration of the imperialist colonial system.[13] The frantic efforts of US imperialism to suppress the national-democratic revolutionary movement provided conclusive evidence of the seething discontent and growing resistance against oppression that now characterized so much of the Third World.

By 1960 the fundamental contradiction in the post-war world stemmed, according to the Maoist analysis, from the conflict between the imperialist states and the colonies and semi-colonies on the one hand, and the divisions among the imperialist countries on the other, rather than from the rivalry between the United States and the Soviet Union. The Kremlin could no longer be considered to be the spearhead of the struggle against imperialism since it was 'panic-stricken by a policy of nuclear war blackmail' and had slid 'from fear of war to fear of revolution'. To ensure the defeat of imperialism and its lackeys, it would be necessary to form the broadest possible united front, which would merge 'the struggle of the people of the socialist countries, the struggle for national liberation of the people of the colonies and semi-colonies, the revolutionary struggle of the proletariat of the capitalist countries, and the fight for peace of the peoples of all lands'.[14] But within this worldwide movement, the most effective element was identified as the independence struggle of Third World countries, with whom China shared the common heritage of a colonial period of political stagnation and economic backwardness, a common hatred of western imperialism and 'comon wishes for developing the national economy and culture'.

The Chinese successes in revolution and construction were in fact described by Chen Yi as providing 'tremendous encouragement to all the oppressed nations and peoples of the world fighting for their liberation'.[15] It is worth noting that, even in its theoretical formulation, China's identification with Third World countries stressed mainly the applicability of the Chinese revolutionary model rather than the value of Peking's military, economic or even diplomatic assistance. In keeping with this general approach, most official pronouncements tended to focus attention on developments that had already occurred or were in the process of occurring rather than on new developments that China might instigate or encourage. Even in its most militant phase, Maoist foreign policy was content to define its revolutionary role mainly in terms of the analysis and endorsement of existing trends rather than the initiation of new and adventurous policies.

Relations with the Indian Sub-continent

Perhaps the earliest and most dramatic break with the Bandung spirit so painstakingly cultivated by China during the mid-1950s arose out of the growing hostility in Sino–Indian relations. Apart from the purely national factor of the territorial dispute, the most divisive element in the relationship stemmed from the fact that both states regarded themselves as pioneers of an alternative tradition and system from which the rest of Asia would draw encouragement and inspiration. But it was the Tibetan uprising of 1959 that precipitated the crisis and contributed most directly to the intensification of the border clashes. By offering asylum to the Tibetan rebels and by allowing the Dalai Lama to establish himself in self-imposed exile on Indian soil, the Nehru government seriously impaired its standing with Peking and left itself open to the accusation that it had broken the spirit, if not the letter, of the Panch Shila.

Another important element in the overall motivation of China's escalation of the dispute into a border war was the desire to probe the pattern of great power relations in the Indian sub-continent. Although the conflict helped to cement closer ties between India and the Soviet Union and to increase Indian military dependence on the West, it is equally significant that Pakistan took advantage of the Sino–Indian dispute to loosen its military and diplomatic alliance with the United States and to develop a much more cooperative relationship with Peking. There is also reason to believe that China was eager to exploit the border dispute in order to highlight the essential weakness of India's position and thereby demonstrate her own emergence as the major power on the Asian continent.

After some initial border clashes in 1956, the Nehru government sought a clarification of China's position, particularly in relation to the North East Frontier Agency (NEFA) region. In his reply Zhou Enlai explained that the Chinese objected both to the name and the demarcation of the MacMahon Line, which they regarded as another by-product of the British colonial legacy, and reminded the Indian leader that China had never given formal agreement to it. Nevertheless, the Chinese premier gave Nehru to understand that, in the light of the Sino–Indian friendship, the MacMahon line might be broadly acceptable to China subject to certain conditions and the approval of the authorities in the Chinese region of Tibet. Taking advantage of the continuing ambiguity of her position, China proceeded to build a road across the Aksai Chin plateau. This route was considered of vital importance for Chinese economic development and military security since it provided the only convenient method of communication between Tibet and Xinjiang enabling Tibet to be supplied by the oilfields and industries of Xinjiang.

After reports of its completion, the Indian government despatched a border patrol to confirm the existence of this strategic route. The very fact that the Chinese had constructed a road on Indian territory, apparently without India's knowledge, must have cast doubt on the validity of the Indian claim. By this time, Zhou Enlai had suggested that India might recognize China's *de facto* occupation of the Aksai Chin area in return for China's *de facto* acceptance of the Indian position in the North East Frontier Agency region. The subsequent Tibetan uprising and the growing Indian sympathy for the Dalai Lama who had taken refuge in India, predisposed the Nehru government to ignore the Chinese suggestion. Meanwhile the Chinese increasingly felt the need to guard all the major passes out of Tibet to prevent insurgents from escaping into India and Nepal, acquiring arms and reappearing in Tibet. Accordingly, Chinese troops completed the physical administration of the border areas, closed the frontier and moved forward. Similarly, Indian troops advanced their position, stretching to the limits India's interpretation of the MacMahon Line. What until then had effectively been a no-man's-land was suddenly converted into a tense theatre of hostilities, which several armed clashes occurring in the late summer of 1959.

Although negotiations on the Sino–Indian boundary continued after 1959, both sides adopted an increasingly intransigent attitude. In September, Zhou Enlai laid specific claim for the first time to the area that had been consistently shown as Chinese on all Chinese maps, but that until then the Indian government had assumed the Chinese would be willing to concede. In 1960, Zhou Enlai made an even more explicit proposal according to which China would give up its claims to the North East Frontier Agency region in return for concessions in Ladakh. Once again, however, the complicating factors of the Tibet and Kashmir disputes made it difficult for Delhi to accept the Chinese face-saving formula. Throughout the period 1959–61, Chinese forces, spurred on by the need to control the Tibetan rebels, took the initiative in expelling Indians from the border post of Longju and arrested Indian policemen at Khurnak. By 1962, domestic pressures within India had reached such intensity that Nehru felt compelled, in spite of a Soviet plea for Indian conciliation and repeated Chinese warnings not to take the dispute to the brink of the precipice, to order Indian troops to drive the Chinese out of all territory claimed by India. Peking, confronted for the first time with a major Indian military offensive into what it regarded as legitimate Chinese territory, charged India with aggression, and on 20 October 1962 launched a fierce counter-attack on Indian positions in both the eastern and western sectors.

With shattering speed, the Chinese were able to overrun Indian military positions and take up possession of most of the disputed territory in both the NEFA and Ladakh regions, thus inflicting the most decisive military and diplomatic defeat experienced by India since independence. In spite of its dramatic victory on the battlefield, Peking did not pursue the advantage it had gained but proposed instead on 21 November a ceasefire and a 12.5 mile retreat. These proposals were unilaterally implemented on 1 December 1962.

In his subsequent account of the boundary question in February 1963, Chen Yi made strenuous efforts to contrast China's forbearance and restraint in the dispute with India's persistant refusal to negotiate.[16] Chinese accusations of

Indian expansionism were supplemented by an unflattering analysis of the Indian political system and the role of the national bourgeoisie whose tendency to vacillate and compromise with imperialism was considered reminiscent of the pre-communist period of China's own recent history. The obvious implication of the Chinese indictment of Indian policies was that Nehru's India could not be entrusted with a leadership role in the Third World, since by its actions against China it had allowed itself 'to play the role of the white man's stooge and to act as an agent-provocateur against a fellow Asian nation'. In so far as the Soviet Union had taken India's side, it had merely betrayed its own collusion with the forces of reaction and imperialism.

But in spite of the bitter propaganda war between the two countries, Peking was at pains to retain an element of flexibility and moderation in its diplomacy and to draw a sharp distinction between the antagonistic policies of the Indian government and the continuing friendship between the Indian and Chinese peoples. In evaluating China's long-term relations with India, Chen Yi denied any 'fundamental conflict of interest between the two countries'.[17] Although China's military action against India diminished her international standing, at least in some sections of the non-aligned group of nations, she was able to make considerable capital out of the resentment caused, especially in Pakistan, by the flow of American military aid to India. Much was made of President Ayub Khan's statement that the large amount of military hardware supplied by the United States, Britain and other countries would enlarge and prolong the conflict between India and Pakistan.

In spite of Pakistan's membership of the CENTO and SEATO alliances and the 1954 Mutual Defense Assistance Agreement with the United States as well as the subsequent bilateral security pact signed in March 1959, China had always left the door open for closer relations with Pakistan. The deterioration of the Sino–Indian dispute provided the necessary catalyst for increased cooperation between the two countries. In 1961 Peking announced that it was ready to engage in border negotiations with Pakistan, and these actually took place during the height of hostilities between India and China in October 1962. The border agreement that was signed in March 1963 ceded to China a small piece of territory previously claimed by Pakistan, but in return the Chinese recognized Pakistan's *de facto* control of Northern Kashmir, thereby gaining additional leverage vis-à-vis India and directly challenging the Soviet position on Kashmir. The joint communiqué issued by the Chinese and Pakistan governments on 4 March 1963 stressed that 'friendly consultation' was the effective way of settling boundary differences.[18] China, for her part, made a point of expressing her appreciation of Pakistan's commitment to a peaceful settlement of the Kashmir dispute.

The boundary agreement was accompanied by a trade accord, and followed, in spite of sustained American opposition, by an air transport agreement. A series of high-level diplomatic exchanges and a Chinese loan of $60 million helped to cement the new friendship and to demonstrate Pakistan's growing independence from the United States. An indication of the strategic value of the new relationship was provided by the Pakistan Foreign Minister, Mr Bhutto, in his statement to the Pakistan Assembly on 17 July 1963 in which he confidently predicted that an attack by India on Pakistan would also involve the security and territorial integrity of the largest state in Asia, clearly implying that in such an eventuality Peking would come to Pakistan's defence. Whether or not Chinese foreign policy actually favoured a military confrontation between India and Pakistan, there is little doubt that the latter's military adventure against India in September 1965 would not have occurred without at least China's tacit endorsement.

The India–Pakistan war served Chinese interests to the extent that it further weakened India's position and provided the Chinese premier with another opportunity to condemn Indian aggression and castigate the United States and the Soviet Union for their interventionist policies in support of Indian expansion. China reaffirmed her support for Pakistan in the Kashmir dispute and warned the Indian government that it had to bear 'full responsibility for all the consequences arising from its extended aggression'.[19] Clearly, the Chinese objective was to apply maximum pressure on India but to stop short of any action that would involve China in a direct confrontation with the United States and possibly the Soviet Union.

In adopting a pro-Pakistan strategy, Peking stood in little danger of American retaliation, since Pakistan's alliance with Britain and the United States precluded the possibility of western intervention on India's behalf, so long as the confrontation retained its predominantly local character. Indeed, it could be argued that in so far as neither the United States nor the Soviet Union was willing to contemplate the complete annihilation of India's adversary, China was unlikely to be called upon to demonstrate her readiness to defend Pakistan's territorial integrity. Apart from her verbal condemnation of US imperialism and Soviet revisionism for their encouragement, support and assistance to 'Indian armed aggression', China was content simply to relieve the pressure on Pakistan by forcing India to deploy a large force on the North Eastern frontier. Accordingly, on 24 September, the Chinese Foreign Ministry accused India of continuing to perpetrate intrusions and provocations against China along the Sino–Indian border and the China–Sikhim border, and issued a warning that was both threatening and ambiguous:

> The Chinese Government has every right to strengthen its defences and heighten its alertness along the border or to act in self-defence. If you insist on keeping up your wilful intrusions, you must bear full responsibility arising therefrom.[20]

Although Pakistan failed in its objective to secure a military victory against India and was subsequently obliged to restore a balance in its relations with all three great powers, China nevertheless remained Pakistan's closest ally. In spite of Russia's prominent role in securing the Tashkent agreement, China was the only power ready to identify completely with Pakistan's claims in the

Kashmir dispute as well as with its wider interests in the Indian sub-continent.

The steady deterioration in Sino–Indian relations from the late 1950s onwards did not signify the abandonment of China's policy of cooperation with neutralist governments. On the contrary, the conflict with India was partly motivated by the desire to detach Pakistan from its military alignment with the West, which also explains the Chinese programme of military aid to the Pakistan armed forces, including a number of agreements providing for joint collaboration in the manufacture of arms. Nor was Pakistan to be an isolated example for China's readiness to normalize relations with her Asian neighbours. By the end of 1963 the People's Republic had concluded satisfactory border agreements with most of the countries with whom it shared a common frontier: with Burma in January 1960, Nepal in March 1960, the People's Republic of Mongolia in December 1962, Pakistan in March 1963 and Afghanistan in November 1963.

In the case of Nepal, Chinese efforts to forge closer relations were also designed to curb Indian influence and thereby fan the elements of tension in the Indo–Nepalese relationship. Apart from offering to come to Nepal's defence should it be attacked by a foreign power, Peking made full use of the friction that had arisen between Nepal and India (as a result of alleged Indian interference in Nepalese affairs) in order to portray China as the Himalayan Kingdom's only true friend. China's diplomatic initiatives were richly rewarded in November 1962 when King Mahendra of Nepal defined his country's attitude to the Sino–Indian border war in strictly neutralist terms. China pursued the same policy in relations with Sikhim and Bhutan, although the attempt to stir up indigenous nationalism and offer Chinese cooperation proved somewhat less successful, especially in the case of Sikhim, which was effectively brought within the Indian defence line soon after the outbreak of Sino–Indian hostilities in October 1962.

Support for Militant Neutralism

The collapse of the Sino–Indian partnership during the late 1950s convinced the Chinese leadership that a country's adherence to a policy of non-alignment offered no guarantee of a close and cooperative relationship. What Peking now required was a more militant form of neutrality which, though it might not ensure a complete coincidence of interests between China and non-aligned states, would at the very least establish an identity of views on such basic questions as opposition to imperialism and independence from great power domination.

What made Burmese neutrality so attractive to the Chinese was, in fact, the tendency of Burmese governments, whether under U Nu or Ne Win, to take a positive stand against the interventionist policies of the western powers as, for example, during the Suez crisis when Burma condemned the Israeli and

Anglo–French involvements in Egypt, supported the establishment of a UN emergency force there, and offered a troop contribution to it. Even more pleasing from Peking's point of view was Rangoon's sensitivity to Chinese interests and its willingness to refrain from adopting attitudes considered antagonistic to Chinese policies. No doubt Burma's discreet silence following China's suppression of the Tibetan uprising in 1959 was one of the main factors that had prompted the Chinese to settle the border conflict with Burma in January 1960 and to sign a treaty of friendship and mutual non-aggression. Following Ne Win's coup on 2 March 1962 and his reaffirmation of the policy of 'radical socialism' at home and 'positive neutralism' abroad, China reinforced her policy of cordiality with Burma and maintained only the most limited support for the Burmese communist movement. At the end of Ne Win's visit to China in July 1965, the joint communiqué issued by the two governments reiterated their commitment to the five principles of peaceful coexistence, expressed the customary opposition to colonialism and imperialism and incorporated the thesis, to which the Chinese now ascribed fundamental importance, that economic independence was a necessary condition for the maintenance and consolidation of political independence.

By the early 1960s the concept of struggle had become the distinguishing characteristic of China's perception of the Third World. In all official statements, Maoist China repeatedly stressed the political, economic and armed resistance that revolutionary movements and non-aligned governments were waging against domestic reactionaries and their imperialist allies in the name of liberation and national independence. Cambodia's neutralist policy was acclaimed by Peking precisely because it was engaged in an intense struggle against American and South Vietnamese aggression. China was therefore willing to endorse Prince Sihanouk's proposal that called upon the participants of the enlarged Geneva Conference convened to settle the Laotian question to provide an international guarantee of Cambodia'a neutrality and territorial integrity.[21] Equally enthusiastic was China's response to the Cambodian condemnation of US actions in Indochina and Sihanouk's decision in 1965 to break diplomatic relations with the United States.[22]

In spite of the complications arising from the presence of a large Chinese minority, it was probably in relations with Sukarno's Indonesia, particularly after the shift to a more radical foreign policy in the early 1960s, that China saw the greatest potential for a militant Asian coalition that would oppose the imperialist policies of the United States. Sukarno's characterization of contemporary international conflict as a struggle between the New Emerging Forces and the Old Established Forces, that is, as a North–South confrontation between the industrialized and the newly emerging nations, closely coincided with China's analysis and, particularly, with the Maoist emphasis on the struggle for liberation. The gradual development of a Peking–Djakarta alliance was reflected in China's diplomatic support for the Indonesian claim to West Irian and Indonesia's reciprocal endorsement of

China's position on Taiwan as well as on the related question of her admission to the United Nations. The cordiality of the relationship was further strengthened when the Chinese associated themselves with Sukarno in his attack on the neo-colonialist character of the proposed Malaysian Federation. An authoritative Chinese statement in September 1963 accused Britain of using the reactionary Malayan ruling group 'to suppress the national liberation movement in this area and thus maintain British colonial interests'.[23]

In supporting the Indonesian policy of confrontation, the Chinese were obviously anxious to demonstrate their revolutionary credentials, their continuing preoccupation with the struggle for the right to self-determination, which they depicted as part of the worldwide struggle against imperialism, against new and old colonialism. The increasing ideological affinity between Peking and Djakarta mirrored the steady deterioration in Indonesia's relations with the United States and Djakarta's growing isolation at the United Nations. In January 1965 Indonesia, in fact, withdrew from the United Nations when Malaysia was accepted as a member of the Security Council for that year. The Indonesian decision was welcomed by Zhou Enlai as a 'revolutionary action' that had greatly advanced the struggle to reorganize the United Nations and terminate its manipulation by the United States and other great powers.

At this juncture China sharpened her own denunciation of the international organization, describing it as a 'US imperialist instrument of aggression' and comparing it to 'a dirty Stock Exchange of international politics in the grips of a few big Powers' in which the sovereignty of small countries was 'often sold and bought there by them like shares'.[24] China had of course several reasons for attacking the United Nations, notably its decision to designate China as the aggressor in the Korean war, its failure to condemn Indian aggression and its refusal to terminate the American occupation of Taiwan and to recognize Taiwan as an inalienable part of China. In order to give vent to these grievances and to her general disenchantment with the structure of international relations, China called for the creation of a 'revolutionary United Nations', which would stage 'rival dramas' in competition with the existing institution. It is more than likely that the Chinese proposal was designed not so much to create an alternative organization as to exert maximum pressure to bring about the reorganization of the world body along lines favourable to Chinese interests and objectives.

At the same time Sukarno began to develop the idea of an axis that would link Indonesia, North Vietnam, North Korea, Cambodia and China. During Chen Yi's visit to Djakarta in August 1965, the two nations reaffirmed their common interest in excluding western influence from Southeast Asia, and there was even a suggestion that China might provide the nuclear facilities for an Indonesian atomic bomb in return for Indonesia's participation in a common military strategy for the region. All these projects, however, were brought to an abrupt halt with the Indonesian coup of September 1965 and the subsequent accession to power of the Suharto military regime in the wake of severe anti-communist and anti-Chinese repression.

Although the attempt to develop an intimate relationship with Sukarno's Indonesia had brought China none of the anticipated benefits, it did provide abundant evidence of China's preference for a militant brand of non-alignment that not only refrained from joining military alliances directed against China, but also denied China's enemies privileged diplomatic or economic positions, and actively sought to contain the military expansion of the United States and other great powers. The Peking–Djakarta axis represented, in effect, an attempt to reconcile two opposing elements in the Maoist conception of the united front. On the one hand, China was anxious to establish a working relationship with other Third World governments in the hope of establishing a third force separate from the two blocs, within which she could exercise a leadership role, and from which she could derive some leverage in her relations with the two superpowers. On the other hand, the Chinese leadership was equally concerned to support national liberation and other revolutionary movements many of which were in direct conflict with conservative and often repressive governments. Sukarno's alliance with the Indonesian Communist Party on the basis of a highly nationalistic and radical foreign policy offered a possible solution to China's dilemma, but the uniqueness of the Indonesian situation precluded the application of that solution to most other Third World countries, and even in Indonesia's case the experiment proved to be short-lived.

The contradictory tendencies in China's united front strategy were perhaps most strikingly evident in her aid policies or, to be more exact, in the material contribution she was willing to make to the anti-imperialist struggle in the Third World, given that the policies of many Asian, African and Latin American governments were far removed from the objectives and aspirations of the revolutionary movements operating in their countries. A policy of indiscriminate support for wars of national liberation was therefore likely to antagonize not only the United States and other imperialist powers but a significant proportion of the underdeveloped countries themselves, which China presumably hoped to lead or influence. Peking was thus confronted with the difficult choice of either leading a reformist Third World trade union of governments or mobilizing and coordinating the often weak and scattered forces of revolutionary insurgency throughout the world. The Chinese Communist leadership sought to reconcile these apparently conflicting interests by balancing a carefully calculated and highly selective programme of economic and military assistance to Third World governments with an equally discriminating policy of support for revolutionary movements and other groups committed to armed struggle.

China portrayed her economic and technical aid to foreign countries as a concrete manifestation of the five principles of peaceful coexistence and as a valuable element in the 'common task of national construction' and the common struggle against imperialism. Much of Chinese assistance before 1957 consisted chiefly of outright grants and, although the emphasis subsequently shifted to loans, these generally carried low rates of interest and, in some cases, were even interest-free. Moreover, the repayment terms of Chinese credits were rather generous, when compared to Soviet and western loans. Credit arrangements with such countries as Burma, Mali, Ghana or Guinea provided for the repayment of the loan in ten annual instalments, the first of which was not required until ten years after the first provision of aid.[25] As a rule, repayment took the form of supplies of local products or local currency. Another important factor contributing to the appeal of Chinese aid was the suitability of Chinese production techniques for the economic conditions existing in most of the underdeveloped, predominantly agricultural societies of the Third World. In addition, the Chinese tended to exclude from their aid materials readily available in the recipient country, thereby maximizing the effectiveness of any given amount of aid. Finally, China's policy of technical cooperation, especially in the industrial field, normally covered all stages of any particular project, including the selection of sites, the drawing up of blueprints and the supply of all necessary equipment and spare parts.

These attractive aspects of Chinese aid policy were to some extent offset by China's inability to provide in sufficient quantity the type of capital goods often required for industrial projects. It has been argued by some analysts that these shortages, attributable in large measure to the backwardness of China's own economy, were responsible for her failure to honour several aid agreements. The fact remains, however, that China was able to develop a substantial assistance programme even in the early 1950s when her resources must have been stretched to the limit by urgent domestic needs. Apart from two lean years in 1957 and 1962, Chinese aggregate aid commitments exceeded 200 million yuan every year from 1955 to 1964, and amounted to 972 million yuan in 1961 and 718 million yuan in 1964.[26] Although three Asian communist countries, notably North Korea, North Vietnam and Mongolia, had received the bulk of China's military and economic aid in the period 1953–64, Burma, Indonesia and Pakistan had also obtained considerable amounts, while the proportion of the total volume allocated to Africa increased significantly, especially after 1960.

Throughout the greater part of the 1960s China was determined to pursue a policy of expanding economic cooperation to win the support of the non-aligned countries of Africa, Asia and Latin America. It was precisely with this end in view that Zhou Enlai outlined China's eight principles of economic cooperation at every major stop during his tour of Africa in December 1963–January 1964. He pledged his government's commitment to the principle of equality and mutual benefit. Chinese assistance would respect the sovereignty of the recipient country, would be given on generous terms and would strive to enhance self-reliance. Experts provided by the Chinese government would share the same living conditions as local experts and would not be entitled to any privileges.[27]

Peking was only too pleased to derive political advantage from the sharp contrast it painted between China's approach to economic and technical cooperation and the aid given by the other great powers. The primary target in

China's denunciation of imperialist aid was of course the United States.[28] In endeavouring to foster a policy of self-reliance among Asian and African nations, China's objective was not simply to propagate the virtues of the Maoist model of economic development, but also to reduce the economic and political dominance currently enjoyed by her principal adversaries in most regions of the Third World.

But if Chinese Communist leaders were to live up to their revolutionary aspirations, then clearly aid dispensed on a government-to-government basis would have to be complemented by some degree of concrete support for 'people's war' in the underdeveloped world. As early as December 1949, Liu Shaoqi had laid particular stress on the desirability and, in many cases, inevitability of armed struggle.[29] According to the Maoist ideology, such struggle had been made necessary by the contradictions between the mass of the people and the ruling circles of these societies, which had themselves become the clients of imperialism and neo-colonialism. It was precisely this kind of contradiction, as for example in Thailand, South Vietnam and Malaysia, that required China throughout the 1960s to proclaim her support for the ideologically most acceptable revolutionary ally in each country. On the other hand, the thesis that revolution cannot be exported safeguarded the Chinese leadership against possible involvement in a regional conflict that might tie China to a losing cause or provoke the full-scale retaliation of a hostile power.

Whatever the theoretical implications of the Chinese notion of 'people's war', it is clear that the People's Republic consistently maintained its practical involvement in domestic military conflicts beyond its borders at a relatively low level. This apparent contradiction between theory and practice is explained not only by the unfavourable conditions for revolution that prevailed in many parts of the Third World, but also by the domestic and external constraints operating on Chinese foreign policy. In the first place, regardless of the claims or requirements of her revolutionary ideology, China was obliged to behave within a fragmented system of states as a territorial power committed to the defence of her own sovereignty, territorial integrity and other vital national interests, which, by their very nature, often precluded the implementation of larger or more internationalist objectives. Similarly, the demands of her own domestic political process, the backwardness of her economy, and the limitations imposed by history and geography often combined to minimize the level of material assistance that could be extended to the revolutionary cause.

But perhaps the most critical limiting factor in China's relationship with external revolutionary movements was her preoccupation with the requirements of state-to-state diplomacy. So long as Asian, African or Latin American governments were willing to adopt an attitude of friendly neutralism, Peking was reluctant to depart from its stated policy of non-interference by offering any significant support or encouragement to anti-government elements, or even to the overseas Chinese who constituted sizeable minorities in many Southeast Asian countries. Rather than engage in subversive activity, the

Chinese tended to rely on such traditional instruments of state policy as aid and trade, border agreements, treaties of friendship and non-aggression, and regular diplomatic exchanges. Such material assistance as was made available to communist parties or other nationalist movements was often minimal and unobtrusive, and designed primarily to provide China with the additional leverage in her ideological dispute with the Soviet Union. While extremely limited in scope, such aid was also useful to Peking as a reminder to Third World governments of the options open to it should their policies prove inimical to Chinese interests.

Although the united front concept was a recurring theme in China's relations with the Third World, its precise definition frequently fluctuated in response to changes in the Chinese analysis of the international situation and to the periodic reassessment of current aims and strategies. Whereas the united front was throughout the 1950s directed chiefly against the United States, after 1960 the Soviet Union became an increasingly important target of China's revolutionary endeavours. It is this shift in perspective that probably best helps to explain the sudden change in Peking's attitude to the second Afro–Asian conference.

Having hailed the Bandung Conference of 1955 and its contribution to the anti-imperialist struggle as an unqualified success, the Chinese leadership argued that the mid-1960s represented an appropriate moment for staging another such conference and thereby further reinforcing the unity of the Afro–Asian bloc. Although Chen Yi recognized at the second preparatory meeting in April 1964 that the time, venue and composition of the meeting might be matters of some debate, he felt confident that a satisfactory solution could be found through friendly consultation. During the early months of 1965, Chinese diplomacy maintained its advocacy of the conference and frequently reaffirmed its confidence that the summit meeting would be held in Algiers as scheduled in June 1965. But it soon became apparent that the issue of Soviet participation and China's total opposition to the proposal would lead to a postponement of the conference. By September Zhou Enlai had made it abundantly clear that China would prefer the conference not to be held at all than to allow Moscow to take part in its deliberations.[30]

Apart from the question of Soviet membership, several other considerations also led the Chinese to the conclusion that the conference would not endorse several of China's key positions, particularly in relation to the United Nations and the Vietnam war. If the Afro–Asian countries could not be persuaded to adopt a common position criticizing the manipulation of the United Nations by a few great powers and condemning US aggression in Vietnam, there was little point in holding the conference. It would seem that at some point during the middle months of 1965 the Chinese leadership reassessed the validity of its united front strategy, which had until then concentrated most of China's energies on creating a loosely structured and ideologically diverse bloc of Third World governments. The progressive radicalization of Chinese foreign policy in the mid-1960s thus resulted in a rapid, though not altogether surprising, reformulation of the united front, reflecting a more intransigent position on the Sino–Soviet dispute, a more hostile attitude towards the 'lackeys' of imperialism and revisionism, and a much greater level of support, mainly in propaganda terms, in favour of revolutionary armed struggle.

The Chinese Presence in Africa

The often contradictory tendencies in China's policy towards the Third World were nowhere more conspicuous than in her fluctuating relations with the African continent. Apart from official diplomatic exchanges, by the early 1960s there had developed between China and Africa a substantial traffic in aid and trade as well as reciprocal missions by cultural delegations, trade union groups, and representatives of student and youth organizations.

Following the establishment of diplomatic relations with Egypt in May 1956 and the adoption of a strongly pro-Arab line in the Suez crisis, China took several steps to inicate her recognition that colonialism in Africa was rapidly coming to an end. Symbolic of this new phase was the decision of the Chinese Foreign Ministry in September 1956 to transfer African responsibilities from the West European and African Affairs Department to the newly created West Asian and African Affairs Department. As first director of the new department, Go Hua made visits to Ghana in 1957 and to North Africa in 1958. Within days of its formation, Peking recognized the Gouvernement Provisoire de la République Algérienne (GPRA) in September 1958, thus emphasizing its intention to pursue an independent policy in Africa distinct in many respects from the positions adopted by the Soviet Union. By the end of 1959, China had established embassies in the United Arab Republic, Morocco, Sudan and Guinea as well as relations with the GPRA.

Paralleling the growth of diplomatic contacts was a flurry of economic activity through the customary channels of trade and aid. By the end of 1961, four African countries had received economic aid from China: a grant valued at $5 million was made available to Egypt in November 1956; Guinea received gifts of 15,000 tons of rice and a three-year $25 million credit in September 1960; Ghana obtained a six-year $20 million loan in August 1961; and aid to Mali was agreed to in principle in March 1961. The favourable terms of all these agreements and the absence of any accompanying conditions or special privileges provided Chinese aid with a degree of influence well in excess of the impact that China's meagre resources would normally have had. Trade agreements were also concluded with Egypt, Guinea, Ghana, Mali, Tunisia, Morocco and Sudan, although in 1960 total trade exceeded $10 million only with Morocco, Sudan and the United Arab Republic. In addition to aid and trade, the Chinese supplied an increasing amount of technical assistance, notably to Mali, Ghana and Guinea. The Sino–Ghanaian Economic and

Technical Co-operation Agreement of August 1961 provided for Chinese experts and technicians to be sent to Ghana, but stipulated, as in all other such agreements, that the salaries of the Chinese personnel were to be paid by China, and that their standard of living would not exceed that of the local personnel of the same grade. Equally significant in enhancing China's image in the eyes of the African public were the touring theatrical troupes used by the Chinese to entertain enthusiastic African audiences, as well as China's regular participation in international exhibitions and trade fairs, in such African capitals as Cairo, Casablanca, Lagos and Conakry.[31]

Another useful indicator of China's efforts to broaden and intensify her activities in Africa was the number of African delegations visiting China, which rose from eighteen in 1958 to thirty-nine in 1959, and eighty-eight in 1960. The number of African countries participating in these exchanges had increased from eight in 1958 to thirteen in 1959 and twenty-nine in 1960.[32] By encouraging the formation of numerous Afro–Asian organizations, and the staging of a variety of small-scale conferences bringing together women, scientists, youth, writers, trade unionists and other representatives, China was seeking to complement its network of official relations with a new form of people's diplomacy in the hope that a whole range of informal contacts, many of them centred around the Afro–Asian People's Solidarity Conference with its headquarters in Cairo, would become the vehicle for the development of new relations, particularly in countries where China lacked diplomatic missions.

Finally, mention must be made of the military instrument in China's African policy, for her compliance with the principles of peaceful coexistence was in no way regarded as incompatible with a measure of support for the various liberation movements struggling to remove the last vestiges of colonial power. Apart from the reported offer of Chinese volunteers to assist the Egyptian cause during the Suez crisis, there is evidence to suggest that several members of the Algerian Army of National Liberation had received their training in China. Moreover, in the last few years of their struggle against the French, the Algerian fighters, who were now upheld by Peking as a model for insurgency in the Third World, received shipments of arms valued at about $10 million. Similar though smaller amounts of military aid were made available to the National Pan-Somali movement in May 1960 and to the Stanleyville regime in the Congo in September 1960.

In spite of the marked retrenchment in the amount of economic aid allocated to Africa in 1961 – the large credits extended to Ghana and Mali in August–September 1961 included the proviso that they could not be drawn upon until July 1962 – there is no reason to believe that Africa had ceased to be a focal point of interest in Chinese foreign policy. The reduction of economic and other exchanges with African countries reflected rather China's decision to curtail most of her activities abroad for that year in the light of serious economic difficulties at home. Indeed, the growing success of the Algerian Liberation Front was interpreted by the Chinese as evidence of the revolutionary upsurge that was about to sweep other parts of the Afro–Asian world, and as confirmation of the Maoist thesis that men and not weapons are the decisive factor in the struggle against imperialism.[33]

China's increasing involvement in African affairs, especially after 1960, was motivated by the desire to contain or neutralize the expansion of Soviet diplomatic and ideological influence. Indicative of the bitter polemic against Moscow's policies in Africa was the leading editorial issued by the *People's Daily* and *Red Flag* in October 1963, which accused Soviet leaders of failing to support the people's armed struggle in Algeria and the Congo.[34]

In contrast to the Soviet emphasis on peaceful coexistence, notably in the context of East–West détente, Chinese policy sought to exacerbate the political and violent upheavals characteristic of many parts of Africa as a means of excluding western influence and promoting a radical united front against the white-dominated regimes of southern Africa. It was partly with this end in mind that Zhou Enlai set off for Africa in December 1963 on a tour that was to last seven weeks and take him to ten countries: the United Arab Republic, Algeria, Morocco, Tunisia, Ghana, Mali, Guinea, Sudan, Ethiopia and Somalia.[35]

But while congratulating every host country for having broken its colonial shackles and freed itself from enslavement, the Chinese leader was anxious to convey to his African audiences the need for continuing struggle along the road of independent development. Political independence was only the first step in the fight against imperialism, for it was still vulnerable to 'the activities of aggression, interference, subversion and infiltration by the imperialists and [other] foreign forces'. Africa could face the future with confidence, but progress would depend on the policies pursued by each country. In his speech at Mogadishu on 3 February 1964, Zhou Enlai stressed the importance of 'correct leadership', 'relying on the strength of the masses' and careful utilization of natural resources.[36] In other words, the struggle for political independence would now have to be complemented by the policy of economic self-reliance.

In every African capital Zhou reiterated with different degrees of emphasis the Chinese contention that imperialist powers were seeking to place the African continent under new forms of political and economic control; he singled out for particular criticism the type of economic aid that merely accentuated the financial and economic difficulties of the newly independent countries. In his report on the results of his visit to Africa, Zhou once again highlighted the unique quality of Chinese aid, which, though small in scale, was 'reliable, practical and conducive to the independent development of the countries concerned'.[37]

China's idealized formulation of her objectives could not conceal the fact that the prospects of two-way trade with Africa remained somewhat limited, given that most African countries were able to supply few of China's needs and yet anxious not to have their relatively small consumer markets flooded by cheaper priced Chinese goods. In spite of these constraints, several agreements were reached in 1964 with Ghana, Kenya, Tanzania, Congo (Brazzaville), and the United Arab Republic. The Kenyan agreement of May 1964 provided for credits of some $15 million to be given in kind over the next five years and repaid after 1975 in goods and convertible free currency. Similar interest-free loans valued at $42 million were extended to Tanzania in June 1964. While Chinese aid was drastically reduced during 1965–66, primarily because of increasing aid commitments to Vietnam, Peking continued to extend various forms of technical and economic assistance, as evidenced by the agreement to finance a joint shipping line with Tanzania in July 1966, which demanded an initial outlay by Peking of $4.2 million, half of which was to be repaid from Tanzania's share of the profits. But all these projects, many of which remained uncompleted by the mid-1960s, were dwarfed by the Tanzania–Zambia railway agreement signed in September 1967, in which China undertook to finance and supervise the construction of the entire railroad stretching from the Zambian copper belt to the Tanzanian port of Dar es Salaam. The Chinese loan was to involve several hundreds of millions of dollars to be repaid over a period of thirty years.

The magnitude of the Tan–Zam railway project, and to a lesser extent the scope of the aid placed at the disposal of Algeria, Mali and Guinea, indicated that the Chinese reserved their most substantial assistance to those countries whose policies were opposed to the existing international order, even if they were not entirely consistent with Chinese ideological preferences. Somewhat ironically, given the new heights of radical fervour achieved during the Cultural Revolution, by the mid-1960s China had apparently resigned herself to the fact that her own revolutionary model could not be readily or immediately applied to the social or economic conditions prevailing in most of Africa. China was willing to maintain and extend diplomatic contacts even with governments that had proved markedly unresponsive to Maoist prescriptions or material inducements. The endorsement and encouragement of armed struggle were thus complemented and partly offset by a patient and gradualist strategy designed chiefly to cement the Chinese foothold in Africa and impede the further expansion of the economic, strategic and diplomatic presence of the two superpowers.

Great Power Rivalry in Asia

Once the Sino–Soviet dispute had reached the stage of a quasi-formal schism, as indicated by the public accusations and counter-accusations at the Twenty-Second Congress of the CPSU in October 1961, the competition for ideological and diplomatic leverage soon became manifest in every corner of the international communist movement. But nowhere was the conflict to be more direct or intense than in Asia, where China enjoyed perhaps a natural advantage, at least in terms of geographical and perhaps cultural proximity. It was, in fact, in East and Southeast Asia that Khrushchev failed most conspicuously to isolate China, for most of the communist movements in these countries decided to adopt a neutralist position between China and the Soviet Union, while some of them evolved a version of neutrality that was distinctly favourable to Peking.

Apart from the unreserved and immediate support gained from the Mongolian People's Revolutionary Party and the Ceylonese Communist Party, the Soviet leadership was also able to command the cautious endorsement of the Indian Communist Party, although in this case the anti-China faction was able to assert its supremacy only after a most acrimonious internal debate and with the aid of the strong anti-Chinese backlash that resulted from the enlarged Sino–Indian border conflict in October 1962. In the case of the three major Asian communist movements, notably the Indonesian, North Vietnamese and North Korean parties, as well as of the smaller parties in Burma, Thailand and the rest of Indochina, China was able to maintain a special relationship or, at any rate, to neutralize Soviet influence.[38]

The mass membership and expanding organization of the Indonesian Communist Party (PKI) made it a focal point of attention in the Sino–Soviet ideological conflict. Once the PKI had clarified its own position, it became clear that, in spite of its official non-alignment, its views on most issues coincided far more closely with the Chinese than the Soviet attitude. In the first place, the Indonesian Communists neither agreed with nor wished to emulate Khrushchev's public criticism of the Albanian leadership. In so far as the Soviet Union had determined its position without prior consultation or negotiation with the other communist parties, its actions were regarded as violating the spirit of the 1960 Moscow statement (see p. 65). On the question of Stalin, the Indonesians were willing to concede the error of the cult of personality, but such criticism, it was agreed, was more than outweighed by the major theoretical and practical contributions made by Stalin to the entire international communist movement over nearly three decades. Moreover, Moscow was not entitled to dictate policy to other communist parties, given that the socialist commonwealth consisted of a group of completely equal and independent parties, each free to apply the principles of Marxism–Leninism to the special circumstances of its own society. The PKI, for its part, was attempting to develop an indigenous adaptation of Marxist ideology by participating in a national front, building the party, and advancing the Indonesian revolution of August 1945. Finally, by identifying with the concept of the 'new emerging forces' and the struggle against the 'old established forces', the PKI was not merely justifying its alliance with Sukarno but highlighting its agreement with the Chinese analysis of the emerging North–South conflict. It is hardly surprising, therefore, that in May 1965 Mao should have sent the PKI a most jubilant message of congratulation on the occasion of its forty-fifth anniversary.[39]

Equally gratifying to the Chinese was the North Korean stand on Albania and, particularly, on Yugoslavia, which was described as a lackey of US imperialism and a divisive force in the socialist camp. Aiming his attack more directly at Khrushchev, Kim Il Sung asserted that no socialist state could dominate or interfere in the internal affairs of a fraternal ally. In the first statement issued in June 1963 by Liu Shaoqi and North Korean President Choi Yong Kun, both sides emphasized their complete agreement on the principles that should guide relations among fraternal parties and countries. They described as impermissible any attempt by one socialist country 'to impair the independence and sovereignty of another country'.[40] Moreover, North Korea, in sharp contradistinction with the Soviet position, gave its full support to China in her conflict with India, reaffirmed the Chinese thesis that peace could not be begged for, but had to be won through struggle against imperialist aggression, and like China paid high tribute to the Cuban people's resistance against the armed attacks of US imperialism without the slightest reference to the role of Soviet military and economic assistance.

For reasons dictated largely by North Vietnam's strategic position and by its reliance on Soviet military and economic aid, the Vietnam Workers' Party tended throughout the 1960s to cultivate the closest possible relations with the Soviet leadership and to eulogize the CPSU for its achievements in socialist construction. It is, therefore, all the more significant that, on 9 November 1961, at the height of the Soviet attack on the Albanian leadership, *Nhan Dan*, the North Vietnamese central party organ, should have given the Albanian Workers' Party its enthusiastic approval. In the midst of the crisis dividing the entire communist world, North Vietnam was thus able to maintain a carefully balanced neutrality that stressed the cordiality of relations between Hanoi and Moscow, but at the same time recognized the very positive contribution of Chinese foreign policy in strengthening the socialist camp, promoting struggles for national liberation and defending world peace. On the occasion of Liu Shaoqi's visit to Hanoi in May 1963, Ho Chi Minh indicated his complete agreement with China's policy of all-out support for 'the five just demands put forward by Fidel Castro', as well as for 'the revolutionary struggle of the people of North Kalimantan against colonial rule', and endorsed China's 'consistent stand' in seeking 'a peaceful settlement of the Sino–Indian boundary question through negotiations'.[41]

Apart from the favourable neutrality of the North Vietnamese and the cautious middle course of the Laotians, China was able to rely in Southeast Asia on the support of most local communist movements. During the 1960s, for example, the Thai communist movement came to model its strategy and tactics more and more on China's revolutionary experience. The announcement of the Communist Party of Thailand in October 1964, proclaiming the formation of a united front 'from below' rather than 'from above' and affirming its determination to overthrow the Thai government, underlined the party's alignment with China. The establishment of the clandestine broadcasting station, the Voice of the Thai People, inside China's borders and the subsequent emergence in Peking of several Thai exiles from obscurity confirmed the closeness of the relationship.

The inability of the Soviet leadership to get widespread acceptance of its position among Asian communist parties may be explained in large part by China's overwhelming physical and ideological presence. The Chinese programme of economic and technical assistance as well as propaganda support for fraternal governments and parties was obviously designed to enhance this presence and expose the Soviet Union's neglect of the revolutionary cause, thus weakening Moscow's leadership of the communist world. In this task, China was considerably aided by the natural appeal of her revolutionary model with its emphasis on the mobilization of the peasantry, the development of united front tactics and the elaboration of guerrilla techniques combining political and armed struggle. Moreover, by stressing such themes as equality, independence and the notion of separate national paths to socialism, China was bound to elicit a favourable response from all those parties with an interest in challenging the Soviet monopoly in the decision-making structure of the international communist system. Any Asian movement deeply dissatisfied with the status quo and sharply antagonistic to American interests was bound to favour the communist power willing to adopt the most explicitly anti-imperialist stance and give the greatest priority to struggles for 'national liberation'.

The gradual shift in Chinese foreign policy, especially noticeable after 1960, which gave rise to an increasingly radical definition of the united front, reflected China's evolving relationship with the United States as much as with the Soviet Union. The policy of promoting a united front from below was prompted principally by a growing conviction that people's war constituted the most effective means of opposing the American military presence in Indochina. Chinese leaders were therefore willing to counter the escalation of American military involvement after the 1962 Geneva accords by pressing for violent revolution in both Laos and South Vietnam. In alleged contrast to the ambivalence of the Soviet position, China was ready to accept certain low-level risks in supporting North Vietnam and its allies rather than jeopardize the excellent prospects of a communist victory. On the other hand, the Maoist leadership was careful throughout the course of the Indochinese war not to allow support for armed struggle to conflict with the requirements of Chinese security.

Although they did not succeed in obtaining the abolition of SEATO, the Chinese lent their signature to the 1962 Geneva agreements primarily because the international recognition of Laotian neutrality imposed at least some limitation on the expansion of the United States military presence, while at the same time facilitating the use of the area as a supply route to South Vietnam. In March 1963, a Sino–Laotian joint communiqué referred to the Geneva settlement as paving the way for the Kingdom of Laos 'to free itself from outside intervention' and 'to realize peace, neutrality, independence, democracy and prosperity'.[42] But as fighting within Laos between the rightist, neutralist and Pathet Lao forces continued to escalate, and as American aircraft operating from military bases in Thailand increased their clandestine reconnaissance and bombing missions within the war-torn country, China accused the United States of scheming to liquidate the middle force in Laotian politics headed by the Prime Minister, Prince Souvanna Phouma, and to subvert the tripartite Government of National Union.

Even as late as June 1964, China's reaction to the Vientiane government's request to the United States for military aid 'for defence of the unity of the country' was surprisingly mild. Although the Chinese now dismissed Souvanna Phouma as a puppet of the United States and the Laotian rightists, they were content to limit their diplomatic response to a proposal that a fourteen-nation foreign ministers' conference be convened in Phnom Penh to discuss the Laotian question. China's relatively low profile in Laos was, however, complemented by an expanded programme of road building in the northern Laotian province of Phong Saly, adjoining Yunnan, as well as by a steadily increasing People's Liberation Army (PLA) presence. The road, far from serving as a route for infiltration or invasion against Thailand, was primarily designed to protect China from a possible hostile thrust. As for the PLA presence, said to comprise by the late 1960s some 14–20,000 men, its main function was to secure for China a viable buffer zone. Peking was content to pursue this low-risk deterrence strategy, confident that the pro-communist forces would in the long run benefit from the protracted military and political conflict. Another important factor in Chinese policy was the decision to leave North Vietnam the more active military role in support of the Pathet Lao, thereby further reducing the possibility of American retaliation against Chinese territory.

China's most significant contribution to people's war was to be her military and economic assistance to the Democratic Republic of Vietnam. For it was North Vietnam that represented, in Chinese eyes, the most important single obstacle to American domination in Southeast Asia and the most effective base from which to assist the liberation struggles of the other Indochinese states. In May 1963, Liu Shaoqi publicly recognized the importance of North Vietnam's role 'in safeguarding the security of the socialist camp, opposing the imperialist forces of aggression and war and safeguarding peace in Southeast Asia and the world'.[43] Following the naval action in the first few days of August 1964 in the Gulf of Tonkin[44] – the Johnson administration used the incident as a pretext for extending the war in Indochina and initiating the bombing of North Vietnam – China issued the most forthright statement of support yet for Hanoi's 'fight against aggression'.[45]

The nature and extent of Chinese military aid may not have been as spectacular or substantial as that supplied by the Soviet Union, but the PLA deployments that began in North Vietnam in September 1965, eventually reaching an estimated strength of 50,000 men, offered Hanoi the most reliable guarantee against a possible American invasion. The greater part of the PLA force was comprised of engineering and construction teams whose main function was to maintain bridges and roads threatened by American aerial bombing. The PLA units were also responsible for building fortifications north-west of Hanoi, thereby providing the North Vietnamese with a safe sanctuary and virtually assuring them of an automatic Chinese response in the event of any attempt by the United States to sever communications lines between North Vietnam and China.[46] In Vietnam as in Laos, China's willingness to risk war was balanced by extreme prudence in the deployment of force so as to avoid provocation. On the other hand, by establishing a deterrence presence, by mounting a worldwide propaganda campaign against the United States, and by supplying an ideological focal point for the Indochinese liberation struggles, China made a significant and perhaps indispensable contribution to the Vietnamese war of attrition against American military intervention. But in defending the North Vietnamese state China was also contributing to her own security.

The Balance Sheet

In the relatively brief span of time between the end of the Korean war and the advent of the Cultural Revolution, Chinese policy towards the Third World underwent several distinct phases, with frequent fluctuations in emphasis and tactics depending on China's domestic and external circumstances. By the mid-1960s, the Chinese objective of promoting the broadest possible united front against US imperialism and Soviet revisionism had suffered several notable reverses. In the first place, China had not gained the necessary support for a second Afro–Asian conference that would exclude the Soviet Union as well as the United Nations Secretary-General from its deliberations, condemn the United States for its aggressive policies in Vietnam, and advocate a policy of armed struggle in support of national liberation. Equally damaging were the events in Indonesia of September–October 1965, which brought an end to Sukarno's rule and inaugurated severe anti-communist and anti-Chinese repression as well as a major right-wing shift in Djakarta's foreign policy. The new military government headed by General Suharto moved rapidly to terminate the 'confrontation' with Malaysia, re-establish close economic ties with the United States, and suspend diplomatic relations with China. In Africa, a series of military coups nullified many of Peking's earlier gains in normalizing and developing relations with newly independent states. Four countries expelled Chinese diplomats and severed relations with Peking: Burundi in January 1965, Dahomey and the Central African Republic in January 1966, Ghana in November 1966. In the period 1965–67, relations with Kenya became particularly tense as several Chinese diplomats and correspondents were declared *persona non grata* following incidents in which they were alleged to have collaborated with the opponents of Kenyatta's government. China's failure, as a result of Soviet pressures, to bring the Fifth Afro–Asian People's

Solidarity Conference to Peking as had been agreed in May 1965 led China in March 1967 to withdraw from the permanent secretariat in Cairo, which she described as being in control of the 'Soviet revisionists'.

Apart from these disappointments, China's leverage and degree of involvement remained extremely limited in many parts of the Third World, notably in Latin America where most communist parties tended to be weak, ineffective and pro-Soviet. In spite of China's skilful propaganda campaign aimed at discrediting Soviet actions in Cuba, in particular Khrushchev's retreat during the crisis of October 1962, Castro continued to depend on Soviet aid and to resist Chinese attempts to create an anti-Soviet faction within Cuba. For the most part, Peking was content to highlight the revolutionary sparks that surfaced from time to time in response to the oppressive political and economic conditions characteristic of most Latin American nations. But, aside from the benefit of her advice, there was little that China could contribute to the struggle of these diverse but scattered elements striving to undermine the status quo.

On the other hand, China's Third World policy, especially during the Cultural Revolution, was the subject of innumerable statements reaffirming the twin themes of the rejuvenation of the Afro–Asian peoples and the irresistible upsurge of revolution. Moreover, despite the setbacks encountered by Peking's united front strategy, the fact remains that China had succeeded in changing her image in the Afro–Asian world from that of a weak and unimportant nation to that of a major power capable of mounting a considerable challenge to the international order established and maintained by the two superpowers. Although the Chinese had been ready to normalize relations with almost any state willing to recognize Peking as the sole legitimate government of China, conventional diplomacy as practised by the Maoist leadership did not dim China's revolutionary vision or undermine her relationship with a wide range of liberation and other revolutionary movements.

For all the tactical shifts that characterized China's external conduct between 1949 and the Cultural Revolution, the anti-imperialist united front strategy may be said to have been a central and distinguishing feature of her foreign policy. Throughout this period the Chinese remained implacably hostile to 'American imperialism', which they perceived as the principal obstacle to the achievement of their national interests and internationalist aspirations. The dispute with the Soviet Union, on the other hand, which emerged during the late 1950s and rapidly intensified in the 1960s, derived largely from Chinese dissatisfaction with Soviet–American collaboration, that is, with the apparent Soviet reluctance to apply effective countervailing power to the American presence in Asia and the rest of the Third World. It remained to be seen, however, whether this peculiar blend of state and people's diplomacy could be indefinitely maintained and whether such a two-pronged strategy directed simultaneously against the United States and the Soviet Union could effectively revolutionize the structure of world power while at the same time fulfilling China's security objectives.

PART II

The Transitional Phase
1969–73

CHAPTER 5

The New Balance of Power

By 1967, when the upheaval of the Great Proletarian Cultural Revolution had reached its peak, China's external relations appeared in danger of irretrievable breakdown. Not only had Peking deprived itself of the means to undertake any new initiatives, but even normal diplomatic conduct was seemingly confined to a series of ad hoc responses much more closely related to domestic circumstances than to the changing international situation. In April 1967, Foreign Minister Chen Yi was publicly criticized by Red Guards for his revisionist tendencies in the formulation and implementation of foreign policy. All of China's ambassadors, with one exception, had been recalled from their overseas posts so that they might participate in the revolution at home. Only Zhou Enlai appeared able to provide any continuity to the functioning of state and government.

The Cultural Revolution and its Aftermath

At the beginning of 1967 Red Guards in Macao had virtually taken control of the Portuguese enclave. Although it was effectively contained by British authorities, similar agitation soon spread to Hong Kong. The banning of three pro-Peking newspapers and the detention of fifty-three Chinese who had taken part in demonstrations in the colony, prompted China to issue in August a 48-hour ultimatum to the British government demanding the release of the detained Chinese and insisting that the newspapers be allowed to resume publication. Following Britain's refusal to accept the note containing these demands, the office of the British diplomatic mission in Peking was burned down and the Chargé d'Affaires placed under house arrest. A few weeks earlier members of the Chinese legation in London had been involved in a violent exchange with London policemen on duty in Portland Place.[1]

Apart from organizing demonstrations against several foreign diplomats and correspondents, Red Guards took temporary control of the Foreign Ministry from senior officials and despatched instructions to overseas posts without the authority of the Minister or any senior official. During this period of acute turmoil, Chinese publications openly acknowledged that China was at odds not only with western and neutralist but also communist governments as well as with the United Nations. The Chinese press began to express open support for a peasant rebellion in West Bengal as a prelude to revolution throughout India. In the case of Burma, the carefully cultivated friendship designed to serve as a model for the policy of peaceful coexistence was abruptly interrupted in June 1967 by a few minor incidents within Burma involving Chinese activists, which rapidly escalated into riots and bloodshed. In spite of Rangoon's repeated affirmations of its neutrality and of its wish to maintain cordial relations with China, Peking reacted by issuing a series of denunciations alleging anti-Chinese activities in Burma, calling for the overthrow of the Ne Win government and praising the heroic armed struggle of the Burmese Communist Party.[2]

Underlying this militant phase in Chinese foreign policy was the notion that Mao Zedong thought had become the critical factor in the spread of revolutionary fervour beyond the boundaries of China. Indeed, at the height of the Cultural Revolution, almost all foreign liberation movements tended to be judged by the extent to which they were willing to identify with and apply the prescriptions of Maoist ideology. On 30 September 1967, the *People's Daily* claimed that the dissemination of Mao Zedong thought was 'carrying forward with the force of a thunderbolt the world revolutionary movement of our time'.[3]

A passionate conviction in the universal validity of the Maoist revolutionary perspective led the Chinese press during this period to ignore revolutionary developments in other parts of the world, for example the abortive rising led by the Che Guevara in Bolivia in March 1967, precisely because these liberation struggles did not conform to the guidelines suggested by the Chinese model. Even after the Cultural Revolution had drawn to a close, as late as December 1969, Mao Zedong thought was still being described as a 'powerful ideological weapon in the hands of the people's fighters in Southeast Asia'.[4]

The domestic and international success of the Cultural Revolution was in fact portrayed as enhancing China's prestige in the world. In spite of the marked deterioration in state-to-state relations with other nations, the Maoist leadership insisted that the international proletariat was on China's side, as were the oppressed nations and oppressed peoples, in fact 'the masses of people who constitute over 90 per cent of the world's population'.[5] China could not therefore be isolated, given the nature of her ideological commitment and her moral and material support for revolutionary struggle throughout the world. In order to uphold its international proletarian responsibility, Peking thus found it necessary to associate itself with the aims of several communist parties in Southeast Asia and elsewhere. Accordingly, the Central Committee of the Chinese Communist Party sent a message of greetings to the Malayan Communist Party in June 1968, endorsing its struggle 'to smash "Malaysia", overthrow the reactionary rule of British imperialism and its lackeys, and win genuine independence, unification and democracy for Malaya'.[6] Similar expressions of support were made in relation to the Burmese, Thai and Indonesian communist parties as well as the Laotian People's Liberation Army and the South Vietnamese National Liberation Front. Indicative of the global character of China's revolutionary objectives was Mao Zedong's statement of 16 April 1968, offering resolute support for the just struggle of the black people in the United States, which he described as 'a new clarion call to all the exploited and oppressed people of the United States to fight against the barbarous rule of the monopoly capitalist class'.[7]

While not disputing the far-reaching changes in domestic and foreign policy wrought by the Cultural Revolution, it would now appear that its disruptive effects have been much exaggerated. In the first place, one must be careful to distinguish revolutionary rhetoric from practical action. In spite of the ferment of public denunciation, big character posters and Red Guard rallies, which began to dominate China's internal environment in 1966, cordial relations were nevertheless maintained with several Third World governments, many of which were hardly noted for their revolutionary outlook. In May 1968, Chen Yi was thus able to describe the development of friendly relations with Nepal as 'a contribution to the Afro–Asian peoples' cause of unity against imperialism and . . . a good example of implementing the five principles of peaceful coexistence'.[8] Exactly the same terms were used to describe China's policy of cooperation with Afghanistan, Pakistan, Zambia and Tanzania.

Although the ideological component in Chinese foreign policy was much more visible during these years, yet even the boldest initiatives were so calculated as to shield China from any unacceptable risk to her security or other fundamental interests. Militant pronouncements normally referred only to general principles and were seldom, if ever, directed towards a specific course of action that might entangle China in overseas military adventures. Far from committing her to any substantial involvement in local or regional conflicts, the main thrust of this apparently radical phase in Chinese foreign policy was to compel the Soviet Union, as the only communist power with a viable nuclear deterrent, to accept the major risks in the struggle against the forces of imperialism, colonialism and reaction.

In spite of the rebel occupation of the Foreign Ministry in the summer of 1967, it is significant that the main guidelines of Chinese diplomacy, inherited from the period before the Cultural Revolution, were neither questioned nor modified. The new wave of revolutionary fervour did nothing to change China's hostility towards both superpowers or to disrupt her programme of nuclear development. The successful testing of the first Chinese hydrogen bomb took place in June 1967, while in September of the same year Peking made its largest aid commitment to the Third World by signing the agreement to build and finance the Tanzania–Zambia railway.

As for the strained relations between Peking and most foreign governments and the resulting loss in diplomatic leverage during this period, they were not perhaps the consequence of a revival of blind xenophobia or of mindless militancy, but a calculated policy designed to produce a polarizing effect on the international relation of forces. In the last analysis, the foreign policy of the

Cultural Revolution was motivated by the Maoist thesis that the inevitably widening gap between the poverty of the underdeveloped countries and the affluence of the industrialized societies could be reversed only if the process of decolonization gave way to genuine economic and social emancipation. Only a policy of self-reliance could help break the vicious circle of dependence in which supposedly nationalist Third World governments had become little more than appendages of the unequal system of international exchange. The Chinese revolution, by the very nature of its cultural extremism, was presented as the shining example of the effort of a backward society to wrench itself, unaided, from the structures of underdevelopment. The rejection of the Soviet model of development, the radicalization of the cultural mechanisms of mass mobilization, and the militant thrust in foreign policy were all different aspects of the same Chinese determination to secure a leadership role in the transformation of the existing world order.[9]

The fact that China's position in the international system generally, and in the Third World in particular, had not been seriously or irreparably damaged by the Cultural Revolution was confirmed by the relative ease with which Peking returned to the international diplomatic and economic arenas once the domestic convulsions had been brought under control. Ambassadors, who had been withdrawn during the Cultural Revolution, gradually returned to their posts, while China's trade resumed its upward growth. Following armed clashes in March 1969 over the disputed islands in the Ussuri River, some limited progress was made towards the normalization of Sino–Soviet relations (see Chapter 6). Paralleling these developments was a noticeable decline in revolutionary propaganda and advocacy of the Maoist strategy of people's war and a corresponding increase in attention to China's defence needs. But undoubtedly the most striking new element in China's external relations after the early months of 1969 was the unprecedented wave of international recognitions extended to her by foreign governments. In 1970, more than ninety overseas delegations, of which some thirty were at government level, visited China, while over fifty Chinese missions, mainly economic and technical, were sent overseas. In the same year, China obtained for the first time a simple majority (51 to 49) in favour of her admission to the United Nations. After January 1971, additional efforts were made to open China's doors to the outside world. A number of study missions abroad were undertaken with a view to expanding China's domestic airline network and providing her industries with sophisticated technology. Foreign diplomats resident in Peking were invited for the first time in five years to inspect several of China's interior provinces, while facilities were made available to foreign journalists, television teams, scientists, technicians, businessmen and sporting groups to visit China. Invitations to the traditional May Day celebrations were extended to some 2000 foreigners from sixty-two countries. In April 1971, the Canton Trade Fair was attended by some 2000 foreign visitors, including 1500 Japanese businessmen representing 800 Japanese firms.

Clearly, Chinese foreign policy had entered a new phase of increased diplomatic activity partly motivated by the perception of the Soviet threat.[10] The Chinese leadership must have come to the conclusion that militant rhetoric or even limited local revolutionary activity could not adequately counter the danger posed by the policies of the two superpowers, but would need to be supplemented by an accelerated programme of national and social reconstruction. On the other hand, both Washington and Moscow were experiencing serious difficulties in maintaining their far-flung empires, which a more assertive Chinese diplomacy might be able to exploit. In Southeast Asia the United States was hopelessly bogged down in a seemingly endless war in an effort to prop up an unpopular and corrupt client regime. As for the Soviet Union, its dominant position in Eastern Europe was increasingly challenged by the nationalist sentiment that was rapidly spreading to many of these countries. To take advantage of these opportunities, Peking would have to complement its revolutionary strategy with a more traditional diplomacy. In this sense the transitional phase in Chinese foreign policy, which began with the end of the Cultural Revolution, reflected the new element of fluidity in international relations.

In June 1968, Zhou Enlai gave the first important hint of what was to be the central theme in China's new diplomatic offensive:

> We will continue to make great efforts to develop our relations with friendly countries on the basis of the five principles of peaceful co-existence. We will unite still more closely with the people of all countries and carry through to the end the struggle against US imperialism and its lackeys and the struggle against modern revisionism![11]

A more explicit outline of the emerging united front strategy was provided by the Chinese Premier on 30 September when he urged Europe, Asia, Africa and Latin America to cooperate in the abolition of military alliances dominated by the superpowers.[12] The central task of Chinese foreign policy was now perceived to be the formation of a loose coalition of nationalist and revolutionary forces throughout the world for the express purpose of containing the hegemonic ambitions of the United States and the Soviet Union. To implement this objective Peking had no alternative but to reactivate and accelerate the application of its long-standing policy of peaceful coexistence.

China's Diplomatic Offensive

Possibly the least complex and ideologically most predictable element of China's new united front strategy was her attempt to resume and, where possible, extend her political and economic relationship with the Third World. Subtle diplomacy and a realistic aid programme were combined with considerable success to exploit the opportunities presented by any country resentful of the interventionist policies of either Moscow or Washington, or increasingly sceptical of the credibility of their commitments. Although Chinese diplomatic initiatives were concentrated in those areas where they were most likely to elicit a favourable response, it is noteworthy that China's offensive encompassed every significant region of the underdeveloped world, including the greater part of black Africa, the Middle East, South and Southeast Asia as well as Latin America.[13]

Apart from its outspoken support for the anti-colonialist wars waged by the various liberation movements in Mozambique, Guinea Bissau and Angola, Chinese propaganda repeatedly championed the African cause against the racist regimes of southern Africa, and highlighted its total opposition to the sale of arms to South Africa and to any suggestion of diplomatic dialogue with the Vorster government. In a long succession of congratulatory messages addressed to African leaders, Zhou Enlai consistently reiterated China's endorsement of their determination to resist the interfering policies of the two superpowers. During the period 1970–71, China considerably expanded her economic, military, and technical aid to several African countries, including Zambia, Tanzania, Mali, Somalia, Mauritania, Congo (Brazzaville), Guinea and Sierra Leone. She fully endorsed the initiatives taken by the Organization of Petroleum Exporting Countries (OPEC) and the Organization of Arab Petroleum Exporting Countries (OAPEC) and extended undisclosed amounts of economic and military assistance to the Palestinian Liberation Organization (PLO), most of it channelled through the Iraqi port of Basra. The establishment of diplomatic relations with Turkey and Iran, the decision to provide Iraq with a $35 million interest-free loan, the expansion of trade with Egypt and Kuwait, the despatch of medical and technical teams as well as military advisers to North and South Yemen and to several Persian Gulf states, were all additional elements in China's concerted campaign to establish a diplomatic and moral presence in the Middle East.

The rather tenuous links that existed between China and most Latin American countries at the end of the 1960s and the limited resources she could realistically expect to inject into the region placed severe limitations on the scope and leverage of her Latin American diplomacy. Nevertheless, by 1970 China was ready to develop her contacts on several fronts. As evidence of its desire to improve relations with Cuba, the Chinese leadership sent a new ambassador to Havana and conveyed a special message of friendship to Fidel Castro. In the case of Chile, the establishment of diplomatic relations in December 1970 was soon followed by a number of important economic agreements and a rapid increase in China's purchase of Chilean copper. Similarly, the normalization of relations with Mexico prepared the ground for the commercial treaty of April 1973 and enlarged trade between the two countries. In 1971–72, China's trade with Peru also rose sharply as shipments of Peruvian copper, lead, and zinc were supplemented by sizeable quantities of fishmeal. Apart from progress in bilateral relations, Peking sought to expand its diplomatic influence by backing Panama and the Dominican Republic in their disputes with the United States, by encouraging Venezuelan attempts to secure a higher return on oil exports, and by supporting the demand of several Latin American countries for a 200-mile territorial limit.

Whatever the benefits accruing from an enhanced presence in the Middle East, Latin America or even Africa, it was in Asia that China's diplomatic offensive was likely to produce the most tangible results. Peking lost no time in taking advantage of the Lon Nol coup of March 1970 against Prince Norodom Sihanouk of Cambodia to act as host for his Royal Government of National Union. In an effort to project an image to the world as the most reliable supporter of the Indochinese people's struggle against the United States, China also hosted the Indochinese People's Summit Conference in April 1970, attended by Prince Sihanouk, North Vietnamese Premier Pham Van Dong, Pathet Lao leader Prince Souphanouvong and South Vietnam Provisional Revolutionary Government President Nguyen Huu Tho. In the same month, Zhou Enlai visited Pyongyang and succeeded in opening a new phase of closer relations with North Korea. Nor were Chinese initiatives confined to contacts with communist governments and revolutionary movements. As from November 1969, relations between Peking and Rangoon steadily improved, culminating in Ne Win's visit to Peking in August 1971 where he was received by both Zhou Enlai and Mao Zedong. Throughout this period China maintained her support for Pakistan in the dispute with India, and in November 1970 made available to the Pakistan government a loan of $200 million followed in May 1971 by another loan of $20 million, both of them free of interest. In the case of Ceylon, in April 1971 China advanced a free-interest loan of $30 million and the Chinese Premier sent a special message to Mrs Bandaranaike supporting her government's efforts to quash the revolutionary insurgency. But perhaps the clearest indication of China's determination to construct a more stable relationship with her Asian neighbours was the perceptible movement towards dialogue with certain member states in the Association of Southeast Asia Nations (ASEAN), especially Malaysia, Thailand and the Philippines. A gift of $200,000 in February 1971 for the flood victims in Malaysia was followed in May by the visit to China of a Malaysian trade delegation resulting in August in a trade agreement with Malaysia involving the purchase of 40,000 tons of rubber and 50,000 tons of timber.

As already indicated, China's opening to the Third World sought to marry diplomatic initiatives with a carefully calculated programme of aid and trade. It is not without significance that Chinese aid to underdeveloped countries, which had declined sharply in 1965–69 – new commitments fell to almost nothing in 1969 – rose dramatically to reach $709 million in 1970 and $467 million in 1971.[14] Of the $2500 million that China had granted in aid to Third World countries by the end of 1971, nearly $1200 million or more than 55 per cent of it was committed during 1970–71. In contrast to its economic assistance, Peking's military aid was relatively modest and was directed only to a few countries. The fact that no country, other than North Vietnam, received a substantial volume of Chinese arms would suggest that Peking did not regard this type of assistance as an effective or reliable means of extending Chinese influence. Much greater stress was placed on various forms of technical cooperation and the employment of a large number of Chinese technicians. Out of a total of 22,165 Chinese technicians abroad in 1972, representing an increase of 3565 over the previous year, over 90 per cent were stationed in Africa.[15] It is worth noting that, although Chinese and Soviet aid to the Third World were more or less comparable in value during 1971–72, the number of Chinese technicians abroad was well in excess of the corresponding Soviet number.

Complementing and reinforcing China's aid policy was the expansion of her trade relations. After recovering to pre-Cultural Revolution levels in 1970, Chinese foreign trade steadily increased from $4246 million in 1970 to $4611 million in 1971, to $5920 million in 1972, and to $9870 million in 1973. In addition to serving the needs of a developing economy, trade provided Chinese diplomacy with a much greater degree of flexibility and penetration. In 1970–72, China's increased diplomatic and political activity was reflected in some twenty-four trade and aid agreements with African states alone. In the Middle East trade agreements were reached with the Lebanon in November 1972, Kuwait in December 1972, and Iran in April 1973. In Latin America similar agreements were concluded with Mexico, Ecuador, Peru, Venezuela, and Argentina, as well as a trade protocol with Cuba and an import–export agreement with Guyana. But perhaps the most dramatic feature of the spectacular increase in China's trade was that by 1973 the non-communist countries had increased their share of China's trade to more than 80 per cent, and that trade with the developed countries had grown in 1973 by more than 90 per cent. The main factors responsible for the sudden rise in Chinese imports included the record purchase of agricultural products, the decision to obtain whole industrial plants and other machinery and equipment from the West and the readiness of Chinese authorities to finance a considerable part of industrial purchases on the basis of deferred payments.[16] Although not the determining factor, China's large purchase of wheat from Canada and Australia and her readiness to acquire the most sophisticated technology from Japan, Western Europe and the United States had undoubtedly facilitated and accelerated the normalization of relations between Peking and the western world.

Starting with the Ninth National Party Congress in April 1969, China's interest in Europe became especially noticeable. The Chinese ambassador to France returned in May 1969 and was thus one of the first senior Chinese diplomats to resume his post after the Cultural Revolution. In the following month, ambassadors were appointed to Rumania and Sweden. Earlier in the year negotiations had already begun for the establishment of diplomatic relations with Italy and Canada. In 1970, relations with Britain improved with the release of four British detainees, Zhou Enlai's message of greetings to the British Prime Minister on the Queen's official birthday and the visit to Britain of an eighteen-man Chinese delegation to discuss the purchase of civil aircraft. Sino–French relations continued to flourish with visits to China by the Minister of Planning, André Bettencourt (July), and by the former Prime Minister Couve de Murville (October).

Apart from the steady expansion of contacts and trade, two main themes now dominated China's relations with Western Europe: support for the enlargement of the European Economic Community, and hostility towards the proposed European Security Conference. The entry of Britain, Denmark, and Ireland into the Common Market was welcomed as part of a process leading to greater European independence from the two superpowers. The future political role of the enlarged Community formed a central part of discussions with French Foreign Minister Maurice Schumann and British Foreign Secretary Alec Douglas Home when they visited Peking in July and October–November 1972, respectively. The visit by West Germany's Walter Scheel in October of the same year, designed to coincide with a formal declaration of the normalization of diplomatic relations, resulted in a trade agreement in December and China's recognition of West Berlin as an integral part of West Germany.

Renewed interest in Europe was by no means confined to western nations or even to neutralist Sweden and Austria. Spurred on, no doubt, by the Soviet Union's armed invasion of Czechoslovakia, Albania Defence Minister Bekir Balluku visited China in October 1968 and came back with a much increased commitment of Chinese aid. At the same time, China began to mend her fences with Yugoslavia, and in February 1969 the first Yugoslav government delegation for nine years arrived in Peking, and negotiated a trade protocol on 17 March. In November of the same year, Yugoslavia elevated its diplomatic relations with China to ambassadorial level, and established a direct shipping line in February 1970. The visit to China by the Yugoslav Foreign Secretary in June 1971 led to the staging of the first Yugoslav industrial exhibition in Peking in December. Plans were subsequently worked out for Belgrade to be a link in China's international airline network. By this time the long-standing ideological polemic between the two countries had completely subsided, and was replaced on China's side by increasing emphasis on Yugoslavia's role as a non-aligned country.

In the meantime, the relationship with Rumania, which China had been cultivating for several years, gained additional momentum with the visit of Rumanian President Nicholas Ceaucescu to Peking in June 1971. Further signs of closer ties were provided by the signing of trade and aid agreements in 1972–73 and the establishment of a Rumanian–Chinese Friendship Association in 1973. Although somewhat less visible, significant improvement in state-to-state relations also occurred with those Eastern European countries that had traditionally been critical of China.

In addition to Europe, Peking was careful not to neglect any of America's Pacific allies, particularly Canada and Australia which had for some time provided China with a significant proportion of her wheat imports. Once Ottawa had recognized the People's Republic in October 1970 and adopted policies distinctly sympathetic to Chinese attitudes on the two related questions of Taiwan and admission to the United Nations, China appeared ready to earmark Canada as her primary source of wheat. In June 1971, an important Canadian ministerial team visited China to discuss the expansion of trade and the possibility of establishing an air link between the two countries. The following month a Chinese delegation arrived in Canada and concluded a major new wheat contract. In the case of Australia, the process of bridge-building proved somewhat slower largely because of the anti-communist obsession of the ruling Liberal government. Nevertheless, the visit to China of the Labour leader, Gough Whitlam, in July 1971 represented a dramatic development in Australian politics, and was soon followed by unprecedented, if still hesitant, hints by the McMahon government that Australia might recognize Peking.

Japan, however, was to confront Chinese diplomacy with a far greater challenge, for relations between the two countries had steadily deteriorated throughout the 1960s. The Japanese–American agreement on the return of Okinawa, Japan's decision to include South Korea and Taiwan within its security perimeter, the automatic extension of the US–Japanese security treaty in June 1970, the rapid expansion of Japan's defence expenditure, the closer economic ties between Japan and the Soviet Union, the increasing Japanese economic stake in South Korea, Taiwan and Southeast Asia, were all contributing elements in China's mounting fear of the resurgence of Japanese militarism and expansionism. Nevertheless, in their visits to China Japanese businessmen were encouraged to believe that, given satisfactory political conditions, Sino–Japanese trade could expand quite rapidly. In March 1971, representatives of Japan's major trading interests were obliged to condemn publicly their government's China policy in return for a Sino–Japanese trade agreement. In July of the same year, growing parliamentary pressure within Japan for the normalization of relations between the two countries provided Peking with additional leverage in its campaign to induce a diplomatic dialogue with Tokyo.

Ultimately, however, the new direction in Chinese diplomacy would depend for its success on a radical shift in Sino–American relations, since it was American antagonism that had largely contributed during the 1950s and 1960s to China's military encirclement and diplomatic isolation. Accordingly, on 26 November 1968, in a statement issued by the Information Department of the Ministry of Foreign Affairs, Peking indicated its willingness to resume the Warsaw talks on 20 February of the following year, and resurrected two principles which, it claimed, had consistently governed its negotiations with the United States: that the United States should undertake to withdraw all its military forces and equipment from Taiwan and the Taiwan Straits; and that China and the United States should 'conclude an agreement on the Five

Principles of Peaceful Coexistence'.[17] The Chinese proposal probably represented the initial step undertaken by the section of the Chinese leadership that had become interested in exploring the possibility of détente with the United States. In effect, the Chinese statement merely restored the *status quo ante* of the ambassadorial talks in Warsaw prior to the Cultural Revolution.[18]

A second and much clearer indication of the new line in Chinese strategy was provided in January 1969, soon after Nixon had taken office, by the joint editorial of the *People's Daily* and *Red Flag*, which pointedly excluded Taiwan, although not the Taiwan Straits, from the list of places from where all US troops had to be withdrawn.[19] That this apparent gesture of goodwill was part of a much larger design was indicated by the whole tenor of Mao Zedong's remarks to Edgar Snow in December 1970:

> In the meantime, he said, the Foreign Ministry was studying the matter of admitting Americans from the left, middle and right to visit China. Should rightists like Nixon, who represented the monopoly capitalists be permitted to come? He should be welcomed because, Mao explained, at present the problems between China and the USA would have to be solved with Nixon. Mao would be happy to talk with him, either as a tourist or as President.[20]

From this point onwards there could be no doubt that a Sino–American rapprochement had become one of the dominant considerations in the formulation of Chinese foreign policy.

Throughout the course of 1971, in remarks made to several foreign visitors, including an American group of academics, Zhou Enlai made it clear that the US treaty of defence with Taiwan need not constitute an insuperable obstacle to the relaxation of tensions between the two countries. Moreover, he indicated that China, far from being committed to the liberation of Taiwan through the use of force, was ready to engage in direct negotiations with Taibei in order to reunify, by peaceful means, the province of Taiwan with the rest of China.[21] Even in demanding the withdrawal of the American military presence from Taiwan, the Chinese leader's use of words suggested that he was more concerned to obtain a satisfactory declaration of intent rather than immediate and physical compliance with an absolute precondition.

The policy of promoting contacts and exchanges between the two countries was given further impetus in April 1971 with the invitation to an American table tennis team to visit China. The team, which was accompanied by two journalists, was to be the first of a large number of visiting delegations, including members of Congress, scholars, doctors, scientists, sportsmen, Chinese-Americans and students. Communications were opened not only between individuals but also between Chinese and American organizations, such as scientific and medical societies, libraries, news services and sports associations.

Perhaps one of the most intriguing aspects of the improvement in Sino–American relations is that it should have occurred at a time when the Nixon administration was still not showing any signs of having recognized the errors of America's Vietnam policy or of wanting to bring the war to a rapid conclusion. Indeed, the United States appeared quite unrepentant as it set about extending the Indochinese conflict, firstly engineering the Cambodian coup in March 1970 and the subsequent South Vietnamese invasion, and later in February 1971 instigating the invasion of Laos, where the CIA had long directed military operations in non-liberated areas. Angered by American actions, Peking described US troop withdrawals from Vietnam as 'a ruse aimed at deception'.[22]

The escalation of the war into a country contiguous with China represented an obvious threat to Chinese security, given that clandestine raids from Laos into Yunnan had reportedly been mounted for some time prior to the invasion by minority and Chinese nationalist agents under CIA direction.[23] An authoritative statement in February 1971 left no doubt as to China's apprehensions:

> Laos is not in Northwest Europe or South America, but in north Indochina. She and China are linked by the same mountains and rivers and have a common boundary of several hundred kilometres. . . . By spreading the flames of aggressive war to the door of China, US imperialism certainly poses a grave threat to China.[24]

Precisely the same argument applied to North Vietnam, where China undoubtedly retained the same fundamental interest in defending a neighbouring ally against attack by a common enemy. China's clear statement of the perceived threat was accompanied by a cautious deployment of force on its borders, specifically designed to convey the protective rather than provocative nature of her intentions. In so doing, the Chinese leadership was able to signal to American policy-makers the risks of continued escalation of the Indochinese conflict, while at the same time indicating that the immediate victory of the communist forces in Indochina was not a precondition for a Sino–American diplomatic dialogue. It is even possible that such a dialogue may have come to be regarded by Mao, but also by the Americans, as a positive contribution to the search for a settlement at the Paris peace negotiations.

Continuity or Change?

Several writers have attempted to characterize the 'new' phase in Chinese foreign policy in terms of a shift from a state of self-imposed isolation to one of global involvement. Such a crude and partial interpretation of a complex set of motives and objectives overlooks the obvious fact that, even at the height of the Cultural Revolution, Peking remained fully committed to an internationalist philosophy. At the very moment when her integration into the international diplomatic system appeared most tenuous, China was seeking to promote a wide range of activities with the express purpose of enhancing revolutionary prospects not only in Asia, but in the Middle East, Africa and Latin America. In reality, as Stephen Fitzgerald has remarked, it is impossible to explain Chinese foreign policy either before, during or after the Cultural Revolution in terms of some simple overriding formula, whether it be nationalism, communism, 'the single-minded pursuit of world domination' or 'the guerrilla mentality of Yenan'.[25]

Such fluctuations as have occurred in China's international behaviour have invariably resulted from a subtle interaction of internal and external factors. What appears to have happened during the late 1960s and early 1970s is that the combination of domestic and international changes brought about a modification in China's external environment, which, coupled with a rapidly changing internal situation, precipitated a reassessment of foreign policy priorities. Of particular significance were the reappraisal and reduction of American global commitments and the corresponding extension of Soviet influence, notably in Asia; the intensifying rivalry of the great powers in such theatres as the Middle East and the Indian Ocean and the growing resistance throughout the world to the international duopoly of power exercised by the United States and the Soviet Union; the changing pattern of European politics and the gradual shift of the diplomatic centre of gravity from the Atlantic to the Pacific; Japan's rise as a major economic power and the growing economic conflicts within the developed capitalist world. Chinese foreign policy could not but be deeply influenced by these shifts in the global balance of power and by the threats and opportunities they implied.

But China's decision to pursue a more active and wider-ranging diplomacy was not the sole product of external circumstances. The much greater emphasis on the art of persuasion and the conventional norms of international conduct characteristic of Chinese foreign policy immediately after the Cultural Revolution reflected to a considerable degree Zhou Enlai's personal ascendancy within the decision-making process and the flexibility and sophistication of his political style. By combining his own institutional power base with the authoritative power derived from Mao, Zhou was able to endow the new diplomatic line with a greatly enhanced degree of legitimacy and continuity.[26] To this extent, the apparent reasonableness and pragmatism of the new phase could be interpreted as part of a campaign intended to take advantage of the new opportunities offered by domestic and international politics.

China's effective performance on the international stage after 1968 may also be regarded as an indication of the flexible and patient diplomacy she had pursued for nearly two decades. A very important though not necessarily the most decisive factor contributing to China's rise as a major actor in world politics was her acquisition of a nuclear capability, which might in due course enable her to threaten directly both the United States and the Soviet Union. Apart from strengthening China's status as a great power and symbolizing her will to national independence, the Chinese nuclear force tended to accentuate the erosion of American commitments to friendly and allied states, decrease the

Soviet Union's capacity for nuclear blackmail, and increase the probability of further nuclear proliferation. All three developments may be said to have made significant inroads into the diplomatic and strategic pre-eminence of the two superpowers. Moreover, China's military performance in the Korean war and in the border conflict with India, as well as the deterrent effect of her geographical proximity in the Indochinese conflict, had already demonstrated her capacity to influence the relation of forces at any point on her defence perimeter.

It remains perhaps to say a word about the state of the Chinese economy and its impact on foreign trade and foreign policy generally. After the withdrawal of Soviet economic and technical aid in 1960, imports of capital goods throughout the 1960s remained much below the level of 1959, partly because of large imports of cereals, partly also because of the insistence on a balanced trade account and the rejection of medium- or long-term credits. Consequently, China's industrialization had to operate without the benefit of any significant inflow of foreign technology. By 1964–65, the Chinese had begun to create an intermediate technology, specially designed for small plants, in which the basic equipment was relatively simple and standardized, thereby facilitating the spread of know-how and ensuring plant maintenance by workers with limited technical qualifications. Although the Cultural Revolution did affect industrial growth, its adverse impact was neither serious nor prolonged. Indeed, after the mid-1960s considerable progress was made in steel-making, chemical fertilizers, transport equipment and the machine-building industry. Steel production, for example, increased from 3.5 million ingot tons in 1957 to 18 million in 1970, while fertilizer output rose from 7,660,000 tons in 1965 to 14,000,000 tons in 1970. Reference has already been made to the recovery of China's trade in 1970 to pre-Cultural Revolution levels (p. 116). Thanks to the many discoveries made during the 1960s, China was fast becoming a major oil producer and in 1973 entered the export market with the supply of one million tons of crude oil to Japan. Although not in contradiction with the fundamental principle of self-reliance, the new trends in China's industrialization and foreign trade pointed to much closer technical cooperation with the outside world, greater exchange of scientific and industrial exhibitions, and a greater willingness to sign contracts involving not only the supply of equipment, but also the design, engineering, procurement, supervision of construction and commissioning of entire plants.[27]

Undoubtedly, China's greater political stability and the renewed stress on economic and military modernization were all important domestic factors contributing to a more confident, more universal, yet more flexible diplomacy. The fact remains, however, that these changes would not have radically altered the form of China's foreign policy equation unless they had been complemented and reinforced by a marked shift in the functions of certain external variables. In describing 1968 as a year of 'accelerated decline' for US imperialism and Soviet revisionism and unprecedented economic and political crisis for the world capitalist system,[28] and in pointing to 'new storms' and to a new era of struggle in international relations,[29] the Chinese leadership was quietly informing the world that Chinese foreign policy was rapidly adjusting to the requirements of a new transitional phase in world politics.

Changing International Environment

One of the most important elements in China's modified understanding of the forces shaping the course of international politics was Japan's rise as a major power. During the greater part of the 1960s, the Indochinese conflict, the Sino–Soviet dispute and the Cultural Revolution had tended to push Japan into the background. However, by 1968 China was openly voicing her mounting concern with the growth of Japanese economic and military power. Although peaceful coexistence was now a dominant theme in China's new-look foreign policy, there remained militant undertones in her relations with the Japanese government. On 27 January 1969, the *People's Daily* advised the Japanese people 'to drive US imperialism out of their soil, put an end to the criminal rule of the US and Japanese reactionaries and achieve genuine independence and liberation'.[30]

The spectre of Japanese militarism was compounded and, to some extent, reinforced by increasing evidence of Soviet hostility, to which the Chinese attributed the escalation of the border dispute and Moscow's concerted effort to extend its economic and diplomatic penetration of Southeast Asia. The Soviet invasion of Czechoslovakia in August 1968 and the subsequent elaboration of the Brezhnev doctrine, which upheld the principle of the collective defence of socialism in any country of the socialist commonwealth, could not but accentuate Chinese fears that the concept of limited sovereignty might, in some future circumstances, be applied to China's situation to justify some form of military intervention. On 16 September 1968, an official Chinese statement protested about Soviet overflights during the preceding year, and, in his National Day address on 1 October, Zhou Enlai openly advised the Chinese people to 'squash any invasion launched by US imperialism, Soviet revisionism, and their lackeys, whether individually or collectively'. On 8 October, Wang Enmao, Vice Chairman of the Revolutionary Committee of the Xinjiang Uygur Autonomous Region, explicitly stated that local PLA units were ready to wipe out the 'Soviet revisionists' should they dare to attack.[31]

But, as we have already seen, China's concern with the Soviet threat pre-dated the Soviet thrust into Czechoslovakia. Speaking at an Army Day reception on 1 August 1968, three weeks prior to the invasion, the PLA Chief of Staff referred to 'a counter-revolutionary ring of encirclement' which 'US imperialism, Soviet revisionism and the Indian and other reactionaries' were striving to form against China.[32] Indeed, as Mao's conversation with the Japanese Socialists in 1964 would indicate, the Chinese leadership had been stressing for some considerable time the aggressive implications of Soviet troop concentration on China's borders. The direct confrontation that occurred in 1969 on the north-eastern and, later, central Asian frontiers were portrayed by the Chinese as the culmination of long-standing Soviet war preparations, possibly for a pre-emptive strike against Chinese nuclear installations. Prompted by security considerations, the Chinese leadership intensified its propaganda campaign against the Soviet Union, ordered practice blackouts and the construction of air-raid shelters and proceeded with the stockpiling of food and raw materials as well as the relocation of troops and industries.

Apart from the immediate physical threat posed by Soviet military power, several other developments were also causing China grave concern. The growing momentum of Soviet initiatives in the direction of Japan, Moscow's increasingly important strategic role in the Indian sub-continent, the expanding Soviet naval presence in the Indian and Pacific Oceans, the attempt to forge friendly links with Asian countries irrespective of the ideological complexion of their governments, were all interpreted as part of a larger policy directed against China. Not unexpectedly, Peking reacted vehemently to the Soviet proposal for an Asian collective security system,[33] denouncing it as a 'tattered flag for an anti-China military alliance' conceived in collusion with US imperialism, and aimed at encircling China and stepping up threats of aggression against her.[34] Somewhat more surprising but equally revealing of the deep-seated nature of China's fears was her adverse response to the process of Soviet–European cooperation and, in particular, her sharp criticism of the Soviet–West German treaty of 1970, which had become one of the cornerstones of European détente. Chinese apprehension about the course of events in Europe stemmed from the realization that the Soviet military threat to China would be considerably greater if the Soviet armed forces did not have to operate simultaneously on two fronts. In effect, the disposition of Soviet forces in 1971 was for the first time in Soviet history greater in Asia than in Europe.[35] Although the difference in actual military concentration was still slight, the significance of the trend was inescapable given that the level of forces in Soviet Asia had increased within the space of a few years from no more than fourteen divisions in 1965 to some thirty-five or forty divisions in 1971. In this sense, the relaxation of tensions in Europe had a direct bearing on considerations of Chinese security.

Many western observers, in fact, attributed Peking's readiness after 1968 to normalize relations with the capitalist world, notably with Western Europe and the United States, to the reassessment of the new external dangers confronting China and above all to the Chinese perception of the Soviet threat.[36] While this interpretation is not without validity, it is at best a partial explanation of a complex policy motivated at least as much by the self-confident awareness of new opportunities as by the fear of a hostile international environment. By the end of 1968, the Chinese leadership was openly claiming that the struggle against US imperialism and Soviet revisionism had entered 'a new historical stage'.

An important element of the Chinese analysis was alluded to by an authoritative article that appeared in the Chinese press on 27 January 1969, which set out to examine the implications of Nixon's inaugural address of 20 January. The presidential speech was actually described as 'a confession by the US imperialists... that they are beset with difficulties both at home and abroad and are in an impasse'.[37] Nixon's own references to the domestic difficulties, internal division and spiritual crisis experienced by the United States were seen as confirmation of the general decline of American power.[38] In contrast to the diplomatic and economic reverses suffered by the United States, China's standing in the world was beginning to rise, while her diplomacy was about to register its most spectacular successes since the inception of the Chinese People's Republic.

China's rise to the front ranks of international politics was closely related to the changing disposition of other countries towards her. Between 1969 and 1971 more than twenty countries recognized Peking as the sole legitimate government of China and were followed by another sixteen in the course of 1972. It is this quick succession of recognitions that constituted the single most important factor in China's changing image in the world and in the expanded diplomatic leverage she was able to exploit promptly and skilfully. Official commentaries emanating from Peking were quick to point out the significance of China's enhanced legal status within the international community.[39] The new wave of recognition was all the more dramatic since it encompassed not only Third World or non-aligned countries but a large number of NATO members, including Italy and Canada in 1970, Turkey, Belgium, Luxembourg and Iceland in 1971, Greece and West Germany in 1972. Other US allies to recognize China were Australia, New Zealand and Japan.

The improvement in China's diplomatic fortunes was not confined, however, to the western world. The persistent Soviet efforts to convene an international conference of communist parties, which would fully endorse Moscow's position in the dispute with China, proved to be a costly and futile exercise. At the preparatory meeting in Budapest in March 1968, the Soviet leadership attempted to use the Vietnam war – and China's refusal to agree to united action in relation to it – as a pawn in the Sino–Soviet conflict, but failed to secure any criticism of the Chinese attitude. Even more damaging to the Soviet cause was the conspicuous absence from the meeting of those communist parties, including the Cubans, North Koreans, Japanese and the North Vietnamese themselves, whose ideological outlook most closely coincided with the revolutionary aims of the South Vietnamese liberation movement. Although seventy-five communist parties subsequently assembled in Moscow for the world conference in June 1969, thirty-two of these were minuscule shadow movements. Absent from the meeting were the Chinese, Albanian, Yugoslav, North Korean, North Veitnamese and Japanese parties. Moreover, other parties expressed objections to the communiqué that the conference issued, while five of the parties that signed, including the Rumanian Communist Party, did so with reservations. Far from reimposing the unity of the international communist movement under Moscow's direction, the meeting merely expressed the new complex and diverse framework of intra-bloc relations, and reaffirmed that these relations were to be governed by the principles of equality, sovereignty and non-interference. Once again, the final communiqué studiously refrained from attacking China, her policies, or the prescriptions of Mao Zedong thought.

The Soviet failure to reduce China's position within the Socialist bloc to that of an outcast may be explained, at least in part, by the desire of several communist parties to emancipate themselves from Soviet domination. To this extent, therefore, all nationalist forces in Eastern Europe, whether communist or not, found a natural ally in China, given the latter's well-orchestrated campaign in favour of greater equality among socialist countries and her explicit denunciation of Soviet expansionism in Europe. It was exactly the same type of reasoning that predisposed most Asian nations to react cautiously and often negatively to the Soviet proposal for an Asian security system. The lessons of the Indochinese conflict and the rapid advance of China's nuclear capability undoubtedly reinforced the unwillingness of most countries in the Asian region to entertain the prospect of a Russo–Chinese war. The Soviet Union's diplomatic and other initiatives in Southeast Asia were therefore treated with suspicion in so far as they were understood to be aimed at the containment of China – a policy that might well involve other Asian countries in a dangerous confrontation with Chinese power.

Perhaps the most concrete indication of the readiness of small and medium powers to accept Peking as a useful weight in the world balance of power was provided at the United Nations where the voting pattern on the question of China's representation changed dramatically in 1970. Until then the proposal to seat the People's Republic and expel the Nationalists had been consistently defeated, although there was a tied vote in 1965, with 47 states for the resolution, 47 against and 23 states abstaining, absent, or not participating in the vote. In 1970, for the first time, the resolution to seat Peking and expel Taibei gained a simple majority of 51 to 49, with 27 states abstaining, absent, or not participating in the vote. In that year, the People's Republic was nevertheless denied its place in the United Nations as a result of a procedure sponsored by the United States whose net effect was to prevent a decision on the occupancy of China's seat unless it received the support of two-thirds of the members present and voting.[40] Before the crucial session of the United Nations General Assembly in October 1971, the United States modified its attitude with the announcement that it would support the admission of the People's Republic but oppose the expulsion of Taiwan. The American 'two Chinas' formula was accompanied by a high pressure lobbying exercise with the apparent intention of defeating the Albanian motion and preserving Nationalist representation at the United Nations. Whether this stratagem was a genuine expression of American policy or simply a token gesture to appease Taibei, the fact remains that in the ensuing vote China was admitted to the

United Nations on her own terms and by an overwhelming majority of 76 to 35, thereby inflicting one of the most humiliating defeats ever experienced by the United States within the international organization.

From the very beginning China had made it clear that she would not accede to any formula that even hinted that the People's Republic did not exercise sovereignty over Taiwan. The Ministry of Foreign Affairs reiterated China's unambiguous position in its statement of 20 August 1971.[41] Confident of the outcome and adamant that there could be no bargaining over principle, the Chinese were happy to leave the canvassing of votes to their supporters. Indicative of China's dramatically improved international standing, especially among Third World countries, was not only the record number of favourable votes on which she could now rely but the enthusiasm with which many governments argued for China's admission. In an explanatory note, accompanying the draft resolution calling for the 'restoration of the lawful rights of the People's Republic of China in the United Nations', Albania, Algeria and the other sixteen sponsoring countries spoke eloquently of the justice of Peking's position, of the valuable contribution of China's peaceful policies and of her importance as a major power in the world.

The historic vote of 25 October 1971 resulting in the admission of the People's Republic and the expulsion of the Nationalists was greeted by many Third World delegates with excitement and jubilation. The fact that for the first time an underdeveloped country, independent of both power blocs, had gained a permanent seat on the Security Council with the right of veto, was widely regarded as symbolic of the Third World's newly found sense of power and self-confidence. Of the 76 countries that had voted for China's admission, 33 were from Africa, 11 from Asia and 7 from Latin America. If to these are added the other 14 Afro–Asian or Latin American countries that refused to cast a negative vote, one gets an overall impression of the substantial success of China's Third World diplomacy. One of the most important implications of the 1971 vote was the possibility of the long-term reorganization of the existing power equilibrium. China's membership of the United Nations and its various agencies was bound to highlight the dissatisfaction of nearly two-thirds of humanity with the prevailing international economic arrangements and their obvious failure to alleviate the dramatic and growing inequality between the haves and have-nots.

The United States Reassesses its China Policy

The very significant strides made by Chinese diplomacy after 1968 in developing a more cooperative relationship with small and middle powers, in Eastern and Western Europe as well as in the Third World, would have lost much of their impact had they not been buttressed by a new understanding with the United States. The strength of China's diplomatic position rested precisely on the fact that the world's greatest power had acknowledged the error of its past policies and taken the first steps towards the normalization of relations, although it is also true that the Maoist leadership proved particularly receptive to American overtures.

The first important indication of a possible shift in American policy was given by Richard Nixon more than a year before his victory in the 1968 presidential elections. In what was widely regarded as a programmatic statement of his new thinking on US relations with Asia, the Republican leader stressed the urgency of reducing the possibility of direct confrontation between the nuclear powers and, for this purpose, advocated the 'development of regional defence pacts, in which nations undertake, among themselves, to attempt to contain aggression in their own areas'.[42] In entrusting the United States with a much diminished role as policeman of the world, Nixon was obviously moving towards a domestic reformulation of the containment policy that had been premised for nearly two decades on the need to isolate China.

Having defined as one of his long-term objectives the improvement of relations with China, Nixon was confronted, on assuming office, with the practical problem of giving substance to this general statement of intent. It will be recalled that after a break of one year, the first ambassadorial meeting between the two countries was scheduled for 20 February 1969 in Warsaw (see p. 118). Although the meeting was cancelled at the last minute by the Chinese, Washington was careful not to engage in recrimination and expressed its readiness to resume the dialogue at the first possible opportunity. On 21 April 1969 Secretary of State William Rogers acknowledged China's central role in the Asian–Pacific region and stressed the American desire to develop a constructive dialogue with Chinese leaders.[43] Perhaps the most revealing aspect of the Secretary's statement was his admission that the United States had been the first to make some conciliatory moves and that it would persist with this policy even in the face of China's negative reaction. In effect, President Nixon decided in July 1969 to relax restrictions on travel to permit almost any American citizens having a legitimate purpose other than tourism to visit China. In 1969 and 1970 the number of passports validated for travel to China totalled 556 compared to 423 from April 1959 to the end of 1968. In July 1969 the United States also waived previous restrictions to permit non-commercial tourist importations of Chinese goods up to a value of $100.

However, these limited gestures were unlikely to persuade Peking to move towards any accommodation so long as the United States did not signify its intention to adopt a more conciliatory position on the central issue of Taiwan. Undeterred by this major obstacle, Mr Rogers reaffirmed on 8 August 1969 his government's determination to bring about a relaxation of tensions between the two countries.[44] But the first decisive demonstration of American goodwill did not occur until November 1969 when the United States announced the termination of the regular patrolling carried out by the Seventh Fleet in the Taiwan Straits. Although the decision was justified on grounds of economy, its strategic and diplomatic implications were immediately conveyed to Peking.[45] In the following month the Nixon administration removed the $100 ceiling on the importation of Chinese goods, and further altered the regulations to permit foreign subsidiaries of US firms to trade with China in non-strategic goods. The United States obviously expected that the cumulative effect of these measures would in due course produce a favourable response. Speaking in a television interview on 23 December 1969, the US Secretary of State struck a more optimistic note and gave an indication that current initiatives could lead to 'improved relations'.[46]

In a major foreign policy message to Congress in February 1970, President Nixon provided further clarification of his China policy, emphasizing once again that the attempt to improve relations between the two countries was unilaterally undertaken by the United States and in the absence of any guarantee that such initiatives would be favourably received by Chinese leaders.[47] In a further bid to reassure them, the American President made it clear that Washington had no intention of taking sides in the Sino–Soviet dispute or of 'joining any condominium or hostile coalition of great powers against either of the large Communist countries'.[48] Although phrased in somewhat ambivalent diplomatic language, the obvious meaning of the Nixon statement was that the United States would do nothing to encourage or assist Soviet plans for an anti-Chinese coalition of Asian states, euphemistically described by Moscow as a system of collective security.

Beginning in April 1970, the United States introduced selective licensing of American-made components and spare parts for non-strategic foreign goods exported to China, while in August 1970 permission was given for the first time to American oil companies abroad to supply their foreign-produced oil to 'free world' ships bearing non-strategic cargoes to Chinese ports. All these measures were intended, in the words of Marshall Green, Assistant Secretary of State for East Asian and Pacific Affairs, 'to convince Peking that we [the United States] are not seeking to "contain and isolate" China and that we favor China's emergence from isolation'.[49] Although, perhaps not unexpectedly, Peking failed to respond directly to these steps, President Nixon announced in his press conference of 10 December 1970 that he would continue with his initiatives in relaxing trade and travel restrictions. In his foreign policy report to Congress on 25 February 1971, he indicated that in the coming year he would carefully examine what further steps the United States might take to 'create broader opportunities for contacts between the Chinese and American Peoples', and how the United States 'might remove needless obstacles to the realization of these opportunities'.

The 'further steps' to which the President had referred came with remarkable speed on 15 March, when the United States lifted all travel restrictions on Americans wishing to go to China. One month later, on 15 April, five new measures were announced, including an offer to expedite visas for visitors or groups of visitors from the People's Republic; relaxation of currency controls to permit the use of dollars by China; authorization to American oil companies to provide fuel to ships and aircraft travelling to or from China; and permission for US vessels and aircraft to carry Chinese cargoes between non-communist ports, and for US owned foreign flag carriers to call at Chinese ports. The President also indicated that he was investigating the possibility of freeing a number of non-strategic goods for direct export to China. However, as he explained to a panel of editors and newsmen on 16 April, it was now time for the Chinese to make the next move in the improvement of bilateral relations.[50]

Apart from easing trade and travel restrictions, it is worth noting that the US President had used, for the first time, in his second report to Congress the term 'People's Republic of China' instead of the more offensive labels 'Communist China' and 'mainland China' traditionally found in US official statements and documents. In the same report, he gave the first indication that his administration was seriously interested in hastening China's entry into the United Nations although not at the expense of Taiwan's exclusion. In April 1971, the Nixon moves were finally reciprocated by China's invitation to an American table tennis team. American diplomacy had apparently succeeded in demonstrating its active commitment to the development of closer relations with Peking and its practical abandonment of the long-standing policy of containment. Greeting the American table tennis team, Premier Zhou Enlai referred to the visit as opening 'a new page in the relations between the Chinese and American people's'. In June, Washington responded to China's gesture of goodwill by lifting the twenty-year-old embargo on direct trade on non-strategic goods with China, thereby removing another important obstacle in the normalization of relations between the two countries.

At this point one may well ask: why was the United States now seeking so assiduously to cultivate a dialogue with Maoist China after having pursued a policy of undiluted hostility towards that country for nearly two decades? Why place so much emphasis on encouraging China to emerge from her supposed isolation, when every previous US administration had left no stone unturned in order to achieve that very isolation? What factors could account for such a dramatic shift in American diplomacy? A partial answer to that question can be found in the growing international influence that China was able to wield, especially in Asia and Africa, in spite of America's sustained efforts to thwart Chinese objectives and aspirations. The increasing recognition that the People's Republic was gaining from many western as well as Third World countries and the steady rise in the number of states supporting Peking's admission to the United Nations must have made Washington realize that, even in the face of total American opposition, China could not be indefinitely denied her rightful place in the world community.

In addition to these considerations, American foreign policy had to take into account the continuing Sino–Soviet hostility and its inescapable impact on Soviet–American rivalry and détente. By developing a triangular relationship with China and the Soviet Union, the United States could derive considerable diplomatic leverage from the dispute between the two communist giants, even while refusing to take sides. More specifically, an improvement in Sino–American relations might make the Soviet leadership more responsive to American pressures on a wide range of international issues, including questions of disarmament, arms control and European security.

But undoubtedly the single most important factor contributing to the Nixon changes in American policy towards China was the profound disenchantment with the Vietnam war. In its initial stages, United States military intervention in Vietnam was conceived as an integral part of the policy of containment and had the support of the majority of the American public. Yet within a few years it became evident that this military adventure would exact a heavy toll in men, money and prestige. Apart from causing widespread anxiety and frustration within the American body politic, the costly and ever-expanding conflict inevitably produced despondency, dissent and mass desertions in the American armed forces. Calls for an end to the bombing and the withdrawal of American troops from Vietnam eventually resulted in a series of congressional initiatives to end the fighting and restrict the powers of the President.

As a consequence of the Vietnam experience, the United States was now much more inclined to reduce its military presence in Asia and to move towards a policy that accepted, however grudgingly, the end of the post-war era of exclusive American hegemony over the non-communist world. By the late 1960s, the intellectual elite and the public at large, as well as a large cross-section of congressional opinion, were ready to replace the bipolar conception of international relations with a more flexible notion of multipolar relationships. By accepting the emergence of China as a great power, whose interests had to be given due consideration, American diplomacy was perhaps hoping that a tacit agreement might be reached between the two countries about their respective spheres of influence. Such an understanding might permit the United States to pursue its policy of military disengagement in Indochina in the knowledge that its political and economic dominance in other parts of Asia would not, as a consequence, be subjected to serious challenge.

Indeed, some observers have argued that President Nixon's underlying objective in fostering the Sino–American rapprochement was to persuade Peking to use all its influence on Hanoi so that American troops might be withdrawn from Vietnam with minimum humiliation to the United States and with sufficient concessions from communist forces in Indochina to allow a political solution to the war compatible with American interests. The Nixon administration may also have entertained the hope that, in return for closer relations with the United States, China would terminate, or at least significantly reduce, her support for insurgency operations and liberation movements in Southeast Asia. There is, however, no evidence to suggest that such an understanding was ever reached, explicitly or even tacitly, between the two countries. China, for her part, consistently maintained that the withdrawal of American forces from the whole of Indochina would, at least in principle, have to precede normalization of Sino–American relations.

Even if one were to overlook China's ideological commitment to the revolutionary struggle in Indochina, Nixon's meandering Vietnam policy would still have remained unacceptable to Peking for security reasons, at least so long as the United States retained in the area the kind of military presence that threatened to unleash a larger confrontation and precipitate China's more direct involvement. Throughout 1970 and the early months of 1971, official Chinese statements continued to describe the American escalation of the war as a threat to the security of the People's Republic and to the peace of Asia and the world. A Sino–Vietnamese communiqué issued in March 1971 reaffirmed in the strongest possible terms China's opposition to American actions in Indochina.[51] As already indicated, such statements were intended primarily to deter the United States from expanding the ground war rather than to set the stage for China's direct military intervention. In other words, the warnings issued by Peking during this period were concerned much more with a potential rather than an actual threat.

In any case, the anxieties experienced by the Maoist leadership with regard to Chinese security were to some extent allayed by the series of messages delivered from Washington to the Chinese government through various diplomatic intermediaries. According to one well-informed observer, the purport of these communications was to assure China of President Nixon's 'new outlook' on Asia and of his determination to withdraw from Vietnam as quickly as possible, while seeking a negotiated settlement of the conflict.[52] An even more important factor in dissipating Chinese fears was the actual process of withdrawal. By August 1969 the departure of the first 25,000 troops from South Vietnam had been completed, and by November 1971 only 196,000 troops remained compared with a peak of 543,000 in February 1969. If the United States had not succeeded in winning the war when its armed strength was at its height, it could scarcely hope to do so with a much reduced military capability. In this sense, the Vietnamization policy was a poorly executed attempt to disguise the inevitable defeat and translate the belated realization that no Saigon army, however well equipped, could withstand for long the tide of popular opposition or the advancing communist forces. Having sought an illusory military victory for nearly a decade, American strategy now had to concede that the Communists had won the decisive political battle in the struggle for the liberation and reunification of Vietnam.

By the middle of 1971, if not earlier, Peking was probably convinced that the United States was finally getting out of Vietnam, although Washington's last minute attempts to find a face-saving formula for a while prolonged the fighting and postponed the Communist victory. Once the Chinese leadership made up its mind that American diplomacy was reconciled to its defeat in Indochina, the movement towards a Sino–American détente gathered considerable momentum. Accordingly, on 17 July 1971 came the historic announcement that President Nixon would visit China before May 1972, and that his National Security Adviser, Dr Kissinger, who had been reported to be indisposed in Pakistan, was actually in Peking conferring with Zhou Enlai. The joint statement announcing the forthcoming visit by the American head of state made it clear that the initiative for the invitation had come from President Nixon himself. There is reason to believe that the While House had made use of the good offices of several well-placed third parties, notably France and Pakistan, to indicate its interest in holding high-level discussions with the Chinese leadership. In the July statement, the two purposes of the Nixon visit were specified as the normalization of relations and an exchange of views on questions of mutual concern.[53] Following a second visit to Peking by Dr Kissinger in October 1971 and several months of consultations, it was finally agreed on 30 November that President Nixon would set off for his historic journey to China on 21 February 1972.

While the seven days the American President and his entourage spent in Peking may not have changed the world, they certainly consummated one of the most dramatic shifts in United States foreign policy since World War II. The joint communiqué issued at Shanghai on 27 February revealed little of the 'serious and frank exchange of views', which took place behind closed doors and covered the whole range of bilateral and international issues. Nevertheless, enough was disclosed to indicate the radical transformation of the Sino–American relationship. Apart from the specific agreements reached with regard to the further development of contacts and exchanges in science, technology, culture, sports and journalism, and the facilitation of bilateral trade, the two sides agreed to maintain close diplomatic contact through various channels, 'including the sending of a senior US representative to Peking from time to time for concrete consultations to further the normalization of relations'.[54] Equally significant was the willingness of the United States to identify with China's formulation of the five principles of peaceful coexistence:

> . . . countries, regardless of their social systems, should conduct their relations on the principles of respect for the sovereignty and territorial integrity of all states, non-aggression against other states, non-interference in the internal affairs of other states, equality and mutual benefit, and peaceful coexistence. International disputes should be settled on this basis without resorting to the use or threat of force.[55]

Indeed, the statement went a long way towards accepting the need to limit great power interests and spheres of influence:

> – both [China and the United States] wish to reduce the danger of international military conflict;
> – neither should seek hegemony in the Asia–Pacific region and each is opposed to efforts by any other country or group of countries to establish such hegemony . . .[56]

It is of course more than likely that neither China nor the United States was altogether sincere in renouncing great power ambitions. Regardless of their real intentions, the statement nevertheless constituted an implicit repudiation of American behaviour, which had attempted to construct over a period of two decades an overwhelming military presence stretching in an unbroken semi-circle from Japan to Thailand, for the explicit purpose of containing China and maintaining in power a loose coalition of anti-communist client states. In China's case, the statement reinforced her claim that she would never be a superpower, that she harboured no great power ambitions, and that she belonged to the Third World through both circumstance and choice. Moreover, this public affirmation of principle underlined China's revolutionary credentials, in particular her recognition of the right of any nation to make its own revolution, and, more importantly, her opposition to the attempts of any great power to frustrate such a revolution.

On the question of Taiwan, the two parties found it necessary to present separate statements of their respective positions. China, for her part, restated her traditional demands:

> The Taiwan question is the crucial question obstructing the normalization of relations between China and the United States; the Government of the People's Republic of China is the sole legal government of China; Taiwan is a province of China . . . the liberation of Taiwan is China's internal affair . . . all U.S. forces and military installations must be withdrawn from Taiwan.[57]

In the case of the United States, there was a clear departure from previously established policy:

> The United States acknowledges that all Chinese on either side of the Taiwan Strait maintain that there is but one China and that Taiwan is part of China. The U.S. government does not challenge that position. It reaffirms its interest in a peaceful settlement of the Taiwan question by the Chinese themselves. With this prospect in mind, it affirms the ultimate objective of the withdrawal of all U.S. forces and military installations from Taiwan. In the meantime, it will progressively reduce its forces and military installations on Taiwan as the tension in the area diminishes.[58]

Implicit in this declaration was the American acceptance of the principle of 'one China', although its realization was left to an unspecified future date. It is worth noting, in this respect, that, while China did not denounce the US–Taiwan treaty, the United States did not reaffirm its commitment to it. The unstated assumption of the American position was that the Taiwan problem would gradually fade away to the advantage of Peking as a result of the phased withdrawal of the American military and diplomatic support that the Chiang Kai-shek regime had enjoyed since 1949.

The net effect of the American presidential visit and the ensuing diplomatic, scientific, cultural and trade agreements was to enhance China's prestige as a great power and consolidate the diplomatic successes she had achieved since the Cultural Revolution. As for the United States, the new dialogue with China formally spelled the end of the containment policy, at least as it had been applied in Asia since 1950, and a re-evaluation of China's role in the international political system. In the words of Marshall Green, speaking before a congressional sub-committee in May 1972:

> . . . in the coming decade China will play a key role in events in Asia and will have a major part in shaping its future. Indeed, its voice will increasingly be heard also in world councils.[59]

Apart from a few pockets of right-wing dissent, the shift in American diplomacy gained widespread approval within the United States. As one would expect, the reaction of most Third World countries and the whole of Western Europe was also positive. Many of these governments had for a long time been advocating a reassessment of American attitudes towards Maoist China. Nevertheless, the reaction of some Asian governments, especially those that depended for their continued existence on US military support, was one of apprehension and, at least in one instance, of outright opposition. The sharp denunciations emanating from Taibei in the wake of the Nixon visit to Peking left little doubt that the Taiwan government was deeply dismayed by the long-term implications of Washington's new China policy.

In order to dispel some of the concerns and misgivings of these governments, the American President sent Marshall Green and a senior staff member of the National Security Council on a tour of thirteen Asian countries to explain and justify the apparent discontinuity in American foreign policy. But no new assurances, however firm, could easily erase the credibility gap that had arisen in America's relations with client Asian states. It was precisely the Asian appreciation of the gradual decline of the American empire that now predisposed even some of the most fiercely anti-communist governments to seek an accommodation with the People's Republic and their other communist neighbours. China had finally won regional acceptance of her dominant role in Asia as well as universal recognition of her vastly enhanced status in the emerging global balance of power.

CHAPTER 6

The Politics of Disorder

China's wide-ranging diplomatic offensive after 1968 and the analysis of the international situation on which it rested were obviously in need of theoretical justification since they appeared to contradict some of the most fiercely defended theses of the preceding period. The much greater emphasis on conventional state diplomacy and the concerted effort to improve relations with the developed capitalist world could not, for example, be easily reconciled with the proposition, frequently advanced during 1966–68, that the great victories of China's Great Proletarian Cultural Revolution and the extensive dissemination of Mao Zedong thought were closely linked with the development of a mass revolutionary movement in Europe and North America.[1] The evolution of the Maoist line was, in fact, gradual and had to overcome the opposition of the Lin Biao faction, which apparently remained wedded to the notion that US imperialism was the principal enemy of world revolution and the 'proletariat and revolutionary people in all countries' the only reliable allies in the worldwide struggle for liberation.[2]

Mao's Revolutionary Diplomatic Line

In his report to the Ninth National Party Congress in April 1969, Lin Biao frequently stressed the dangers posed by Soviet revisionism and even made passing reference to the principles of peaceful coexistence. But the main thrust of his argument was that, apart from making preparations against a possible war of aggression launched by either superpower, China should ignore Soviet and American attempts to isolate her diplomatically and concentrate her energies on developing a united front with those 'genuine Marxist–Leninist parties and organizations of various countries, which are composed of the advanced elements of the proletariat'.[3] The main Chinese objective was defined as uniting with the revolutionary struggles of the people of Vietnam, Laos, Thailand, Burma, Indonesia, India, Palestine and other Third World countries. Also included in this 'new rising force' were the proletariat, the students and youth and the masses of the black people of the United States struggling against the US ruling clique, the proletariat and labouring people of the Soviet Union seeking the overthrow of the Soviet revisionist renegade clique, and the people of all other countries resisting aggression and oppression by US imperialism and Soviet revisionist social-imperialism.[4]

During the course of 1970 and the early months of 1971, Chinese diplomacy under the direction of Zhou Enlai became progressively more responsive to American overtures and to the other opportunities for enhanced international recognition. The new conventional wisdom continued nevertheless to be opposed by several dissenting voices, which subscribed to the view that the international front against US imperialism remained the keystone of China's foreign policy. In May 1971 an authoritative editorial issued by the *People's Daily*, *Red Flag* and the *Liberation Army Daily* claimed that:

> The international united front against US imperialism is an important magic weapon for the world people to defeat US imperialism and all its running dogs.[5]

The statement went on to describe US imperialism as 'the common enemy of the world people' and advocated a policy that would 'isolate and strike at the chief enemy to the utmost'. This thinly disguised attack on the new diplomatic line formulated by Zhou and approved by Mao, and the implicit opposition to the improving climate in Sino–American relations, were not finally overcome until Lin Biao's departure from the political stage. In August 1971, 'Chairman Mao's revolutionary diplomatic line' was already being hailed as signalling the failure of the American containment strategy and the beginning of a new era in Chinese foreign policy.[6]

The new Maoist line, however, represented much more than the mere defence of China's flourishing diplomatic activity. Central to the emerging Chinese analysis was the revised assessment of the current state of US imperialism and a much clearer appreciation of its gradual decline. The profound disturbances experienced by the international monetary system in the late 1960s were interpreted as the outward sign of the much deeper and more general 'political and economic crisis of capitalism'. Far from stemming the tide, American imperialist adventures, it was argued, 'drained away US imperialism's limited financial and material resources'.[7] A major editorial statement published on New Year's Day in 1970 confidently predicted the advent of a transitional era in international relations characterized by 'the new development of the fundamental contradictions of the world'.[8] Although allusions to the revolutionary potential of people's wars were still frequently made, much greater emphasis was now placed on two contradictions regarded as the critical factors in the decline of American power. The first involved domestic conflicts in American society such as the black power and anti-war movements, while the second related to inter-imperialist rivalries resulting from the revival of the European and Japanese economies and their growing resistance to American dominance.

It was, in effect, the Maoist reading of these contradictions that encouraged China to pursue a policy of détente with the United States. A classified but almost certainly authentic Chinese document, identified as 'Outline of education on situation for companies' and issued by the Political Department of the PLA Kunming military region in April 1973 provides valuable insights into the new Chinese thinking:

Our invitation to Nixon to visit China proceeds precisely from Chairman Mao's tactical thinking: 'exploiting contradictions, winning over the majority, opposing the minority, and destroying them one by one'. And this by no means indicates a change in our diplomatic line . . . we act in the light of changes in situations, tipping the scale diversely at different times . . . having a correct recognition of questions and correctly laying a firm hold on contradictions, Chairman Mao sent out all at once our pingpong teams and invited Nixon to visit China.[9]

Indeed, the need for such tactical flexibility had been clearly outlined as far back as November 1968 when the official media republished an instruction originally issued by Mao in 1949, which stressed the value of waging 'covert' as well as 'overt' struggle 'against the imperialist'.[10] Several years, however, were to elapse before the outside world was to perceive the function of this old Maoist directive in changing the direction of Chinese foreign policy.

The shift to a more subtle and flexible conception of anti-imperialist struggle represented to some extent a rationalization of China's failure during the mid-1960s to mobilize a revolutionary third force in the intermediate zone. On the other hand, it is equally apparent that the reorientation of policy was strongly influenced by the Maoist analysis of rifts in the enemy camp and the unprecedented opportunities they offered for a greater Chinese presence on the world stage. It is not altogether coincidental that the first issue of *Red Flag* to appear after the announcement of Dr Kissinger's initial visit to China in July 1971 should have included a theoretical piece calling for study of Mao's essay 'On Policy' of 1940. The article, which was reprinted in the *People's Daily* on 17 August after a delay of two weeks, underlined the desirability of taking advantage of all 'fights, rifts and contradictions in the enemy camp and turning them against our present main enemy'. By applying this basic strategic principle to the contemporary international situation, a policy 'combining alliance and struggle' was formulated which called for the broadest possible united front in order to isolate the main enemy and maintain the integrity of China's revolutionary commitment.[11] The strong inference of this and subsequent official and semi-official statements[12] was that the opponents of the Sino–American rapprochement had been guilty of the most serious error in failing to distinguish between temporary and permanent alliances and between primary and secondary enemies.

China's reassessment of the international situation thus paved the way for the revival of the policy of peaceful coexistence, which, in any case, had never been totally abandoned. On the other hand, it is worth remembering that the Chinese had always sharply contrasted their brand of peaceful coexistence with the Soviet version. For them, coexistence between countries with different social systems was possible only because the international balance of class forces had become increasingly favourable to socialism. In other words, imperialist powers had been compelled to restrain their aggressive designs by the growing realization of their relative weakness vis-à-vis socialist countries and revolutionary movements throughout the world. In keeping with this interpretation, the Chinese leadership was able to explain the movement towards détente with Washington in terms of the decline of American power rather than of the diminution of its hegemonic intentions. The Nixon decision to renounce for the United States the policeman's role implicit in the long-standing policy of containment was seen as the unavoidable result of successive American military and diplomatic defeats, particularly in Asia and most recently in Indochina.

Various forms of political and diplomatic struggle were regarded, then, as constituting an integral part of the notion of peaceful coexistence. Nor did the policy exclude the possibility of armed struggle should local circumstances indicate reasonable prospects of revolutionary success by military means. In this context, it is highly significant that Peking should have remained firm in its support of the communist forces in Indochina even during the most delicate stage of the emerging Sino–American dialogue. Classified information, to which reference has already been made, reveals that China continued to expect a military solution to the Vietnam conflict even after the Paris peace agreement of January 1973.[13] Although anxious to secure a leading role on the stage of world politics, China, at least during this transitional phase, was still not reconciled to passive acceptance of the international status quo.

Far from advocating acquiescence in the prevailing world order, Mao's revolutionary diplomatic line made the concept of disorder the most distinctive element in China's analysis of the international situation. By the early 1970s the notion of upheaval ('luan'), perhaps better translated as chaos or confusion, had become the central theme and the unifying theoretical framework of Chinese foreign policy. The world was repeatedly described by innumerable articles, speeches and other public statements as being in a state of 'great upheaval'. A major editorial published in January 1972 painted the following picture:

> The basic contradictions in the contemporary world have sharpened. In particular the contradictions between U.S. imperialism and Soviet revisionism on the one hand and the people of the world, including the American and the Soviet people, on the other, and the contradictions between the two superpowers in their scramble for world hegemony and spheres of influence have become even more acute and widespread. . . . Various political forces are in the process of further division and reorganization. The characteristic feature of the world situation today can be summed up in one word 'upheaval', or 'global upheaval'.[14]

In his address to the UN General Assembly in October 1972, the leader of the Chinese delegation, Qiao Guanhua, drew the same conclusions. In spite of the apparent progress of détente in East–West relations, he argued that 'the struggle between aggression and anti-aggression, interference and anti-interference, subversion and anti-subversion, control and anti-control was bound to continue for a long time'.[15] In the Chinese view, the relaxation of tensions was at best a temporary and superficial phenomenon that should not be allowed to delude the people of the world or lull them into a false sense of security.

In his report to the Tenth National Party Congress, Zhou Enlai, using the Leninist thesis of imperialism as the principal theoretical basic of his analysis, once again characterized the international situation as one of 'great disorder on earth', and pointed to 'the awakening and growth of the Third World' and its struggle 'against hegemonism and the power politics of the superpowers' as a major event in contemporary international relations.[16] This formulation of the Chinese perception of disorder was subsequently given a new twist by Vice-Premier Deng Xiaoping in his address to the Twenty-Eighth Session of the UN General Assembly in April 1974. The sharpening of world contradictions, it was claimed, and the law of the uneven development of capitalism were helping to undermine 'the old order based on colonialism, imperialism and hegemonism'. More specifically, it was argued that the world currently consisted of three parts, which were 'both interconnected and in contradiction to one another'.[17] The United States and the Soviet Union made up the First World; the developing countries of Asia, Africa and Latin America constituted the Third World; while the developed countries between the two made up the Second World.

This new categorization of the principal actors on the international stage represented a considerable extension and refinement of the previously bipolar model of the world that had traditionally postulated a direct confrontation between the forces of reaction and revolution. But the most significant feature of the revised Maoist outlook was the definition of the major cleavages in the world as those between the two superpowers and the medium and small countries. In sharp contrast to the class analysis explicitly outlined during the Cultural Revolution, the polarization characteristic of the international political system was now expressed primarily in terms of inter-state relations. Instead of references to the 'international class struggle', to the 'development of the world people's revolutionary movement' or to the dominance of the 'East Wind' over the 'West Wind',[18] attention in the early 1970s was focused almost exclusively on the hegemonic and exploitative policies of the superpowers, and on the resistance they aroused among medium and small powers anxious to shake off 'superpower enslavement or control' and to safeguard 'their national independence and integrity of their sovereignty'.[19]

What may appear as the failure to provide any clear theoretical exposition of China's new diplomatic posture was, in reality, a carefully calculated attempt to preserve the revolutionary image of Chinese foreign policy. The Maoist leadership could not therefore restrict its initiatives to identifying the various contradictions in contemporary world politics and highlighting the ensuing divisions and upheavals. In this sense, it was both logical and necessary for Peking to stress the desirability of international disorder and indicate its willingness to give the trend every possible encouragement. Accordingly, when addressing the Tenth National Party Congress, Zhou Enlai spoke in glowing terms of the turmoil currently prevailing in inter-state relations:

Such great disorder is a good thing for the people, not a bad thing. It throws the enemies into confusion and causes division among them, while it arouses and tempers the people, thus helping the international situation develop further in the direction favourable to the people and unfavourable to imperialism, modern revisionism and all reaction.[20]

The phenomenon of disorder, as perceived by the Chinese, had thus provided them with a ready-made and relatively inexpensive instrument with which to demonstrate their revolutionary credentials. It was doubtful, however, whether such a blanket endorsement of international disorder could indefinitely conceal the emerging contradiction in Chinese foreign policy, or the growing gap between diplomatic action and revolutionary rhetoric.

Superpower Dominance

Once China's foreign policy-makers perceived the changing character of the global balance of power, they were quick to exploit the new tendencies and integrate their revised assessment of the international situation into their analysis of contradictions. Having detected signs of a growing opposition throughout the world to the policies of the two superpowers, notably within the ranks of underdeveloped and non-aligned countries, Peking shifted the focus of its attention from 'imperialism' to 'superpower hegemonism', from 'oppressed classes' to 'medium and small powers'. The shift in diplomatic emphasis was clearly discernible in Zhou Enlai's interview with a group of French correspondents in July 1970. Though one or two superpowers were contending for world hegemony, he argued that the days when they decided the destiny of the world were gone forever.[21] Even Mao's statement of May 1970, in spite of its references to revolution and armed struggle, had acknowledged the nation (or state) as the principal agent likely to undermine the existing international order:

A weak *nation* can defeat a strong *nation*, a small *nation* can defeat a big *nation*. The people of a small *country* can certainly defeat aggression by a big *country*, if only they dare to rise in struggle, take up arms and grasp in their own hands the destiny of their *country*. This is the law of history.[22] [italics added]

The widely published New Year's Day editorial of 1971 made the new Maoist formulation of international struggle still more explicit by claiming that 'many medium-sized and small nations have risen against the power politics of the two superpowers, US imperialism and social-imperialism'.[23] The task of opposing hegemonic control was thus assigned to states and governments rather than to exploited classes. The 'power politics' practised by the United States and the Soviet Union and the leverage accruing to them by virtue of their dominant military and economic positions were regarded as the decisive factors capable of welding together a united front of all other countries.[24]

What made the threat to the independence of medium and small powers particularly acute, in the Chinese view, was the growing trend towards collusion between the two superpowers. Washington's acquiescence in the Soviet invasion of Czechoslovakia and Moscow's passive diplomacy in the face of United States aggression in Vietnam were interpreted as irrefutable evidence of Soviet–American collaboration. In the words of the communiqué issued at the conclusion of the Twelfth Plenum of the Eighth CCP Central Committee on 31 October 1968, shortly after the Czechoslovakian incident, 'the US imperialists and the Soviet revisionists [were] trying in vain to redivide the world'.[25] A similar evaluation was made of the Soviet–American relationship in the Middle East where the collaboration of the two powers was described as an 'attempt to redivide the world', and their proposals for a 'political solution' were seen as a 'swindle' to make the Arab people surrender and nullify the Palestinian armed struggle.[26]

Although the Maoist line on foreign policy had not overtly abandoned the main guidelines enunciated in the 1950s and 1960s, the context of its application had undergone drastic modification. Possibly the most far-reaching change was the perceived ideological retrogression of the Soviet Union from a socialist to an imperialist power. The social-imperialist label was first applied to the Soviet Union in a commentary published by the *People's Daily* on 23 August 1968. The CPSU leadership was accused not only of restoring capitalism in the country but of 'pressing ahead with their imperialist policies abroad and stepping up their counter-revolutionary global collusion with US imperialism in a vain attempt to redivide the world'.[27] Once the Chinese concluded that revisionism had degenerated into imperialism, they lost little time in describing the Soviet Union as the primary accomplice of US imperialism.[28] By the time of the Ninth National Congress, Moscow had already been ascribed an independent imperialist status. Social-imperialism was now placed on a par with US imperialism in respect of all four major contradictions (see p. 9), the only difference being that no rivalries were specified between social-imperialist countries, since the Soviet Union was the only great power that sought to disguise its imperialism under the flag of socialism.

Having denounced the hegemonic ambitions of the superpowers, particularly the expansionist designs of the Soviet revisionist leadership, China was bound to reaffirm her own determination not to become a superpower. Accordingly the New Year's Day editorial of 1971 asserted that the Chinese people stood for 'equality among all nations big or small'.[29] In keeping with this general declaration of intent, China pledged not to subject other countries to aggression, subversion, interference, control or bullying, not to participate in nuclear disarmament negotiations behind the backs of non-nuclear countries, not to be the first to use nuclear weapons, not to attach any conditions or ask for any privileges in return for aid, not to become a munitions merchant. All these undertakings were intended to demonstrate the sincerity of her adherence to the principles of equality, sovereignty, territorial integrity, mutual benefit and peaceful coexistence in relations among states. Maoist China was using normative concepts of international behaviour developed by the West to highlight the gap between theory and actual practice. For the interventionist policies of the great powers, in particular the United States and the Soviet Union, had made nonsense of the principles of sovereignty and equality and transformed the international system into a pyramidal power structure whereby the two superpowers, situated at the apex of the pyramid, could exercise economic, military, diplomatic and legal dominance over the rest of the world.

It is true that, by reason of her history and civilization, the vast dimensions of her land and population, her strategic position, her industrial and agricultural development, her large military forces and her nuclear potential, China was destined to be a great power in her own right. While recognizing these geopolitical realities, the Maoist leadership was nevertheless adamant that China would not act as a superpower. In making this claim, the Chinese developed a subtle distinction between the legitimate and coercive exercise of power, between influence that is compatible with the five principles of peaceful coexistence and influence that thrives on inequality and interference in the domestic affairs of other countries.[30] By consistently preaching the virtues of self-reliance, China was hoping to contrast the egalitarian, non-interventionist thrust of her own praxis with the strategic collusion of the two superpowers and their expansionist and neo-colonialist policies. To this end, Peking pledged to support all the just propositions of the underdeveloped countries, to work for the creation of a new international economic order, and to oppose all hegemony and spheres of influence.

But glib references to the aspirations of Third World countries could not indefinitely obscure the conflict, at times very intense, between Third World governments strategically and economically integrated into the capitalist system and national revolutionary movements committed to a programme of socialist development and national independence. Significantly, it was during this transitional phase that Peking chose, presumably with Mao's blessing, to align itself with Yahya Khan's government in Pakistan and with Bandaranaike's government in Ceylon in clear opposition to the nationalist and revolutionary struggles in those countries. Similarly, cooperation was established with the military junta in Chile and assistance extended to the CIA-backed factions in Angola. By failing to recognize, let along act on, this fundamental cleavage in the political economy of many Third World societies, Chinese foreign policy in the last few years of Mao's life lost much of its former radical edge.

New United Front

Although China had since the early 1960s consistently opposed the Soviet–American rapprochement and denounced it as evidence of superpower collusion, her analysis after the Cultural Revolution underwent a subtle but significant change. While still the target of vehement attacks, the 'unholy alliance' between the United States and the Soviet Union was no longer regarded as necessarily leading to world hegemony. China now stood to gain from East–West détente in so far as the resulting structural contradictions in the international system were likely to foster the growing independence of Soviet and American allies, in Western and Eastern Europe as well as in other parts of the world. To the extent that middle and small powers had developed greater confidence and leverage in asserting their rights vis-à-vis the superpowers, China found it ideologically congenial and diplomatically expedient to support their demands, especially on such economic issues as territorial water limits, control over natural resources, foreign investment and international trading arrangements. American reverses in Southeast Asia, Soviet difficulties in Eastern Europe, increased economic rivalry between the major centres of capitalism, and the rising mood of revolt within the Third World had all combined to persuade Peking that the world was witnessing a new tide of opposition against superpower hegemony and the emergence of a new united front.

It will be remembered that in China's domestic revolutionary experience the united front concept had justified the formation of a worker–peasant alliance supported by the more progressive elements of the national bourgeoisie (see pp. 12–13, 16). Applied to the international context, the same concept now dictated at least a tacit understanding between the Third World and the Second World (comprised principally of Western Europe and Japan). By widening the united front so as to include the two intermediate zones (see pp. 19–20), Chinese foreign policy has abandoned the simple formula that pitted the cities against the countryside and reverted to a less abrasive but far more complex position. The previous emphasis on protracted armed struggle and people's war was thus replaced by a more flexible conception of change and the recognition that in certain circumstances non-revolutionary groups could be viewed as effective opponents of the existing international order and, therefore, as objective allies of the revolution.

In relations with the first intermediate zone, Peking shifted its attention from revolutionary movements to established governments, inviting the latter to reassess their policies towards the superpowers, to question the international system of exchange which condemned their countries to permanent backwardness, and to foster a greater commitment to self-reliance as the only means of tapping the most dynamic and creative energies of their societies. The Chinese were obviously hoping that this loose coalition of Third World governments would achieve, despite their many ideological and other differences, sufficient cohesion to thwart the designs of the two superpowers. In the case of the second intermediate zone, the accent after 1968 was on the role of inter-imperialist rivalries and the efforts of America's European allies to reassert their diplomatic and economic independence. Concern with the working-class struggles and the political and economic crises experienced by these countries gave way to renewed interest in the prospects of European integration and in the growing rift between Western Europe, Japan and the United States on issues of international trade and monetary policy.

In spite of its apparent logic, the notion of promoting cooperation between the first and second intermediate zones as a step towards a possible coalition was fraught with difficulties. One illustration may suffice to indicate the nature of the Chinese dilemma and the inescapable conflict of interests dividing the rich industrialized Second World from the underdeveloped and exploited Third World. In endorsing the cutback in oil production and the steep price increases imposed by oil-exporting countries in the wake of the Yom Kippur war, Chinese leaders were understandably anxious to demonstrate their solidarity with the Arab cause and with the Third World in general. On the other hand, by raising energy costs the OPEC decision was bound to have a disruptive effect on the Japanese and West European economies, whose very lifeline depended on large and regular flows of OPEC oil. While mindful of these contradictions in the relationship between the two intermediate zones, China nevertheless persisted throughout the early 1970s with the theme of national independence, which she described as the common demand of all nations striving to free themselves from Soviet–American control. As the authoritative article published in *Red Flag* in November 1972 explained, opposition to the 'power politics and hegemonism of the superpowers . . . [was] a trend of world history'.[31]

So enthusiastic was Peking in its application of the united front principle to foreign policy that it was now willing to extend the concept in order to include many of the East European countries, which were portrayed as the victims of 'fairly tight Soviet control'. In keeping with this strategy, the Soviet military intervention in Czechoslovakia was roundly condemned for having violated the rights of a sovereign state even though the Dubcek experiment, denounced for having taken the capitalist road, was viewed as equally reprehensible. However, in criticizing the misguided policies of the Czechs, the Maoist leadership was also at pains to deny Moscow the right to impose on other communist parties, by force or threat of force, its own interpretation of communist orthodoxy. To be more exact, the Chinese took advantage of the Czechoslovakian episode to expose the hegemonic inclinations of the Soviet leadership and, by implication, to convince fraternal parties as well as neighbouring countries that such behaviour was totally foreign to China's own conception of international relations. In this sense, Maoist united front tactics may be said to have been both a cause and a consequence of the Sino–Soviet dispute.

Having substituted the fluid notion of the intermediate zone for the more rigid class analysis of the fundamental contradictions in the world, and having blurred the distinction between US imperialism and social-imperialism, Maoist theory was able to inject a new element of polarization into the international system and to redefine the major axis of conflict. By reviving the policy of peaceful coexistence and reformulating the united front strategy, China was able to substantiate and give added impetus to her leading role in world history. As early as September 1970 the communiqué issued by the Second Plenum of the Ninth CCP Central Committee had explicitly linked the successes of Chinese diplomacy to the revised Maoist line.[32] On the basis of correct diplomatic behaviour and support for the demands of small and middle powers, regardless of their ideological complexion, China was seeking to undermine the Soviet–American duopoly in international relations.

Towards a Plural Balance

As the Cultural Revolution receded further into the distance, it became increasingly evident that the Maoist leadership regarded a multipolar world as the kind of international system most likely to satisfy the dual objective of reducing the power of the Soviet Union and the United Stated while at the same time extending China's own freedom of diplomatic action and ideological sphere of influence. In the Chinese view, the ambivalent adversary relationship between Moscow and Washington was conducive to the breakdown of bipolarity. However, it should not be inferred from this proposition that the Chinese were committed to some crude theory of pentagonal balance of the type propounded by the Nixon administration. While recognizing the emerging role of China, Japan and Western Europe in world affairs, Chinese foreign policy during this period remained attentive to the powerlessness of power, at least as traditionally understood, to the growing importance of transnational actors, whether they be liberation movements or multinational corporations, and to the rise of the Third World as a new factor in international relations.

In so far as the fragmentation of international decision-making had become an important Chinese objective, Japan and Western Europe assumed particular significance in China's strategy for a revised world order. Having restored its diplomatic links with all the major capitals of Western Europe, Peking became a very active advocate of West European integration. Franco–Chinese cooperation, which had symbolized since 1964 the mutual rejection of bipolarity, was now extended to encompass Britain, West Germany and Italy. France's determination to develop an independent nuclear deterrent received consistent diplomatic support and was portrayed as the model of national independence to be imitated by other European powers. An economically united Western Europe was strongly favoured because it hastened the decline of American economic dominance in Europe, but primarily because it provided a powerful counterweight to Soviet power in Eastern Europe and prevented Moscow from mobilizing all its economic and military resources for the confrontation with China. In the communiqué issued at the end of President Pompidou's visit to China in September 1973, Peking expressed strong support for European 'independence, sovereignty and security'.[33] China's favourable attitude to the enlarged European Common Market[34] clearly indicated her reassessment of the European balance and her conviction that the European political climate had become much more favourable to the notion of a third force independent of both superpowers. As we shall see in chapter 9, the same kind of rationale was to underlie the improvement in diplomatic and economic relations with Japan.

From what has already been said, it should be readily apparent that Maoist strategy was not directed simply towards the creation of a multipolar system. An equally important objective was to encourage the polycentric tendencies operating within both alliance systems. This aspect of the Chinese plan was perhaps most visible in the attempts to contain Soviet power within the international communist movement, notably in Eastern Europe. In fostering closer diplomatic and economic relations with Albania, Yugoslavia and Rumania, China was obviously intent on strengthening their resolve to assert and maintain their independence from the Soviet Union. By ceasing or moderating her attacks on the domestic policies of fraternal parties, China was hoping not only to normalize her bilateral relations with Eastern European countries but to demonstrate her favourable attitude to 'communist neutralism'. The ideological element in China's dealings with other communist parties was now in rapid decline. By the early 1970s Peking was ready to abandon its demand for total loyalty from ideological supporters, and was even willing to make common cause with the Italian and Spanish parties, which had previously been condemned for their rightist, revisionist tendencies. This latest application of the united front principle was clearly designed to create within world communism as large a coalition of anti-Soviet forces as possible, comprised of parties and movements representing almost every position on the ideological spectrum. By multiplying the incentives and the opportunities for dissidence within the international communist system, by highlighting the exploitative character of Soviet dominance, China would perhaps force Moscow into concentrating more of its energies on rebuilding Soviet controls in the socialist commonwealth, thereby weakening its capacity for détente with the United States and its allies. ·

Although China still lacked sufficient economic and military resources to conduct a global diplomacy on the scale of either superpower, her enhanced diplomatic status, her psychological and ideological influence in the Third World, and, above all, her geopolitical importance in Asia had forced the United States and the Soviet Union into a triangular relationship. By the late 1960s China represented, in the Soviet view, not only nuisance value but a major threat to Soviet political and strategic interests. The Soviet leadership was now confronted with the possibility of two hostile fronts instead of one. Paradoxically enough, through its confrontation with Moscow, Peking also gained added leverage with Washington, since the Sino–Soviet dispute had become an unpublicized but significant variable in the Soviet–American equation. In effect, one of the primary aims of Mao's revolutionary diplomatic line was to take advantage of the interacting forces in the Moscow–Washington–Peking triangle to weaken the Soviet Union, under-mine the Soviet–American duopoly and reinforce China's identification with the interests and aspirations of small and medium powers.

One of the most interesting characteristics of the triangle is that, while each party was antagonistic to the other two, yet none of the three bilateral relationships or sides of the triangle (i.e. US–USSR, USSR–China, China–US) was exclusively antagonistic.[35] All three contained elements of cooperation as well as rivalry, although the adversary relationship between Moscow and Peking appeared far less likely of resolution or even partial accommodation than that between Moscow and Washington or Washington and Peking. To the extent that each antagonism was diluted or complemented by some degree of collaboration, there was a natural tendency for the third party in each case to denounce such collaboration as collusion, in order to discredit the other two or acquire the role of arbiter. For China, the principal objective in playing the triangular game was to reduce Soviet–American collusion to a minimum, mount opposition to the two superpowers by highlighting such collusion, and contain Soviet expansionism by threatening collusion with the United States.

At this point it is worth remembering that, even at the height of the cold war, the American–Soviet conflict was less direct or all-embracing than has often been imagined. Not only did Russian and American soldiers never fight each other on the battlefield, but the protagonists gradually came to acknowledge the legitimacy of their respective imperial boundaries. By the early 1960s both superpowers had abandoned any intention of interfering in the core of each other's sphere of influence; hence their mutual acceptance of stalemate in the Berlin and Cuban crises. Faced with the risk that even the most minor clash could escalate into a major nuclear exchange, the United States and the Soviet Union elaborated a series of tacit and formal agreements designed to regulate their strategic relationship, demarcate their respective defence perimeters, and consolidate their privileged position vis-à-vis lesser or aspiring nuclear powers.

During the greater part of the 1960s, the Soviet Union's attitude to détente was motivated primarily by the need to inject a measure of stability into the nuclear balance as well as by the desire to win full acceptance by the United States as an equal in status, power and prestige. In this sense, both the security objective and the search for diplomatic pre-eminence impelled the Soviet leadership towards a *modus vivendi* with the United States. However, by the late 1960s the Soviet perception of external threats was somewhat modified to take account of the intensified hostility and expanding military capability of the Chinese adversary. Détente with Washington thus assumed even greater importance in Soviet calculations, since it afforded Moscow the only realistic opportunity to gain some leverage over the developing Sino–American relationship. Moreover, the diplomatic thaw with Washington could be expected to encourage a reduced American military presence in Europe and a European security agreement, which would, in turn, reinforce the territorial status quo in Europe and thereby enable the Soviet Union to concentrate more of its energies and resources along the southeastern border with China.

The early 1970s did, in fact, witness a spate of East–West accords, as instanced by the successful implementation of West German's Ostpolitik, the limited agreements reached during the first phase of the SALT negotiations, and the growing volume of trade between communist and capitalist countries. Nevertheless, tension and competition still characterized the Soviet–American relationship, particularly on such critical issues as the Middle East conflict where opposing strategic and economic interests precluded the possibility of a peaceful settlement. Nor could the intermittent efforts of the superpowers to contain or moderate their arms race achieve meaningful or lasting success so long as the political economies of both states remained tied to an increasingly pervasive military–industrial complex, each dependent on the other for its survival and continued expansion. A partial détente was mutually advantageous to Moscow and Washington in so far as it helped to stabilize the balance of terror. On the other hand, a complete rapprochement was incompatible with the dominant domestic and external interests of either the Soviet or American power structure.

The strategic constraints and moderating influences acting on the Soviet–American relationship were less evident in the Sino–Soviet dispute. Whereas the Soviet Union and the United States have no common border, the Russians and the Chinese share the longest frontier in the world. Whereas the Soviet–American antagonism was of relatively recent origin, the Moscow–Peking confrontation was the continuation of long-standing disputes originating with Tsarist expansion in the Far East and Central Asia. Whereas in the Soviet–American rivalry the ideological factor had degenerated into little more than a convenient cloak for the pursuit of narrowly conceived state interests, the conflict between Soviet Russia and Maoist China (at least during the revolutionary and transitional phases of Chinese foreign policy) assumed all the intensity of an ideological schism, with each side appealing to the same shared doctrine and claiming to be its only faithful exponent.

The division between two rival churches, both obsessed with notions of authority and orthodoxy, inevitably predisposed the leadership on each side to aim for the liquidation of the other's heresy. In other words, neither Moscow nor Peking could rest until the ideological position of the opponent had been rectified or his power base destroyed. Mao's China was attempting not merely to undermine the Soviet system of alliances but to penetrate the very heart of the Soviet empire by alleging a fundamental conflict of interests between the Soviet people and their government. A 'revisionist renegade clique' was accused of having usurped power in the Soviet Union and replaced the dictatorship of the proletariat with a 'bourgeois dictatorship over the masses of workers, peasants and revolutionary intellectuals'.[36] The Soviet Union for its part charged the 'military–bureaucratic regime' of Mao Zedong and his entourage of taking the Chinese people on a 'ruinous path' that could only lead to 'new ordeals and defeats'.[37] The position could be reversed only with a return to socialism based on the principles of Marxism–Leninism and proletarian internationalism, which in Moscow's language meant a return to the Soviet fold and acceptance of the Kremlin's leadership within the socialist commonwealth. Given the direct and pervasive character of their confrontation, both Moscow and Peking were likely to remain highly suspicious of each other's intentions and extremely sensitive about possible interference in each other's internal affairs. There was little likelihood that the Soviet Union would abandon its claim to primacy within the communist camp or that China would rejoin the camp on Soviet terms.

In the case of the Sino–American relationship, I have already observed in Chapter 5 how the American military withdrawal from Indochina, the decline in American support for the Taiwan regime, and the change in the American attitude towards Chinese representation at the United Nations all contributed towards the decline of past hostility between the two countries. China's favourable response to American overtures was partly motivated by the desire to expand the Chinese presence in the United Nations, improve relations with American allies, notably Japan, and gain greater access to western technology. Another, and perhaps more important, objective was to thwart Moscow's strategic ambitions which hoped to pit China against the United States. Indeed, from the Chinese point of view, the great value of the rapprochement with Washington was the possibility of arresting the progress of détente between the two superpowers and of keeping alive the fear of a major Soviet–American nuclear confrontation. In a sense, China wanted to deter a possible Soviet strike by raising the prospect of American as well as Chinese retaliation.

In the event of nuclear war, United States forces stationed in the Korean peninsula and in other parts of the Asian rimlands could scarcely remain unaffected if for no other reason than the resulting fall-out. Indeed, the American military presence could be expected to perform a deterrent role even if the Soviet Union were contemplating only a conventional attack on China. Now that the United States was no longer regarded as a threat to Chinese security, the maintenance of American military and political influence in the region constituted a useful barrier to the penetration of Soviet power. The Asian theatre had thus witnessed a gradual but significant shift from Soviet–American to Sino–American collusion. The 1950s and 1960s had been notable for the parallelism of Soviet and American policies in restricting China's freedom of action in relation to Taiwan and in supporting India in the border conflict with China. By contrast, the 1970s ushered in a new era of Chinese–American collaboration as evidenced by their joint support for Pakistan[38] and their well-orchestrated campaign against the alleged build-up of Soviet naval power in the Indian Ocean.

Sino–Soviet Hostility

In analysing the various components of the dispute between the two communist giants, it is important to realize that by the end of the Cultural

Revolution many of the original policy issues that had fuelled the conflict during the late 1950s had largely disappeared. As a nuclear power with an undisputed role in world affairs, China no longer had any need of Soviet economic or military assistance to achieve her principal objectives. As for the Soviet Union, there was now little danger that it would be drawn against its will into risky adventures in support of its former ally. What remained, however, over and above the lingering ideological quarrel, was the Soviet determination to curb the rise of Chinese power and influence and China's natural interest in countering Moscow's containment strategy.

In Russian eyes, the emergence of China as a major power in Asia represented a potential long-term threat to Soviet security. Admittedly, China's acute military inferiority, especially in nuclear capability, ruled out the possibility of Chinese territorial expansion at Russia's expense. Nevertheless, China's inexhaustible manpower resources could conceivably endanger Moscow's defence perimeter in Soviet Asia, an area twice as large as the United States but with barely 60 million people, two-thirds of whom were non-slavic, and where, presumably, the Chinese would have an interest in encouraging and assisting separatist movements. In the diplomatic arena, the Soviet Union was understandably disturbed by the continuing challenge to its authority within international communism and by the possible erosion of its power in Eastern Europe. But perhaps Moscow's most acute anxiety had grown in direct proportion to the improvement in Sino–American relations, which threatened to end the bipolar structure of international politics and, together with it, the Soviet Union's privileged relationship with the United States.

Soviet apprehensions about the Washington–Peking dialogue became particularly evident after the announcement of President Nixon's forthcoming visit to China. Several articles appearing in the Soviet press tended to interpret this new development as a political manoeuvre directed against the Soviet Union. A leading commentary published in *Pravda* on 10 August 1971 placed little confidence in official American assurances that the normalization of relations with China would not be at the expense of other countries. The much less reassuring conclusions of the *Washington Post* were regarded as a more accurate indication of United States policy and were quoted at some length:

> In spite of all American public denials, Nixon Administration officials privately express an opinion that it is not in the interests of the U.S.A. to allay fully the Soviet Union's suspicions concerning the U.S.–Chinese agreements that may displease Moscow or make her uneasy.[39]

The Soviet analysis of Chinese and American intentions, which now had the possibility of Sino–American collusion as one of its dominant themes, was frequently accompanied by dire warnings about the serious damage such collusion would inflict on Soviet–American détente:

> A dialogue has been going on for a long time between the U.S.A. and the U.S.S.R. The dialogue is highly important but very difficult. . . . What could deal a stronger blow to trust than unscrupulous diplomatic manoeuvres, backstage intrigues and equivocation?[40]

More explicitly, the Soviet Union accused the Nixon administration of trying to change China into a 'new colony and army supply base', of encouraging Peking's anti-Soviet propaganda and of using the rapprochement with China as a means of neutralizing potential opposition to the bombing of North Vietnam as well as for domestic electoral advantage.[41] China's readiness to cooperate in such imperialist designs was advanced as proof of her complicity and her total betrayal of the revolutionary cause.

One should not, of course, be too easily deceived by the ideological facade behind which the Soviet leadership tended to evaluate the Sino–American connection. The public preoccupation with ideological purity could hardly conceal the overriding concern with the expansion of Chinese influence. It was precisely this concern which had forced the Soviet Union to pursue since the end of the 1960s a traditional balance of power diplomacy. The Soviet proposal for an Asian security scheme, the attempt to forge friendly links with Asian countries irrespective of the ideological complexion of their governments, the increasing naval activity in the Indian and Pacific oceans, the formidable array of armour and missiles along the border with China, the dismemberment of Pakistan, and the growing overtures to Japan were all part of a larger policy designed to contain China through the establishment of a pervasive Soviet presence in Asia.

As might have been expected, Peking's response to Soviet initiatives was characterized by suspicion and apprehension. During the late 1960s Chinese leaders seriously feared the possibility of a Soviet nuclear attack, although these fears subsequently diminished as China's nuclear deterrent became progressively more credible. The military threat had assumed particular importance in Chinese eyes following the Soviet enunciation of the 1968 Brezhnev doctrine and the explicit justification of Soviet interference in the internal affairs of another socialist state. Nor did such interference depend on the use of military means. The Soviet Union could, for example, involve itself in Chinese politics, possibly during a succession crisis when its support might affect the outcome of the power struggle. This appreciation of Soviet intentions led Peking to initiate a wide-ranging counter-attack against the Soviet containment policy. To this end – although, as we have seen, it was by no means the only motivating factor – Maoist China proceeded to normalize her relations with near and distant countries, both Asian and European as well as with the United States.

Sino–Soviet border tension, which dated back at least to the early 1960s, reached its height following Moscow's decision in February 1969 to intensify the patrolling of its forces along the Amur and Ussuri Rivers. On 2 March, Soviet troops were authorized for the first time to fire on Chinese patrols found on territory claimed by the Soviet Union. According to the generally accepted account of the clash that took place on the disputed island of Zhen Bao (known as Damansky by the Soviets), the Chinese retaliated by ambushing and inflicting heavy casualties on an outnumbered Soviet unit. The Soviet side responded by virtually annihilating a Chinese unit with greatly superior firepower on the same island on 15 March. Both parties attempted to exploit the border incident for political advantage, but neither was prepared to attempt further inroads into the other's military position.

Although Soviet intentions remain somewhat obscure, it is more than plausible that the Soviet thrust was partly intended to strengthen Moscow's position within the Warsaw Pact and bring into line recalcitrant members such as Rumania. By making it appear that it was merely reacting to Chinese aggression, the Soviet Union may also have been seeking to extend its influence over India. However, it is more than likely that the most important Soviet objective was to intimidate the Chinese into a partial rapprochement. While some elements within the Soviet leadership may have advocated a conventional or even nuclear attack on China, the Kremlin was obviously not prepared to undertake such a risky adventure. It was probably only after the violent incidents allegedly involving attacks by Red Guard units against Soviet diplomatic personnel in Peking, and the realization that no improvement in Sino–Soviet relations was possible in the foreseeable future, that Moscow decided on a massive increase in the number of troops deployed along the border.

While China was certainly alarmed by the Soviet use of force and by the vastly expanded Russian deployment of mechanized and rocket divisions along the frontier, the Kosygin proposal for negotiations, conveyed personally to Zhou Enlai on 21 March, was politely but firmly rejected. In the ensuing exchange of statements between the two governments, Moscow continued to press for consultations, with the threat of force as the implicit sanction, while Peking maintained the view that no agreement could be reached unless the Soviet Union recognized in principle the 'unequal' character of the nineteenth-century boundary treaties. On the other hand, the Chinese government went to considerable pains to emphasize the reasonableness of its position, stressing its readiness to 'take these unequal treaties as the basis for determining the entire alignment of the boundary line'.[42] China, in effect, pledged not to demand any of the Soviet-held territories except for certain relatively small areas in the Far East and Central Asia allegedly seized by the Soviet Union in addition to the areas it had acquired under the 'unequal treaties'. In the meantime, China proposed that each side should maintain the status quo of the boundary, refrain from extending its line of actual control, and studiously avoid recourse to the use or threat of force.

Irritated by the Chinese refusal to engage in negotiations on Soviet terms, Moscow issued a three-months deadline for consultations and accelerated the concentration of its conventional and strategic forces in the border region, including the Mongolian People's Republic. Through a series of renewed border clashes and deliberately manufactured rumours of a possible surgical strike against Chinese installations, the Soviet leadership brought further pressure to bear on the Chinese government and finally secured, shortly after

Kosygin's visit to Peking on 11 September 1969, China's agreement for negotiations on the border at the deputy foreign minister level. Indicative of China's increasingly moderate line in the face of a possible Soviet attack was the official statement of 7 October which argued for the continuation of normal state relations on the basis of the five principles of peaceful coexistence.[43] The statement also reaffirmed the defensive purpose of China's nuclear development, stressing the country's determination to resist threats of nuclear war and its readiness to oppose aggression, if necessary by fighting a 'revolutionary war'.

The improved climate between Moscow and Peking was not, however, translated into progress in the border negotiations. Both sides had probably agreed to the talks not with a view to a lasting settlement but rather in order to avoid the danger of military confrontation while keeping each other's nerves on edge. Some months after the commencement of negotiations, the Chinese placed complete responsibility for the failure of the talks on the Soviet Union, which, they claimed, had refused to disengage its armed forces from the disputed areas.[44] A joint editorial published on 1 August 1970 by the *People's Daily, Red Flag*, and the *Liberation Army Daily* denounced Moscow's expansionist designs and called upon the party, the army and the people to be ready at all times to face aggressive war from social-imperialism and US imperialism.[45] By agreeing to participate in border talks, China had found a way of defusing the military crisis with the Soviet Union while at the same time maintaining the conflict in a condition of stalemate. By demanding that Moscow acknowledge the 'unequal' nature of the existing treaties, the Chinese had placed Soviet leaders in the unenviable dilemma of either laying themselves open to later substantive demands or adopting a seemingly intransigent attitude which might precipitate an escalation of hostilities.

Although Sino–Soviet border tension appeared under control by the early 1970s, each country remained the principal target of the other's polemics, and both sides continued to show their concern for the future by steadily increasing their military deployments along the frontier. By 1970 the Soviet build-up of conventional forces along the frontier had reached at least thirty-five combat divisions with another twenty-five divisions ready to reinforce them. In addition, Moscow had expanded its border airforce bases, constructed several new landing strips and vastly increased the number of tactical nuclear missiles and rockets deployed in the region. China, for her part, had constructed a new missile-testing complex near Peking and significantly augmented her military and para-military strength along the northern border.

The Soviet capacity to inflict unacceptable damage on China was subsequently enhanced by raising the level of its troop deployments from Xinjiang to the Pacific coast to some forty-five divisions, and equipping them with the nuclear armed SS-12 'scaleboard' tactical missile (500-mile range). Soviet ground forces were grouped mainly around the Trans-Baikal Command (stretching from central Siberia to Outer Mongolia), the First Far East

Command (centred on Vladivostok and mustering a total of twenty divisions) and the Second Far East Command (centred on Khabarovsk). These forces were supported by 1200 tactical aircraft based mainly on new airfields built in western Siberia and by a number of nuclear bases deploying a variety of IRBM–MRBM missiles (1200–2300-mile range). To reduce the vulnerability of their trans-Siberian railway and to increase their logistic capacity, the Soviets were also constructing the Baikal–Amur railway, as well as several main highways and lateral roads. The provision of new barracks, family accommodation, permanent training grounds and air defence installations, all tended to suggest that the Soviet Union was set on creating a balanced, hard-hitting and permanent military capability designed not only to contain any possible Chinese attack but, should circumstances require it, to launch a major assault on the industrial heartland of Manchuria.

Given China's conventional and strategic inferiority vis-à-vis the Soviet Union, it was only natural that her response should include a strategy of passive defence. In keeping with the policy 'dig tunnels deeper, store grain everywhere and accept no hegemony', the Chinese proceeded with the large-scale construction of shelters, which, it was claimed, were able to provide by 1975 protection for over 80 per cent of the population in Peking and the other major cities. Complementing these arrangements were military preparations designed to bog down the attacking force in the Chinese hinterland by both nuclear retaliation and a protracted guerrilla campaign.[46] The seventeenth nuclear test explosion at Lop Nor in Xinjiang on 17 October 1975 was probably part of a programme to produce new tactical weapons in the low 20-kiloton range. China's rapidly expanding nuclear production capacity was being used to equip Soviet-made bombers acquired before the break with Moscow, as well as China's small but growing medium-range missile force. In 1975 it was estimated that 20–30 IRBMs (up to 3500-mile range) were already deployed, mostly in Manchuria, while another 50 MRBMs (1500-mile range) were sited further west, and presumably targeted on Soviet Siberian airfields, the trans-Siberian railway and the two main cities of Khabarovsk and Vladivostok. The IRBMs enabled China, for the first time, to threaten directly the Baku oilfields and such industrial centres as Tashkent and Novosibirsk. At the extreme end of their range they could even reach targets in the European part of the Soviet Union. Progress with the construction of hard silos and tests for a 6000-mile ICBM tended to suggest that it would not be long before China could boast a retaliatory capability that could threaten intolerable destruction on the Soviet Union, thereby sharply reducing the probability of a Soviet pre-emptive strike.

But even before the development of a viable Chinese nuclear deterrent, a swift Soviet strike, using both conventional and nuclear means, would encounter serious difficulties, especially if the Chinese airforce retained a measure of control over the battlefield. Once the attack had penetrated deep inside Chinese territory, local forces, notably those stationed in the Peking–Tianjin area, would be able to counter-attack by striking at Soviet supply lines. The problems, then, likely to confront any Soviet thrust into China were of such a magnitude as to deter the Kremlin leadership. Admittedly a Russian invasion would impose on China massive human and material losses, but there was still no guarantee that such an exercise would result in the installation of a viable Chinese regime subservient to Soviet wishes. In this sense, Moscow's costly investment in manpower and military hardware in the inhospitable wastes of eastern and central Asia and China's elaborate defence preparations could be interpreted not so much as a prelude to war but as one facet of a larger and more pervasive struggle for diplomatic and ideological supremacy.

The most explosive issue in the Sino–Soviet conflict – the border dispute and the resulting military build-up – were part of a more complex Asian game, in which each power was attempting to establish a strategic political equilibrium that would prevent the other from dominating the area. While it might be possible to reach a measure of accommodation in central Asia that would reduce the stance of both parties from one of active confrontation to deterrence, there was little likelihood that their diverging interests would be reconciled in the rest of Asia. By the very nature of their vastly different geopolitical situations, Moscow and Peking were likely to compete for power and influence not only in South and Southeast Asia, where both were seeking to develop client relationships, but also in Northeast Asia where both were attracted by the prospect of an economic partnership with Japan and anxious to forestall the establishment of a political alliance between Japan and the other side.

The Soviet endeavour to legitimate and institutionalize a widespread Asian presence through a network of bilateral and multilateral agreements, and the corresponding Chinese attempts to undermine the Soviet Union's credentials as an Asian power, may be seen as the most conspicuous manifestation of a quarrel that had as its theatre the whole of the Third World. A long series of attacks on Chinese foreign policy, which appeared in the Soviet media in the early 1970s, left no doubt that Moscow was considerably disturbed by China's not altogether unsuccessful efforts to cast the Soviet Union in the role of a superpower whose interests were generally antagonistic to those of the Third World. A radio commentary broadcast in January 1972 rejected the notion of 'two superpowers' as an anti-Marxist view designed to alienate the Third World from the socialist countries.[47] Moscow's sensitivity to Chinese accusations of hegemonism led the Soviet leadership to insist that the confrontation between the two world systems, socialism and capitalism, was the most fundamental issue in international relations. In lumping together all small and medium powers and pitting them against the superpowers, the Chinese, it was claimed, were trying to find allies even 'among the most reactionary and anti-communist circles'. The underlying Chinese objective was described as the 'unprincipled forming of blocs on an anti-Soviet basis with any forces, even the most reactionary'.[48]

It was perhaps the Middle East conflict that provided China with one of the most convenient sticks with which to beat Soviet diplomacy. Accordingly Moscow's attitude to the Yom Kippur war was harshly denounced for its betrayal of the Arab cause. On 26 October 1973, the *People's Daily* condemned the Soviet failure to provide timely and adequate military assistance to the Arabs and charged Moscow with capitulating to American pressure.[49] Soviet revisionism was also accused of exploiting Soviet Jewish emigration in pursuit of its own interests and against those of the Palestinian people. As for Soviet arms sales to the Middle East, they were described as extortionary and a lever used by Moscow to press buyers to repay debts on earlier purchases.

A leading article reviewing the 'sordid behaviour' of social-imperialism during 1974 listed the following examples: attempts to keep superpower colonial interests intact at international conferences (e.g. Special Sessions of the UN General Assembly, Law of the Sea Conference); creation of tensions in the Indian sub-continent and arms build-up in the Indian Ocean; huge profits registered by speculating in the international market at the expense of Third World countries.[50] Moscow was also accused of using aid as a device for gaining 'control over key industrial sectors in a number of developing countries'.[51] Through the avenue of 'joint-stock enterprises', it was argued, the Soviet Union had reaped colossal profits, plundered the cheap labour and natural resources of underdeveloped countries and at the same time disposed of Soviet-made industrial products for which there was no ready market anywhere else in the world.

China's very weakness in relation to Soviet economic and military power had presented her with the necessity of opposing superpower domination but also with the opportunity to identify with the aspirations of Third World countries by calling for the creation of a new international order. By discrediting Soviet economic and military aid as the self-interested exercise of a superpower and by developing relations with Afro–Asian and Latin American governments, irrespective of their ideological complexion, Maoist China was obviously hoping to reinforce Third World resistance to Soviet penetration and thus further erode the bipolar structure of world politics.

Peking and the Moscow–Washington Adversary Relationship

By the mid-1970s the Chinese appraisal of the world situation was substantially different from that of the 1960s. The overriding condition of the international system was now defined in terms of disorder, characterized by the formula 'countries want independence, nations want liberation, and the people want revolution'. The Third World had grown in strength and become a major force in the international arena. On the other hand, side by side with the mounting rebellion against a bipolar world was the intensifying struggle of the superpowers for world hegemony. In this fierce contest for power and influence, the Soviet Union was on the offensive, the United States on the defensive. While American power had been shrinking, Soviet military capability had been steadily growing. Moscow was waiting for the United States to bring home its troops from Europe before asserting its political dominance on the western side of the iron curtain. The Soviet Union had already established its position in the Indian sub-continent, was rapidly exploiting the power vacuum left by the American military defeat in Indochina and was in the process of carving out spheres of influence in other parts of Asia and Africa. The turbulence created by Soviet actions and American counter-actions pointed to the growing threat of a new world war. The so-called balance of power was only transient and superficial and could not be depended on to maintain the peace.[52]

But of the two superpowers the Soviet Union was clearly the more aggressive. The Soviet police of détente was dismissed by the Maoist leadership as a propaganda exercise intended to conceal the imperialist ambitions of the Soviet revisionist leadership. China's conception of her own role in confronting this challenge was essentially two-fold: to alert the world to the real nature of hegemonism and to mobilize a new united front capable of defeating it.[53] It was in order to pursue this struggle and form the broadest possible united front against Soviet social-imperialism that China had moved towards détente with the United States.

But China's compromise with US imperialism was perceived, or at least presented, as radically different from Soviet–American collusion. To explain this difference Zhou Enlai had drawn the distinction at the Tenth National Party Congress between giving money and firearms to bandits 'in order to lessen the damage they can do and facilitate their capture and execution' and giving these things to bandits 'to share in their loot'.[54] The first strategy had been the one followed by Lenin in formulating his peace programme and in signing the Brest-Litovsk treaty of 1918, while the second typified the 'doings of Khrushchev and Brezhnev, both betrayers of Lenin'. China's temporary concession to US imperialism, it was argued, derived logically from Mao's revolutionary diplomatic line and offered four distinct advantages:

> (1) it frustrates the strategic deployment of the Soviet revisionists . . . (2) it aggravates the contradictions between the U.S. and the Soviet Union . . . (3) it aggravates the contradictions between U.S. imperialism and Asian countries . . . and (4) it benefits our liberation of Taiwan. . . .[55]

By the early 1970s Chinese foreign policy was committed to extracting every possible advantage from the new triangular relationship with the United States and the Soviet Union.

Being a much weaker military and economic power than the other two, China was able to make capital of her very weakness by disclaiming any superpower ambitions and by championing the cause of the poor and the proud. The triangular game also permitted her to play upon the persisting tensions and divisions between the Soviets and the Americans and, by default, to act as a balancer between the two competing powers. By the very nature of the triangle China was thus able, at least partially, to neutralize the threatening options available to the Soviet Union and to prevent its rapprochement with the United States from unduly restricting the assertion of Chinese interests. At the same time, she was careful not to confine her initiatives to the construction of a triangular or even pentagonal balance of power. Chinese leaders valued the gradual erosion of international bipolarity and its replacement by a multipolar system of inter-state relations not as an end in itself but as a means to an end. They regarded the current transitional phase, which they were trying to accelerate, as favourable to their objectives because it provided them with greater freedom of manoeuvre and sharply limited the dominance of the two superpowers. Whatever China's long-term ambitions, her attitude to the perceived turbulence and disorder in international relations suggested that she had yet to accept the permanence of the existing world order or its implicit power structure.

PART III
The Post-Revolutionary Phase
1973–

CHAPTER 7

Domestic Upheaval

With the benefit of hindsight it can be argued that the Tenth Party Congress in August 1973 ushered in a new phase in Chinese politics even though the formal reports and communiqués emanating from the Congress gave little indication of the profound changes that were soon to occur. The demarcation of phases in the evolution of a political system is in many ways an arbitrary exercise since any period is likely to contain important elements of continuity as well as change. This is especially true of this period given the sharp fluctuations in the political fortunes of the key protagonists and the equally abrupt shifts in policy formulation. Yet, despite the intensity of ideological conflict and the vehemence of the leadership struggle, particularly during 1973–76, it is possible to interpret Deng Xiaoping's political re-emergence in 1973 as signalling the ebb-tide of the Great Proletarian Cultural Revolution. Many of the trends that had characterized China's external relations during the previous transitional phase were now confirmed and given added impetus by the greater synchronization of domestic and foreign policy.

True enough, the period after 1973 did not see the abandonment of all the objectives of the Chinese revolution. After all, many of the veteran leaders who were rescued from political oblivion and restored to positions of power had themselves played an active role in the victory of Chinese communism and were firmly committed to the creation of a viable socialist state. On the other hand, it is doubtful whether they had ever accepted Mao's larger revolutionary goals or the convulsive political and educational campaigns that he periodically unleashed to maintain the fervour and moral purpose of the revolution. To the extent, then, that bureaucratic pragmatism became in the mid-1970s a dominant political theme, one may legitimately speak of the post-revolutionary phase in Chinese foreign policy, at least in so far as events within China reinforced and accentuated trends that had already become apparent in her external conduct. One must, however, avoid the premature conclusion that these trends are necessarily permanent or that conflict and contradiction have been eliminated from Chinese political life. Despite the outward appearance of stability achieved in the aftermath of the fall of the 'gang of four', this latest phase may well prove to be simply another transitional stage in the continuing evolution of the Chinese communist experiment.

Ideological Conflict and the Struggle for Power

Although the exponents of uninterrupted revolution, notably Zhang Chunqiao, Jiang Qing, Yao Wenyuan and Wang Hongwen and many of their followers, attained powerful positions in the party and gained formal acceptance for several of their radical concepts, their control of the party and state bureaucracies was never adequate enough to ensure the thoroughgoing implementation of 'the new born things' of the Cultural Revolution. By the end of 1971 the demise of Lin Biao and the purge of his associates had already strengthened the hands of the moderate camp, thereby facilitating the rehabilitation of veteran cadres, which culminated in April 1973 in the return to public life of Deng Xiaoping, the Party's former Secretary-General and the man condemned by Red Guards as the 'second top capitalist roader in the Party'. The advance of young cadres, many of whom were promoted during the Cultural Revolution, was obstructed and eventually reversed.

True enough, the revolutionary spirit was upheld in the official reports presented to the Tenth Party Congress. The election of Wang Hongwen, the fast rising star within the Shanghai group, to the third ranking position in the Politburo pointed in the same direction. Wang argued that 'cultural revolutions were to be carried out many times in the future' and stressed the 'right of the masses to exercise revolutionary supervision over all ranks of the Party and state organs'.[1] Even Zhou's report was radical in tone, praising the achievements in 'struggle–criticism–transformation in all realms of the superstructure' and supporting the Maoist line on revolution in literature, art, education and public health.

But despite the reassertion of revolutionary themes and slogans and Mao's apparent support for the radical faction, the gradual restoration of bureaucratic control over the party was already under way. At the Tenth Party Congress Deng Xiaoping was elected to the Central Committee and admitted into the CCP Politburo, and in December 1973 he was made a Vice-Chairman of the Party's Military Affairs Commission. Though Mao may have acquiesced in Deng's return to power, perhaps because his skills and contacts were needed to tighten political control over the military establishment, the fact remains that his philosophy and style of work were dramatically opposed to those advocated by the radicals. The various views expressed by Deng over the years, including his statement in 1961 'it doesn't matter whether it is a white cat or a black cat, any cat that catches mice is a good cat', tended to attach much less importance to ideological rectitude and were widely regarded as promoting material incentives, greater importation of foreign technology and the need to put economics rather than politics in command. He was also known to be hostile to the radical innovations in education introduced by the Cultural Revolution as well as to the rapid elevation of young cadres, once again an important plank in the radical platform.[2]

Following Zhou's illness, Deng Xiaoping gradually assumed control of the administrative system, a role that was confirmed in January 1975 when he was named a Vice-Chairman of the party, Senior Vice-Premier of State Council and Chief of Staff of the PLA. At the same time, the party's supremacy was reasserted by the Fourth National People's Congress from which Mao was noticeably absent, while party control over the government apparatus was explicitly acknowledged in the Constitution. Zhou Enlai's 'Report on the work of the government', which was a summation of past policies and a blueprint of future tasks, once again went out of its way to praise the achievements of the Cultural Revolution, endorsing the three-in-one revolutionary committees, the proletarian revolution in art and literature, the May 7 schools, and the worker–peasant–soldier Marxist study groups.[3] He even characterized the struggle between the two classes as 'long and tortuous and at times even . . . acute'. But while situating economic development in a political context and integrating economic tasks with class struggle and revolution in the superstructure – Zhou had always been more adept than Deng in handling the dialectical relationship between economics and politics – he placed his full authority behind an ambitious two-stage development programme. The first five-year stage ending in 1980 called for building 'an independent and relatively comprehensive industrial and economic system'. A second twenty-year stage was envisaged that would bring about the 'comprehensive modernization of agriculture, industry, national defence and science and technology' (subsequently referred to by the Hua Guofeng–Deng Xiaoping leadership as the 'four modernizations'), thereby enabling the national economy to advance 'in the front ranks of the world'.

Whereas the basic goals of the economic programme were not at issue within the leadership, there was considerable dispute about means and priorities. Taking advantage of Zhou's declining health, Deng was now pressing ahead with his more technocratically oriented conception of growth. Several new appointments, notably the re-establishment of the Ministry of Education under Zhou Rongxin, an education official who had been purged during the Cultural Revolution, led the radicals to conclude that 'a right deviationist wind [was] trying to reverse correct verdicts'.[4] This rightist or revisionist current, increasingly personified by Deng Xiaoping, became the target of a series of ideological campaigns, including the anti-Lin Biao anti-Confucius campaign of 1973–74,[5] the campaign launched in February 1975 to study 'the theory of the dictatorship of the proletariat', and finally the campaign to criticize the classic novel *Water Margin*, a thinly veiled attack against present-day 'capitulationists' accused of submitting to revisionism and betraying Mao's revolutionary line.[6]

The vehemence of these campaigns, far from indicating the political strength of their exponents, simply pointed to the desperate attempts of the radical coalition to defend itself against the pragmatist offensive and to its increasing reliance on the media, which were now one of its few remaining levers of power. Throughout most of China, with the exception of Shanghai and one or two other provincial centres, the radicals did not enjoy sufficient regional support to block the return of moderates to positions of power. Despite their emphasis on the role of the urban militia, only in Shanghai were the radicals able to create an independent force free from party or army control. Similarly, though they gained the support of some PLA units, the bulk of the military forces remained hostile to their policies and ideology.[7] It was partly because they understood so well the combined strength of the interests opposed to them that they chose to target their campaign against one individual, namely Deng Xiaoping whom they were able to portray as 'the Party person in power taking the capitalist road', and the man 'who has clung to the revisionist line of Liu Shao-chi and Lin Piao and has to this day refused to mend his ways'.[8]

Inevitably Zhou Enlai's death on 8 January 1976 brought matters to a head and persuaded the radicals that this was an appropriate time, perhaps their last opportunity, to reverse the trends of the previous three years. On 7 April 1976 they achieved a major victory with the dismissal of Deng Xiaoping from all posts both inside and outside the party. But two aspects of the decision set clear limits to its significance. In the first place, Deng was allowed to retain his party membership, thus leaving open the possibility of his future rehabilitation. Secondly, the positions of First Vice-Chairman of the party and Premier of State Council were assigned to Hua Guofeng, a relatively unknown factor in the leadership struggle and certainly not someone closely associated with the radical cause in recent years. Moreover, all the evidence suggests that the 'gang of four' owed much of their tactical success to the support, however qualified, that Mao had given them. Though Mao was unlikely to have been directly aligned with any of the contending factions, his endorsement of the various political campaigns and his stress on the need to prevent the resurgence of capitalism, especially within the party, were crucial in legitimizing the actions of the radicals and in temporarily tilting the political balance in their favour.

The precariousness of the radical position was revealed soon after Mao's death with the arrest on 6 October 1976 of the whole leadership core of the Cultural Revolution. Apart from the 'gang of four', many of their followers were also arrested or purged, including most members of the Shanghai Municipal Party Committee. Two weeks later a mass rally in Peking celebrated Hua's appointment as new Chairman of the party. His appearance in military uniform symbolized the critical role of the army in the success of this political coup. Equally revealing was the editorial published on 27 October 1976 by the *Liberation Army Daily*, which credited Comrade Hua Guofeng with having 'averted a major retrogression in Chinese history and a great disaster for our people, thereby winning the complete trust of the whole Party, the whole army and the people of all nationalities throughout the country'.[9] The PLA's intervention is not difficult to explain given the deep-seated animosity that had existed between the PLA leadership and the radicals, most of whom were closely identified with the actions of the Red Guards during the Cultural Revolution and with anti-military and anti-professional attitudes. By backing

Hua and his allies, the army was able to form a coalition with the ruling organs of party and government, which could defeat the radicals swiftly and decisively. The military thus became an important prop for the new regime during the transitional period, contributed to the rehabilitation of veteran cadres and the reassertion of pragmatic policies and, in the process, strengthened their own position within the central decision-making apparatus.[10]

The ensuing campaign against the 'gang of four', who were now accused of 'revisionism' and of 'weaving plots and intrigues', was paralleled by a gradual abatement of the criticism levelled against Deng Xiaoping. In January 1977 several demonstrations calling for his return were reported, and at the end of June 1977 the *People's Daily* praised Deng for the very ideas for which he had been previously condemned. In July, Deng recovered all his previous posts and a few weeks later made the closing speech at the Eleventh Party Congress. Unlike Hua, whose position in the Chinese hierarchy greatly depended on the claim that he was Mao's legitimate successor,[11] Deng Xiaoping had a far more extensive power base within both the civilian and military bureaucracies. His position was considerably strengthened as more and more of his close collaborators resumed their former key posts in party and government organs in both central and provincial departments. Deng was therefore far less restricted than Hua in the extent to which he could depart from the spirit and letter of Mao's revolutionary line. He made no secret of his belief that China's modernization programme required the creation of an elitist scientific community that would enjoy material incentives, prestige and extensive interaction with the international community. In so far as Mao's ideological legacy stood in the way of such a project, Deng was quite prepared to reject the radicalism of the Great Proletarian Cultural Revolution and to abandon many of the Maoist concepts that had been propagated and applied with varying degrees of enthusiasm during the previous three decades.

Deng's modernization strategy rested then on the restoration of a technical–bureaucratic elite in Chinese society and was justified by the claim that the overwhelming majority of intellectuals had become members of the working class. The communiqué issued in December 1978 after the Third Plenary session of the Eleventh Central Committee stated that 'the large-scale turbulent class struggles of a mass character have in the main come to an end'.[12] The same communiqué announced the appointment of four new members of the Politburo, all believed to be supporters of Deng's policies, and the promotion or restoration to full membership of the Central Committee of nine people, most of whom had previously been denounced by the Red Guards as 'revisionists'. Directives previously issued by the Central Committee in regard to the movement 'to oppose the right deviationist wind to reverse correct verdicts' were now cancelled and described as 'erroneous' documents. Conversely the Tian An Men events of April 1976, which saw a commemorative occasion in favour of Zhou Enlai turn into a major political demonstration against the 'gang our four', were now characterized as 'entirely revolutionary actions'. This dramatic revision of recent history and the refusal to carry out a systematic assessment of the achievements and significance of the Cultural Revolution were revealing indicators of Deng Xiaoping's personal ascendancy and of the general realignment of power within the Chinese political system.[13]

The restoration of professional administrators, their increasing cooperation with the military and the re-establishment of the party's organizational structure together with its various channels of control were seen as providing the administrative and economic basis for the implementation of the 'four modernizations'. The new political programme was expected to mobilize the support not only of the majority of veteran cadres but of several other interest groups that were also likely to benefit from the shift in priorities. These included scientists, technicians, senior officers, engineers, skilled workers, foremen, intellectual youth and peasants anxious to develop private plots or other sideline occupations. To this extent the reversal of policies implicit in Deng Xiaoping's strategy was probably buttressed by a good deal of popular support, though the precise nature and extent of that support remained unclear. Much less open to doubt was the general thrust of the new policies, which envisaged a decreasing reliance on mass mobilization and the development of a more predictable, efficient, hierarchical system, in which workers and peasants would enjoy the pleasures of privatism and greater material-consumption in return for observing the discipline imposed by cadres and technicians. While Maoism would remain the official ideology, it would no longer serve as an operational system of knowledge or provide a revolutionary vision of world order. Its main function would now be to provide a symbol of continuity and legitimacy reinforcing the position of the new elite and rationalizing the pragmatic or even bureaucratic formulation of policy.

While this may have been the underlying intention of Deng and his associates, there were obvious limits to such an enterprise. The concern with participatory, egalitarian and communitarian values, which had been the distinguishing feature of Maoism, was likely to continue to exercise a powerful appeal for important sections of Chinese society. Presumably the political system could not easily tolerate the creation of new inequalities. Beyond a certain point income and status differentials between urban and rural areas, between skilled and unskilled workers and between the working class and the intelligentsia would provoke explosive discontent. To this extent revolutionary idealism and self-interest might still combine to prevent the full restoration of the bureaucratic instinct.

The Four Modernizations

The more pragmatic ordering of society and pattern of economic development favoured by China's post-Maoist leadership was premised on the desire to transform China into a strong, modern power. Indicative of the new thinking was the decision in December 1976 to resurrect Mao Zedong's April 1956 speech 'On the ten major relationships', a relatively conservative statement dating back to the period prior to the Great Leap Forward when Mao, conscious of the 'rightist' atmosphere then prevalent, made a tactical retreat after a rapid burst of collectivization in 1955. Few of the relationships analysed by Mao in 1956 were readily applicable to the vastly different conditions of 1976. The importance of the speech lay not so much in its specific prescriptions as in its more generally conventional approach to decision-making and its stress on material incentives to reward skill and productivity.

The main themes of the new economic programme were outlined in a series of national conferences. Two Conferences to Learn from Dazhai in Agriculture were organized, the first in the autumn of 1975 and the second in December 1976. The Dazhai model was now used principally to focus attention on quantitative production achievements, including grain production, mechanization, growth in income and contributions to the state. In April 1977, a National Conference to Learn from Daqing in Industry was convened, at which it was projected that one-third of China's enterprises would become Daqing-type units by 1980. These forums, which were concerned with the overall development of agriculture and industry, were complemented by national conferences of narrower scope dealing with individual branches of the economy, namely petroleum in November 1976, coal in January 1977, light industry also in January 1977 and railways in March 1977. Conferences were also convened to discuss capital construction, machine-building and communications work on 3, 4 and 11 April, respectively. In February, several conferences had been called to study various aspects of national defence, including scientific research and production.[14] Most of these conferences, which received heavy media attention, were primarily intended to remove bottlenecks or restructure economic sectors that had failed to develop to their full potential.

The magnitude of China's projected modernization programme was revealed by Hua Guofeng in his keynote speech to the Fifth National People's Congress on 26 February 1978. He announced that in the course of the current ten-year plan China would construct 120 large-scale projects, including ten in iron and steel, nine in non-ferrous metals production, eight coal mines, ten oil and gas fields, thirty power stations, six trunk railroad lines, and five harbours. By 1985, China would produce 400 million metric tons of food grain and 60 million tons of steel annually. It was also planned to increase industrial output over the next eight years by an annual rate of more than 10 per cent and agricultural output by 4–5 per cent.[15] These projections were supported in the ensuing twelve months by numerous pronouncements, articles and editorials, all of which stressed the same growth objective. Figures released in 1979 pointed to the increase in production registered in the preceding year.[16] In his report to the Fifth National People's Congress in June, Hua Guofeng announced that total grain output had risen by 22 million tons to 304,750,000 tons (an increase of 7.8 per cent over the previous year), steel output from 20,460,000 tons to 38,780,000 tons, coal output from 483 million tons to 618 million tons, and crude oil production from 87 million tons to 104 million tons. Electricity generation had increased by 26 per cent, and the total volume of imports and exports by 53.7 per cent.[17]

Speed was regarded as crucial to the success of the programme, hence the repeated exhortations to boost production and the preference for 'those trade and branches of the economy that will produce *quick results*, earn more profits and foreign exchange and that can compete on the international market so as to accumulate more funds, import advanced techniques and *quicken the pace of construction*' (italics added).[18] In keeping with the same objective, efficiency was now to be accorded a much higher priority. To this end managers were encouraged to adopt sound management principles, make greater use of material rewards, stress specialization and professionalism and upgrade scientific research. Former industrialists and businessmen were to have restored to them their bank deposits and high salaries of which they were deprived during the Cultural Revolution. Their work was to be rearranged to enable them to assume managerial positions and professional titles.[19] In addition, economic management was to be reorganized by giving added emphasis to 'economic means', 'economic organization' and 'economic laws' and by sending managerial personnel abroad to study and acquire advanced experience.[20] The National Conference on Learning from Daqing in Industry stressed the following principles: leadership unity, strict discipline to be observed by workers, scientific management, technical innovations and fulfilment of state plans. Similarly, the Dazhai model for agriculture was now identified with quantitative production criteria, including rapid growth rates, accelerated mechanization and wage increases. In the early part of 1979, there were indications that the commune system itself might be radically modified to allow for the partial break-up of production teams into groups of families or even single families, although several provincial authorities subsequently issued statements strongly warning against the pursuit of individual affluence.[21]

Parallel trends in education policy meant the reintroduction of examinations for admission, promotion and graduation in institutions of higher learning, greater status and authority for teachers, greater stress on basic and applied scientific research, revival of academic titles, and specialized schooling for academically gifted students.

In the area of defence, PLA deficiencies were now acknowledged with remarkable candour. The army's decisive role in the succession struggle provided it with added leverage in pressing its demands which were, in any case, favourably viewed by the new leadership. Given the budgetary constraints arising from scarce resources, the quest for weapons modernization could be expected to bring the military into conflict with the civilian bureaucracy. On the other hand, there was considerable agreement among policy-makers on the need for a much higher level of military professionalism. In a report on the international situation delivered in July 1977, Foreign Minister Huang Hua made abundantly clear his government's commitment to military modernization:

> By merely relying on our consciousness, not modern weapons, we cannot win the war. Over the past few years we have suffered from this. . . . The barrels of the new submachine guns the PLA fighters carried at Chenpao Island became red hot after firing several chips of shells. . . . Poorly trained fighters could not correctly operate their equipment, and thus sacrificed their lives under the wheels of tanks.[22]

The need to improve the weapons and equipment of the Chinese armed forces thus had the support of civilian as well as military leaders.[23] But the procurement of a modern defence system also required the acquisition of complex skills, hence the increasing stress on the specialized training of officers in military academies and the importance of material incentives to ensure a steady inflow of competent personnel.

The resurgence of professionalism and the corresponding downgrading of the militia found expression in an expanded programme of research into military technology and growing interest in the procurement of foreign weapon systems. The military, for their part, were prepared to concede that national defence construction would depend on the modernization of science and technology, but speed was of the essence:

> We cannot afford to let time slip through our fingers because time waits for no one. If we act slowly we will lag behind and will have to passively receive the blows.[24]

In the view of the civilian leadership, however, economic development had to take precedence over weapons development, for military modernization presupposed economic construction. Only by developing 'the metallurgical, machine-building, fuel, chemical, power, meters and instruments, electronics and other basic industries' would it be possible to lay 'a solid national foundation for strengthening national defence'.[25]

From this brief account of China's modernization strategy as it unfolded in the early stages of the post-Mao era, one can detect a distinct shift away from the twin Maoist concepts of self-reliance and permanent revolution. On the other hand, the break in continuity is perhaps less radical than is often claimed. To begin with, the changes tentatively introduced during the final years of Zhou's administration did not receive universal support within China. Nor did it always prove possible to translate the rhetoric of modernization into concrete and effective policies. Nevertheless, the fact remains that in ideological and policy terms the fall of the 'gang of four' did reflect the decline, however partial or temporary, of the radical conception of socialist construction that envisaged a labour-intensive agricultural policy, a political programme of mass mobilization, the elimination of social and economic inequality and the creation of the selfless and self-disciplined man. Though many of these goals were not openly or categorically rejected during this later period, the very commitment to rapid economic growth necessitated increasing emphasis on the development of large, capital-intensive complexes and sophisticated technologies, both of which in turn required a more prominent role for the intelligentsia, cadres and specialists, and greater reliance on foreign capital, foreign technology and foreign managerial techniques. Although Mao had also supported on several occasions a much faster growth rate in agricultural and industrial production and recognized the positive contribution that foreign technology might make, he had remained adamant that the acceleration of economic development would have to be combined with an intensive inculcation of socialist values and ideas, and heightened ideological and political struggle within the superstructure.

The lower priority now attached to intermediate technologies and labour-intensive small- and medium-scale industries was accompanied by a revised educational policy based on merit and the introduction of bonuses and other wage differentials. The net effect of these measures was likely to advantage the cities as against the countryside, skilled as against unskilled workers, and mental as against manual labour.[26] Not surprisingly, every effort was now being made to minimize the role and significance of class struggle both as a tool of social analysis and as a guide to policy. The struggle between 'modern ideology and the vestiges of old ideas' was to be the substitute of class struggle, thereby justifying the rejection of radical demands on the grounds that they were incompatible with the development of productive forces. The new ideological line enabled the intellectual/bureaucratic elite to strengthen its position not only by imposing a much stricter labour discipline on peasants and workers but by legitimizing its leading role in the four modernizations.[27] An interesting indicator of this trend was the decision announced in January 1979 to remove the designation of landlords and rich peasants on the grounds that only a handful of counter-revolutionaries now existed in China.[28] Yet Mao had argued as late as 1976 that the bourgeoisie had entrenched itself right inside the Communist Party. A new concept was gradually emerging equating socialism with state ownership. Indeed, the leading role of the state in controlling the economy was advanced as a decisive argument against the existence of major contradictions within Chinese society.

By discarding or downgrading the importance of class analysis, it was possible to argue that the introduction of advanced technology, whatever its source or method and rate of application, would be neutral in terms of its class effects and have a generally beneficial impact on the socialist economy.[29] The previously established notion that technology and managerial institutions were not neutral but inextricably linked with the class relationship from which they originated was abandoned. In opposition to the radical perspective, which stressed the importance of national economic independence and self-sufficiency, a correct political line on class struggle and the weeding out of class enemies, the new leadership was committed to increased exports of coal and oil in exchange for the import of new technology and equipment. The net effect of this policy was to foster a framework of trade and financial relations not unlike the system of unequal exchange that had traditionally tied the Third World to the international market economy.

While there is little doubt of the main thrust of China's economic strategy as enunciated by Deng Xiaoping or of the enthusiasm with which it was pursued, there were nevertheless several factors limiting the new regime's freedom of action. In the early months of 1979 it became clear that the acquisition of foreign technology would have to proceed at a slower rate than originally planned because of China's rapidly dwindling foreign exchange reserves and the prospect of a drastically increasing foreign debt. At home, construction projects were outstripping available human, material and financial resources. China's decision to freeze several foreign contracts and delay the signing of new ones, the downward revision of projected steel production, and the abandonment of all-round agricultural mechanization were only some of the indicators pointing to the severe economic and political – not to mention military – pressures tending to retard or even deflect the policy of the four modernizations.[30]

Foreign Policy Implications

Although the foregoing analysis has concentrated on the changing complexion of Chinese domestic politics, the loss of revolutionary momentum was equally apparent in China's external conduct. Indeed, the declining influence of traditional Maoist concepts as determinants of foreign policy had already become apparent during the late 1960s and early 1970s. This transitional phase witnessed a clearly discernible shift from class to state relations as the basis for interpreting the world situation and the substitution of the Soviet Union for the United States as China's principal enemy. The restructuring of Peking's perception of the world, which partly reflected the rapidly changing internaional environment, thus paved the way for a more cooperative relationship with the United States.

As early as December 1971, Zhou Enlai had described the antagonism with the Soviet Union as the essence of Chinese foreign policy, rather than opposition to the two superpowers:

> That we oppose the two superpowers is a slogan. The essense lies principally in opposition against this most actual enemy, Soviet revisionist social-imperialism, and in the combat against this social-imperialism.[31]

The concept of Soviet social-imperialism enabled Chinese leaders to portray the Soviet Union as guilty of territorial expansion, economic encroachment, military intervention, and political infiltration and subversion. On this issue at least the radical and bureaucratic factions in Chinese politics were largely in agreement, though for sharply divergent reasons.

The radical position, which continued to have wide public currency even after the demise of the radicals, was premised on the view that the Soviet Union was out 'to subvert the dictatorship of the proletariat and the socialist system in China and to restore capitalism',[32] that is, to impose its revisionist line on the Chinese Communist Party. It followed that the Soviet threat had to be resisted not so much by greater military preparedness as by a persistent and vigilant domestic class struggle that alone could isolate and eventually remove the actual or potential agents of Soviet social-imperialism.[33] The pragmatists, on the other hand, viewed the Sino–Soviet conflict in more conventional military and diplomatic terms. For them, Soviet expansionism necessitated and justified China's closer relations with the Second World, that is, with the industrial countries of Europe and Japan. But even more important was the rapprochement with the leading capitalist power, which had been enshrined in the principles of the Shanghai communiqué. For both factions, then, domestic and foreign policy considerations were inextricably interwoven and attitudes to both sets of issues were seen as complementary and mutually reinforcing.

The gradual decline of the radical position in Chinese politics was paralleled by a significant shift in foreign policy, but was partly obscured by the persistence of the Sino–Soviet dispute. Apart from consolidating the new strategic and economic relationship with the advanced capitalist world, Deng Xiaoping and his associates were anxious to develop a more pragmatic policy towards the Third World. While continuing to pay lip service to the importance of resisting superpower domination, the Three Worlds theory enunciated by China in April 1974 was, in reality, directed principally against the Soviet Union. Rather than American imperialism it was Soviet social-imperialism that was now identified as the principal source of colonialism and neo-colonialism. According to Huang Hua, Soviet actions in Czechoslovakia, Angola, the Middle East, South Asia and the Indian Ocean provided conclusive evidence that 'the newly-emerging biggest, most despicable colonialist, social-imperialism ha[d] become more and more flagrant in taking the place of old line imperialists and in expanding brutality throughout the world'.[34] This rather crude version of 'imperialism versus the Third World', which emerged in embryo in the last few years of Mao's life and became part of his so-called 'revolutionary diplomatic line', meant that China was often obliged to make common cause with some of the most conservative Third World governments, many of which were closely integrated into the western economic and strategic orbit. Clearly, the desire to cultivate close relations with President Mobutu of Zaire, the Shah of Iran or the various ASEAN governments had much less to do with the requirements of revolution than with the dictates of *realpolitik*. To justify this development the Chinese leadership introduced the concept of 'phased revolution', according to which the revolutionary process had to pass through several stages, each stage requiring distinctive policies and tactics appropriate to it. To the extent that anti-hegemonism was currently 'the mainstream of world struggle', it was deemed inopportune for the proletariat to strive for socialist revolution or 'the single-handed seizure of power'.[35]

Although the likelihood of a Soviet attack against China had greatly diminished after 1973, the conflict between the two countries continued to colour the whole complexion of Chinese foreign policy. While Soviet military capabilities were now considered inadequate for the task of subjugating China, most official pronouncements claimed that Soviet ambitions lay elsewhere, that is, in a global strategic contest with the United States and in more localized attempts to extend the Soviet sphere of influence, particularly in Europe and the more vulnerable regions of the Third World. In this sense, the Sino–Soviet relationship was subject to contradictory pressures. In so far as the Soviet military threat posed to China had receded and the intensity of the ideological dispute subsided in the wake of Mao's death and the downfall of the radicals – it could even be argued that a certain ideological affinity now existed between the two social systems – there were grounds for anticipating a reduction in Sino–Soviet hostility. Peking's willingness to maintain correct diplomatic relations with Moscow, to enter into border negotiations and to release the Soviet helicopter crew that had been captured in Xinjiang in March 1974, pointed in this direction. Yet, if one is to judge by the acrimonious character of Sino–Soviet exchanges throughout this period, culminating in China's formal decision in April 1979 to terminate the Sino–Soviet alliance, it is difficult to avoid the conclusion that the conflict was still as far as ever from resolution. The border dispute and its strategic implications, the rivalry for power and prestige in the Third World, the competition for spheres of influence, particularly in East, South and Southeast Asia, all pointed to conflicting long-term, interests that could not be easily or quickly reconciled. Moreover, Mao's legacy made it difficult for Peking to reach a compromise with Moscow, given that important elements of the new leadership depended for the legitimacy of their position on a continuing public commitment to the struggle against 'Soviet revisionism'.

But perhaps the most decisive factor inclining the Chinese to maintain their policy of hostility towards Moscow was the conviction that closer relations with the West were likely to prove far more advantageous, at least in the foreseeable future, than the easing of tensions with the Soviet Union. Western capital and technology were deemed more vital to the success of China's four modernizations than anything Russia could provide. In the military field, Chinese interest in foreign equipment and technology dated back to the early 1960s when the termination of Soviet aid obliged Peking to seek alternative sources of supply. Although no contracts were actually signed, preliminary approaches were made to Sweden, Switzerland and France. China's concern for her vulnerability to aerial penetration resulted in the early and mid-1970s in renewed efforts to acquire a more effective air defence capability, particularly through the purchase of European military hardware. In addition to prototypes and outright transfers of weapons systems, China was anxious to procure the means of production themselves. In December 1975, she signed an agreement with Great Britain that provided for the purchase of fifty supersonic Spey jet engines, a licence to manufacture these engines in China, and the furnishing of facilities and technical expertise for engine testing and maintenance. The Spey contract was especially noteworthy in that it bypassed the scrutiny of the Western Consultative Committee (Cocom) for technology transfers, the implication being that China would now have access to western military technology, if not from the United States, at least from its allies. Other defence-related contracts included helicopters, radar, aircraft and missile-tracking equipment from France and helicopters from West Germany. In 1977–78 negotiations were under way for the purchase of HOT and MILAN anti-tank and Crotale anti-aircraft missiles from France, electronic guidance systems from Italy, West German leopard tanks and helicopters equipped with anti-tank missiles, patrol aircraft from Japan, and Harrier fighters from Hawker Siddeley of Great Britain.[36]

Nor was the interest in foreign technology confined to the military sector. Chinese imports of machines and equipment rose from $240 million in 1968 to $2165 million in 1975.[37] To secure the foreign exchange needed to sustain her modernization programme China was compelled to raise the level of her own exports. Petroleum sales, which were to play a crucial part in this regard, became a new item on China's export list in 1973 and totalled $910 million in 1975. However, petroleum exploration, extraction and processing in turn required large investments and sophisticated equipment, thereby accentuating China's dependence on technology imports. In the early to mid-1970s, oil exploration machinery, oil rigs, coal dressing equipment, petrochemical and fertilizer plants, fertilizers and agricultural machinery accounted for more than 80 per cent of China's imports from Europe and Japan, while foodstuffs, raw materials and energy fuels accounted for more than 65 per cent of her exports to these countries. Between 1971 and 1975 Chinese imports from the advanced capitalist world increased from $1000 million to $4000 million, while the value of China's two-way trade rose from $4290 million to $14,090 million. The rate of trade expansion was somewhat reversed in 1976, partly because of opposition from the radicals, but the upward trend was resumed in 1977. Following the establishment of a China–EEC joint trade committee, Peking let it be known that it wanted to increase its imports from Europe from $2700 million in 1978 to $25,000 million by 1985. According to one estimate, Peking's spiralling capital requirements would result in an import bill between 1978 and 1985 of $200,000 million. Even if such projections were dismissed as far-fetched, the more conservative estimate of $120,000 million still entailed an average annual growth rate of 15 per cent.[38]

In their eagerness to increase export earnings, China's new leaders were willing to establish processing zones whereby plant sites and cheap labour would be made available to foreign industrialists – many of them overseas Chinese – who would then re-export the processed products to overseas markets. In pursuit of the same objective a concerted effort was also being made to develop a tourist industry, which was perceived as another useful method of exploiting China's cheap and abundant labour. However, as these measures were insufficient to keep pace with the accelerating demand for foreign technology, Peking was obliged to devise other ways of financing her imports, including deferred payments, joint-production projects, more flexible forms of borrowing and reciprocal accounts between the Bank of China and European and Japanese banks. China's modernization strategy was now firmly based on increased commercial, financial and technological interaction with the advanced capitalist economies.

The convulsive ideological and power struggle that China had experienced during the 1970s, the subsequent triumph of pragmatic–bureaucratic policies and institutions, and the new economic priorities implicit in the four modernizations were bound to have far-reaching implications for China's external conduct. The foreign policy impact of these internal political realignments would have been even more drastic and immediate had it not been for the fact that external pressures and Mao's changing perception of the international configuration of forces had already set the stage for a wide-ranging accommodation with the world capitalist system. A series of concessions from both sides, reflecting to some extent the diminished economic and strategic bargaining power of the United States, had made possible the resolution of several outstanding differences and a much greater degree of Sino–American cooperation in bilateral relations as well as on a broad range of multilateral issues. The same external and domestic factors had resulted in a more diversified and less ideologically oriented policy towards the Third World. The Sino–Soviet conflict rather than the contradiction between revolutionary struggle and colonialism or neo-colonialism was now the principal determinant of China's relations with the countries of Asia, Africa and Latin America. Though support was still extended to several liberation movements and sympathetic communist parties, opposition to Soviet policies and influence had become the essential prerequisite for such support. The national and ideological confrontation, which had for two decades pitted China's revolutionary strategy against America's conception of world order, had by the late 1970s largely subsided. By contrast, the Sino–Soviet quarrel, though less ideologically centred than in the past, had become a keystone of Chinese foreign policy and one of the principal axes of international conflict.

CHAPTER 8

Sino–American Rapprochement

After the initial euphoria generated by the 1972 Nixon visit, the relationship between the two countries did not make the rapid or substantial headway that some observers had expected, and negotiations on most outstanding issues reached virtual stalemate. A case in point was Peking's apparent reluctance to reach agreement on the question of "assets and claims", which revolved around $196.9 million in US claims for American property confiscated by China after 1949 as against $76.6 million in Chinese assets frozen by the United States. Similarly, the issue of most favoured nation status for Chinese exports to the United States, which would lower tariffs and make them more competitive in the American market, had been under consideration since mid-1973 but had yet to be finalized. During 1974–75, Peking became increasingly sensitive on the Taiwan question raising several problems that had previously been over-looked. The number of American newsmen admitted to China, other than those assigned to cover official visits, declined, while the exchange of resident correspondents was postponed until the establishment of formal diplomatic relations. Reciprocal visits by non-official delegations continued, but Peking took great care to encourage those exchanges that were most likely to enhance pro-Chinese sentiment in the United States. The announcement in late 1974 of President Ford's planned visit in 1975 gave fresh impetus to the process of 'normalization', but subsequent developments did little to advance the relationship. The uncertainty surrounding America's policies in Asia following its defeat in Indochina, powerful opposition within the United States to any further disengagement from Taiwan, and China's increasing determination not to expand bilateral ties even in relatively non-controversial fields until further progress had been made on the Taiwan problem, combined to diminish the political impact of President Ford's trip to China. The exchange of views at the summit level merely demonstrated the desire of both countries not to jeopardize the existing dialogue.

Diplomatic Entente

Of all the unresolved issues Taiwan was perhaps the chief obstacle to the establishment of ambassadorial relations, but also the most reliable indicator of the changing disposition of the two sides.[1] Although the United States had progressively reduced its military presence on Taiwan in keeping with the pledge it had given at Shanghai, other initiatives taken after 1972 tended to reinforce American ties with Taiwan. Trade between the two countries increased from $1500 million in 1971 to $4500 million in 1976, far exceeding the value of Sino–American trade, which in fact declined from $934 million in 1974 to $336 million in 1976. As of December 1975, American loans and guarantees extended to Taiwan amounted to more than $1700 million making it the largest customer of the Export–Import Bank after Brazil. There were now thirteen American banks represented on the island, while US investment in various Taiwanese industries was estimated in July 1976 at $476 million, bringing total investment since 1952 to nearly $1300 million. Large US financial interests had obtained concessions from the Nationalist regime for oil and gas exploration and were planning the construction of five to ten production platforms in the Taiwan Strait at a cost of about $150 million each. In addition to expanded cultural exchanges, five new Taiwan consulates were established in the United States. But probably the most disturbing trend from Peking's point of view was the level of US arms sales to Taiwan, which increased from $196 million in 1974 to $293 million in 1976 and included a highly advanced radar air defence system, Hawk ground-to-air missiles and F-5E jet interceptors.[2] The steady expansion of military and economic links suggested that the United States still regarded Taiwan not only as a vital strategic interest in the Asia–Pacific region but as a useful lever in negotiations with China.

Though not underestimating the difficulties posed by the Taiwan issue, there is reason to believe that the progress in Soviet–American détente had also contributed to the Sino–American diplomatic standstill. After all, the Nixon–Kissinger opening to China was in no small measure designed to exploit the Sino–Soviet conflict in order to induce the Soviet Union into a more cooperative relationship with the United States. The Ford–Brezhnev meeting in November 1974 and the resulting set of understandings directed towards the signing of a SALT II agreement confirmed Chinese fears of Soviet–American collusion, particularly as the site chosen for the meeting was Vladivostok, which Peking claimed was part of Chinese territory forcibly seized by Tsarist Russia.

In spite of the foregoing constraints, which were considerably magnified by the leadership crisis in both countries, by the end of 1976 it was possible to detect new signs of movement in Sino–American relations. The visit to China in September 1976 by former US Defence Secretary James Schlesinger (known for his hawkish views on the Soviet Union) underlined China's unhappiness with US–Soviet détente policy but also her desire for a more substantial strategic relationship with the United States. Though Schlesinger's trip occurred within days of Mao's death, he was able to meet with senior Chinese leaders and was accorded the privilege of visiting Inner Mongolia, Tibet and the nuclear weapons testing centre at Lop Nor in Xinjiang.

Equally significant was the softening of China's Taiwan position, which was discernible prior to Mao's death but became particularly noticeable after the fall of the 'gang of four' and the gradual consolidation of Deng Xiaoping's foreign and domestic policies. Whereas Chinese leaders had as recently as July 1976 given the impression to visiting Americans that Taiwan might have to be 'liberated by force',[3] less than two months later but two months prior to Mao's death, Geng Biao, head of the international Liaison Department of the CCP Central Committee, delivered a secret speech in which he advocated a cautious and patient attitude to the Taiwan issue. Geng Biao's analysis of Chinese objectives was remarkably frank and deserves to be quoted at some length:

> To liberate Taiwan is our set policy, but it depends on the development of the international situation as a whole and our own preparation. If it cannot be solved by force, peaceful liberation is the best. For the present it is better to sustain the status quo. . . . At this moment, just let the U.S. defend us against the influence of Soviet revisionism and guard the coast of the East China Seas so that we can have more strength to deal with the power in the north and engage in state construction.[4]

Exactly the same sentiments were expressed a year later by Chinese Foreign Minister Huang Hua who went even further by indicating that China would not liberate Taiwan by armed force within the next ten years even if the United States normalized relations with the People's Republic, abrogated its mutual defence treaty with Taiwan, and withdrew all its armed forces from the island.[5]

It is against this background and the apparent wish of the Carter administration to speed up the process of normalization that Secretary of State Cyrus Vance visited China in September 1977. By this time, Peking had already communicated its readiness to improve trade relations as well as scientific, educational, cultural and sports exchanges even prior to any agreement on diplomatic recognition. Access to American advanced technology and know-how, including sophisticated equipment, research facilities and management techniques, was now considered vital to China's economic modernization. However, to the apparent disappointment of the Chinese the Vance visit brought no visible breakthrough and Sino–American relations remained in the state of semi-normalization that had prevailed since 1974. Once again, Washington seemed more intent on stabilizing its relationship with Moscow and placating the powerful pro-Taiwan lobby than on cementing the connection with Peking.

It was not until May 1978, when President Carter's national security adviser Zbigniew Brzezinski travelled to China for three days of talks, that the United States gave the first unequivocal indication that it would move rapidly to establish full diplomatic relations with China. Brezezinski, who gave Chinese officials an unprecedented briefing on the status of the Soviet–American strategic arms talks, explained to his Chinese hosts that the United States recognized and shared their resolve to 'resist the efforts of any nation which seeks to establish global or regional hegemony'.[6] His discussions in Peking were described as the fullest consultations held with the Chinese since contacts were established in 1971. In Brzezinski's own words, 'the basic significance of the trip was to underline the long-term *strategic* nature of the United States relationship to China' (italics added).[7] Moscow's predictable reaction was to warn Washington against the formation of an anti-Soviet Sino–American bloc that it claimed, would 'close the possibilities for co-operation with the United States in reducing the danger of nuclear war and limiting arms'.[8] Although the Taiwan issue had not yet been fully resolved, the clear impression that relations between the two sides were rapidly improving was confirmed with Peking's announcement of its intention to send students to America, an action that it had previously insisted would have to await the establishment of diplomatic relations. The agreement reached in October 1978 provided for 500 Chinese students and scientists to go to the United States the following year, with sixty American students and scholars going to China in exchange.

Two crucial but closely interrelated factors were responsible for the more cooperative climate between the two countries: the intensification of Sino–Soviet and Sino–Vietnamese hostility on the one hand and the growing coincidence of Sino–American interests on the other. Of particular concern to Peking was Hanoi's increasing alignment with Moscow, which eventually resulted in the signing of a Soviet–Vietnamese treaty of friendship and cooperation in November 1978. By contrast there was now no significant conflict of interest between China and the United States. Indeed, Chinese foreign policy positions closely accorded with those of the United States, at least with respect to containment of Soviet military and political power not only in Southeast Asia, but in Africa, Western Europe and the Indian Ocean. This striking parallelism in strategic orientation greatly facilitated the negotiating process, which finally led on 15 December 1978 to the simultaneous declaration in Peking and Washington that relations between the two countries would be normalized as from 1 January 1979,[9] thus completing the process begun with President Nixon's visit to China and the Shanghai communiqué of 1972.

In the diplomatic compromise reached by the two sides, the United States accepted China's three principal conditions: diplomatic ties with Taiwan were to be severed, the US–Taiwan mutual defence treaty abrogated, and the 700 remaining American military troops withdrawn from the island.[10] In return, Peking conceded that the treaty should have a year's grace and lapse on 1 January 1980 (China had earlier insisted on immediate termination), an option spelt out in the pact itself. As a trade-off for this Chinese concession, designed to cushion the shock of American disengagement both in Taiwan and in the United States, the Carter administration agreed to include in the communiqué an anti-hegemony clause – Chinese code for the Soviet Union. At the same time, Washington acquiesced in Peking's refusal to offer an explicit guarantee of its peaceful intentions in relation to the liberation of Taiwan. Deng Xiaoping firmly reiterated China's view that 'the return of Taiwan to the embrace of the motherland and completing the process of reunifying the country is entirely an internal Chinese affair'.[11] However, the position was made somewhat more palatable for the United States by Deng's qualification that China's intention was to solve the matter peacefully and patiently. The Carter administration was also able to argue that the People's Republic did not have the military capability to launch a 120-mile attack against a heavily fortified and heavily armed Taiwan.[12] In any case, the forceful seizure of Taiwan would risk alienating Japan, the United States and many of the countries of Europe and Asia with which China was seeking an increasingly intimate economic and strategic relationship.

As a further sign of its commitment to Taiwan's security, the United States unilaterally declared that it reserved the right to continue supplying the territory with defensive weapons. In an unprecedented press conference televised throughout China, Chairman Hua Guofeng voiced strong opposition to the continued shipment of arms to Taiwan after normalization, arguing that it was 'detrimental to a peaceful settlement of the Taiwan question' and to 'peace and stability in the Asia–Pacific region'. However, his next sentence: 'Our two sides had differences on this point. Nevertheless we reached an agreement on the joint communiqué'[13] provided ample evidence of the pragmatic readjustment in China's foreign policy. Normalization was not expected to alter the substance of the economic and political relationship between Washington and Taibei. Although special congressional legislation might be necessary for the purpose, the Carter administration was confident that the establishment of the American Institute of Taiwan (which was to be paralleled by the Taiwanese Co-ordination Council for North American Affairs in Washington) would provide the necessary framework for the continuation of bilateral trade, US arms sales and various loan arrangements.

Peking, for its part, was prepared to take a longer-term view of the Taiwan question, and formally substituted the notion of reunification for that of liberation,[14] which had previously characterized its more militant approach to the problem. In keeping with the new mood of moderation, the Standing Committee of the Fifth National People's Congress addressed a message to the people of Taiwan, which stressed the goal of reunification, pointed to the stability and unity within China, invited negotiations with the Taiwanese authorities, and announced an immediate end to the sporadic shelling of the Dajinmen and Xiaojinmen, Dadan, Erdan and other islands.[15] Several subsequent public statements reaffirmed Peking's readiness for the gradual exchange of people and goods, the peaceful negotiating of differences and the landing in China of Taiwan commercial aircraft headed for Tokyo.[16] It was even suggested in some quarters that after reunification Taiwan might be allowed to keep its armed forces and present economic system as a special province within China. Although these appeals and gestures of goodwill were flatly rejected by Taibei, China's overtures had undoubtedly embarrassed President Chiang Ching-Kuo, who was now faced with the painful option of either agreeing to discussions with Peking, and thereby undermining the legitimacy of his regime, or of rebuffing China's conciliatory initiatives but at the cost of intensified debate, criticism and even outright opposition from those sections of Taiwan society sceptical of the need for high levels of military spending and eager to gain a greater say over the political future of the island state.

Whatever the eventual outcome of the political manoeuvring on either side of the Taiwan Strait – US–Taiwan ties might still cause a measure of friction between Peking and Washington[17] – conditions now seemed ripe for a new *entente cordiale* between China and the United States. Certainly, the Chinese made great play of the euphoria prevailing in the immediate aftermath of normalization. The establishment of Sino–US diplomatic relations was described as 'an inevitable trend of historical development'[18] and as 'opening up vast vistas for friendly intercourse and co-operation between the two peoples'.[19] During his visit to the United States in January 1979, Deng Xiaoping made no secret of China's preoccupation with the Soviet Union's alleged expansionism or of her newly found enthusiasm for the extension of American naval strength in the Indian and Pacific Oceans. The Vice-Premier's call for greater military preparedness in Japan and a more concerted defence effort within the Association of Southeast Asian Nations (ASEAN) represented not only a dramatic departure from the orthodoxy of the 1950s and 1960s but an undisguised realignment of Chinese foreign policy with current American strategic thinking. The scientific, technological and cultural agreements concluded at the end of Deng Xiaoping's visit together with several other accords on the establishment of consular relations and increased exchanges in education, agriculture, space and high energy physics[20] were presumably intended as a taste of things to come.

Economic Dimensions of the Relationship

Notwithstanding the importance of military and diplomatic considerations, there can be little doubt that the economic motive played a considerable part in the decision of both countries to hasten the process of normalization. For the United States, a stable and cordial relationship with China offered the prospect of access to rich oil and other energy resources as well as a large market likely to require increasing inputs of foreign technology. For the new Chinese leadership on the other hand, the great attraction of expanded trade with the United States was the possibility of acquiring the heavy and sophisticated machinery deemed essential for economic growth. In other words, in exchange for China's rich natural resources and her cheap and abundant labour the United States could explore ways of adapting its advanced technology to China's evolving economic infrastructure.

Such a theoretical notion of economic complementarity, however, has to be assessed in the light of the changing pattern of trade relations between the two countries. The total value of US–China trade, which had increased from $4.9

million in 1971 to $935.2 million in 1974, declined in the following three years reaching a low of $357 million in 1976. Until 1971 the absence of any trade was a direct expression of the American policy of containment and isolation. The changing diplomatic climate of the early 1970s combined with the crystall-ization of Peking's new foreign economic policy and China's disappointing 1972 agricultural harvest to produce a sharp rise in US farm exports to China in 1973 and 1974 (nearly 80 per cent of US sales to China during this period were agricultural). When the boom of grain exports subsided in 1975, not only was there no offsetting rise in industrial exports but even in the agricultural area the Chinese market could no longer be regarded as a dependable outlet for American exports.[21] As for the sale of complete industrial plants, the United States supplied only eight out of the 100 plants purchased by China between 1972 and mid-1975, the bulk of sales being accounted for by Japan and Western Europe. The same situation prevailed in relation to Chinese imports of machinery and equipment. America's poor performance in the capital goods sector is explained in part by Japan's more advantageous geographical and cultural location but also by the more attractive financial and credit arrangements it was able to offer the Chinese. In this sense, the absence of formal relations, the unresolved claims–assets dispute and the lack of most favoured nation status placed US industrial exporters at a considerable disadvantage vis-à-vis their Japanese and European competitors. But perhaps the most significant limiting factor in Sino–American trade, at least in the short-term, was the advent of a severe world recession in 1973 coupled with high levels of inflation, which inevitably resulted, despite several corrective measures, in the largest trade deficit incurred by the People's Republic since 1949.

Even though the value of Sino–American trade in 1978 regained the ground lost over the previous three years, much of the increase was accounted for by a sale of 3.7 million metric tons of wheat. On the other hand, normalization of diplomatic relations promised to create a major upsurge in the flow of US investment and technology to China. American corporate interests were now confidently forecasting that the value of trade between the two countries might rise to $5000 million by 1981 and $10,000 million by 1985, compared with only $374 million in 1977 and $1000 million in 1978. This predicted sharp increase in trade was expected to be in industrial and agricultural equipment, mining, oil technology and aircraft purchases, compared to the previous emphasis on grain imports. The visit to China in July 1978 of a high-level delegation of American scientific and technical advisers indicated that the Chinese were ready to press ahead with bilateral cooperative ventures in the science and health areas as well as with exchanges in scientific, technological and educational personnel between the two countries.[22] During 1978 China sent several agricultural delegations to the United States with a view to acquiring American agricultural technology. In mid-November, a US delegation headed by Agriculture Secretary Bergland reached agreement on the exchange of scientific and technological information and was presented with a memorandum outlining a diversified list of agricultural products that China hoped to acquire from the United States, including food-processing equipment, livestock, feed mills and agricultural chemicals.

In October 1978 the US Secretary for Energy, James Schlesinger, visited Peking for detailed discussions on a broad range of energy questions, underlining the special attention devoted to the fuel and power industries in China's modernization programme. No formal agreements were announced, but the talks produced a list of possible joint projects in such areas as oil (China's oil reserves were estimated at about 100,000 million barrels, or three times the known reserves of the United States) gas, coal, renewable energy and hydroelectric power. Cooperation was also envisaged in high energy and nuclear physics, and although no public proposals were made for the direct transfer of American nuclear technology or equipment, China's decision to purchase two nuclear power plants from France would almost certainly have required American acquiescence since much of the technology involved in the French nuclear contract originated from the United States. While endeavouring to expand all aspects of primary energy production, with the benefit of foreign assistance, China was primarily concerned to develop the coal industry, which provided the basis for her domestic economy, and oil output, most of which was earmarked for export to help pay for the huge capital import programme now gathering momentum. Significantly, Schlesinger's visit to China was preceded by high-level delegations from five major US petroleum companies, which discussed the possibility of contractual relationships for offshore oil development, most probably in the South China Sea, whereby they would obtain access to Chinese oil as payment or at least part payment for their capital investment.

In the months immediately following normalization several large US corporations reported considerable progress in their dealings with Chinese officials. Apart from oil exploration and production contracts involving Exxon Union oil, Pennzoil, Phillips Petroleum and Standard Oil (Indiana), which were currently under consideration, more than a dozen multi-million dollar contracts had either been signed or were in various stages of negotiation. Bethlehem Steel had signed an agreement to develop an iron ore mine at a cost of $100 million, while United States Steel was engaged in negotiations for coal and steel projects whose total value was expected to range from $1000 million to $5000 million. Intercontinental Hotels, a subsidiary of Hyatt and Pan American Airways, had signed contracts and was negotiating several offers to build and operate hotels in various parts of China totalling 10,000 rooms at an estimated cost of $1300 million. Fluor had signed an $800 million contract to design and manage a large copper mine and concentrator project at an undisclosed location in China. Ford motors was negotiating for the establishment of a major assembly plant; Pullman was discussing contracts for railroad stock and fertilizer plants; Boeing had agreed to sell China three long-range 747 jetliners for nearly $200 million and was expected to supply at least a dozen shorter-range aircraft in the near future at a cost of more than $1000 million; and General Electric, Ford Aerospace and Hughes Aerospace were competing for contracts to supply communications satellites estimated at between $500 million and $2000 million.[23] Even in the very sensitive area of arms transfers, the United States was expected to become more sympathetic to Chinese requests, especially if, as seemed likely, Chinese inquiries were in the first instance directed to communications equipment rather than actual weapons systems. Indicative of the change in attitude was the notification sent by US Secretary of State Cyrus Vance to NATO members in November 1978 informing them that Washington would no longer obstruct their military exports to China. Negotiations for the sale of an American communications satellite to China and its launching by the United States represented another significant step towards the transfer of sophisticated American technology.

But for the United States to participate fully in the burgeoning China trade, several outstanding issues in the bilateral relationship had to be resolved. The long-delayed conclusion of an agreement on the frozen assets and claims issue, achieved during the visit to Peking by the US Treasury Secretary Michael Blumenthal in March 1979, removed one of the most serious impediments in two-way trade. Under the agreement China would pay $80.5 million in Chinese assets. The initial Chinese payment of $30 million would be made on 1 October 1979, at which time the United States would unfreeze all Chinese assets blocked since 1950. The Chinese balance was to be repaid by October 1984 in five annual instalments of $101.1 million each.[24] Two months later, US Commerce Secretary Juanita Kreps and Chinese Foreign Trade Minister Li Qiang initialled a trade agreement that was designed to provide a more stable framework for commercial and financial exchanges, extend reciprocal most favoured nation status and greatly facilitate the granting of official credits to China.[25] Not all difficulties, however, were thereby automatically eliminated. For example, the very considerable gap in the technical standards and specifications acceptable in each country and the restrictions imposed by the United States on China's textile exports were bound to remain a source of frustration.

In the longer term, however, apart from the impact of Japanese and European competition, the principal constraint on the future expansion of Sino–American trade was likely to arise from the domestic obstacles to China's ambitious modernization plans. Even with the accelerated development of natural resources it was by no means certain that China would be able to pay for the industrial imports envisaged by those plans. By the end of 1978 Chinese foreign currency reserves stood at little more than $2000 million. If all projects planned for the following six years were to come to fruition, the cost of Chinese imports over the period would total $120,000 million (less conservative estimates put the figure as high as $200,000 million). According to the US Department of Commerce, China's debt to the West would rise to $20,000 million by 1985. Fears about future indebtedness, coupled with a long-standing aversion to foreign borrowing and increasing concern about the industrial and institutional bottlenecks that became painfully evident by late 1978, convinced Chinese leaders of the need to decelerate the pace of economic modernization. Although Deng Xiaoping, Fang Yi and other Chinese officials confidently reassured US businessmen and members of Congress that the introduction of advanced technology and capital funds from abroad was not in jeopardy, the early months of 1979 witnessed a marked contraction of targets and a rearrangement of economic priorities. Several contracts already signed failed to get the necessary import licensing even though in many cases such approval was overdue. Negotiations that had been making good progress gradually lost momentum; some were postponed and others altogether abandoned. It remained to be seen whether this period of 'readjustment' was merely a temporary pause to be followed by a resurgence of frenetic modernization or whether Chinese economic and political institutions would compel a slower rate of industrialization and prevent the country's headlong integration into the world capitalist economy.

The Sino–Soviet–American Triangle

While the prospect of economic complementarity and a flourishing trade relationship held considerable attraction for both China and the United States, it would be misleading to suggest that it had been the decisive factor sustaining or hastening the process of normalization. As already indicated in Chapter 6 (pp. 147–50, 157–9), throughout the 1970s China's attitude to the United States, indeed her overall foreign policy orientation, was formulated primarily as a response to the perceived threat of Soviet–American collaboration. The various steps taken in the late 1960s and early 1970s to achieve a more stable and less antagonistic relationship with the United States were obviously central to China's revised diplomacy. A second and closely related element in China's initial strategy (also characteristic of the transitional phase) was the attempt to discredit the policy of détente by describing it as a mixture of collusion and rivalry. Détente, far from representing the dominant trend in the evolution of bipolar politics, was portrayed as a subsidiary phenomenon that served the temporary interests of the two superpowers as each struggled for ascendancy over the other. According to the Chinese analysis, the various attempts by the United States and the Soviet Union to introduce a measure of stability and cooperation into their relationship was dictated by their desperate need to moderate domestic political and economic crises and contain the rising tide of opposition to their dominance in world politics. Yet, such collusion and compromise could only be partial, temporary and relative.

In his address to the Sixth Special Session of the UN General Assembly in April 1974, Deng Xiaoping referred to Soviet–American agreements as 'a facade and a deception' calculated to disguise their increasingly fierce rivalry.[26] The continuing escalation of the nuclear and conventional arms race was viewed as unmistakable evidence that Moscow and Washington were intensifying their contention, and that such arms control initiatives as the SALT negotiations were essentially a propaganda exercise that would do little to impose quantitative or qualitative restrictions on the military preparations of either superpower. Similarly, the agreements reached by the European Security Conference were described as a smokescreen 'to deceive and lull the people of all lands into a false sense of security'.[27] They were a mere scrap of paper, which had no binding force on the Soviet Union and could in no way safeguard the security of the European countries. The stipulation about advance notice of military manoeuvres contained in the document entitled 'On confidence building measures and certain aspects of security and disarmament' was considered equally empty of substance, since the announcement of military exercises could do little to prevent the transition of the exercise to a war operation. As for the agreements in the fields of economics, science and technology, they were the result of negotiations in which the Soviet Union, the United States and other western countries had acted at cross purposes and with ulterior motives. Moscow needed economic cooperation with the West in order to overcome its agricultural problems and technological backwardness. By promoting economic relations it could also hope to widen the divisions already existing between the major western countries. On the other hand, the United States and the European Economic Community were bound to take advantage of increased commercial and technological interaction to increase their economic and political penetration of the Soviet Union and Eastern Europe.

Even the outwardly innocuous agreement of November 1975, in which the United States undertook to sell annually to the Soviet Union 6–8 million tons of grain over the next five years, was interpreted as a sign of fierce rivalry between the two superpowers. Having declared the accord to be 'an official proclamation of the complete bankruptcy of Soviet agricultural policy' and 'a concrete manifestation of the grave political and economic crises of Soviet social-imperialism', the Chinese proceeded to argue that the purchase of US grain was also a convenient means of building up a strategic reserve of grain that the Soviet Union might use as part of its war preparations, its 'expansion and aggression abroad and scramble for world domination'.[28] For its part, the United States had found not only a stable foreign market for its surplus grain but a useful lever with which to resist Moscow's expansionist policies.

But by 1975 this seemingly evenhanded critique of détente had been subtly but substantially qualified to suggest that a dramatic increase in Soviet offensive military power, particularly in the European theatre, now constituted the greatest threat to peace. Apart from expanding its armed forces in Central Europe and re-equipping them with new arms, the Soviet Union was also accused of stepping up 'expansionist manoeuvres for the purpose of an outflanking movement' and of 'actively plotting to seize vital strategic points and passages in Northern Europe'.[29] According to the Chinese assessment, the increased Soviet capability of fast shipment of massive armed forces in the Arctic and Baltic areas was complemented by the rapid build-up of the Soviet naval presence in the Mediterranean, which now consisted of a standing fleet of some fifty to sixty vessels. In order to extend the sphere of constant operations of its navy, the Soviet Union, it was claimed, was now engaged in a concerted search for new bases on the southern coast of the Mediterranean and on the Iberian peninsula. As part of its offensive against NATO's 'soft under-belly' Moscow was also staging frequent manoeuvres as a means of applying pressure on 'those Balkan countries which refused [d] to bow to Soviet hegemonic domination'.[30] Equally significant, in the Chinese view, were Soviet attempts to sow discord among southern European countries, notably in Cyprus, by exploiting their domestic and regional conflicts. In the Asian theatre, Moscow's strategy was to create a cordon of military power around the continent from the Mediterranean, to the Red Sea, the Indian Ocean, right up to Vladivostok, 'using Vietnam as its hatchetman, in its central thrust to seize the whole of Indochina and then dominate southeast Asia and South Asia and edge the United States out of Asia'.[31]

Given the nature of Soviet strategic objectives, the commitment to détente in the West was criticized as tantamount to appeasement since it cherished 'the illusion that peace can be maintained through compromise and concessions'.[32] In other words, the basic flaw in the theory and practice of détente was no longer that it concealed a global contest between two superpowers for world supremacy, but that it diverted attention away from the central issue of world politics, namely the Soviet Union's insatiable appetite for expansion and the need to contain that expansion through the application of effective countervailing power. Though Moscow attempted after Mao's exit from the political stage to improve relations with Peking, it was soon made clear, in spite of some slight progress in border negotiations, that the new Chinese leadership would not be any less vehement in its denunciation of Soviet 'expansionist activities'. Indeed, Peking went out of its way to warn the United States of the dangers of isolationism. Far from achieving the hoped for strategic equilibrium between East and West, a policy of appeasement and conciliation would encourage the Soviet Union to fill the vacuum left by the United States and take 'advantage of US weaknesses to make expansionist and infiltrative moves', thus confronting 'other countries, including nations in the Second World, with a more dangerous and horrendous enemy'.[33]

To deal with the Soviet threat it was necessary to establish a new united front comprising the Third World, the Second World but also the United States, for only such a coalition would constitute an effective deterrent to 'Soviet hegemonism'. On the other hand, by joining forces, these countries would be able to expose the vulnerability of Russia's strategic position in the Middle East, Africa and the Indian Ocean. In an interview with foreign journalists in October 1977, Deng Xiaoping argued that, despite its edge in military preparedness, the Soviet Union would be seriously disadvantaged in time of war by the backwardness of its industry and agriculture. He went on to characterize the American policy of selling wheat to Russia as 'feeding her population and building up her reserves' and therefore a form of economic appeasement.[34] During his visit to the United States in January 1979, the Chinese Vice-Premier was even more explicit in his advocacy of practical cooperation between the United States, China, Japan and Western Europe:

> The threat to international peace, security and stability comes from the Soviet Union. So the thing that we can all do is that we should try to hamper whatever they do, undermine whatever they do and frustrate what they try to do in any part of the world.[35]

Peking's obsessive anti-Sovietism and the distorted and exaggerated accounts of the global strategic balance on which it rested were partly motivated by the desire to prevent China's strategic encirclement by the Soviet Union. At the same time, the propaganda campaign against 'hegemonism' afforded China a useful and relatively low-risk device with which to achieve a degree of leverage over the Soviet–American relationship.

But the increasingly close alignment with the United States was also a reflection of China's limited military capabilities. At the nuclear level, the Chinese deterrent remained almost exclusively dependent on dated delivery systems consisting principally of intermediate range bombers and liquid-fuelled, soft-site medium and intermediate range missiles.[36] Although every effort had been made to disperse, camouflage and diversify these delivery systems in order to reduce their vulnerability, their lack of mobility and sophistication and the absence of a nuclear submarine capability indicated the enormous strategic advantage enjoyed by the Soviet Union and China's consequent dependence on the countervailing power of the United States.

While the Sino–American relationship did not entail any formal military arrangements, an implicit understanding seemed to emerge by the mid-1970s whereby the United States would provide a measure of undefined military assistance to China in the event of a Soviet attack. More significantly, the United States appeared increasingly willing after 1972 to exert diplomatic and strategic pressure with a view to deterring such an attack. This quasi-strategic alliance did not, however, imply a complete identity of interests. Whereas the United States, as one of the two superpowers, was committed to a policy of détente as the only way of maintaining the adversary relationship with the Soviet Union below the threshold of nuclear violence, China, as a non-superpower, strategically inferior to the Soviet Union, was much freer to adopt an implacable cold war stance in which détente had little or no place. Moreover, unlike China, American policies towards the Soviet bloc were constrained by the operation of the Atlantic and other western alliance systems, which obliged the United States to take into account the interests and perceptions of its allies, the vast majority of whom strongly opposed a return to the tensions and hostility of the cold war period. In any case, a working relationship with Peking would be to Washington's advantage only in the context of a Soviet–American *modus vivendi*. Thus, for example, while taking note of Chinese warnings, the Carter administration could not allow the successful completion of its negotiations with the Soviet Union for a SALT II agreement to be jeopardized by Peking's criticisms and its apparent alignment with the more hawkish elements of the US Congress and the military establishment. For a long time to come the Soviet Union would remain the principal focus of American global strategy, and even in the Asia–Pacific region Japan was likely to occupy at least as important a place as China in the minds of US policy planners.

Notwithstanding these limitations, the Sino–American partnership was likely to play a central role in the diplomatic and strategic conduct of both countries. From China's point of view, Soviet–American relations, though not as intensely confrontational as she would ideally like to see, were nevertheless likely to retain their competitive character indefinitely into the future. Despite developing trade links, the Helsinki agreements, the Berlin accords and the SALT II negotiations, détente was unlikely to provide the Soviet Union with sufficient security on its European flank to enable it to concentrate all its energies and resources on the conflict with China. The connection with the capitalist world, and with the United States in particular, was therefore bound to remain a prominent feature of Chinese foreign policy, since it afforded Peking the opportunity to exert at least marginal influence over the evolution of East–West relations. Evidence of the strategic benefit that might accrue to Peking from its opening to the West was provided by the American response to China's invasion of Vietnam in February 1979. The statement issued by President Carter a few days after the Chinese military thrust, indicating that US forces would be used 'if necessary' in the defence of vital American interests,[37] was widely interpreted as a warning to the Soviet Union not to intervene in the war, the net effect of which was to allow Peking a freer hand than might otherwise have been the case.

The United States also stood to gain from its new relationship with China. In a briefing to US businessmen in January 1979, Brzezinski emphasized the 'long-term, historic significance' of normalization, pointed out that China had a population of nearly one billion and the third largest defence budget in the world, and drew attention to the parallel interests of the two countries in establishing conditions of peace and stability in Asia, enabling nations to be 'free of outside dominations'.[38] Though such statements did not amount to an acceptance of China's proposal for an anti-Soviet alliance, the choice of words was remarkably similar to Chinese rhetoric. No doubt the Brzezinski line represented only one facet of American thinking shared mainly by those cold war elements on Capitol Hill and in the Pentagon who viewed the Soviet Union as an aggressive power and China as a useful counterweight to it. The more moderate members of Congress and the State Department were much less inclined to accept the premises or implications of this line of analysis. Significantly, whereas the Secretary of State Cyrus Vance was preoccupied with the Middle East and SALT negotiations, it was left to Brzezinski to speed up the process of normalization with China and take charge of Deng Xiaoping's visit to the United States. In this sense, the China card endowed American diplomacy with much greater flexibility, enabling the United States to speak with two voices and to combine in its dealings with the Soviet Union elements of hostility and conciliation, the relative weights of which could be varied depending on domestic or external circumstances.

But the rapprochement with China fulfilled another and perhaps more important objective, for it facilitated the application of the Nixon doctrine in the aftermath of America's failure in Vietnam. Far from signifying a policy of withdrawal from Asian rimlands, the doctrine involved a redefinition of the boundaries of the American empire and less risky or conspicuous forms of engagement in the defence of American strategic and economic interests. The role ascribed to China by the new American thinking was perhaps most concisely expressed by Brzezinski:

> The United States has great economic and security interests around the rim of Asia: in Japan, South Korea, all the Pacific islands down to the Philippines and in Southwest Asia as well.
> To protect our interests, we retain a strong military presence in the region, we maintain appropriate weapons sales throughout the region, and we are prepared to act on our interests should the need arise. Few actions will contribute more to the security and stability of our important positions around the rim of Asia, however, than a constructive involvement with China. As we improve our relations with Peking, China will also wish to keep us involved in the region and not, as in the past, seek to drive us away.
> For the first time in decades we can enjoy simultaneously good relations with both China and Japan. It is difficult to overstress the importance of this fact. Normalisation consolidates a favorable balance in the Far East and enhances the security of our friends.[39]

In other words, the relationship with China was designed to stabilize the Asia–Pacific region in which the United States retained major trade and investment interests. Given the population, natural resources and strategic importance of the Pacific basin it is hardly surprising that both the United States and Japan should have become increasingly dependent on its orderly development and political and economic integration. But just as the military alliance with Japan contributed to America's ability to support her other strategic interests and commitments in the Pacific with reduced risk and greater efficiency (the supposed identity of American and Japanese interests was somewhat shattered by the worldwide economic recession and the intensification of trade rivalries), so the diplomatic and economic partnership with China was expected to reduce the probability of a Sino–American conflict and confront the Soviet Union with the threat of a two-front war in Asia and Europe. At the same time, Washington had reason to believe that closer links with Peking would result in increased Chinese support for the American military presence in Asia and reduced Chinese pressure on anti-communist, pro-American regimes in the region. For the United States, the trans-Pacific coalition with China and Japan had become the cornerstone of its Asian strategy not simply because china offered a lucrative market for American and Japanese goods at a time of serious contraction in the world market economy, but rather because both Chinese and Japanese participation was now seen as crucial to the success of the new economic and political order it was seeking to create in the Pacific basin.

There can be little doubt that the Sino–Soviet conflict contributed enormously to the Sino–American rapprochement, and that both Peking and Washington saw the shift from confrontation to partnership as providing them with increased leverage in their relations with Moscow. On the other hand, it would be unwise to assume too readily that the Sino–Soviet dispute was so fundamentally irreconcilable as to preclude any form of meaningful contact between the two countries. A slight easing of tensions was discernible half-way through 1977 as a result of the reconvening of the Sino–Soviet border water navigation negotiations. At the end of August, China named a new ambassador to Moscow, a post that had remained vacant for eighteen months, and on 6 October several minor agreements were reached at the twentieth routine session of the border talks. Though Peking subsequently decided not to renew the Sino–Soviet Treaty of Friendship, Alliance and Mutual Assistance due to expire in April 1980, in communicating its decision to Moscow it reaffirmed its readiness to maintain normal state relations on the basis of the five principles of peaceful coexistence and proposed negotiations 'for the solution of outstanding issues and the improvement of relations between the two countries'.[40]

Following a Soviet request for greater clarification of her proposal, China suggested in May 1979 a wide-ranging negotiating framework separate from the border talks and whose object would be to formulate general principles to govern their bilateral relationship, to eliminate obstacles to normalization, and to promote commercial, scientific, technological and cultural exchanges on the basis of equality and mutual benefit.[41] The most noteworthy aspect of the proposal was that for the first time since 1969 China had not set any prior conditions to the opening of talks. There was no longer any demand for the withdrawal of Soviet troops from Mongolia – which Peking had insisted on as recently as the spring of 1978 – or even for Soviet disengagement from the disputed areas along the border. The stipulation that had featured in all previous Chinese pronouncements on the issue had been described by Moscow as utterly unacceptable. The Chinese note thus confirmed the more conciliatory approach suggested by several other minor yet significant gestures.

On 5 May 1979 the *People's Daily* published a remarkable article that conceded that China had no monopoly on authentic socialism and went on to argue:

> We should sum up our practice over the last 30 years since the founding of the People's Republic in real earnest and modestly learn from the experience of other socialist countries so as to closely integrate the universal truth of Marxism–Leninism with the concrete practice of socialist construction in China.[42]

Such views were far removed from the bitter denunciations levelled only recently against Soviet revisionism. Additional evidence of the improving diplomatic climate was the rehabilitation of Wang Jiaxiang and Liu Xiao, two former Chinese ambassadors to the Soviet Union who presumably favoured the reactivation of the Sino–Soviet relationship. Wang Jiaxiang's political re-emergence was especially instructive not only because he had been China's first ambassador to Moscow after October 1949 and therefore closely associated with the preparation of the 1950 alliance treaty, but because the Chinese media now portrayed him as a victim of Lin Biao and the 'gang of four', whereas he had been accused during the Cultural Revolution of having spoken in favour of an arrangement with revisionism. Such rewriting of history was open to several interpretations, but a perfectly legitimate conclusion to be drawn from this and other related developments is that ideological opposition to revisionism was no longer high on Peking's list of political priorities. The announcement in June 1979 that the Soviet Union had agreed to enter into high-level negotiations with China in July or August provided further indication that both communist states were ready to explore the possibility of renewed dialogue.

The increasingly pragmatic character of Chinese politics, the loss of revolutionary zeal and the accompanying decline in the ideological battles of the past, together with the preoccupation with economic modernization, could not but have a profound impact on China's relations with the two superpowers. Although strategic considerations and the continuing rivalry for spheres of influence might still dictate a high level of Chinese hostility and suspicion towards the Soviet Union, the ideological factor of the dispute had largely subsided, thereby considerably improving the prospects for normalization. In any case, the possibility of a costly and perhaps uncontrollable military confrontation had also exerted a moderating influence on Peking and encouraged both sides to retreat from the brink. But quite apart from these factors, both the Chinese and Soviet governments stood to gain from more flexible policies, which would enable them to emphasize either the antagonistic or the cooperative aspects of their relationship depending on current circumstances. From China's point of view, the relaxation of tensions with the Soviet Union might produce positive spin-offs, either in regional terms, for example by reducing Vietnam's freedom of action, or by way of increased economic cooperation. More importantly, both the Chinese and Russians had come to realize that so long as their relationship remained one of undiluted enmity, the United States would continue to hold a unique advantage in the great power triangle. Despite their many differences, China and the Soviet Union might be able to achieve a sufficient measure of agreement to compel the United States to make concessions that might not otherwise be feasible. An opening to Moscow could well provide Peking with additional leverage in its relations with Washington, whether on bilateral issues such as Taiwan and trade or on more general questions pertaining to the global strategic balance. In the foreseeable future the triangular relationship would remain highly fluid with none of the three powers likely to promote friendship with one purely at the expense of the other. While the Sino–American connection gave every indication of prospering, it was by no means impossible that Sino–Soviet relations might also emerge from the frozen state in which they had languished for nearly two decades.

CHAPTER 9

Sino–Japanese Relations

Although the Sino–American rapprochement had confirmed the importance of China's role in the new triangular political relationship linking her with the two superpowers, she was still by far the weakest member of the triangle. Neither her deterrent capability nor her industrial might could match the military and economic muscle of the two giants. By the early 1970s most Asian countries had normalized their relations with Peking and recognized China's enhanced status in world affairs. But many had yet to fashion a stable and cooperative relationship with their powerful neighbour, while some still harboured the fears and suspicions of the past. Apart from being flanked on the west and north by a hostile superpower, China had also to contend in the east with a sophisticated and expanding industrial state, Japan.

The Chinese were obviously anxious to take advantage of the gradual breakdown of international bipolarity in order to reduce or at least restrict Soviet and American dominance in the Asia–Pacific region. However, as we have already seen in Chapter 6, after the Cultural Revolution the Soviet Union gradually displaced the United States as the primary target of Chinese hostility. The Sino–Soviet conflict was, in fact, most acute in Asia for it was here that China felt most directly threatened by the perceived Soviet attempt at encirclement, strikingly symbolized by the proposed establishment of a Moscow-inspired system of collective security. It was precisely in order to offset Soviet, and to a much lesser extent American, initiatives inimical to her interests that China favoured the emergence of multipolarity and the rise of new focal points of international diplomacy. This objective assumed particular significance in relations with Japan where Peking faced the prospect of increased Soviet penetration. In an effort to counter Soviet strategy, Chinese foreign policy sought to capitalize on the growing number of opportunities for bilateral cooperation and consultation and to apply a whole range of balance of power techniques made possible by the progressive diffusion of power and influence in international politics.

The Prelude to Normalization

Before analysing in any detail the factors contributing to the Sino–Japanese détente and its implications for Sino–American and Sino–Soviet relations, it may be instructive to place recent developments in their historical context. For more than 2000 years China and Japan have had a history of close though intermittent contacts based on cultural affinity and· geographical proximity. Apart from sending embassies to some of the dynasties in China, Japan adopted or adapted Chinese learning and methods of administration while at the same time rejecting what seemed incompatible with its own social and political traditions. Buddhism and to a lesser extent Confusianism were to prove important vehicles for Chinese civilization in Japan. For all their many differences, the Chinese and Japanese nations can be said to have enjoyed a prolonged period of artistic and cultural interaction as well as a continuing sense of Asian identity in relation to the West. In the modern period these ties were somewhat loosened by the Sino–Japanese struggle for ascendancy in Korea, but above all by Japan's withdrawal from the Confucian tributary system and its acceptance of the concepts and rules governing the western system of sovereign states. The Sino–Japanese war of 1894–95, China's internal disunity during the greater part of the nineteenth and first half of the twentieth centuries and Japan's territorial and economic expansionism tended to highlight the elements of conflict and discord in Sino–Japanese relations. Yet despite the striking divergence of their economic and political development and the ideological differences separating communist China from capitalist Japan, the cultural bonds between the two countries have not lost their vitality. Indeed they have been reinforced by the increasing complementarity of their respective economies. Whereas China with a vast population and a relatively backward economy wants to gain access to foreign sources of advanced technology, Japan, which is now a highly sophisticated industrial society, feels compelled by the very structure of its economy to expand its trade in order to satisfy the growing demand for raw materials and secure export outlets for its vast manufacturing industries.

On coming to power in 1949 the Chinese Communist leadership had to reconcile itself to an extensive and prolonged American presence in Japan as the unavoidable legacy of the Second World War. Nevertheless, the Chinese government stressed on more than one occasion its willingness to develop trade links with Japan and to discount the question of war reparations. As a further indication of its goodwill, and in spite of the peace treaty concluded by the Japanese with the Chiang Kai-shek regime in Taiwan, Peking agreed to the repatriation of thousands of Japanese citizens and to the release of a considerable number of Japanese war criminals held in China. At the same time, one of the main obejctives of Chinese diplomacy was to drive a wedge between Tokyo and Washington. For in the Chinese view, unless the Japanese terminated their alignment with the United States there was little likelihood that they would abrogate their treaty with Taiwan. A neutral Japan was regarded as a precondition for the normalization of relations between the two countries. In response to the direct threat posed by American military bases in Japan, Okinawa and Taiwan, and the far-reaching implications of collusion between American imperialism and Japanese capitalism, Peking attempted to sow discord between Japan and the United States and to encourage those forces within Japanese politics favouring a policy of ideological and military neutrality.

During that initial phase, China's position was premised on three specific principles:

(1) Japan would need to eschew policies inimical to Chinese interests;
(2) Japan would have to reject unequivocally the two Chinas' fiction;
(3) Japan should not hamper attempts to normalize Sino–Japanese relations.

The fact that Tokyo, under pressure from the United States, was unwilling to comply with these conditions helps to explain the lack of progress in political relations between the two countries during the 1950s and 1960s. The diplomatic stalemate did not, however, prevent China from concluding a series of commercial agreements with Japan, using private organizations as inter-mediaries. Moreover, as part of a major programme of cultural exchanges, Chinese theatre companies entertained enthusiastic Japanese audiences, while Japanese commercial, professional and artistic delegations were warmly received in China.

The advent of the Ikeda government, after the political crisis surrounding the signing of the security treaty with the United States in January 1960, was regarded by some as foreshadowing a more favourable Japanese attitude towards China. However, far from resolving the traditional ambiguity in Japan's China policy, the new Prime Minister considerably aggravated relations with Peking by engaging in negotiations with the South Koreans. The Chinese reaction was prompt and vehement. Tokyo was accused of colluding with Washington and Seoul and of promoting a military coalition whose aim was the domination of the Northeast Asian region. It was not until 1963 that signs of a thaw began to appear. An industrial Japanese exhibition held in Peking and Shanghai provided the opportunity for thousands of Japanese businessmen to visit China. Following a fishing agreement and several important trade contracts, Japan agreed to grant China long-term credits to finance the purchase of a rayon plant. The Japanese Foreign Minister declared that his government would have no part in any policy designed to isolate China. In 1964, agreement was reached on the reciprocal establishment of unofficial trade legations in China and Japan; a regular cargo service was inaugurated between Osaka and Shanghai; and commercial and cultural contracts continued to expand.

In spite of the unmistakable growth in the range and depth of relations between the two countries, particularly at the economic level, political considerations were still impeding a diplomatic rapprochement as well as cooperation in other areas. Nowhere was this more evident than in the field of trade. After 1963, Sino–Japanese commercial relations were conducted through the dual channels of 'friendly trade' and 'memorandum trade', each governed by different political and economic objectives. The relative importance of these two forms of commercial intercourse fluctuated in accordance with the changing priorities of Chinese diplomacy. Peking's obvious intention was to use trade as a lever with which to influence Japanese politics and thereby extract concessions from the Japanese government in respect of its China policy. Friendship trade was initiated in 1960 when, on the recommendation of the Japan–China Trade Promotion Council, Peking agreed to trade with a few 'friendly' Japanese companies that had promised to adhere to China's three political principles and to oppose the US–Japan Security Treaty.

Notwithstanding the benefits of 'friendship trade', it soon became evident that most of the friendly companies were small and economically weak. They could satisfy neither China's demands for long-term credits, industrial machinery and fertilizers nor her expectations of political leverage. Accordingly, in an effort to enhance the effectiveness of Sino–Japanese trade, Zhou Enlai enlisted in 1962 the support of Matsumura Kenzo, a senior Diet member of the ruling Liberal–Democratic Party (LDP), in initiating memorandum trade between the two countries as a prelude to the eventual normalization of economic and diplomatic relations. The agreement signed in September 1962 covered the period 1963–67 and provided for an average two-way trade of about $100 million per year, the exchange of trade liaison personnel between Peking and Tokyo, and a method of deferred payment and medium-term credit for China's purchases of Japanese industrial plants. Unlike friendship trade, it was envisaged that commercial transactions covered by the memorandum would be negotiated collectively each year between the Chinese government and a group of Japanese companies and industries. Memorandum trade thus acquired semi-official status, especially as a result of the endorsement it received from a section of the LDP leadership and the fact that it was being partially financed by government-approved credit arrangements.

Although Sino–Japanese trade increased dramatically during the period 1963–67 from $47.5 million to $557.7 million and gave rise to a vastly expanded exchange of economic delegations, technical experts and industrial exhibitions between the two countries, serious political complications developed in relation to the Taiwan question. In response to pressures from the Taiwanese government, Tokyo arranged in May 1964 for the former prime minister, Yoshida Shigeru, to send a 'private letter' to Taibei giving assurances that the Export–Import Bank would no longer be used to finance Japanese industrial sales to China. Peking decided therefore to de-emphasize memorandum trade in favour of friendship trade whose value in fact rose from $24 million in 1963 to $266 million in 1968. During this period memorandum trade as a proportion of total Sino–Japanese commercial transactions fell from 46.7 per cent to 20.4 per cent.[1] This form of controlled retaliation and the consequent uncertainty about the future of trade relations between the two countries – several warnings were sounded by Japanese politicians and businessmen who were concerned that memorandum trade might be totally suspended after 1968 – enabled China to influence the factional struggle within the ruling Liberal Democratic Party (LDP). Indeed, trade had become one of the main weapons in China's well-orchestrated campaign to modify the direction of Japanese foreign policy.

In retrospect, it seems clear that the end of the Ikeda administration in November 1964 and its replacement by the Sato administration produced a steady decline in diplomatic relations. On 25 November 1964, the Chinese press published a strong attack on the new Japanese Prime Minister condemning him for his anti-China policies, and particularly for his refusal to permit a Chinese delegation to attend the Ninth General Congress of the Japan Communist Party, his criticism of China's nuclear testing, his opposition to Chinese representation at the United Nations and his close ties with the Nationalist regime in Taiwan.[2] Another attack was launched on 12 February 1965 when the Japanese government was critized for its refusal to allow Export–Import Bank credits for plant exports to China.[3] Peking's subsequent cancellation of orders for Japanese industrial equipment. Tokyo's moves to restore ties with South Korea, and the beginning of formal negotiations for the extension of credits to Taiwan, all contributed to the deterioration in Sino–Japanese relations.

In December 1968 Japan was accused of acting as 'a bridgehead for aggression in Asia', of collaborating with 'US imperialism's massacre of the Vietnamese people' and of seeking to revive 'the Greater East Asia Co-Prosperity Sphere'.[4] The alleged revival of Japanese militarism, which now became a dominant theme in Chinese propaganda, served to reinforce earlier accusations of expansionism, and especially the charge that Japanese capitalist interests were scheming to take control of Taiwan through the subterfuge of the two-Chinas policy. Sato's visit to Taiwan in September 1967 and the Sato–Nixon joint statement of November 1969 announcing the return of the Ryukyu Islands to Japanese administration merely confirmed Chinese suspicions. What Peking found particularly offensive was not only the retention of American military bases on the islands but Japan's redefinition of its security perimeter to include both Taiwan and South Korea.[5] The Nixon–Sato communiqué was interpreted as further evidence of collusion between Japanese militarism and United States imperialism. The security implications of Japan's new self-proclaimed role as assistant policeman of the Far East were completely unacceptable to the Chinese.[6] But for all China's protestations, there seemed little chance that the Sato government would depart from the general direction that Japanese foreign policy had followed since the conclusion of the peace treaty with Taiwan. After all, the triangular contest between Peking, Taibei and Tokyo was essentially a product of the Asian cold war or, to be more precise, of the American policy of containment. Japan was unlikely to modify its two-Chinas policy so long as the United States remained wedded to the defence of Taiwan.

Moreover, while the Japan–Taiwan connection may have originally been designed to serve as a link in the American chain of diplomatic and military containment of an allegedly expansionist China, Taiwan soon assumed special significance for Japanese economic and military interests.[7] In 1965 Japan extended to Taiwan a long-term low-interest credit valued at $150 million, and in 1970 promised to make available on a project by project basis, credits totalling some $250 million. By 1971 two-way trade between the two countries had exceeded $1000 million, while the Japanese export surplus was estimated at $500 million. Moreover, Japanese investments in Taiwan, which amounted to $68 million or 19 per cent of the total foreign investment in the island, involved some 350 firms and 316 technical cooperation projects with local enterprises. When one also takes into account the interests of the 3000 Japanese residents in Taiwan and the question of war indemnities,[8] which might be raised by the conclusion of a new peace treaty with the People's Republic, it is not difficult to understand Tokyo's reluctance to jeopardize the Japan–Taiwan relationship. Several factors, then, had tended to produce the deteriorating climate between Tokyo and Peking. Japan's decision to include South Korea and Taiwan within its security perimeter, the automatic extension of the US–Japan security treaty in June 1970, the rapid expansion of Japan's defence expenditure, the accelerating Japanese economic penetration of South Korea, Taiwan and Southeast Asia, were all contributing elements in China's mounting fear of the resurgence of Japanese expansionism.[9] Even the return of Okinawa to Japan was interpreted by the Chinese government as promoting the process of remilitarization.[10]

Gradually, however, the preoccupation with Japan–US relations and the American role in Japanese rearmament was complemented by the fear of Soviet–Japanese collaboration. China's apprehensions were in large measure based on her perception of the Sino–Soviet border conflict. In Peking's view, the massive Soviet military build-up along the Chinese border had been made possible by the redeployment of Soviet forces normally stationed on the Pacific coast. Such a major strategic readjustment, it was argued, was unlikely to have occurred without a corresponding thaw in relations between Moscow and Tokyo. Similarly, the Soviet policy of containment, as reflected in the call for an Asian collective security system and the expansion of the Soviet economic presence in Southeast Asia, might in the foreseeable future be considerably facilitated by Japan's acquiescence, if not active cooperation. The successive Soviet–Japanese negotiations for the joint economic development of Siberian resources served to confirm Chinese fears and suspicions, and were no doubt partly responsible for Peking's decision to sustain its anti-Japanese campaign until early 1972, some twelve months after the first overt steps had been taken towards détente with the United States.

In spite of this daunting array of obstacles to improved Sino–Japanese relations, the fact remains that Chinese attitudes and perceptions were far from static. Peking could hardly ignore the possibility that a policy of frozen hostility towards Japan might well drive it towards precisely the kind of diplomatic and military initiatives deemed prejudicial to Chinese interests. A campaign of denunciation against the revival of Japanese militarism might well promote rather than hinder higher levels of Japanese defence spending and the acquisition of nuclear weapons. Moreover, a Chinese strategy designed to highlight the alleged existence of Japanese–American collusion might hasten the reduction of the United States military presence in the Asian rimlands at a time when such a presence was still needed to counter the perceived Soviet threat. If Chinese diplomacy was to prevent an alliance between Japan and any of China's actual or potential enemies, if, for example, it was to impede a Soviet–Japanese rapprochement or place effective restraints on relations between Japan and Taiwan, then a more subtle, more complex and less antagonistic policy might prove more effective.

By the early 1970s, the Maoist leadership was ready to consider a much wider range of options than had previously been canvassed. Even if one of China's long-term objectives was to drive a wedge between Japan and the United States, such an outcome might be better obtained by emphasizing the common interests shared by Tokyo and Peking rather than their differences. China could also try to keep the Soviet Union at a distance by offering Japan more attractive economic arrangements. By trading Chinese raw materials for Japanese producer goods and guaranteeing to supply oil in sufficient quantities to satisfy a significant proportion of Japan's energy needs, China could perhaps successfully outbid the Soviet Union. Even on those issues where it might be necessary to oppose Japan directly, for example in such areas as rearmament or economic and military relations with Taiwan and South Korea, it might be preferable to proceed on the basis of 'people-to-people' rather than state-to-state diplomacy. By playing an active role in Japanese internal politics, by favouring those domestic groupings opposed to government policy, by encouraging exchange visits with their representatives, China might be able to bring about a change in the Japanese administration favourable to her interests.

Evidence of China's capacity to influence Japan's domestic political process was demonstrated by the willingness of several former Japanese cabinet ministers to join in Chinese denunciations of Tokyo's 'militarist' and 'expansionist' policies. The relative strength of China's bargaining position was also reflected in Zhou Enlai's enunciation in April 1970 of the four principles that were to guide China's future trade with Japan. China, it was stated, would not carry out any transactions with Japanese firms that assisted Korea or Taiwan, had big investments in these two countries, produced weapons for use in the Vietnam war or were involved in joint American–Japanese commercial operations. Although these conditions were not strictly enforced, the fact that all of Japan's major steel firms, banking institutions, shipping lines and industrial conglomerates had accepted them in principle was indicative of the powerful political movement that had arisen in support of radical change in Japan's long-standing China policy.

In the meantime, pro-Peking sentiment within the Liberal Democratic Party itself had steadily increased, and by the end of 1970 a coalition of all major .

political parties was formed under the name of the League of Dietmen for the Promotion of the Normalization of Japan–China Relations. The organization, headed by Fujiyama Aiichiro, was composed of 379 Dietmen including well over 40 per cent of the LDP parliamentary membership. Political opposition to Sato's policy intensified as did the pressure for immediate Japanese recognition of the People's Republic.[11] In July 1971 a Komeito (Clean Government Party) delegation visiting Peking issued a joint statement with the China–Japan Friendship Association, in which five principles were listed as preconditions for the normalization of Sino–Japanese relations. The five Chinese demands, supported by the Komeito, basically an anti-communist party and, at that time, the second largest opposition party in Japan, were as follows:

(1) there is only one China, and the government of the People's Republic represents the whole of China;

(2) Taiwan is a province and an inalienable part of China;

(3) the Japan–Taiwan treaty is illegal and must be abrogated;

(4) the United States must withdraw all its armed forces from Taiwan and the Taiwan Straits area;

(5) the legitimate rights of the People's Republic must be recognized in all United Nations organizations and the Nationalist representatives expelled.

In due course, partly as a result of Peking's entry into the United Nations and the accelerating Sino–American détente, the fourth and fifth principles disappeared from the joint statements issued by the various Japanese delegations visiting China. However, by late 1971 the dissenting faction within the LDP and all the opposition parties, including the left-wing of the Japan Communist Party, were united in their acceptance of the first three principles.[12]

By this time, even the 'mainstream' faction of the LDP was beginning to re-examine the general direction of Japanese foreign policy. A succession of heavy-handed and unilateral moves by the Nixon administration had seriously impaired the Japanese–American relationship. The sudden announcement in July 1971 of the forthcoming Nixon visit to China had been made without any prior consultation with the Japanese government. Nor did the White House subsequently attempt to inform Japanese leaders of American intentions and expectations. Following the July 'shock', the Sato administration was again confronted a few weeks later with a *fait accompli* when the United States announced a series of protectionist measures, including a 10 per cent surcharge on all dutiable imports covered by quotas. This commercial ultimatum, which was reinforced by the decision to suspend the gold convertibility of the dollar, was obviously designed to force a revaluation of all other major currencies, including the yen, and thereby reduce the competiveness of America'a major rivals within the international trading system.

Something of the new friction in relations between Tokyo and Washington was conveyed by Sato himself, following his inconclusive meeting with President Nixon in January 1972.[13] Against this background many influential Japanese voices began to question the value of the security treaty with the

United States. Once it had become evident, as a result of the Nixon 'journey for peace', that Washington no longer regarded China as an aggressive nation – the Shanghai communiqué conceded the principle that Taiwan was part of China and declared the ultimate objective of the United States to be the withdrawal of all its forces and military installations from Taiwan – serious doubts arose as to whether Japan was anything more than a logistic link in the chain of America's residual military obligations in East Asia. While these doubts may have been somewhat premature, they nevertheless helped to highlight the growing divergence of interests between the two allies. That Japan could no longer afford to have its foreign policy determined by directives from Washington was made painfully obvious by the humiliating defeat incurred by the Sato government at the United Nations when it agreed to co-sponsor the American-inspired resolution designed to prevent Taiwan's expulsion.

Just as new forces were propelling Tokyo and Peking towards a diplomatic détente, so old obstacles were gradually declining in importance. By the end of 1971 the Taiwan question, which had been regarded as an insuperable problem, was now viewed in a different light. Taiwan's role in the Japanese economy proved to be an issue that had been vastly overstated. After all, exports represented only 10 per cent of Japan's annual Gross National Product and Taiwan accounted for less than 4 per cent of those exports. While individual Japanese firms might suffer considerable losses should Taibei decide on economic retaliation in response to the latter's recognition of Peking, the fact remained that such retaliatory measures were far more likely to disrupt the Taiwanese than the Japanese economy. In any case, Japan had been trading simultaneously with both China and Taiwan since 1950. There was no reason to believe that China would demand the termination of Japan's lucrative trade with Taiwan as a precondition for the establishment of diplomatic relations. The Chinese had already, for political reasons, turned a blind eye to the failure of several large Japanese companies to observe the four conditions laid down by Zhou Enlai in April 1970 as guidelines for future Sino–Japanese trade relations (see p. 202). As for the question of war indemnities, Chinese leaders had made it known through several semi-official channels that they would waive any claim against Japan for war reparations.

In the area of Sino–Japanese trade the President of the Nippon Steel Corporation was led to understand by the Chinese that they would be favourably disposed to receiving export credit facilities provided that the terms offered were comparable to those on the international market. Peking also indicated its readiness to allow Japanese participation in oil exploration in China, to export crude oil to Japan, and to send specialist missions to Japan to discuss trade prospects in relation to steel, heavy electrical goods, oil and agricultural products.[14] These concessions on China's part were reciprocated by several Japanese overtures. In July 1972 Japanese Foreign Minister Ohira made it known that the diplomatic recognition of Peking would mean the automatic abrogation of the peace treaty with Taiwan.[15] In the same month, the

Japanese government reversed the policy implicit in the eight-year old 'Yoshida Letter' and approved the use of state funds to finance the export of industrial sales to China. In August agreement was reached between the two countries on the settlement of accounts in both Japanese yen and Chinese yuan. In September the Japanese Ministry of Justice lifted existing restrictions on the re-entry into Japan of those Chinese residents who had visited the mainland. These conciliatory gestures were reinforced by a series of statements and semi-official meetings with Chinese envoys designed to demonstrate Japan's readiness to engage in a diplomatic dialogue with Peking.

But perhaps the single most important factor responsible for the thaw in Sino–Japanese relations was China's drastically altered perception of the US–Japan security treaty. In conversations with several Japanese delegations prior to the summit talks of September 1972, Zhou Enlai stressed China's appreciation of the difficult and delicate adjustment that Japan would have to make to its ties with the United States. However, it was readily conceded that such an adjustment would come about only as a result of hard and protracted negotiations that would need to take account of the emerging Soviet threat. Significantly, after August 1971 Japanese political groups visiting Peking failed to include the usual call for the removal of United States bases from Asia. Three months after the establishment of diplomatic relations, Zhou Enlai gave, in the course of a conversation with a former Japanese minister, Takeo Kimura, the frankest exposition yet of the Chinese perspective:

> The Japan–United States security treaty would become unnecessary in Sino–Japanese relations because it would be unbecoming of an independent nation like Japan. . . . However, since Japan needed United States nuclear protection it would be 'unavoidable' for Japan to keep the pact vis-a-vis the Soviet Union . . .[16]

This far-reaching reappraisal of Japan's continued military alliance with the United States was paralleled by a much less hostile attitude to Japan's proposed military build-up. The fourth five-year defence programme (1972–76), which called for a total expenditure of $15,400 million, was no longer perceived as a threat to Chinese security. Indeed, Zhou went so far as to argue that an increase in Japanese defence capability, provided that it did not 'mark the beginning of Japanese militarism', might be a legitimate exercise in self-defence for 'there ha[d] emerged a new problem over the Asian horizon—the shadow of the Soviet Union'.[17]

The marked change in Chinese perceptions was no doubt brought about to some extent by increased Chinese anxiety over the confrontation with the Soviet Union. American military bases around China's periphery may have been originally aimed at Peking, but in the 1970s they might serve to enhance China's security by acting as a deterrent to a Soviet thrust against Chinese territory. The temporary retention of American aerial and naval power in Asia might offer China the necessary protection until such time as she had developed her own nuclear second-strike capability. Peking's willingness to improve relations with Japan was also inspired by its appreciation of the decline of

American power. A residual American presence was now acceptable precisely because it no longer formed part of a containment policy against China. Such a presence was indeed welcome in so far as it reduced the probability of Japan joining a Soviet-dominated security system or acquiring an independent nuclear capability. The Japanese alliance with the United States could also be particularly useful in neutralizing or at least mitigating the impact of Soviet–Japanese collaboration in the development of Siberian oil and natural gas resources.

The Emerging Pattern of Détente

The new phase of cooperation between Tokyo and Peking was inaugurated by Tanaka's visit to China in September 1972, during which he formally subscribed to the three principles enunciated by the People's Republic, that is, recognition of Peking as the sole legal government of China, acknowledgement that Taiwan was part of China, and rejection of the 1952 peace treaty between Tokyo and Taibei. However, an element of ambivalence remained in Japan's position on the status of Taiwan. Article 3 of the joint Sino–Japanese statement issued on 29 September at the end of the Tanaka visit was expressed in the following terms:

> The Government of the People's Republic of China reaffirms that Taiwan is an inalienable part of the territory of the People's Republic of China. The Government of Japan fully understands and respects this stand of the Government of China and adheres to its stand of complying with Article 8 of the Potsdam Proclamation.[18]

It has been argued that 'understanding and respect' for China's stand was not equivalent to complete acceptance of the Chinese claim.[19] Nor was the reference to Article 8 of the Potsdam Proclamation devoid of legal ambiguity. According to Kenzo Yoshida, a senior officer of the Japanese Foreign Ministry, Japan, by agreeing to comply with Article 8 of the Potsdam Proclamation, which was itself a reaffirmation of the 1943 Cairo Declaration, was simply restating its former acceptance, under the San Francisco Peace Treaty, of the political reversion of Taiwan to China. On the other hand, neither the People's Republic nor the Republic of China was a signatory of the San Francisco Peace Treaty. In any case, Peking had since 1952 consistently denounced both the San Francisco treaty and Japan's peace treaty with Taiwan as 'illegal and void'. Such legal uncertainties about the status of Taiwan could not, in fact, be finally removed until China and Japan had concluded a new peace treaty, as provided under Article 8 of the Zhou–Tanaka statement.

Pending the conclusion of such a treaty, it was also difficult to determine whether the state of war between the two countries had technically come to an end. Although the preamble to the statement specifically referred to 'the termination of the state of war and the normalization of relations between

China and Japan' as expressing the 'wishes of the two peoples', it was not made clear whether the statement itself should be taken as having formalized the ending of the state of war, or whether such formalization would have to await the signing of a peace treaty. Article 1 of the joint statement, it is true, explicitly stated that 'the abnormal state of affairs which has hitherto existed between the People's Republic of China and Japan is declared terminated on the date of publication of this statement'. But the very use of the term 'abnormal state of affairs' implied that it had not been possible to make a substantive statement about the 'state of war'. On the other hand, the whole purpose of the Tanaka visit and the joint statement was not to resolve complex legal problems but to give concrete political expression to the desire for a more cooperative relationship between the two countries. Apart from China's renunciation of war indemnities and the mutual commitment not to use force or threat of force in the settlement of disputes, the statement also provided for a whole range of negotiations aimed at the conclusion of a treaty of peace and friendship and several other agreements on matters of trade, fishing, navigation and aviation. Equally significant, although not mentioned directly in the statement, was Foreign Minister Ohira's declaration:

> The Japanese Government holds that as a result of the normalization of Japan–China relations, the Japan–China [i.e. Japan–Taiwan] treaty has lost the meaning of its existence and is declared to be terminated.[20]

The political readjustments resulting from the Zhou–Tanaka talks were the first hesitant attempts on the part of China and Japan to adapt their relationship to the changing international equilibrium.

After the normalization of relations, Sino–Japanese trade continued to expand. In addition to long-term iron and steel import contracts, China began to take advantage of Export–Import Bank credits to purchase complete sets of industrial plant and related technology. By 1974, two-way trade had risen to $3300 million after reaching $2010 million in 1973, which was nearly double the volume for the previous year. Equally dramatic was the increase in Japan's trade surplus, which rose from $72 million in 1973 to $679 million in 1974. Within two years of the joint statement of September 1972, the two governments had concluded an undersea cable accord, a memorandum for the increase of resident news correspondents in each country, a three-year official trade agreement providing for most favoured nation treatment with respect to tariffs and customs clearance, as well as an aviation agreement. A fishery agreement was announced in August 1975.[21]

In spite of the very considerable progress in the interchange of visits and goods between the two countries recorded during this relatively short period, several difficulties continued to impede the full development of political and economic relations. First, there remained the perennial dispute about the status of Taiwan despite Japan's severance of formal diplomatic ties with the Chiang Kai-shek regime. In the period 1965–73, Japan's trade with Taiwan had amounted to $8321 million, resulting in a favourable balance for the former of approximately $3173 million. Moreover, it was estimated that, by the end of 1973, Japan had a total investment of $153 million in Taiwanese industry, in addition to government and private loans amounting to some $330 million.[22] In 1973, Taiwan was, in effect, Japan's third biggest purchaser and the fourth largest recipient of Japanese investment in Asia. Peking was obviously disturbed by the magnitude of these conomic ties for their net effect was to reinforce the obstacles hindering a settlement of the Taiwan question. In a report released in November 1973 and clearly directed against Taiwan's main trading partners (Japan and the United States), the Chinese accused Taibei of selling out national interests to foreign monopoly capital.[23] By making Taiwan an appendage of foreign economic and military interests, the Japanese were, in Peking's view, assisting the Nationalists to erect new barriers against eventual reunification.

An even more divisive issue looming on the horizon was the prospect of increased Soviet–Japanese economic collaboration. Following the resumption of diplomatic relations in 1956, bilateral trade developed at a modest pace. By 1970, Japan had become the Soviet Union's main capitalist trading partner, the total volume of their trade amounting to $653 million. In the ensuing four years, the value of their transactions reached $873 million in 1971, $1196 million in 1972, $1564 million in 1973 and $2511 million in 1974. This seemingly large increase was not, however, an accurate indication of the real growth in the volume of trade for it concealed the very substantial price rises that occurred between 1970 and 1974. In effect, the average index of Japanese import prices doubled during this period. As a percentage of Japan's total trade, Soviet–Japanese trade had remained more or less constant at just over 2 per cent. Although Japan's trade with the Soviet Union had steadily expanded during the 1970s, the increase was far from dramatic and less than expected.

The planned growth in trade was, in reality, dependent on the successful conclusion of negotiations on a variety of investment projects in Siberia, in which it was envisaged that Japan would provide the necessary amounts of capital in return for assured access to Siberian reserves, namely coal, low-sulphur petroleum and liquefied natural gas. The most significant of these proposals, in both economic and strategic terms, was the Tyumen oil project, which called for the building of a pipeline and a parallel highway from Nakhodka to Irkutsk, connecting the already existing pipelines from the latter point to Tyumen. In addition, the project also involved the construction of a refinery at Nakhodka, from which it was originally expected that Japan would receive an annual delivery of 40 million tons of refined oil for a period of twenty years. Other projects encompassed by the Siberian programme included: a $3000 million project for the production of liquefied natural gas, which would supply Japan with 10,000 million cubic metres annually; a coking-coal scheme for which the Soviet Union requested $585 million in exchange for the supply of 500 million tons of coal beginning in 1982; a development project along

Sakhalin's continental shelf requiring Japanese loans of $200 million for the exploration of oil and natural gas deposits; the export of 16.8 million cubic metres of Siberian timber in return for Japanese industrial goods valued at $500 million.[24]

Following the inconclusive Soviet–Japanese summit talks in October 1973, the Japanese government encouraged private financial and commercial interests to undertake negotiations with the Soviet Union, presumably on the understanding that Export–Import Bank funds for up to 80 per cent of capital costs would be made available. A protocol was signed in late April 1974 providing for credit of $1050 million in tied loans at 6.375 per cent interest for eight years. These funds were earmarked for the development of south Yakutia coking coal, the exploration of Yakutia natural gas and the exploitation of Siberian timber. In exchange, the Soviet Union agreed to purchase from Japan machinery, ships, construction material and consumer goods related to these projects, and to repay the loan by deliveries of coal, gas and timber. At the same time, the Soviet Union, Japan and the United States signed a memorandum on natural gas exploration. The Soviet Union was requesting some $200 million in Japanese and American loans to finance Soviet industrial imports, in return for which it offered to supply annually to each country 10,000 million cubic metres of natural gas for a period of twenty-five years.

As Japanese involvement in the development of Soviet resources began to gather momentum, Chinese disquiet became increasingly evident. The proposed Tyumen oil project was regarded by Peking as a potential threat to China's security, since both the oil and the highway would run very close to the Chinese border where a large Soviet military complex was already located. Accordingly, the Chinese cautioned Japan to minimize the military significance of the project, arguing that the Soviet strategic build-up posed a threat as much to Japan's as to China's security. For its part, Peking made it clear that it would be forced to take 'appropriate measures' should the Soviet–Japanese economic partnership lead to further expansion of the Soviet military potential in the Far East.[25] These warnings were obviously intended to counter the many incentives inducing Japan to participate in the development of Siberian resources. China could hardly ignore the strong attraction for Japan of closer sources of raw materials for its steel, power, construction and paper industries, as well as of an expanding market for Japanese industrial and consumer goods. Increased Soviet trade might also have the added advantage of promoting increased industrial production along the western Honshu sea coast. Moreover, the appeal of Siberian development tended to grow with the increasing doubts about the reliability of Middle East oil and gas. Finally, Japan was naturally anxious to develop economic relations with the Soviet Union as a means of securing more favourable Japanese fishing rights, facilitating the reversion of the disputed northern islands and benefiting generally from the new diplomatic manoeuvrability that had followed the decline of the cold war.

In an attempt to undermine or at least restrain Soviet–Japanese collaboration, the Chinese launched a major propaganda offensive designed to highlight and exacerbate the conflict of interests separating the two countries. Apart from the legacy of military hostilities, traditional Japanese antipathy towards the Soviet Union was accentuated by the Soviet decision in 1950 to form an alliance with China directed specifically against Japan, by the subsequent Soviet veto on Japan's entry into the United Nations, by the exclusion of Japanese fishermen from Peter the Great Bay and the Sea of Okhotsk in 1957 and 1959 respectively, and by Moscow's indifference to Japanese concern with the radioactive fall-out from Soviet nuclear tests during 1959–60. But possibly the greatest bone of Soviet–Japanese contention was Tokyo's continuing demand for the restoration of the Soviet-controlled islands of Kunashiri, Etorofu, Habomai and Shikotan.

Taking advantage of these elements of friction in the Soviet–Japanese relationship, China consistently supported Japan's efforts to regain its lost territories. Statements to this effect made by Japanese Foreign Minister Kiichi Miyazawa during his visit to the Soviet Union in January 1975 were quoted approvingly by the Chinese press.[26] The strategic importance of the islands, particularly of Etorofu which became a Soviet air base as well as a fortified naval part and a listening-post for American underground nuclear tests in the Aleutians, provided Peking with further ammunition for its denunciation of Soviet objectives.[27]

Another important and closely related source of tension that the Chinese endeavoured to exploit was the question of fishing rights. It is estimated that, as a result of the Soviet occupation of the northern islands, some 1400 Japanese fishing vessels and 12,000 fishermen were detained between 1946 and 1973. The Soviet fishing fleet comprising a 10,000-ton mother ship and scores of large trawlers and transport ships were accused of intruding into the seas near Japan, interfering with the operation of Japanese fishermen and seriously threatening their security.[28] Nor was the Soviet threat confined to these harassing tactics. Moscow's campaign to bring Japan into the Soviet sphere of influence was characterized as a mixture of economic blandishments and military threats.

The main thrust of Peking's strategy was not hard to discover. To obstruct Soviet–Japanese collaboration, China would use every possible opportunity to underline the expansionist nature of Soviet objectives. In this, she was greatly assisted by the several contentious issues that surfaced periodically in the bilateral relationship between Tokyo and Moscow. Even the prospect of economic cooperation in the development of Siberian resources was not without its difficulties. In the first place, the Russians tended to drive hard bargains with the Japanese, in the belief that, especially after the 1973 oil crisis, Japan had no alternative but to diversify its sources of energy. Accordingly, the amount of oil Japan was to receive each year from the Tyumen oil project was reduced from 40 to 25 million tons. Moreover, the Soviet Union modified its original proposal whereby Japan would have financed a pipeline along the Sino–Soviet frontier, and insisted instead on the construction of a second

Siberian railway of some 3200 kilometres between Irkutsk and Sovetskaya Gavan. The new project, which was bound to increase Soviet military and naval capability in the Far East, immediately aroused Japanese anxiety for the Soviet plan represented a major challenge not only to Chinese but also to American and Japanese security interests.

Treaty of Peace and Friendship

The scope and limitations of China's diplomatic efforts to retard or contain the Soviet–Japanese collaboration became fully apparent in the protracted negotiations for a China–Japan treaty of peace and friendship. Although the Zhou–Tanaka statement of September 1972 had affirmed that 'neither of the two countries should seek hegemony in the Asia–Pacific region' and that both of them were 'opposed to efforts by any country or group of countries to establish such hegemony', the two sides subsequently found it extremely difficult to agree on a formula that would incorporate this so-called 'anti-hegemony' clause in the treaty. While prepared to accede to Chinese demands for its inclusion, Tokyo was at the same time anxious not to become a pawn in the Sino–Soviet conflict or to be regarded as China's subservient ally.

After the initiation of official treaty talks in November 1974, Chinese optimism about the prospects for an early conclusion of the treaty was soon dissipated. Peking's insistence on spelling out the 'anti-hegemony' clause so as to aim it directly at the Russians obviously disturbed the Japanese who were committed to a policy of equidistance between Peking and Moscow. In an attempt to break the negotiating deadlock, the Japanese government informed the Chinese ambassador in April 1975 that it might agree to the inclusion of the first part of the 'anti-hegemony' clause (renouncing mutual hegemony aspirations) in the preamble rather than in the operative part of the treaty, but would oppose the insertion of the second part of the clause, which referred to a third country's 'hegemonism'.[29] In May 1975, Prime Minister Miki reaffirmed his intention to seek an early peace treaty with China on the basis of the principles enunciated in the 1972 joint communiqué.[30] However, the Chinese insisted that an unequivocal condemnation of 'hegemony' had already appeared both in the 1972 joint Sino–Japanese statement and in the Shanghai communiqué of February 1972 without occasioning any Soviet protest. Why should Moscow suddenly take exception to the reaffirmation of an established and almost universally accepted principle?

Faced with the added complication of the public disclosure of the content of the talks between the two parties, Miki announced in June 1975 that the Japanese ambassador to Peking had been instructed to impose strict secrecy on current treaty negotiations. However, the shift to secret diplomacy produced no immediate results and no discernible softening of the Chinese position. In early 1976 the Japanese hinted that they might agree to the inclusion of the 'anti-hegemony' clause provided that the Chinese indicated their understanding and acceptance of Japan's interpretation of its meaning, which was that the clause expressed a principle of universal application and not one restricted to the Asia–Pacific region or directed against any specific third country.[31] In spite of this apparent concession, China's uncompromising stand coupled with the Soviet Union's increasingly vehement denunciation of the proposed treaty and its 'anti-hegemony' clause once again brought the negotiations to an impasse.

But Soviet diplomatic intervention was by no means the sole factor hindering the conclusion of a treaty. While both the Chinese and Japanese governments had agreed to set aside the difficult political issue of Taiwan and to tolerate a measure of ambiguity in their respective attitudes to the problem, the fact remained that Tokyo's policies were based on the expectation of Taiwan's indefinite separation from the Chinese mainland. While Peking was willing for the time being to forgo the use of force as a means of achieving reunification, it still had the option of exerting renewed pressure at some future date in order to force Japan's hand on this key unresolved issue. The Japanese, on the other hand, had a clear preference for the maintenance of the status quo, while influential pro-Taiwan elements within the ruling Liberal Democratic Party, which stood to lose heavily in the event of a sudden or violent disrupion of Japan's economic links with the island, were pressing strongly for a cautious approach to the negotiations. These pressures could not be easily ignored, given the Miki government's precarious domestic situation and the persistence of fierce and prolonged intra-party faction fighting. Were Miki to have yielded too much or not enough to the Chinese position, his opponents within the party would almost certainly have seized on the issue as an additional weapon in their campaign to topple him.

The Sino–Japanese deadlock was thus the result of several interacting factors. But, clearly, the probable deterioration in relations with the Soviet Union remained the most difficult problem to resolve, for Tokyo had not only to contend with Soviet opposition but also take into account the question of Soviet–Japanese economic collaboration as well as concurrent efforts to conclude a peace treaty with Moscow. Moreover, Japan's room for diplomatic manoeuvre was narrowly circumscribed, for it lacked the necessary leverage to extract from China the kinds of concessions that may have yielded a compromise acceptable to Soviet leaders. In the event, talks for a Soviet–Japanese treaty also reached stalemate largely because of sharp differences over the disputed islands. At their fifth ministerial meeting in January 1978, the two countries failed to issue a joint statement or communiqué, thereby fuelling speculation that their respective positions remained far apart.[32] Moscow's subsequent decision to make public the draft treaty it had proposed at the consultations merely exacerbated relations with Tokyo and exposed Soviet attempts to neutralize the Japan–US security treaty and incorporate Japan into an Asian collective security system.[33] In the area of economic cooperation, progress proved considerably slower than had originally been expected, and the project to develop the Tyumen oilfields, which had been regarded the showpiece of Japanese involvement in Siberian economic development, came to a virtual standstill after the autumn of 1974. Japan's trade with China had surpassed that with the Soviet Union every year since 1972 with the exception of 1976, when political turmoil within China probably contributed to the decline. In 1975 the total value of Sino–Japanese trade amounted to $3800 million, compared with $2800 million for Soviet–Japanese trade.

By the middle of 1978 Japan's rapidly developing economic links with China and its deteriorating relationship with the Soviet Union had contributed to a much more favourable climate for the signing of the Sino–Japanese treaty of peace and friendship. Nevertheless, a contentious issue that had remained dormant for several years did arise in April 1978, when about 100 Chinese fishing vessels entered the area covered by the Senkaku (Tiaoyu) Islands in defiance of Japanese warnings. Although there had been little interest in these five small islands (situated in the East China Sea, about 200 miles from China and 100 miles west of Japan's Ryukyu Islands) until 1968 when a US-sponsored survey predicted that the surrounding seabed contained large oil deposits, both the Chinese and Taiwanese governments subsequently disputed Japanese territorial claims to the islands.[34] The Chinese and Japanese then agreed to 'shelve the issue' in 1972 to facilitate normalization of relations, and the same understanding was reached in 1978 during the final stages of their treaty talks. The quick withdrawal of the Chinese vessels from the disputed area following the April 1978 incident and the agreement not to allow the Senkaku Islands to prejudice the treaty negotiations were in sharp contrast to the Soviet–Japanese deadlock over territorial claims to the Kurile Islands and Japan's fishing rights in the newly established Soviet 200-mile economic zone. Similarly, the agreement between the Japanese and South Korean governments on 'Joint development of the continental shelf' in June 1978, while it provoked Peking into lodging a strong protest against Japan's alleged infringement of Chinese sovereignty,[35] was not allowed to hinder the process of détente and cooperation.

In spite of continuing difficulties over the wording of the 'anti-hegemony' clause, the visit to Peking by the Japanese Foreign Minister in August 1978 resulted in the signing of the long-awaited peace treaty. In defending the agreement, which was widely welcomed by Japanese public opinion,[36] he claimed to have elicited from Deng Xiaoping verbal pledges that there would be no repetition of incidents with respect to the Senkaku Islands as had occurred in April 1978 and that China would soon move to abrogate the 1950 Sino–Soviet pact. These apparent gestures of goodwill on China's part were presumably meant to compensate Japan's key concession, embodied in Article II of the Treaty, which required both contracting parties not to 'seek hegemony in the Asia–Pacific region or in any other region' and to oppose 'efforts by any other country or group of countries to establish such hegemony'. Peking had succeeded not only in inserting an 'anti-hegemony' clause in the treaty, but in keeping a specific reference to the 'Asia–Pacific region'. On the other hand, Tokyo had managed to weaken the thrust of the clause by the inclusion of the phrase 'or in any other region' and by modifying the wording from 'each country will oppose' to 'each country is opposed to', thereby sidestepping the possible implication of positive joint action against hegemonism by a third country. In Japan's view, the addition of a separate qualifying clause in Article IV, stipulating that the treaty would not affect the relations of either Japan or China with third countries, also helped to dilute the anti-Soviet flavour of the text.

On the basis of these limited modifications to the draft originally favoured by the Chinese, Japan disclaimed any intention of aligning itself with China against the Soviet Union. Great play was made of the fact that the treaty did not require of either party any obligations other than those already imposed by the UN Charter and the 1972 communiqué. Japan, it was argued, in keeping with its 'omni-directional' policy, would be opposed to any type of hegemonism, but would not agree to defining any particular country as having hegemonic objectives. In a press conference given in Peking after the signing of the treaty, the Japanese Foreign Minister stated: 'Japan cannot permit itself to be involved in the dispute between your country [China] and the Soviet Union and this is the opinion of the Japanese people'.[37] On the other hand, the terms of the treaty could be legitimately construed as evidence of Japan's decision to give its relations with China precedence over those with the Soviet Union. The very fact that Tokyo had agreed to the inclusion of the 'anti-hegemony' clause despite Soviet warnings did not seem capable with an 'equidistant diplomacy' towards the two communist powers. Regardless of the particular explanations offered by the Japanese government, it was difficult in the context of the intense Sino–Soviet confrontation to avoid the conclusion that the treaty had an anti–Soviet character that was bound to incur Soviet hostility. In some sense, the Soviet–Vietnamese treaty could be seen as a response to the growing evidence of Sino–Japanese cooperation and an attempt to give new impetus to the Soviet concept of an Asian collective security system. Of particular concern to the Soviet Union was the emerging three-way connection between the United States, China and Japan, which had become an important element of American diplomacy under the Carter administration. To this extent, the Peking–Tokyo entente represented not so much a radical departure from as a new phase in Japan's post-war alignment with the United States.

China, for her part, made little effort to conceal what she regarded as the anti-Soviet significance of the treaty. In a major article on 14 August devoted to an evaluation of the agreement, the *People's Daily* described the development of friendly relations between China and Japan and the signing of the treaty as having 'put a thorn in the flesh of the Soviet Union' and as proclaiming 'the ignominious bankruptcy of the Soviet social-imperialist plot to interfere and sabotage'.[38] During his visit to Japan in October 1978, Deng Xiaoping left his hosts in little doubt as to the limitations of their 'omni-directional' policy. He not only characterized 'anti-hegemonism' as 'the nucleus of the China–Japan Treaty of Peace and Friendship', but went on to add that the 'omni-directional' concept, while legitimately advocating a policy of friendship with all countries, had also to come to terms with hegemonism, which was 'the root cause of insecurity and instability in the world'.[39] The formal ratification of the treaty on 23 October 1978 thus inaugurated a new era of Sino–Japanese diplomatic and economic cooperation and a significant shift in the Asian balance of power. A few outstanding issues, notably the prospect of closer links between Tokyo and Moscow, Japan's relationship with Taiwan and the disputed Senkaku Islands remained a potential source of friction. The contention over the Senkaku Islands briefly re-emerged on 29 May 1979 when China protested against Japan's intention to build a heliport and conduct scientific surveys on one of the islands. But these irritants were unlikely to undermine the emerging pattern of compromise and détente between the two countries. As for the strategically sensitive question of Korea, where a precarious equilibrium existed between the two Korean governments and the major powers, recent trends had significantly diminished the gap between the Chinese and Japanese positions. Although Peking continued to give strong support to its North Korean ally, its previous opposition to the American military presence and Japanese economic influence in South Korea was now far more restrained. Given that a new Korean war was likely to have an adverse effect on China's relations with both Japan and the United States, Chinese policy now appeared firmly committed to the preservation of the status quo or at least to gradual and peaceful change. Indeed, it was by no means inconceivable that Peking might now be willing to apply pressure on Pyongyang to prevent any initiative that might conflict with China's global strategy aimed at containing the perceived threat of Soviet encirclement.

Economic Parnership

While the implications of the Sino–Japanese treaty of peace and friendship were obvious and far-reaching, it was generally expected that its most immediate impact would be in the economic arena, for it is here that the policies of the two governments were likely to achieve the greatest degree of complementarity. The expansion of economic exchange between the two countries promised to provide China with the necessary capital and technology for her 'four modernizations' (see Chapter 7) and Japan with a lucrative market and access to vitally needed resources, notably energy fuels. The enthusiasm with which Japanese business circles welcomed the treaty was largely based on the expectation that the dream of exploiting China's gigantic market was about to come true. Japanese industrialists were obviously hoping that Chinese interest in the acquisition of petrochemicals, steel and machinery would help to offset sluggish domestic demand for these products, which represented the economic sector hardest hit by the prolonged recession in the industrialized western world. An expanded market in China could also help to offset mounting competition from Japan's Asian industrial rivals and relieve the pressure resulting from American and European protectionism. Japan–China trade, which had already increased in dramatic fashion over the last three decades, from $59 million in 1950 to $3485 million in 1977, was now projected to grow at an even faster rate.

By the mid-1970s Chinese petroleum had already become an important factor in Sino–Japanese trade. China's steadily increasing oil output had enabled her oil exports to Japan to rise from 1 million tons in 1973 to about 8 million tons in 1975. In 1977, crude oil accounted for 38.6 per cent of China's exports to Japan, thereby providing her with $600 million in foreign exchange. And, as the Japanese Minister for International Trade and Industry, Kōmoto Toshio, explained before his visit to China in September 1978, current projections indicated an increasing Japanese dependence on Chinese oil, perhaps up to 10 per cent of all the oil imported by Japan in the next ten years and some 50 million tons of oil by 1985.[40] The development of China's oil industry, however, was crucial not only to Japan's energy needs but also to the solution of China's potentially large balance of payments deficit with Japan. Needless to say, the success of this effort was dependent on Peking's acquiescence in the rapid exploitation of this valuable non-renewable resource and the availability of financial support for the establishment of refining facilities for heavy oil.

Enough will have been said to indicate that by 1978 the economic and political conditions were ripe for a major breakthrough in Sino–Japanese trade relations. The signing of the 'Long-Term Trade Contract' between the two countries on 16 February 1978 was, in fact, designed to provide a major impetus to the 'export of technology, plants, building materials, and machine parts from Japan to China, and Japanese imports of crude oil and coal from China'. The eight-year treaty, which envisaged over the period a total of $20,000 million in two-way trade divided equally between the two countries, was perceived by both sides, and particularly by the Japanese business community, as cementing the Sino–Japanese economic relationship. During the first five years the contract envisaged that Japan would more than double its imports of Chinese crude oil, from 7 million tonnes in 1978 to 15 million tonnes in 1982. Over the same five-year span Japan would purchase between 5.1 and 5.3 million tons of coking coal for its steel industry and between 3.3 and 3.9 million tons of steaming coal for power generation. In return, the Chinese agreed to buy from Japan $7000–$8000 million of plant and technology and $2000–$3000 million of construction materials and equipment during the same five-year period. In addition to the $10,000 million of Japanese sales to be generated directly by the trade agreement, Japanese business leaders expected a substantial amount of subsidiary trade – estimated by Doko Toshio, president of Keidanren (Japan Federation of Employers' Associations), to reach some $4200 million by 1982.[41]

To a very large extent the 1978 trade agreement and the many contracts that followed in quick succession had been facilitated by the substantial modifications in China's trade policy, which were eventually crystallized at the National Conference on Finance and Trade held from 20 June to 9 July 1978. The main conclusion to emerge from the conference was China's readiness to expand the import of advanced technology and equipment on a deferred payment basis through compensatory trade and to develop 'export-oriented industrial areas, construction of specialized factories, processing of raw materials . . . and assembly work'.[42] These and other measures designed to increase China's export capacity gave additional impetus to trade relations with Japan. One of the most important results of negotiations between the two countries was the protocol exchanged between the New Japan Steel Co. and the Chinese Public Corporation on Advanced Technology on 23 May 1978, which provided for the construction of the Baoshan steel plant in Shanghai expected to produce 6 million tons of unprocessed iron annually. Negotiations were also under way for the construction of another steel plant of similar size in the eastern part of Hebei province as well as for Japanese technological assistance towards the modernization of existing steel plants. A contract was also signed in June–July 1978 for the export of colour television plants from Japan to China amounting to $300 million.

Other projects agreed to or under negotiation in the months following the National Conference on Finance and Trade included the manufacture of over 300,000 tons of ethylene annually by Nikki Co. which was to invest $132 million; the construction of several petrochemical plants involving Mitsui Engineering and Shipbuilding, Mitsui Petrochemical Industries, Tokyo Engineering, Tokyo Bussan, Nippon Sokubai, Mitsubichi Heavy Industries, Shinetsu Chemical Industries and numerous other firms; the remodelling of Peking's national stadium; the establishment of oil, copper and aluminium refineries; the expansion of port facilities at Tianjin, Qinhuangdao, Shanghai and Guangzhou; and joint development of a $32,500 million hydroelectric power scheme involving four power stations on the Yangtze and Yellow Rivers. Although many of these plans had not advanced beyond preliminary discussions, the stage had been set, as a result of reciprocal visits by several study missions, including high-level ministerial delegations, for a vastly expanded framework of economic collaboration. Particularly important in this respect was the meeting in September 1978 between the Japanese Minister of International Trade and Industry, Komoto Toshio, and the Chinese Vice-Premier Li Xiannian. The two governments agreed in principle on the extension of the trade pact for another five years until 1990 and on the doubling or even trebling of the currently projected volume of trade. Agreement was also reached on Japanese assistance in the fields of science and technology, on the establishment of a Japanese trade office in Peking, and on Japanese involvement in the development of coal mining and several non-ferrous metals such ás lead, aluminium, tin and tungsten. In the course of subsequent negotiations, it emerged that the Chinese were also anxious to involve the Japanese in the exploitation of oil resources in the Gulf of Pohai and the Pearl River estuary. In the light of these ambitious plans and the emerging boom in Sino–Japanese trade (estimated to have totalled $5000 million in 1978), Japanese economic analysts were now predicting that bilateral trade might expand to as much as $20,000 million by 1985.[43]

Eventually, however, the euphoric mood generated by the magnitude of the supply contracts concluded in 1978 gave way to a more restrained and realistic assessment of the Sino–Japanese economic partnership. Peking's decision in February 1979 to suspend many of the contracts it had negotiated with Japanese suppliers was an apt reminder of the economic and institutional limitations on China's capacity to absorb sophisticated foreign technology and of the inadequacy of traditional supplier credits to finance these enormously expensive imports. Most of the 1978 contracts amounted to basic agreements that left the details of financing to be worked out at a later date. Early attempts to resolve the problem were constrained by China's long-standing ideological opposition to foreign borrowing and by the OECD guidelines that required Japan to set a minimum interest rate of 7.25 per cent for trade loans of up to five years and 7.5 per cent for longer-term loans.[44] Although Japanese exporters were ready to offer more favourable terms by juggling prices and blurring the designation of the projects to be financed, further difficulties arose from China's marked preference for borrowing US dollars rather than Japanese yen. Given the steady appreciation of Japanese currency in recent years, China was reluctant to see the enlargement of her foreign debt through continuing currency fluctuations.

On the other hand, by the latter half of 1978, the Chinese attitude to commercially based finance had undergone significant change. In August it was confirmed that the Bank of China would agree to accept direct loans from the Japanese Export–Import Bank. But it was only in May 1979 that the thorny issue of trade financing was settled, at least temporarily, by agreement on a multi-million dollar loan comprising funds from both government and private sources. One component of the package involved a loan by the Export–Import Bank of Japan of approximately $7000 million in yen-donominated credits. These long-term loan funds, which carried an attractively low annual interest rate of 6.25 per cent, were earmarked for the development of China's coal and oil reserves but were likely to be spread over a much greater range of mineral and other projects. This arrangement was supplemented by long-term credits estimated at $7000 million to be provided in dollar-denominated funds by a consortium of twenty-two Japanese commercial banks at a yearly interest rate floating at 0.5 per cent over the London inter-bank offered rate (Libor). In addition, a group of thirty-one Japanes commercial banks were to supply a short-term loan amounting to $6000 million at an annual interest rate floating at 0.25 per cent over Libor. It was hoped that the inflow of Japanese commercial credit would help the Chinese to revise the contracts for Japanese plant technology and machinery, estimated at $2600 million, that had been suspended in early 1979.

Notwithstanding the breakthrough in trade financing, Japanese businessmen and government officials were now more cautious in their forecasts of the future growth of trade with China. Though Chinese leaders, particularly Deng Xiaoping and his associates, were determined to maintain the momentum of their modernization programme and to preserve China's credibility with international suppliers, practical considerations had already compelled a 'readjustment' of economic policy involving a reduction in the number of heavy industrial projects, notably in the petrochemical sector, and a scaling down of plant capacity. The complementarity between the Chinese and Japanese economies had clearly been exaggerated, for the two societies were not only at vastly different stages of economic development but their social and political priorities were hardly identical or even easily reconcilable. Nor could either country point to a widespread or stable consensus on societal goals and appropriate strategies for their implementation. Indeed, the domestic and foreign policies of both China and Japan were in a state of flux and under considerable internal as well as external challenge. It remained to be seen how the Chinese and Japanese responses to these challenges would affect the attitudes and perceptions of the two countries. Though the Sino–Japanese partnership appeared by the late 1970s to be built on more solid foundations than at any time since World War II, the relationship retained nevertheless a good measure of ambivalence. Peking's and Tokyo's common strategic dependence on the United States, their deep mistrust of Soviet intentions and their economic pragmatism might not always be sufficient to offset continuing and newly emerging elements of conflict and competition. How relations between the two most powerful Asian nations developed in the early 1980s and beyond would depend on the nature of domestic political change as well as on the rapidly shifting regional and international balance of power.

CHAPTER 10

Southeast Asia: The Realignment of Power

China's interest and involvement in the affairs of Southeast Asia date back almost 2000 years. Over the centuries the countries now comprising Indochina, Burma, Thailand, the Malay peninsula and the Indonesian archipelago had evolved a tributary relationship with the Chinese empire based on trade and the acceptance of Chinese suzerainty. The system of state relations was irrevocably shattered in the nineteenth century by the intrusion of European military and economic power and replaced by a wide-ranging network of colonies and spheres of influence. By the mid-1970s the emancipation of the entire region from foreign domination had not yet been completed, although the Second World War, the Communist Chinese victory of 1949 and the defeat of the United States in Indochina were important landmarks in the achievement of independence. A new stable relationship between the People's Republic of China and the nations of Southeast Asia had not yet emerged, but the Sino–Soviet conflict and traditional Sino–Vietnamese tension gave some indication of the way in which historical influences, geopolitical realities and ideological attitudes were likely to coalesce into a new pattern of diplomatic and economic interaction.

The Global Balance

It will be remembered that throughout the 1950s and 1960s Chinese leaders were primarily concerned with thwarting the American policy of containment (see Chapter 2). Peking opposed American intervention in the Indochinese conflict, partly because it considered the introduction of US troops as posing a major threat to Chinese security. It was, therefore, of the utmost importance that these forces should not advance past the 17th parallel. In a very real sense, North Vietnam was to remain an important buffer zone between China and the United States throughout the duration of the war. It is not without significance that China's only threat to intervene directly in the conflict was explicitly designed to forestall the possibility of an American ground invasion of North Vietnam.[1] With the resignation of President Johnson and the gradual departure of US troops from South Vietnam, one of the key conditions for the

220

establishment of a new dialogue between Washington and Peking had thus been satisfied.

China's admission to the United Nations in October 1971, and the subsequent visit of President Nixon to Peking in February 1972, inevitably complicated China's Vietnam policy and exercised a restraining influence on her denunciation of American actions in Indochina. Nevertheless, only a few weeks prior to the American President's historic journey to Peking, the Chinese Ministry for Foreign Affairs felt obliged, in deference to North Vietnamese sensibilities, to issue one of its most critical statements on the US role in the Indochinese war.[2] Even in the joint communiqué signed at the end of the Nixon visit, which was meant to usher in a new era in Sino–American relations, Peking reiterated its commitment to revolutionary struggle and explicitly reaffirmed its support for the peoples of Vietnam, Laos and Cambodia, and more particularly for the seven-point proposal of the Provisional Revolutionary Government (PRG) of South Vietnam.[3] In the same spirit, Peking was careful not to allow the Nixon visit to prevent a series of aid agreements with Hanoi in January, June and November 1972 providing for the gratuitous supply of military equipment and materials during 1973.[4] According to one estimate, China supplied the Vietnamese Communists with 500,000 tons of oil, more than 1 million tons of rice and some $300 million in other aid annually during the early 1970s.[5]

It is true that the American decision in May 1972 to impose a military blockade on North Vietnam produced a rather muted reaction from China. Peking may have even been instrumental in getting the Vietnam peace negotiations off the ground by persuading Hanoi to give up the precondition of the removal of the Thieu regime. Furthermore, it may be argued that China's enthusiastic acceptance of the provisions of the Paris Peace Agreement of 27 January 1973 betrayed an eagerness to maintain the momentum of détente with the United States rather than any desire to secure 'self-determination, peace and unity for the Vietnamese people'. The agreement, which was hailed as a 'major victory for the Vietnamese people' with far-reaching implications for the 'anti-imperialist struggle' throughout the world,[6] did not in fact bring an end to the fighting. Instead of the promised cease-fire, the Paris agreement was followed for more than two years by continuous and escalating warfare throughout much of South Vietnam.

After the Tenth Party Congress China engaged in renewed and vigorous criticism of US politics in relation to Indochina, Taiwan and several other unresolved issues. The scale of military operations subsequently undertaken by North Vietnam and the PRG made it difficult for China to continue pressing for a negotiated settlement that would fall short of Hanoi's proclaimed political aims. Indeed, a Chinese military delegation that visited Hanoi in October 1974 was responsible for accelerating the movement of supplies to North Vietnam through a base set up at Nanning in southern Guangxi province. A subsequent visit by a ten-member military mission headed by Yang Yong in

February–March 1975 was the prelude to the rapid escalation of the war in Indochina and to the decisive collapse of the pro-American forces in both Cambodia and South Vietnam. In a long series of official and semi-official statements issued in April–May 1975, China welcomed 'the victorious development of the Vietnamese people's just struggle' and drew attention to the bankruptcy of United States gunboat diplomacy.[7]

Following the communist liberation of Phnom Penh on 17 April 1975 an editorial in the *People's Daily* saw in the disintegration of the Lon Nol regime confirmation of the Maoist view that no imperialism can ultimately withstand the resistance of the oppressed.[8] The Vietnamese victory was hailed in the Chinese press – still under the strong influence of the radicals – as the vindication of the principle of people's war.[9] But in proclaiming the event as a major blow against US imperialism, Peking was also reminding the world, and particularly its neighbours, of China's unique contribution to the struggle,[10] and of her desire to have a voice in the future direction of Southeast Asian politics.

Moreover, endorsement of the communist success in Indochina no longer endangered the prospects of dialogue with the world's major capitalist power, which had abandoned, or at least downgraded, its role as global policeman. The new compatibility between Chinese and American interests had obvious but far-reaching implications. For the end of the Vietnam war and even of American military intervention in Asian affairs did not necessarily affect the US strategic position in the South-West Pacific. By contrast, China was still a very small naval power and had only limited short-range aerial strength. To the extent, therefore, that China feared the military penetration of the Soviet Union into Southeast Asia, and so long as she remained in a position of strategic inferiority vis-à-vis the two superpowers, a residual American presence in the region could operate to China's advantage as a counter to Soviet influence. At the end of 1973, Zhou Enlai was reported to have conveyed to the Australian Prime Minister China's preference for a gradual US military withdrawal from Southeast Asia and the West Pacific, warning that a precipitate disengagement would provide an opportunity for the Russians to move in behind the retreating Americans.[11] By 1975, the Soviet threat in Southeast Asia had become one of the main recurring themes in Chinese propaganda.[12] China's obsessive preoccupation with the expansion of Soviet power, which was bound to assist the process of bridge-building with the five member countries of the Association of Southeast Asian Nations (ASEAN) – Indonesia, Malaysia, Singapore, Thailand, Philippines – pointed to the subtle and flexible combination of ideological objectives and power perceptions in Chinese foreign policy and to the substantial scope for accommodation in Sino–American relations.

As I have already observed (pp. 149–50), the diplomatic rapprochement with the United States was paralleled by a steady deterioration in Sino–Soviet relations. The two trends appeared to accentuate one another. In each case,

China's support for revolutionary movements was both an asset and a liability. Throughout the 1960s, Peking was able to embarrass Moscow and weaken the latter's leadership of the communist world by pointing to the Soviet Union's neglect of the revolutionary cause. After the late 1960s, however, there was little evidence to suggest that Peking was seeking the leadership of an ideological bloc. Its attitude, which depended for its validity and credibility on the maintenance of a militant line in support of liberation wars, was rather aimed at denying the Soviet Union a military or diplomatic foothold. In the Southeast Asian context, China was able to rely on the support of most local communist parties, with the exception of the Laotians and North Vietnamese who insisted on steering a cautious middle course between Moscow and Peking.

During the Cultural Revolution the theory and practice of people's war was enthusiastically endorsed by the Burmese, Thai and Malayan parties and by the remnants of the Indonesian Communist Party in Borneo. The military wings of these movements (e.g. Thai People's Liberation Army, Indonesian People's Armed Forces, Burmese People's Armed Forces) received extensive propaganda support from Peking, as indicated by a stream of statements and articles appearing in the Chinese press.[13] In return they were willing to associate themselves with China in denouncing Soviet interference in the affairs of their countries. In July 1975, the 'Voice of the people of Thailand' accused the Soviet Union of 'intensifying expansion and infiltration in Thailand' and of 'slandering the People's Republic of China in a bid to obstruct and sabotage relations between Thailand and China'.[14] In spite of Peking's lower revolutionary profile since the purging of Lin Biao and his followers and the less elevated role ascribed to people's war, China was able to maintain a considerable degree of influence over these movements. On the other hand, none of these communist parties was sufficiently large to have any noticeable impact on the political struggle within international communism, nor were sustained gains likely to be made against existing local governments, at least in the foreseeable future.

The quandary confronting Chinese leaders as they tried to prevent the extension of Soviet influence in Southeast Asia was even more striking in relation to the Indochinese conflict. In March 1970, China took advantage of the Lon Nol coup against Prince Norodom Sihanouk of Cambodia to act as host to his Royal Government of National Union, in order to project an image to the world as the most reliable supporter of the Indochinese people's struggle against the United States. Cambodia thus became a testing ground of the relative influence of the two communist giants. By continuing to recognize the government in Phnom Penh, the Soviet Union had allowed the initiative to pass into Chinese hands. The anti-Soviet statements of Prince Sihanouk were especially gratifying to Chinese ears. In August 1973 he accused Moscow of 'obstinately maintain[ing] diplomatic relations with the moribund regime of the Phnom Penh traitor's,[15] and described the so-called support accorded by the Soviet Union to FUNK (National United Front of Kampuchea) as devoid of all 'value and credibility'. At the non-aligned summit conference in Algiers, the prince reiterated his profound misgivings about Soviet intentions.[16]

At the Twenty-Ninth session of the UN General Assembly the chairman of the Chinese delegation Qiao Guanhua launched a sustained diplomatic campaign to unseat the Lon Nol government from the United Nations in order to have it replaced by the Royal Government of National Union.[17] Although the vote was narrowly lost, China was thereby able to demonstrate her support for Prince Sihanouk's government-in-exile. It was not surprising, therefore, that in the wake of successive victories on the battlefield and the long drawn out seige of Phnom Penh, the Khmer Rouge should have sent their special envoy to Peking for high-level negotiations with the Chinese leadership to determine guidelines for Sino–Cambodian relations in the post-war situation. Following the victory of the Khmer Rouge, Khieu Samphan led a delegation to Peking in August 1975, the first visit abroad by the new Cambodian government since the liberation of Phnom Penh. While acknowledging the 'unprecedented revolutionary heroism' of the Cambodian people, the Khmer Rouge leaders went to considerable lengths to express gratitude for China's contribution to the struggle, which was described as 'many-sided, extensive, concrete and pure'.[18]

Enough will have been said to indicate that China's involvement in Southeast Asia, whether of a substantial kind as in Indochina or of a more token variety as in the rest of the region, was in part designed to pre-empt any significant Soviet inroads into China's ideological or diplomatic sphere of influence. On the other hand, Peking had come to realize that if it were to place too heavy a stress on its liberation strategy, it could easily undermine its prospects of normalizing relations with conservative Southeast Asian governments. It was partly in order to exploit this Chinese dilemma that the Soviet Union had sought to expand its own diplomatic and trade relations with the ASEAN countries.[19] Accordingly, discussions were initiated with the Filipino government with a view to the signing of a trade pact and the creation of a joint shipping line. Soviet aid to Malaysia, which was growing, had already made possible the construction of the Tembeling hydroelectric station in Pahang state. It was estimated that the Russians were now buying one-quarter of Malaysia's total rubber output. Another diplomatic success for Moscow was the readmission of Soviet technicians to Indonesia after 1970.

To respond to this challenge China was obliged to broaden her own relations and extend areas of mutual cooperation with Southeast Asian countries, in the hope of imposing more effective restraints on Soviet influence. China's efforts to create in the eyes of her southern neighbours an image of respectability and credibility will be the subject of a more detailed discussion (pp. 238–47). For the moment, suffice it to say that Peking's propaganda campaign was aimed at highlighting the Soviet Union's 'superpower' interests and ambitions. To this end, the Chinese reacted sympathetically to the neutrality concept, and contrasted their favourable attitude to the Malaysian neutralization proposal with the Soviet Asian collective security scheme, first enunciated in 1969 and subsequently rejected by both Malaysia and Indonesia. Particularly encouraging for China was the refusal of Southeast Asian countries to promote Soviet at the expense of Chinese interests. In October 1973, Ghazali Bin Shafie, a senior Malaysian minister, made it clear that the ASEAN countries would do nothing to advance the Soviet cause in the Sino–Soviet dispute.[20] China, for her part, denounced on more than one occasion Soviet naval ambitions in East Asia, and portrayed the Soviet call for the 'internationalization' of the Malacca Strait as 'a violation of other countries' sovereignty over their territorial waters' and as part of a grand design to establish hegemony in the vast waters between Vladivostok and the Indian Ocean.[21] She consistently stressed the right of small and medium powers to extend their sovereignty beyond the 12-mile territorial limit, contrasting this position with that held by all great powers, including the Soviet Union.[22]

The New Indochinese Conflict

While China's role in the great power triangle provides valuable insights into the interaction with her Southeast Asian neighbours, her policies towards the region were not the mere product of the great power balance. A variety of local factors as well as Peking's intricate but fluid regional strategy also helped to shape Chinese attitudes and perceptions. In any case, Southeast Asia represented an amalgam of aligned and non-aligned nations, radical and conservative political systems, deeply entrenched and highly vulnerable governments. Even when consistently pursuing the same objective, an effective foreign policy towards these countries required careful attention to these national variables. Communist Vietnam, neutralist Burma and pro-western Thailand had to be treated as quite separate and diverging entities.

Without doubt, Hanoi posed the most difficult challenge to Peking's diplomacy, for while there had previously existed a substantial identity of views on a broad range of issues, Chinese and Vietnamese interests were far from identical. Regardless of ideological affinities, China was unlikely to view with equanimity the prospect of a powerful and unified Vietnam capable of shifting the local balance of power. Even before reunification, it was North Vietnam, rather than China, that had the decisive influence over communist military operations in South Vietnam, Cambodia and Laos. At no stage had China participated directly in the Indochinese war. Although she provided military and economic aid to Hanoi and to all the other dissident groups, it was North Vietnam that supplied at the most critical juncture the bulk of the manpower needed to neutralize the massive influx of American troops and sophisticated military equipment. In order to pursue the war effort in South Vietnam, much of Laotian and Cambodian territory had to be occupied by North Vietnamese troops. It was not beyond the realm of feasibility that Hanoi might wish to use this presence to achieve a more lasting diplomatic sphere of influence, possibly in conflict with Chinese aims and objectives. Nor was it by any means certain that Peking would always be assured of Hanoi's cooperation in the preservation of Cambodian or Laotian neutrality. These considerations were no doubt responsible for China's decision to establish a physical presence in the area, for example by building an extensive road system across the north of Laos.

Chinese misgivings about North Vietnamese intentions were seemingly reinforced when Hanoi attempted to move closer to Moscow in the Sino–Soviet dispute, perhaps because of increased military and economic dependence on the Soviet Union. In March 1973, Zhou Enlai had forecast that in response to the Soviet policy of 'infiltration' Vietnam would 'strive to maintain an equilibrium between Soviet and Chinese influence', although he recognized that Chinese actions would also have an important bearing on Vietnam's attitude.[23] In August 1975, Deng Xiaoping came close to naming Vietnam outright as the principal focus of Soviet military ambitions in the region.[24] Deputy-Premier Chen Xilian, who led the Chinese delegation to North Vietnam's thirtieth anniversary celebrations, renewed the standard Chinese attack against superpower contention as a means of conveying Peking's fears of Soviet ambitions towards the Indochinese peninsula.[25] China's repeated emphasis on the role of the '*South Vietnamese* people and armed forces in the war against US aggression' and her subsequent support for the admission of both Vietnams to the United Nations were perhaps intended to reinforce the division between the two Vietnams and thereby retard the process of reunification.[26] The Chinese now tended to view every Vietnamese initiative, whether domestic or external, as the consequence of Soviet influence. Even the not unexpected Vietnamese decision in late 1975 to reunify the two halves of the country and the establishment of the Lao People's Democratic Republic in December were considered a reflection of Soviet wishes and the first steps towards the creation of a Vietnamese-dominated Indochinese federation.

For its part, North Vietnam had been troubled for some time by the implications of the Sino–American rapprochement. Throughout the duration of the war the United States remained the primary enemy and no strategic or tactical redefinition of Chinese objectives could alter that fact. Although China was not openly criticized, there was little enthusiasm for the Shanghai communiqué, which was regarded as part of a larger American design aimed at accelerating the distintegration of the socialist camp. Vietnamese sources also claimed that immediately after the launching of their spring offensive in 1975 to liberate the South, Peking had warned Vietnam not to engage in a major military operation against the United States. According to Hanoi, such advice was motivated by China's hostility to the emergence of a powerful and reunified Vietnam. As for Peking's attempts to court ASEAN countries, they were interpreted as an attempt to achieve Vietnam's diplomatic encirclement. In other subsequent disclosures, Vietnamese spokesmen accused the Chinese leadership of striving to impose Maoism on Vietnam and coerce it into an alliance with China against the Soviet Union. In October 1978, Hoang Tung, a member of the Central Committee of the Communist Party of Vietnam and editor of *Nhan Dan*, went so far as to describe Chinese foreign policy, especially after 1972, as 'non-socialist' and as 'collaborating with the imperialist forces against the world revolutionary forces'.[27]

Vietnamese suspicions about Chinese intentions were seemingly confirmed when Le Duan, Secretary General of the Vietnamese Communist Party, visited Peking in September 1975. Despite the lavish welcome extended to the Vietnamese delegation, Deng Xiaoping left little doubt that Sino–Vietnamese amity would depend on Hanoi's readiness to join China in condemnation of superpower hegemonism, which, in Chinese parlance, was now virtually synonymous with Soviet social-imperialism. While profusely thanking China for her past assistance, Le Duan did not accept Peking's ideological position and took pains to point out that 'our victory is inseparable from the profound sympathy and great and valuable assistance that the people of the *other fraternal Socialist countries* and all progressive mankind extended to our just patriotic struggle' (italics added).[28] The Vietnamese delegation left China earlier than expected, without signing a joint communiqué or receiving any promise of long-term aid, and proceeded to Moscow where it signed an agreement estimated to have committed $2600 million in Soviet aid to Vietnam's 1976–80 five-year plan.[29]

It is against the background of the rapidly deteriorating climate in Sino–Vietnamese relations that one must therefore assess the attitudes of the two countries to the communist regime that assumed control of Cambodia (now called Kampuchea) in April 1975. Although the Vietnamese and Cambodians had cooperated in the latter stages of their long-drawn-out struggle for liberation, relations between them had not always been cordial. During the war against the United States, the Vietnamese were able to establish, with Prince Sihanouk's acquiescence, bases and transit facilities through Cambodian territory. In return, the Vietnamese and their allies did nothing to assist the Khmer communists when Sihanouk was out to eliminate them as an internal threat to his regime. It was not until the Lon Nol coup in 1970, which threatened to cut off the Vietnamese supply lines on Cambodian soil, that the Vietnamese agreed to give open backing to the Khmer revolutionary movement, which had been developing since 1968. However, after the 1973 Paris agreement the Cambodians, having resisted Vietnamese pressure to negotiate a peace settlement with Lon Nol, were left to bear the brunt of American bombing.

Recent history had thus combined with the legacy of long-standing animosity between the two countries to produce from the outset considerable tension in the relationship between the two communist governments. Hanoi's call for 'Indochinese solidarity' was received with extreme scepticism by the Kampuchean regime, which lost little time in making known its hostility to

Vietnam's continued military presence on Kampuchean soil. The Pol Pot leadership then proceeded to expel tens of thousands of Vietnamese civilians, many of whom had lived in Kampuchea for generations, and asserted its sovereignty over several disputed islands in the Gulf of Thailand, including Puolo Wai. In apparent respect for the Brévié line – this was the line originally drawn by the French in 1939 to divide the administrative and police jurisdiction between the colony of Cochin China and the protectorate of Cambodia – Hanoi later returned Puolo Wai to Phnom Penh but refused to accept the line as the boundary of the territorial waters or economic zone. The breakdown of border talks in May 1976 was depicted by the Kampuchean side as evidence of Vietnamese 'plans of annexation of a big part of the seas of Kampuchea'.[30] Vietnam, on the other hand, had made every effort, particularly in the early stages of the dispute, to settle outside differences through negotiations, carefully avoided any criticisms of Kampuchea's domestic policies and maintained official support for Phnom Penh's international actions. It was only after repeated Kampuchean attacks on Vietnamese territory and the intensification of internal opposition to the Pol Pot leadership that Hanoi began to criticize the regime's 'brutal and infantile peasant egalitarianism'.[31] Once the dispute reached the point of an irrevocable schism, Pol Pot was openly accused of abandoning the 'path of unity' and of embarking 'on the path of terrorism and destruction of all opposition'.[32]

According to the available evidence, the first serious Kampuchean attack came in April 1977 along the border near Ha Tien and Chau Doc towns and was followed on 24 September 1977 by a major attack when the Pol Pot forces mounted an offensive along a 150-kilometre front in Tay Ninh province, penetrating deep into Vietnamese territory. Significantly, Phnom Penh's military threat had been preceded by Pol Pot's visit to China, during which he attended the Chinese National Day Celebrations as a guest of honour and reaffirmed his country's adherence to Mao Zedong thought. In return, the Chinese leadership, despite some reservations about Pol Pot's domestic policies, gave oblique but unmistakable support for the defence of Kampuchea's territorial integrity. Hanoi for its part, frustrated by Phnom Penh's intransigence and angered by reports of Kampuchean atrocities against Vietnamese civilians, launched a major counter-attack, thrusting deep into Kampuchean territory, possibly in the hope of forcing a negotiated settlement. Following a thorough investigation of the prisoners taken during the hostilities, the Vietnamese learned that Chinese advisers and instructors were playing a major role in Kampuchea's war effort.[33] This assessment was subsequently confirmed by US intelligence, which estimated that as many as 10,000 Chinese military personnel were stationed in Kampuchea, two-thirds of whom were working on the construction of roads and railway lines.

On 31 December 1977 Phnom Penh broadcast a bitter attack on Hanoi, in which it announced the breaking off of diplomatic relations and accused the Vietnamese of trying to create a parallel Kampuchean communist party and army with 'a handful of Khmer traitors and hooligans'. Encouraged by substantial arms deliveries from China, including heavy artillery, tanks and armoured personnel carriers, Kampuchea flatly rejected Vietnam's three-point proposal in February 1978 for an end to hostilities,[34] continued shelling Vietnamese border towns and generally maintained its belligerent posture. Vietnam, which could have occupied much of Cambodia after its successful military thrust in early January 1978, instead chose to withdraw once again in the hope that the Khmer forces might seek a political compromise. However, Kampuchea's refusal to negotiate over the deteriorating border problem, the detrimental effects of the war on Vietnam's reconstruction programme (some 321,400 refugees were estimated to have fled from Kampuchea into Southern Vietnam since 1975, most of them in 1977–78), and especially the damage done to agricultural production in the border zones, eventually convinced the Vietnamese leadership of the need for a military solution to the problem.

The other factor that no doubt strongly influenced Hanoi's thinking was Peking's abandonment on the occasion of the Fifth National People's Congress in February 1978 of any semblance of neutrality. In his Political Report to the Congress, Hua Guofeng accused Vietnam without actually naming it of seeking regional hegemony. The Chinese ambassador in Vietnam subsequently confirmed China's lack of interest in a quick settlement of the conflict by predicting a 'long, long war' between the two Indochinese states. Chinese denunciations reached a new peak on 12 July when the *People's Daily* launched a virulent attack on Vietnam for its 'aggression' against Kampuchea, charging that its victory against the United States and its acquisition of vast amounts of US weaponry had 'made the Vietnamese authorities' heads swell and their hands itch'. Vietnamese pressure on Kampuchea through 'armed aggression and subversion' was seen as evidence of Hanoi's 'dreams of becoming the overlord in Southeast Asia' and the first step in 'the rigging up an "Indochina federation"'.[35] Although Peking was reluctant to make a clear and public commitment of total support for Kampuchea, nevertheless it received in August 1978 a high-level military delegation from Phnom Penh, headed by Son Sen, the Kampuchean Deputy Minister in charge of National Defence. The visit was described by the Chinese press as having 'achieved complete success', and Chinese Vice-Premier Chen Xilian declared that 'the Chinese people and the Chinese People's Liberation Army [would] always stand on the side of the Kampuchean people and the Kampuchean Revolutionary Army'.[36] Son Sen was privately informed by his hosts that China would not be able to intervene directly in the conflict but would provide every possible support. The Chinese also advised the Khmer leadership to prepare for a long-drawn-out guerrilla resistance, in support of which they subsequently made available large quantities of arms, tinned food and communications equipment to be stored in the jungle and mountain areas of Kampuchea.[37]

China's advice to the Pol Pot regime was premised on the assumption that a decision to abandon the capital in the face of Vietnamese and insurgent attacks would not only expose Vietnam's 'aggressive designs' and reinforce the fears of its Southeast Asian neighbours, but would eventually defeat the Vietnamese by pinning them down in a costly and unwinnable guerrilla war. Inevitably, Peking's advocacy of a 'fierce, protracted and arduous struggle' was interpreted by Hanoi as a formula for mobilizing anti-Vietnamese forces in Indochina until the completion of China's projected industrial modernization allowed her to take more decisive action against Vietnam.[38] Whatever the validity of this scenario, and despite the mutual reservations Hua Guofeng's China and Pol Pot's Kampuchea may have had about each other's domestic policies, the two countries were now clearly linked by a marriage of convenience which they hoped would seriously circumscribe the range of options open to Vietnam. Not unexpectedly, Hanoi responded to what it perceived to be Sino–Kampuchean collusion by pointing to 'the blood-stained hands . . . of the Pol Pot–Ieng Sary clique' and by denouncing 'the main culprits', that is, the Chinese rulers who were 'running headlong down the road of hegemonism and [were] full of hegemonistic ambitions'.[39] The Vietnamese gradually reinforced their troops on the border, formalised their strategic relationship with the Soviet Union in November 1978 and by the end of the 1978 rainy season were ready for a major military offensive. The announcement on 4 December 1978 of the formation of the Kampuchean National United Front for National Salvation thus legitimized and paved the way for Vietnam's decisive military intervention on 27 December.

According to western intelligence sources, the force that was unleashed to unseat the Pol Pot regime consisted of more than 100,000 Vietnamese troops and some 20,000 Khmer insurgents aided by Vietnamese tanks, armoured cars and other vehicles and supported by bombing sorties. Several factors had no doubt contributed to the nature and timing of the military operation, but none was more important than the realization that the Kampuchean leadership, under strong pressure from Peking, was gradually changing its diplomatic style and taking small but effective steps to restore its international respectability, particularly in the eyes of the western world. Hanoi may well have regarded the installation of the Heng Samrin regime in Phnòm Penh following a lightning military campaign as a last opportunity to remove the Kampuchean threat to its security and programme of economic reconstruction, while at the same time reducing the likelihood of an enhanced Chinese presence in Indochina. On the other hand, it remained to be seen whether the new Vietnam-backed government in Kampuchea could swiftly quell the Khmer Rouge insurgency that was now cooperating with an assortment of right-wing guerrilla groups, and whether it could head off the support that China and neighbouring Thailand might be willing to offer them.

But the Kampuchean conflict was by no means the only factor contributing to the rapid deterioration in Sino–Vietnamese relations. After April 1975, it became increasingly evident that Chinese aid to Vietnam was being reassessed and that any continuing assistance would rapidly decline. In August, a North Vietnamese economic delegation led by Deputy-Premier Le Thanh Nghi visited Peking with the express purpose of securing aid, but failed to reach any agreement. A subsequent visit by Le Duan in late September produced an agreement on an interest-free loan and supply of general goods to North Vietnam in 1976, but gave no indication that China was ready to contribute significantly to Vietnam's post-war economic recovery or to honour Zhou Enlai's promise made in June 1973 that Chinese economic and military aid to Vietnam would continue for another five years at the 1973 level. By mid-1976, Hanoi, conscious of China's increasingly insistent demands for adherence to an anti-Soviet line and attracted by the prospect of substantial Soviet military and economic aid, rapidly abandoned the careful balancing act between the Soviets and Chinese that it had maintained throughout the duration of the war against the United States.

Although the political upheaval surrounding Mao's death generated hopes of a possible improvement in the Sino–Vietnamese relationship, these were soon dispelled following the visits to Peking by Vietnamese Defence Minister General Vo Nguyen Giap and Premier Pham Van Dong in June 1977. Having terminated all non-refundable aid in 1975, China subsequently decided not to make available any new loans, and the only assistance given in 1977 was for projects begun in earlier years.[40] Chinese actions undoubtedly dealt a severe blow to Vietnamese reconstruction plans, particularly at a time when anticipated western aid failed to materialize, and when a series of natural disasters had virtually crippled Vietnam's war-ravaged economy. In May–July 1978 Chinese policy was brought to its logical conclusion when Peking cancelled all aid projects to Vietnam, withdrew all technicians (as a result of which several important industrial installations were partially paralysed), closed three Vietnamese consulates in southern China[41] and recalled her ambassador from Hanoi. China defended these measures on the grounds that Vietnam had 'stepped up . . . its ostracism of Chinese residents in Viet Nam' and 'destroyed the minimum conditions required for the con-tinued stay of Chinese experts in Viet Nam to carry on the aid projects'.[42] Chinese technicians, it was later argued, had been flown out to compen-sate China for the costs involved in coping with the resettlement of nearly 160,000 ethnic Chinese expelled from Vietnam.[43] However, Hanoi countered by accusing Peking of supporting Kampuchean aggression against Viet-nam and of inciting Chinese residents to leave Vietnam by whipping up a provocative propaganda campaign of fear and hatred. According to the Viet-namese, these gestures were part of a premeditated plan designed to compel Vietnam to adopt an anti-Soviet line. Having failed to achieve her objectives, China, it was claimed, decided to cut off aid by way of punish-ment and as a means of preventing or slowing down the 'building of socialism'.[44]

The increasingly tense relationship with China, coupled with the failure to normalize relations with Washington and to draw increased economic assistance from the West, inevitably led Vietnam to seek closer ties with the Soviet Union. Despite several ideological differences between the two countries, Hanoi realized perfectly well that the Soviet Union remained the only significant source of military assistance, while Moscow recognized that Vietnam (especially after the defeat of Mrs Indira Gandhi's regime in India) was by far its most secure diplomatic and strategic foothold in Asia. A series of visits to Moscow by Vietnamese ministers in 1977 yielded a Soviet pledge to supply two destroyers and four squadrons of MIG-21 fighters, and were followed by the arrival in Vietnam of two Soviet military delegations, presumably to assess the country's military requirements. In May 1978, US intelligence sources claimed that 5000 Soviet experts were stationed in Vietnam, 'engaged on tasks from training the army to use new equipment and operating Soviet aircraft and ships', and that the Soviet Union had established an electronic listening point at Cam Ranh Bay enabling it to keep track of US and Chinese fleet movements and to pinpoint the exact location of Chinese command headquarters.[45] There was, however, no evidence that the Soviet Union was about to use the sophisticated base facilities built by the United States at a cost of $2000 million.

There was nevertheless a price that Vietnam had to pay for its increasing economic and military reliance on the Soviet Union. After initial resistance to the idea, Vietnam was finally obliged to join Comecon as a full member in June 1978. A few months later Le Duan and Pham Van Dong visited Moscow, and on 3 November signed a Treaty of Peace and Friendship and Co-operation, Article 6 of which contained a pledge by both parties to consult each other with a view to taking 'appropriate and effective measures' in the event that either was attacked or threatened with attack. In order to soften the diplomatic impact of the treaty and reassure Southeast Asian governments, Vietnamese spokesmen stressed that the treaty was intended as a 'strategic deterrent' against an 'adventuristic' China and in no way curtailed Hanoi's autonomy. The treaty, it was argued, did not make Soviet intervention automatic, since it was dependent on consultation between the two sides and Hanoi's prior agreement. But for all the stress on independence and non-alignment as the continuing touchstone of Vietnamese foreign policy, it was difficult to avoid the conclusion that economic and political necessity had compelled Vietnam to establish increasingly intimate ties with the Soviet Union and that China was the principal object of this alliance. Peking responded to the treaty in predictably hostile fashion, portraying it as a prelude to the establishment of Soviet military bases on Vietnamese soil and 'an important component part of the Soviet global strategy in Asia which will also increase the hegemonic acts of the Cuba of Asia'.[46]

In addition to the regional and global aspects of their strategic conflict, Peking and Hanoi had to grapple with two other divisive issues – the mass exodus of ethnic Chinese from Vietnam and the border dispute – which, though they did not lie at the origin of the tension between the two countries, nevertheless significantly exacerbated it. According to China, the forced repatriation of some 160,000 Chinese settlers in Vietnam known as the Hoa people was the result of a calculated policy of discrimination and repression which was, in turn, a direct development of Moscow's policy of strategic encirclement. After several alleged attempts to resolve the problem through negotiation, Peking published a bitter denunciation of Vietnam that set the tone for a deluge of articles in the official media and in Hong Kong's pro-Peking papers. The Vietnamese were accused of compelling Chinese residents 'to take up Vietnamese nationality on penalty of losing their work papers, have their staple and other food rations cut, paying heavy taxes and even being deported'.[47] Hanoi's abandonment of the principle of voluntary choice of nationality, it was claimed, violated the agreement between the two sides and ran counter to the general principles of international law.

China's claim of 'persecution' was probably related to the Vietnamese effort to abolish 'capitalist private trade' and reform the currency, which affected everyone engaged in business, regardless of ethnic origin or the nature and scale of the enterprise. However, most of the Chinese businessmen resided in South rather than North Vietnam, principally in Cholon (the Chinese area of Ho Chi Minh City) and tended to leave by sea to Thailand, Malaysia and other capitalist centres. In Ho Chi Minh City alone, perhaps 30,000 shops and businesses were closed and their contents confiscated. The big outflow of 'boat people' from southern Vietnam started in April 1978. Of the 163,000 people who left Vietnam between March 1978 and mid-1979 for nearby non-communist countries, 65 per cent were from Vietnam's Chinese minority.[48] Only a small number of southern Chinese would have managed to make the hazardous trip to the Chinese border. The majority of those who reached Yunnan, Guangxi and Guangdong provinces were much more likely to have been longtime residents from the North. Although the small Chinese-dominated private trade sector in Hanoi and Haiphong was no doubt affected by the Vietnamese government's clampdown on private trade and the private hoarding of money in March 1978, it would seem that an equally and perhaps more important factor in the mass exodus that got under way at the end of March was the tense political climate and anti-Chinese feeling within Vietnam arising from the conflict with Kampuchea. To the extent that China was known to be actively supporting the Pol Pot regime in its feud with Hanoi, the local Chinese community may well have felt their position to be especially vulnerable. Nor can one exclude the possibility, as Vietnamese sources subsequently alleged, that Peking took advantage of the situation and initiated a rumour campaign warning Hoa people of the inevitability of a Sino–Vietnamese war, in which they would presumably become the target of Vietnamese hostility.[49] Hanoi, in fact, accused China of exploiting the overseas Chinese issue to lower the prestige of Vietnam, and of deliberately inciting Chinese workers and technicians to return to China with a view to causing maximum disruption to the North Vietnamese economy. Although the two parties engaged in several consultations, ostensibly with a view to resolving the issue, it was soon evident that the negotiating process and the resulting proposals and counter-proposals were merely a pretext for the exchange of insults and, for the Chinese in particular, a justification for the controlled escalation of the conflict.

Another irritant in the dispute and perhaps a more accurate indicator of the worsening crisis in Sino–Vietnamese relations was the increase in border tension, which had emerged in the early 1970s but greatly intensified with the escalation of the fighting between Kampuchea and Vietnam. In February 1978, incidents at Don Van and Mong Cai resulted in some thirty Vietnamese casualties, and were followed by sporadic exchanges of gunfire and propaganda diatribes over public address systems. By the end of August, both Vietnam and China had built up their forces along the border, with each side accusing the other of intensifying preparations for war. It is quite feasible that the Chinese were deliberately provocative in order to create a diversion that would oblige Vietnam to fight on two fronts, thereby reducing its military effectiveness in the conflict with Kampuchea. Peking may also have intended the border incidents to be taken as a warning to Hanoi that further attacks against the Pol Pot government would invite Chinese retaliation along the Sino–Vietnamese border.

Apart from these larger considerations, local factors may also have played a role in the dispute. The Vietnamese, for example, were concerned that the two dozen or more tribes living in the mountainous autonomous zones of northern Vietnam might establish a closer affiliation with relatives and officials across the ill-demarcated border in China's Yunnan and Guangxi provinces. But the manipulation of the border tension was also related to the disputed jurisdiction of several islands in the South China Sea. Attempts to deal with the problem in 1973–75 had led both sides to strengthen their claims by actual occupation, which in turn contributed to the further aggravation of the conflict. In December 1973, the Vietnamese informed China of their intention to proceed with oil exploration in the Gulf of Tonkin and proposed negotiations for the demarcation of the border. In January 1974, Peking replied affirmatively to the Vietnamese proposal, but immediately pre-empted any negotiated settlement by forcibly seizing the Paracel (Xisha) Islands from the Saigon regime. A year later, Vietnam responded in kind by 'liberating' the Spratly (Nansha) Islands, thereby forestalling a possible Chinese occupation. Claiming all disputed islands to be 'an inalienable part of Chinese territory since ancient times',[50] China refused repeated Vietnamese requests for negotiations over the Paracels and warned that any attempt by Hanoi to exploit the resources on the Spratlys and their surrounding seabeds would provoke China into retaliatory action.[51]

In the absence of a clear delineation of the disputed territory, Chinese and Vietnamese fishermen were involved in several incidents, but these were the result not so much of legal ambiguity as of the deepening mistrust between the two countries. Similar influences prevailed with respect to the contested border area which, Chinese Vice-Premier Li Xiannian readily admitted, involved a mere sixty square kilometres scattered along the length of the boundary and, in one place, a dispute over an area less than one square kilometre. It is difficult to believe that these opposing claims for minuscule pieces of territory could have been responsible for the rapidly deteriorating border situation, for the substantial concentration of forces on either side, or for the increasing frequency of border clashes.

During his visit to the United States and again in Japan on his way home, Deng Xiaoping repeated on several occasions that Vietnam would have to be taught a lesson. When China did invade on 17 February 1979, she claimed it was in retaliation for Vietnamese aggression. According to Peking, Vietnam had been responsible for more than 1100 border provocations in 1978, for 705 incidents between August 1978 and the eve of China's 'counterattack' and for armed incursions into Chinese territory at 162 places, resulting in 300 Chinese frontier guards and civilians being killed or wounded.[52] The final decision for the military offensive, which was taken immediately after Deng's return from the United States, involved some 75,000–85,000 troops out of the seventeen divisions China had deployed near the border. Chinese forces crossed the 450-mile frontier at more than twenty points with their four main concentrations driving towards Cao Bang, Lang Son, Lao Cai and Lai Chau. Although the Chinese government was at pains to emphasize that the invasion was purely punitive in nature and 'limited in time and space', the precise objectives of the exercise were never clearly spelt out. Part of the ambiguity may have derived from China's need to redefine her war aims in the light of her performance on the battlefield.

Initially, the impression was created that the Chinese army was out to destroy Vietnamese military installations near the border, consolidate China's territorial claims and, if possible, seriously weaken Vietnam's military capability. But subsequent Chinese statements indicated somewhat more limited military objectives (this may have been a rationalization of China's limited military success) and much more extensive political goals. As Chinese forces rolled deeper into Vietnamese territory, Hanoi lost several border positions and suffered considerable casualties, but the defiant tone of Vietnam's propaganda and the problems of supply, transport, communications and command coordination encountered by the Chinese operation dimmed any hope of repeating the surgical strike that had humiliated the Indian army in 1962. The Vietnamese were able to mount a competent defensive action relying mainly on well-trained regional forces and militia dug into the hills but without introducing their regular divisions or airforce (neither China nor Vietnam made extensive use of air power).[53] Disclaiming any intention of a strategic victory over the Vietnamese army, Peking contented itself with the brief capture of Lang Son, claiming that the principal military objective of the exercise had been to explode the myth of Vietnamese invincibility. On closer scrutiny, however, it did appear that, for Peking at least, the invasion fitted neatly with the Clausewitzean notion of war as the continuation of politics by other means.

In his address to the UN Security Council on 23 February, China's representative Chen Chu was careful to stress that his country had been 'compelled to make limited counterattack in self-defence of China's frontier as a result of the wanton provocation of border conflicts on the Sino–Vietnamese border by the Vietnamese authorities'.[54] Yet the greater part of his speech was taken up with a bitter denunciation of Vietnam's invasion of Kampuchea and the link between that 'act of aggression' and 'harassment of Chinese border areas'. A few days later, Chen Chu made the linkage between the two conflicts even more explicit by challenging the Vietnamese authorities to commit themselves to withdraw all their invading forces from Kampuchea. To the extent that the collapse of the Pol Pot regime had seriously tarnished China's image as the protector of Kampuchea, her punitive action against Vietnam was intended to restore her prestige by diverting Vietnamese troops from Kampuchea, weakening Vietnamese 'hegemony' in Indochina, diluting Soviet influence in Hanoi and demonstrating Peking's readiness and ability to frustrate Soviet objectives in the region.

After formally ending her invasion on 5 March and completing the withdrawal of her forces on 19 March, China claimed that the PLA had attained its 'set goals in the self-defensive counter attack'.[55] The sixteen-day campaign had enabled the Chinese to gain control of several small but strategic positions on the mountainous border, which they might be able to use as a bargaining lever in a general settlement of the territorial dispute. As for Peking's broader strategic objectives, the war had perhaps demonstrated the limits of Hanoi's freedom of action and compelled Vietnam to divert resources in a way that was likely to hamper its internal consolidation. On the other hand, there was little evidence that China's action had lessened Vietnam's dominance in Indochina or its military and economic dependence on the Soviet Union. It could be argued, however, that by the very timing of its action, coming so soon after the conclusion of the Sino–Japanese treaty and the normalization of Sino–American relations, Peking had succeeded in casting doubts on the reliability of the Soviet Union as an ally.

During the course of the war, Moscow limited its reaction to some verbal warnings and the despatch of a dozen ships to the South China Sea, thus giving the impression that it was not prepared to intervene directly, either because it wished to avoid a conventional war with China or because it feared the possibility of American involvement. Paradoxically, by insisting that President Carter had given tacit encouragement if not full approval to China's invasion plans and yet maintaining such a low-key response,[56] the Soviet Union had indicated that its strategic relationship with the United States (and perhaps the prospect of a SALT II agreement) would have to take precedence over its obligations to Vietnam.

Although China and Vietnam subsequently agreed to hold negotiations for the resolution of their conflict and to exchange prisoners captured during their sixteen-day war, the border tension continued unabated. At the first few sessions of the talks, Vietnam repeatedly accused China of continuing to occupy Vietnamese territory, of massing about half a million troops in the border region, and of deploying twelve divisions with thousands of artillery pieces along the border.[57] Peking countered these allegations by accusing Vietnam of intrusions into Chinese territory, resulting in several Chinese casualties, and of stepping up the expulsion of Chinese nationals from Vietnam. These charges and counter-charges were paralleled by proposals and counter-proposals. Inevitably, China rejected the Vietnamese three-point proposal of 16 April, calling for the creation of a demilitarized zone and the exchange of prisoners, the restoration of normal relations between the two countries, and the settlement of the border and territorial dispute on the basis of the Franco–Chinese agreements of 1887 and 1895. Instead, Peking put forward on 26 April an eight-point proposal which, among other things, required Vietnam to renounce hegemony in Indochina, to withdraw its troops from Kampuchea and Laos, to respect Chinese sovereignty over the Paracels and the Spratlys, and to take back those Chinese nationals who had been driven to China.[58] As could be expected, the Vietnamese negotiator, Phan Hien, dismissed the Chinese package as designed to impose a 'Chinese peace which is even worse than the "Pax Americana" of the past'.[59]

Hanoi was certainly not going to concede at the negotiating table what China had clearly failed to gain on the battlefield. As long as Vietnamese self-confidence and military strength remained intact, there was little likelihood that China would be able to compel Hanoi to accept any erosion of its independence and sovereignty or to downgrade its strategic and diplomatic association with Moscow. The Chinese, it seemed, had seriously under-estimated the depth of Vietnam's determination not to return to the pattern of dependence and subservience that, in previous centuries, had frequently characterized its relations with China. The relationship with the Soviet Union provided the Vietnamese with a unique opportunity to maintain their independence vis-à-vis China by introducing a strong countervailing force in the regional balance of power. Far from inclining Hanoi to reassess its perceptions and objectives, Chinese actions and propaganda merely reinforced its commitment to established policies. In this sense, Chinese warnings about Soviet and Vietnamese hegemonism had become self-fulfilling prophecies. It remained to be seen whether China would accept, however grudgingly, the new strategic reality of a powerful Vietnam closely linked to the Soviet Union, or whether it would seek to modify the status quo by another punitive expedition that might well provoke a stronger Soviet reaction and prove even costlier than the previous confrontation.

It remains to say a word about China's dwindling presence in Laos, which stemmed from and closely paralleled the deterioration in Sino–Vietnamese relations. In spite of its close ties with Vietnam and the signing of a twenty-five-year treaty of friendship and cooperation between the two countries in July 1977, Laos persisted for some time with its increasingly difficult tightrope act between Hanoi and Peking. However, after the open Kampuchea–Vietnam rupture in December 1977, Laos felt obliged to reaffirm its support for Vietnam's struggle against 'imperialism and other international reactionary forces'. In 1978, the Laotian government attempted to reduce the Chinese presence in the country by requesting the withdrawal of army engineering units and military equipment brought in by the Chinese to defend the road network they began constructing during the war against the United States. In December 1978, the road-building project was dealt another blow when Laos requested the closure of the Chinese economic counsellor's office in Oudomsay. On the other hand, by virtue of their involvement in northern Laos for nearly eighteen years, the Chinese had apparently gained the respect and confidence of the local population, many of whom had benefited from Chinese aid for public works, sanitation, medical care and the supply of consumer goods.

China's prestige in the area was of paricular concern to the Laotian authorities who feared that it might provide the basis for a rebellion against the government. The suspicion that China was training commando units and assisting dissident elements operating in Phong Saly, Oudomsay and Nam Tha provinces was an additional factor helping to sour relations between the two countries. Not surprisingly, after the Chinese invasion of Vietnam, Laos condemned Peking for the first time by name. The Vientiane statement, which firmly aligned Laos with Hanoi and the Heng Samrin government in Phnom Penh, was the result of intense Vietnamese pressure designed to create a common Indochinese front against the perceived Chinese threat.[60] The subsequent expulsion of the remaining Chinese road-builders from northern Laos and the sharp reduction in the number of Chinese embassy staff in Vientiane further weakened Peking's position in Indochina. The ensuing Chinese attacks on the Pathet Lao regime, which was accused of allowing tens of thousands of Vietnamese troops to be stationed in Laotian territory and of sending Lao troops to Kampuchea 'to serve as common fodder in the Vietnamese aggression against the country',[61] provided striking confirmation of the almost total eclipse of Chinese influence in Indochina.

The ASEAN Connection

It is perhaps ironical, but an accurate indicator of the changing direction of Chinese foreign policy, that Peking's declining fortunes in communist Indochina and especially the escalating intensity of 'its conflict with Hanoi should have been accompanied by and contributed to China's rapprochement with non-communist Southeast Asia. Needless to say, the process of diplomatic normalization with the ASEAN governments was a delicate operation requiring a good deal of patience and diplomatic flexibility to overcome the years of mutual suspicion and ideological animosity. The task was greatly facilitated, however, by the fact that both China and the ASEAN states now shared a common interest in the maintenance of a substantial American military presence in the Asian rimlands. This community of interests was to a large extent made possible by the Sino–American rapprochement in the early 1970s and was given additional impetus in the mid-1970s by the growing convergence between Chinese and ASEAN attitudes towards Vietnam.

The first notable breakthrough in China's search for a dialogue with ASEAN occurred in Sino–Malaysian relations, and culminated in the joint communiqué issued on 31 May 1974 at the end of Tun Abdul Razak's visit to Peking. The agreement provided for the establishment of diplomatic relations between the two countries on the basis of the five principles of peaceful coexistence. China recognized the independence and sovereignty of Malaysia, while Malaysia acknowledged the People's Republic of China as the sole government of China and Taiwan as an unalienable part of Chinese territory. Malaysian recognition of Peking, however, had come only after a long series of initiatives. In a major speech in January 1971, Tun Abdul Razak had given the first clear indication that Malaysia was in the process of reassessing its China policy.[62] Peking's favourable response to the shift in Malaysian foreign policy was soon reflected in the growing number of reciprocal visits by sporting teams, technical experts and trade missions. By 1972, the Malaysian National Corporation had approved 4000 applications by Malaysian traders to import Chinese goods worth M$110 million. During 1971 China purchased 40,000 tons of Malaysian rubber, and in the first two months of 1972 another 12,000 tons, which was more than double the amount for the corresponding period of 1971. During the 1973 rice shortage, Malaysia bought 100,000 tons of rice from China. The increasing scope for trade relations between the two countries was matched by a progressively more cordial diplomatic climate. Even before the Malaysian Prime Minister's visit to Peking, the Chinese had shown signs of being seriously interested in Malaysia's neutralization scheme, which they interpreted as a useful device for limiting foreign penetration in the Southeast Asian region.

The new spirit of cooperation between Peking and Kuala Lumpur could not conceal, however, the difficulties surrounding two major unresolved issues: on the one hand, the political future of the overseas Chinese community in Malaysia and China's attitude to it, and, on the other, the perennial problem of Chinese support for communist insurgency.

China's difficulty in devising an acceptable policy with respect to the overseas Chinese, in Malaysia as in several other Southeast Asian countries, was attributable, in part, to the sharp economic divisions among the overseas Chinese themselves. While the wealthy class of Chinese merchants and entrepreneurs tended to be strongly opposed to communism, many of the poorer Chinese were attracted to left-wing politics and tended to look to the People's Republic as their protector. Peking was able to extract some benefits from the rich overseas Chinese through their remittance of large sums of money to their families and relatives in southern China, resulting in the entry of valuable foreign exchange. As for the contribution that the more radical and less privileged Chinese minorities might make towards the progress of revolutionary struggle, Peking was mindful of the fact that Chinese leadership of any movement was likely to minimize the chances of securing non-Chinese support. Given that in most Southeast Asian countries the Chinese constituted a minority, often mistrusted by the rest of the population, the development of revolutionary zeal among them might serve merely to reinforce hostility and resentment not only against the Chinese community but against China herself.

Enough will have been said to indicate that the overseas Chinese were as much a liability as an asset in Peking's relations with Southeast Asia. For this very reason it had not supported Chinese education amongst the overseas Chinese and had sought, wherever possible, to disengage itself from the problems of ethnic integration confronting many Southeast Asian societies. After the Cultural Revolution, China continued with this policy as was demonstrated by her complete non-involvement in the communal strife that led to the 1969 Malaysian riots and resulted in further inroads into Chinese political rights. China's attempts to defuse this potentially explosive issue were taken to their logical conclusion in the joint Sino–Malaysian communiqué of May 1974, which stated:

> ... The Chinese Government considers anyone of Chinese origin who has taken up of his own will or acquired Malaysian nationality as automatically forfeiting Chinese nationality. As for residents who retain Chinese nationality of their own will, the Chinese Government, acting in accordance with its consistent policy, will enjoin them to abide by the law of the Government of Malaysia, respect the customs and habits of the people there, and live in unity with them, and their proper rights and interests will be protected by the Government of China and respected by the Government of Malaysia.[63]

The formula contained in the statement however, left unresolved the position of those stateless Chinese variously estimated at between 150,000 and 250,000. Nor did the agreement between the two governments provide any hint of a possible solution to the problem posed by the economic strength and political weakness of the Chinese minority, which, though constituting some 40 per cent of the Malaysian population, enjoyed less than 15 per cent representation in the national parliament.

A separate but closely related question of compelling importance to the Malaysian government was China's relationship with the local communist movement. On his return from Peking, the Malaysian Prime Minister gave an enthusiastic account of the assurances he had received in Peking that communist insurgency would be treated as a purely internal matter for the Malaysian government to deal with as it pleased. Clearly, Tun Abdul Razak was hoping that the new association with China would undercut the prospects of the revolutionary movement by undermining its morale and by making it diplomatically unrewarding for the Chinese to maintain their current level of support. In a bid to frustrate this strategy the Malayan Communist Party sought to demonstrate its continuing links with Peking, hence the proud claims of the Voice of the Malayan Revolution that its broadcasts commemorating the twenty-fifth anniversary of the Malayan National Liberation Army had been re-broadcast by Radio Peking in several languages. There was, in reality, no reason to expect that the establishment of diplomatic relations with Kuala Lumpur would lead Peking to abandon its dual strategy. Although solidarity with Southeast Asian communist parties and advocacy of armed struggle were no longer given the same priority or overt encouragement as in previous years, they were not altogether abandoned. On the other hand, China's revised global strategy with its increasing emphasis on anti-hegemonism was helping to bridge the diplomatic gap between Peking and many of the rightist governments of Southeast Asia.[64]

As with Malaysia, so with the other four ASEAN countries the Chinese government tried to facilitate the process of bridge-building by an adroit mixture of diplomatic contacts and trade incentives. As a result of the first Filipino trade mission to China in 1971 arrangements were made for Filipino coconut oil to be exchanged for Chinese rice. Early in 1972 Peking was host to President Marcos' brother-in-law, Governor Romualdes, and to Senator Salvador Laurel. The following year saw the despatch of another trade delegation to Peking and to the Canton Fair, and a reciprocal Chinese mission to the Philippines. Adding momentum to these contacts, Zhou Enlai expressed to the Filipino visitors his confidence that trade relations would soon expand and 'develop into diplomatic relations'.[65] The Philippines was obviously interested in securing a regular supply of crude oil from China while expanding its sales of sugar, coconut oil and wood products. The visit to Peking by the President's wife, Mrs Imelda Marcos, in September 1974 consolidated the diplomatic and economic relationship between the two countries and led to an agreement whereby China would supply the Philippines with no less than one billion barrels of crude oil at 'reasonable prices'.[66]

By 1974, it was clear that oil had become an important element in Peking's diplomacy in Southeast Asia and in its efforts to normalize relations with both Thailand and the Philippines. In December 1973, the Thailand Foreign Ministry disclosed that negotiations to buy oil from China were under way between the Thai and Chinese delegations at the United Nations. In the same month, the Deputy Foreign Minister. Chatichai Choonhavan, accompanied by the Defence Minister, Marshall Dawee Chullasapya, visited Peking and concluded a deal with China for the delivery of 50,000 tons of diesel oil at 'favourable prices'.[67] A long-standing impediment to improved trading relations between the two countries, the Revolutionary Party Decree No. 53 introduced in 1959 in order to restrict all contact with communsit states, was progressively eliminated and finally repealed after the overthrow of the Thai military regime in October 1973. Following the visit of a Thai trade delegation to China in October 1972 it was announced that China had ordered 60,000 tons of maize, thus bringing Thailand 120 million baht in earnings and making

China Thailand's best customer for maize.[68] In January 1975, a further agreement was concluded providing for the sale of another 75,000 tonnes of Chinese highspeed diesel oil to Thailand.

Both the Philippines and Thailand finally agreed to establish diplomatic relations with China in 1975. At Chinese insistence, the Zhou–Marcos communiqué of 9 June and the Zhou–Pramoj communiqué of 1 July each contained an anti-hegemony clause.[69] Both Manila and Bangkok recognized the People's Republic as the sole legal government of China and agreed to remove all official representation from Taiwan within one month from the signature of the agreement. Peking, for its part, reaffirmed that it did not recognize dual nationality for overseas Chinese. On the other hand, it would respect the right of Chinese residents in Thailand to retain Chinese nationality and would protect their proper rights and interests provided that they abided by the laws of Thailand, respected the customs and habits of the Thai people and lived in amity with them.

The steady acceleration of trading and diplomatic links did not altogether bypass China's relations with Singapore and Indonesia, though in the latter case the pace was distinctly slower and the political climate far less favourable. After 1971, Singapore, which enjoyed the advantage of a substantial two-way trade with China, sent several trade missions and technical delegations to China, but still insisted on dissociating economic from diplomatic relations. On the subject of recognition, Prime Minister Lee Kuan Yew indicated that Singapore would prefer to adopt a wait-and-see attitude and leave the initiative to its Southeast Asian neighbours. He did not share Malaysia's confidence that China would always respect the sovereignty and independence of Southeast Asian countries, maintaining that, once the influence of the other great powers in the region had been effectively checked, China might seek to expand her own presence and activities. In contrast to the Malaysian position, Singapore espoused the view that it would be preferable for great power rivalry to remain a factor in Southeast Asian politics, with a continuing American presence helping to offset China's growing influence. Singapore's attitude was partly inspired by such domestic considerations as the need to create a viable Singaporean identity and prevent the growth of a vigorous political opposition to the ruling government. By the same token, the attraction of increased economic and cultural cooperation with China and the appreciation of the power realities in Asia had gradually encouraged the kind of conciliatory diplomacy that Malaysia, the Philippines and Thailand had already initiated. A high-ranking mission headed by the Foreign Minister, Sinathamby Rajaratnam, visited Peking in March 1975 and was followed by Lee Kuan Yew in May 1976. Singapore's Prime Minister reiterated that there would be no early exchange of ambassadors between the two countries as his government wished to be the last of the ASEAN member governments to normalize relations with the People's Republic. On the other hand, he was ready to pursue the development of bilateral relations in those fields where there was 'basic agreement', and indicated that Peking had undertaken to accept the way in which the Singapore government dealt with communists inside its territory as a domestic matter.[70]

It was now clear that the greatest obstacle to the normalization of relations between China and the ASEAN countries derived not so much from the hostility of Chinese diplomacy as from the domestic situation of Southeast Asian States. Nowhere was this more evident than in the murky atmosphere that still prevailed between Peking and Djakarta in the early 1970s. The Suharto government, which had frequently claimed that recognition of Peking was not a priority issue, had rejected several Chinese overtures, including the seemingly innocuous invitation in 1971 to send a table tennis team to China. Foreign Minister Adam Malik was reported as saying that diplomatic relations would not be restored for another five or even ten years.[71]

He attributed the delay in diplomatic normalization to the problems associated with the integration of the Chinese community into Indonesian society, and indicated to Chinese Foreign Minister Ji Pengfei at the Paris Conference on Vietnam in early 1973 that 'Indonesia would need time to educate its Chinese population to be loyal to Indonesia and not to have their orientation toward Peking'.[72] It is true that Indonesia's difficulty in dealing with the overseas Chinese was compounded by their apparent preference for ambiguous citizenship status. On the other hand, it is equally true that the government's policy was marked by procrastination and indecision and a tendency to reinforce popular Indonesian suspicions of Chinese loyalties and life-styles. There was, moreover, little evidence that the Suharto regime had fashioned a coherent programme for the political and economic integration of the Chinese minority. On the contrary, the separate existence of this ethnic community was likely to be maintained so long as it provided a convenient scapegoat for local popular discontent. This type of stereotype response was in evidence in the Djakarta riots of January 1974, even though the main target of attack appeared to be overseas Japanese rather than local Chinese business interests.

There was, however, no reason why the thorny question of China's relations with the overseas Chinese could not be resolved to the mutual satisfaction of both sides. With the passage of time, agreements could be devised to deal with the problem of the stateless Chinese not only in Malaysia but also in the Philippines, Thailand and Indonesia.

If the overseas Chinese did not constitute an insuperable obstacle to improved relations between China and Southeast Asia, neither did the question of revolutionary insurgency. By the mid 1970s the Malaysian, Filipino and Thai governments had all come to the conclusion that a policy of diplomatic and economic cooperation with Peking might even help to moderate its advocacy of armed struggle and reduce the level of its material assistance to liberation struggles. In the case of Thailand, the return of military rule after the October 1976 coup, which reversed most of the foreign policies of the 'democratic' period, helped to slow down the development of relations with both China and the Indochinese states. However, the bloodless coup of October 1977 which brought General Kriangsak to power restored the policy of détente with China, who was now endeavouring to cement an informal alliance with Thailand and Kampuchea as a means of countering the growing links between Moscow, Hanoi and Vientiane. In December 1977, Prime Minister Kriangsak reaffirmed his country's commitment to 'constructive cooperation' with China and described the insurgency problem as 'an internal affair of our own that has to be solved by ourselves',[73] thereby effectively removing it as an obstacle to closer ties with Peking. During an official goodwill visit to China by the Thai Prime Minister in March–April 1978, two agreements were concluded, one on trade and the other on scientific and technical cooperation. For her part, China restated her full support of ASEAN and endorsed the Association's aim to establish a zone of peace, freedom and neutrality in Southeast Asia, first proposed by Malaysia and subsequently endorsed by the Kuala Lumpur ASEAN Declaration of 27 November 1971. It should be added, however, that many aspects of the neutralization scheme were never clarified. Although the ASEAN countries had requested the great powers to recognize and guarantee the neutrality of the associated states, the precise nature of ASEAN had yet to be defined. Was it a group of nations striving for a non-aligned and genuinely independent policy, or was it to be the nucleus of a new coalition, perhaps a new alliance arrangement closely linked to and dependent on the United States? Or was the zonal concept an attempt to establish a new 'co-prosperity sphere' dominated by Japanese and American corporate interests?

These ambiguities were much less important to the Chinese leadership than the political milage to be gained from increasing cooperation with non-communist Southeast Asia. During his visit to the Philippines in March 1978 Vice-Premier Li Xiannian commended the government of President Marcos for opposing 'hegemonism and power politics', praised the progress made by ASEAN in regional economic cooperation and endorsed 'the positive proposal of the ASEAN countries for the neutrality of Southeast Asia'.[74] Before the end of the visit it was announced that the two countries had agreed to settle in 'a spirit of friendliness and conciliation' the dispute over the Spratly Islands, which were claimed by the Philippines as well as China and Vietnam. A few months later, a five-year trade agreement was signed in Peking, which provided for the import of 1,200,000 tonnes of crude oil per year as from January 1979, thereby making the Philippines the second largest importer of Chinese oil after Japan.

By 1978 the strengthening of bilateral and multilateral ties with the ASEAN countries had become a crucial aspect of the Sino–Vietnamese contest for influence in Southeast Asia and, therefore, one of the primary objectives of Chinese foreign policy. The goodwill mission to ASEAN countries by Vietnamese Foreign Minister Nguyen Duy Trinh in early 1978 was part of a concerted campaign to convince them of Vietnam's good intentions and dispel any fears of a Vietnamese military threat. He was followed in July by Deputy Foreign Minister Phan Hien who visited Singapore, Malaysia and Thailand, and two months later by Prime Minister Pham Van Dong who made a quick tour of all five ASEAN members, partly in order to pre-empt any diplomatic leverage China might gain from a similar trip that Deng Xiaoping was scheduled to make in November. Hanoi took advantage of these diplomatic contacts to stress the need for all the countries in the region to maintain their independence and sovereignty, and to be wary of Chinese expansionism and of the dangers posed by the overseas Chinese, who were described as a latent fifth column for Peking. Pham Van Dong also proposed a treaty of friendship, cooperation and non-aggression between Vietnam and the ASEAN countries, as well as several other agreements dealing with cultural exchanges, scientific and technical, postal and telecommunications and maritime cooperation.[75] He assured his hosts, particularly Malaysia and Thailand, that Vietnam would not assist communist insurgency in their countries and was careful, when visiting the Philippines, not to raise questions about such sensitive issues as the future of American military bases or the disputed Spratly Islands. Vietnam even went so far as to advocate a Southeast Asian zone of peace, independence and neutrality, that is, a modified version of the ASEAN concept, which was to encompass both the ASEAN region and Indochina. Hanoi now insisted that its previous opposition to ASEAN referred only to the grouping's military tendencies. Clearly, Vietnam's intention was to establish a more intimate association with ASEAN, thereby placing China in the dilemma of having either to recognize Vietnam's new role in Southeast Asia or risk incurring the displeasure of the ASEAN states.

Predictably, the response of ASEAN leaders to Vietnam's proposals and softer diplomacy was polite but guarded. While Malaysia was more accommodating to Vietnamese initiatives than many of its neighbours, no member of ASEAN was ready to enter into treaty relationships that could be interpreted as a tilt towards Hanoi and against Peking, or as a departure from the previously accepted meaning of the ASEAN concept of a zone of peace, freedom and neutrality. Although Deng Xiaoping insisted during his trip through Southeast Asia in November that China would not withdraw her support from local revolutionary movements, he was adamant that such support was separate from and compatible with cordial state-to-state relations. The Chinese leader argued that the Vietnam–Soviet treaty, by contrast, was directed not only against China but against the peace and security of the Asia–Pacific region. He linked explicitly the 'global hegemonism' of the Soviet Union with the 'regional hegemonism' of Vietnam, and invited all Southeast Asian nations wishing to safeguard their sovereignty and independence to oppose 'hegemonism big or small'.[76] In this context, ASEAN was described as securing the interests of peace, stability and prosperity in Southeast Asia and the world at large. In other words, Chinese diplomacy was only too willing to exploit the pro-western and anti-Soviet inclinations of ASEAN governments and particularly their preoccupation with internal security which implied increasing dependence on the United States for access to sophisticated military equipment, communications and transporation systems and surveillance capabilities.

It was not, however, until Vietnam's full-scale military intervention in Kampuchea in December 1978 that China was able to take full advantage of anti-Vietnamese sentiment within ASEAN. Following the meeting of ASEAN foreign ministers in January 1979, a statement was issued deploring 'the armed intervention threatening the independence, sovereignty and territorial integrity of Cambodia' and calling for 'the immediate withdrawal of all foreign troops from Cambodian territory'.[77] At the meeting convened by the Security Council on 11 January, Singapore's representative argued that his country and others in Southeast Asia would, in the light of Vietnam's earlier assurances that it would not interfere in the internal affairs of other countries, entertain 'serious doubts on the credibility of Vietnam's word and its intentions'.[78] The stage was thus set for Peking to draw ASEAN into taking sides in the intensified struggle for influence between the two communist nations.

The erosion of Thailand's neutrality in the conflict, following the flight of Pol Pot forces into Thai territory, was greatly accentuated by Chinese offers of support in the event of 'Vietnamese aggression' against Thailand.[79] A similar pledge of support was conveyed to the Philippines government. The obvious implication of Peking's position was that ASEAN should align itself with China in her battle with Vietnam. Though the Malaysian government was fearful of the consequences of such an alliance or quasi-alliance, its position was considerably weakened by the steady flow of boat people from Vietnam to the ASEAN countries. With 76,000 'refugees' already in Malaysia, Foreign Minister Tunku Ahmad Rithauddeen warned in June 1979 that further arrivals would 'mar' relations between the two countries. Thailand, Indonesia and Singapore also hit out at Hanoi, giving notice that they would not accept any more refugees and accusing Vietnam of deliberately tolerating the exodus, partly as a means of destabilizing the five-nation grouping. As could be expected, Peking sought to capitalize on the situation by highlighting the 'tremendous difficulties' experienced by China in common with Southeast Asian countries as a result of the Vietnamese policy of 'aggression, ethnic discrimination and human trafficking'.[80] The influx of refugees and the Indochinese conflict thus provided ASEAN with a pretext for a concerted anti-Vietnamese propaganda campaign and an expanded programme of military cooperation, particularly in relation to the Thai–Malaysian border. As further evidence of its wish to collaborate with ASEAN, Peking announced in July that it would encourage the Communist Party of Thailand to join with the army-backed Thai government in a *de facto* united front against Vietnam and its Indochinese allies.

China's programme of bridge-building with ASEAN formed, then, part of a much larger plan aimed at the diplomatic and economic isolation of Vietnam, in a manner remarkably reminiscent of American attempts to ostracize China during the 1950s and 1960s. The Chinese policy of containment, which was fully supported and partly inspired by American diplomacy, was directed as much against the Soviet Union as against Vietnam. The net effect of the policy was to widen the gap separating China from communist Indochina and to align Peking more closely with the new Asian–Pacific order favoured by the United States and Japan, in which ASEAN was expected to play an increasingly prominent strategic and economic role. The growing complementarity and coordination of American and Chinese policies, which had become progressively more apparent since Brzezinski's visit to China in May 1978, were thus given added impetus by China's rapidly expanding connection with ASEAN.

Epilogue

By whatever standards we may wish to judge the achievements of the Chinese Communist Revolution, there is no denying its far-reaching impact on China's role and visibility within the international community. In the space of less than two decades, the Communist leadership had succeeded in restoring China's political unity, territorial integrity and sense of national pride to a degree unmatched since the late eighteenth century. Despite the periods of intense domestic turmoil and considerable external conflict often involving one or both super-powers, Mao's China was able to neutralize serious threats to her security and to develop a distinctive foreign policy and diplomatic style that commanded the attention of small and great powers alike. During the greater part of the 1950s and 1960s, Maoist China injected a new element of polarization into the international political system, not in the crude sense that she became the standard bearer for armed revolution the world over, but in the more subtle, yet more radical sense that she was willing to challenge the prevailing notions of world order and the underlying structures of power and authority.

By the early 1970s, however, significant changes had occurred in China's domestic and external environment. Her enhanced security, status and influence, coupled with the steady decline of the bipolar system of international relations, gradually undermined the identity that had hitherto existed between national interest and ideological commitment. Though China was still far from reconciled to a policy of the status quo, her newly acquired sense of power and prestige inevitably moderated her disenchantment with the prevailing balance of power and diluted the revolutionary content of her diplomacy. Her increasingly close association not only with the United States but with the other major capitalist powers, and the much lower priority accorded to Third World struggles against colonialism and neo-colonialism, pointed to the loss of revolutionary momentum in Chinese foreign policy. Although these changes did not become fully apparent until the mid-1970s, the evidence suggests that they gained considerable momentum almost immediately after the Cultural Revolution and that, generally speaking, they enjoyed Mao's blessing, which greatly helped to legitimize them.

Domestically, the accent was now on high-speed industrialization and an economic programme designed to bring China by the end of the century into the front ranks of the world's great powers. The main responsibility for the realization of this goal was assigned to the state and its vast, centralized bureaucratic apparatus which was to oversee and co-ordinate the inputs by the various sectors of the economy. During the second plenum of the Fifth National People's Congress held in late June and early July 1979, Hua Guofeng unveiled a new three-year programme to 're-adjust, restructure, consolidate and improve' the national economy. Many of the ambitious targets that had been previously announced as part of the modernization strategy, particularly in steel and grain production, were now abandoned. The re-adjustment of economic policy did not, however, reverse Peking's fundamental decision to open its doors to direct foreign investment and accept loans from foreign banks.

Explaining the recently adopted law on joint Chinese and foreign enterprises, Vice-Premier Li Xiannian conveyed to a visiting US industrial research delegation in July 1979 China's expectation that the proportion of investment by foreign companies would in many cases be higher than 50 per cent. Such joint enterprises could operate for twenty years or even longer, and foreign profits derived from them could be sent abroad so long as foreign investors abided by Chinese laws and tax policies. In October 1979, Vice-Premier Gu Mu even raised the possibility that some foreign firms might invest in China as sole owners of enterprises. Special export-oriented zones were now taking shape not only near major industrial centres such as Shanghai and Tianjin but also in areas in Guangdong province including Shenzen, Zhuhai and Shantou. In an effort to facilitate and speed up international arrangements, the provinces of Guangdong and Fujian were granted extraordinary commercial authority to deal directly with foreign firms. Cooperation with foreign capital was envisaged particularly in the electric power industry, development of energy resources, including oil and coal, transport and communications, raw or semi-processed materials, precision machinery, and the mechanization of agriculture. As regards long-term crude oil strategy, Chinese planners appeared increasingly committed to offshore development with its unavoidable high foreign technology participation and its advantageous location in relation to the large Japanese market. But the actual extent and timetable of foreign involvement in China's oil expansion programme had yet to be determined. In any case, the acceleration of China's crude oil exports would ultimately be limited not only by the rising costs of crude oil extraction but also by China's huge domestic requirements.

As part of the re-evaluation of the modernization strategy, steps were also taken in 1979 to provide the Bank of China with greater authority, particularly over major capital import decisions. By the end of the year, China had completed or was on the verge of finalizing between $20,000 million and $30,000 million worth of foreign credits. It was estimated that loans and credit facilities of roughly comparable magnitude would be available to China in 1980. In addition, joint equity venture investments over the next five years were likely to yield ancillary external resources valued at $10,000 million to $20,000 million. In spite of the availability of direct commercial loans, Chinese planners were nevertheless expected to adopt a cautious approach to such financial arrangements and to complement them with joint equity ventures, counter trade and other payback schemes. In the area of foreign trade, however, the import of technology continued to accelerate with the volume of business in 1978 equalling twice the total for the five years from 1973 through 1977. Total two-way trade in 1978 represented a 30 per cent growth over the previous year. During the first seven months of 1979, Chinese exports totalled $6,960 million, that is, an increase of 40 per cent over the corresponding period of the previous year, whereas Chinese imports totalled $8,400 million, an increase of 70 per cent.

Enough will have been said to indicate that the modernization project was to be facilitated by the transfusion of substantial financial and technological resources, which only advanced capitalism could provide. Once the hurdles of diplomatic normalization had been overcome, China was in a position to expand her trade links with the West, which she hoped would enable her to gain access to Western capital, technical know-how and military hardware. A good example of this trend was provided by America's opening into China's electricity market following the signing of the protocol on hydroelectric power and water resource management during Vice-President Walter Mondale's visit to Peking in August 1979. Although the agreement carried no immediate sales of technology it was expected to lead eventually to a variety of consulting, engineering and construction contracts. Another major stumbling block in the development of Sino–American trade was removed in January 1980 with the approval by Congress of the agreement conferring most-favoured-nation status on China. The agreement was likely to encourage a significant increase in China's exports to the United States by sharply reducing tariffs on Chinese goods. As a result of this arrangement, the US Export-Import Bank was now free to enter into negotiations for extending credits and credit guarantees to China, thereby enabling American firms to compete more effectively with their European and Japanese counterparts.

But quite apart from its value for the economic modernization programme, a more cooperative relationship with the capitalist world was perceived as a necessary response to China's conflict with the Soviet Union. For the time being at least, an equidistant relationship with all great powers was deemed neither feasible nor desirable. During his tour of Western Europe in October–November 1979, which included France, Germany, Britain and Italy, Hua Guofeng returned time and again to the theme of Soviet hegemonism and to the need for 'all peace-loving states' to block the Soviet Union's 'aggressive' and 'expansionist' designs. He encouraged West Europeans to 'put missiles before detente' and argued that a strong, united Germany was in the interests of world peace, presumably because a reunited Germany would mean the erosion of the Soviet bloc, and serve as a useful counterweight to Soviet power. By magnifying and dramatizing the alleged Soviet threat, thereby fuelling

European fears and suspicions, Peking was perhaps also hoping to acquire more readily and with fewer strings the economic assistance it was seeking. In each of the four countries the Chinese leader signed new agreements for greater economic, scientific and cultural cooperation. In Germany, it was announced that, in addition to the $869 million in credits which German banks were making available, the German government would underwrite another substantial credit guarantee of approximately equal value. German firms were expected to play a leading role in China's energy research, energy technology, outer space research, raw material research, farming, medicine, sea and oil exploration, and chemical research, as well as in China's plans to modernize electrical and communications networks.

A particularly powerful attraction for Mao's successors was the prospect of acquiring sophisticated Western armaments, which would hasten the development of China's military capabilities, while at the same time cementing a strategic connection deemed essential to the containment of Soviet power. The question of arms transfers certainly featured prominently in the discussions between Hua Guofeng and his European hosts in October–November 1979. In Britain, the Chinese Premier let it be known that China was greatly interested in concluding a licensing agreement with Rolls-Royce to manufacture advanced engines such as the Pegasus engine used by the Harrier. In Italy, missile guidance systems, helicopters and rapid-fire cannon were the main objects of attention. An even more significant breakthrough in Chinese military cooperation with the West occurred soon after when US Secretary of Defense Harold Brown visited Peking in January 1980. He used the occasion to promote wider security links between the two countries; called on China to join the United States in finding 'complementary actions' to counter growing Russian expansion, and offered her access to the sophisticated Landsat-D surveillance satellite.

The gradual but steady re-orientation of Chinese diplomacy was thus reflected in and reinforced by political and economic developments within China, which also pointed to the blurring of the revolutionary vision, the partial abandonment of the Maoist principle of self-reliance and the increasingly enthusiastic adoption of western-inspired notions of modernization.

No doubt, the Chinese state would seek to monitor and control China's participation in the international market economy and regulate the activities of transnational corporations and international banking and other financial institutions to ensure their compatibility with Chinese objectives. On the other hand, the wholesale incorporation of capitalist technology, with its emphasis on technical rationality and bureaucratic organization, would of necessity widen the economic and cultural gap between town and country, accentuate income differences within the industrial labour force, intensify the elitist structure of the educational system and reinforce the process of political stratification. Given the priority accorded by the Deng Xiaoping–Hua

Guofeng leadership to the modernization objective, it is hardly surprising that many of the propositions central to the Maoist critique of capitalism should have been substantially modified and, in some instances, altogether discarded.

Several of the verdicts arising from ideological campaigns over the previous two decades were being gradually eroded; others were totally reversed. The revisionist and long-discredited policies associated with Liu Shaoqi were once again in official favour as was Peng Dehuai's critique of Mao's radical programmes. In a major speech delivered on behalf of the Party Central Committee in September 1979 to celebrate the thirtieth anniversary of the People's Republic, Vice-Chairman Ye Jianying offered the most negative appraisal yet of the Cultural Revolution and its achievements. The period of political turbulence which began in 1966 was now described as a 'calamity' and 'the most serious reversal to (the) socialist cause' since the founding of the People's Republic. All the main proponents of the Cultural Revolution were accused of vilifying the four modernizations, and of deliberately disrupting production. The principal lesson to be drawn from this experience, according to Ye Jianying, was the need to 'liberate the productive forces' and constantly raise labour productivity. From now on the work of every district, every department and every unit, right down to every single individual, was to be judged 'by its direct and indirect contribution to modernization'.

Closely allied to this revised criterion of socialist development was the contention that a fundamental change had occurred in China's class structure. The capitalist class had ceased to exist. Workers, peasants and intellectuals could therefore be integrated into a united front which also included 'compatriots' in Taiwan, Hong Kong and Macao. The overriding task of this new united front was no longer class struggle but the realization of the four modernizations and the 'reunification of the motherland'. The decisions reached by the Party Central Committee in February 1980 further consolidated the new political line and the emerging power structure. Several of Deng Xiaoping's close collaborators including Hu Yaobang, Zhao Ziyang, Wan Li, Wang Renzhong, Fang Yi, Gu Mu, Yu Qiuli, were placed in strategic positions within the Party hierarchy. On the other hand, four senior members of the Politburo, Wang Dongxing, Ji Dengkui, Wu De and Chen Xilian were removed from all posts both inside and outside the Party, presumably because they were considered to have radical leanings and to be too closely identified with the Maoist policy line. Equally symbolic of the new order but even more far-reaching was the posthumous rehabilitation of Liu Shaoqi, whom Mao himself had labelled a 'renegade' and the leading 'capitalist-roader'. At the same time the decision was taken to delete Article 45 of the Constitution which recognized the right of citizens 'to speak out freely, air their views fully, hold great debates and write big-character posters'.

The foreign policy implications of the new course on which China had embarked were wide-ranging but not always immediately apparent. In the first place, the conscious desire to maximize the interests and power of the Chinese state, which was not altogether absent from Mao's own conception of China's destiny, now entailed a much more unqualified acceptance of the pyramidal structure of decision-making than had previously been the case. The tacit repudiation of the more radical and egalitarian strand in the Maoist vision, which had until recently accompanied and strongly influenced the conduct of domestic politics and state diplomacy, was now compounded by the almost exclusive recourse to traditional instruments of party control and statecraft. China was currently intent not only on modernizing her economy and making her way to the top of the international ladder but on developing for the purpose increasingly intimate links with the two pre-eminent institutions of contemporary capitalism, namely the advanced industrial state and the transnational corporation.

Whatever its economic and diplomatic advantages, the rapprochement with the West, and particularly with the United States, represented a sharp reversal of many of the fundamental positions that had governed China's external conduct during the 1950s and 1960s. After all, one of the earliest factors contributing to the Sino–Soviet dispute had been China's hostility to the Soviet concept and practice of peaceful coexistence. Moscow was bitterly attacked for betraying the interests of the socialist bloc and the cause of liberation in the Third World. Yet, it was Peking that was now most assiduously pursuing a policy of détente with the United States and seeking a degree of diplomatic, strategic and economic interaction and co-ordination with the capitalist system that no Soviet leader had probably ever contemplated. The strident denunciations of domestic repression and external aggression that had dominated the Maoist interpretation of western capitalism were rapidly receding into the past. What accounted for this drastic revision of China's perception of the outside world? Was capitalism no longer the 'paper tiger' of former years? Had it undergone such profound transformation as to make the previous analysis obsolete? Or had capitalist decline advanced so far as to render it innocuous? Peking's remarkable silence on these questions suggested that they were no longer central to the concerns and preoccupations of the new Chinese leadership.

Ironically this process was occurring at a time when the capitalist system was experiencing its most serious economic crisis since the Second World War. The continuing instability of the international monetary system, the declining capacity of national governments and their financial institutions to direct money markets and corporate transactions, the increasing incompatibility of the North American, Western European and Japanese economies, the emerging conflict of interests between oil consumers and oil producers and the persistence of recessionist conditions, all pointed to a progressively more fragmented and competitive international market economy. Short-term compromises might for a time obscure the nature of the crisis but were unlikely to arrest the decline of the international economic order established under the aegis of *Pax Americana*. It was by no means clear that China's policy-makers had fully appreciated, or even begun to formulate a coherent response to the economics of scarcity and the politics of disorder, which were likely to dominate world politics in the early 1980s and beyond.

As already indicated, the corollary of China's opening to the West was her continuing animosity towards the Soviet Union and its allies. Nothing could illustrate more graphically the direction of China's anti-Soviet diplomacy than Chairman Hua's visits to Rumania, Yugoslavia and Iran in August 1978. Peking's readiness to abandon old ideological quarrels and jettison old allies (Albania) for new ones (Yugoslavia) reflected above all its determination to support any country willing to oppose Soviet policies and hinder the extension of Soviet influence. China's determined efforts to restore her relations with the Eurocommunist movement and the highly publicized visit to Peking in April 1980 of Italian Communist Party leader, Enrico Berlinguer, pointed in the same direction. True enough, anti-Sovietism did not constitute *prima facie* evidence of declining revolutionary zeal. After all, had not Peking defended its initial estrangement from Moscow on the grounds that the Soviet leadership had abandoned its commitment to revolution at home and abroad? On the other hand, the Chinese argument about Soviet social-imperialism had not thus far implied that any government or political movement that relied to some extent on Soviet military or economic aid was necessarily pursuing counter-revolutionary policies. Yet this is precisely the interpretation that was now being placed on the attitudes and actions of several Third World countries, notably Cuba and Vietnam.

The Moscow-backed coup in Afghanistan in December 1979 offered the Chinese yet another, though not altogether unexpected, opportunity to attack the Soviet Union's 'hegemonist ambitions'. In this particular instance, however, Peking was able to exploit the fact that the Soviet use of force had been directed against a 'non-aligned and Islamic country of the Third World'. The Soviet occupation of Afghanistan held out the prospect of important political gains for Chinese diplomacy. In the first place, the Islamic fury which until now had been vented almost exclusively on the United States, partly because of its policies on Iran and the Middle East, was now beginning to turn against the Soviet Union. Secondly, Chinese leaders were able to portray the Soviet use of force as a prelude to a more adventurous strategy aimed at gaining access to Indian Ocean ports and eventually threatening the Western world's Middle Eastern oil supplies. In other words, the Chinese condemnation contributed to the hardening of America's response.

At relatively little cost to her own security, at least in the short-term, China was able to take advantage of the virtual collapse of the Salt II agreement, and, by giving limited assistance to Muslim rebels, was partly instrumental in getting the Soviet war machine bogged down in the inhospitable mountain areas of Afghanistan. But undoubtedly, the most pleasing aspect of the Soviet military intervention, from China's point of view, was its beneficial impact on relations with Pakistan, and especially with the United States. The considerable importance attached by both sides to Harold Brown's visit to China in January 1980, and the inclusion in the American delegation of senior officials from the State Department, the CIA and the National Security Council provided ample evidence of the desire of both Washington and Peking to harmonize their policies on this issue and intensify the level of their strategic cooperation.

China's attitude to the Afghanistan crisis clearly reflected the changing direction of her Third World policy. Because of its implacable hostility towards Moscow, Peking now felt obliged to make common cause with some of the most conservative political forces in the Afro–Asian world. Chinese support for the South-African backed National Front for the Liberation of Angola or for the anti-communist governments of General Numeiry in Sudan, President Mobutu of Zaire, President Sadat of Egypt, the Shah of Iran before his overthrow, President Zia-Ul-Haq of Pakistan, or the ASEAN grouping in Southeast Asia was obviously dictated by considerations other than the Third World struggle for emancipation. This is not to say that Soviet policies were any more likely to advance the interests of national or social liberation in the Third World. On the other hand, China's fixation with the Soviet threat was rapidly undermining her credibility as the self-proclaimed 'champion of the poor and the proud'.

The Three Worlds theory enunciated in 1974, supposedly under Mao's instructions, may have originally been intended to salvage something of China's faith in the Third World's revolutionary potential. The concept of a united front of Third World nations directed against the interventionist policies of the two superpowers did perhaps imply, despite the noticeable absence of any notion of class conflict, a lingering element of radicalism in China's analysis of the international situation. However, with Mao's death and the fall of the radicals, support for the New International Economic Order became a rhetorical exercise increasingly devoid of practical content. Third World governments, communist parties and liberation movements could now expect to receive Chinese support only to the extent that they identified with Peking's anti-Sovietism. Conversely, criticism of the western world's entrenched economic and strategic interests in Asia, Africa and Latin America was now much less frequent and usually low-key. The containment of Soviet military power in the Middle East, the Persian Gulf area, the Indian Ocean and South and Southeast Asia was now considered much more crucial to China's national interests than support for Third World liberation struggles. The anti-American united front of the 1950s and 1960s had thus given way to the anti-Soviet united front of the 1970s.

China's attempts to maximize her strategic position vis-à-vis the Soviet Union had, in effect, transformed her relations with the Third World. In the process, Chinese leaders had deprived themselves of a theoretical basis for the analysis of the domestic and international structures of economic exploitation, and hence of any coherent strategy for the more equitable allocation of the world's resources. As a result of the very growth of her power and influence,

China's challenge to the prevailing global equilibrium lost much of its former breadth and intensity. Her concern with the redistribution of power was now largely limited to her own aspirations for enhanced status and authority within the existing framework of international decision-making. It remains to be seen whether China's friends and clients will indefinitely accept and cooperate with this new strategic orientation. To the extent, for example, that the interests of the North Korean regime, the Palestinian Liberation Organization and many of the Southeast Asian communist parties are likely to be prejudiced by China's diplomatic entente with the United States, Sadat's Egypt and ASEAN, respectively, Peking's policies can be expected to meet with increasing resistance. Other external pressures are also likely to influence the future direction of Chinese diplomacy. The embryonic trilateral association with the United States and Japan in the Asia-Pacific region, particularly if it acquires increasing strategic importance, could well prove a major destabilizing factor in Soviet-American relations. Should the Soviet Union decide that its military security and other vital national interests are threatened by the emergence of such a coalition, it will almost certainly seek to offset or neutralize this new version of containment by expanding its own presence in several strategic regions of the world, notably in southern Africa, the horn of Africa, the Middle East, the Persian Gulf, the Indian Ocean and Southeast and Northeast Asia. The net effect of the renewed scramble for spheres of influence will be to fan the flames of regional conflict, intensify the pressures for vertical and horizontal nuclear proliferation and significantly escalate the tension in Sino–Soviet relations.

China's policy-makers are unlikely to view any of these possible consequences as compatible with Chinese interests. Considerations of regional stability and the wish to avoid dangerous provocation of the Soviet Union may therefore incline Peking to the view that the rapprochement with Washington and Tokyo ought to be balanced by the normalization of relations with Moscow. It is probably this factor which more than any other contributed to the resumption of Sino–Soviet negotiations. This is not to say that China was ready to make substantial concessions. Although Peking had dropped its earlier demand than the Soviet Union terminate specific 'hegemonic' practices (e.g. the stationing of Soviet forces in Mongolia) as a prerequisite for holding such talks, she was still determined to make Soviet 'hegemonism' in general and the issue of a Soviet military withdrawal from Mongolia in particular a central feature of the negotiations. The Afghanistan crisis inevitably exacerbated the difficulties of the negotiating process but did not altogether destroy it. In this context, it is not without significance that on 2 April 1980 the *People's Daily* should have challenged for the first time in twenty years the validity of the theoretical arguments underpinning the Sino–Soviet doctrinal schism. Most of the Chinese criticisms, whether they dealt with Stalin's role, Yugoslav socialism, relations with liberation movements, peaceful co-existence, relations within the international communist movement, or the nature of Soviet communism, had hitherto revolved around the concept of revisionism. It was now argued that the origins and characteristics of revisionism had not been correctly or scientifically analysed. Indeed, it was claimed that the attempts of a proletarian party to develop the productive forces of the economy should not have been labelled 'revisionist'. This ideological reversal, dictated largely by the evolution of China's internal situation, was bound to have wide-ranging ramifications for China's external conduct. While deep-seated conflicts of national interest were likely to continue to dominate Sino–Soviet relations, the virtual elimination of the ideological factor from the dispute might make for a more flexible framework of diplomatic bargaining.

If the relationship with the Soviet Union held some faint prospect of future dialogue, the same could not be said of Sino–Vietnamese hostility. The publication in early October 1979 of a Vietnamese publication entitled *The Truth about Vietnam–China Relations over the Last Thirty Years* underscored the remoteness of any rapprochement. The dossier conceded that during the Second Indochina war tens of thousands of Chinese 'logistic troops' had been sent into Vietnam's northern border provinces to help repair roads and railways damaged by American bombing. But it asserted that the main task of the Chinese contingent was 'to gather information, infiltrate into areas inhabited by ethnic minorities and engage in propaganda for the Cultural Revolution'. The Hanoi document also alleged that as from the early 1950s China's primary aim had been to keep Vietnam divided, thereby removing the only force capable of containing Chinese expansionism in Indochina. China's failure to endorse fully the Vietnamese position at the 1954 Geneva Conference, her attempts to discourage Hanoi from launching a revolutionary war in South Vietnam, her unwillingness to intervene in the war against US intervention, the enormous hurdles she placed in the path of aid supplies from the Soviet Union, the cessation of all military assistance after 1973, were all designed, according to the dossier, to weaken Vietnam and prevent it from achieving its goal of unification and socialist reconstruction. Peking's reaction to these charges was predictably hostile, with several Chinese publications stressing the substantial economic, military and moral assistance provided by China in Vietnam's liberation struggle, and denouncing Hanoi for deliberately distorting the historical record as part of its anti-China policy.

Throughout 1979 the Sino–Vietnamese talks remained deadlocked with both sides repeatedly restating their position, and both accusing the other of armed border provocations. In March 1980, the Chinese Foreign Ministry issued a stern warning to Vietnam against further infiltration and called for the suspension of the talks until the latter half of the year. During this period Peking maintained an intense propaganda campaign against Vietnam and made great play of the defection to China of veteran Vietnamese leader, Hoang Van Hoan, and of the house arrest of at least four other communist leaders in the Vietnamese capital. At the same time, rivalry over interests in the South China Sea continued to intensify. Contracts China had signed with American companies for the exploration of the disputed waters around Hainan Island were seen by Vietnam as an attempt to gain de facto international recognition of the disputed border line. The concession could also be interpreted as a bid to apply naval pressure against Vietnam, since the presence of US-controlled work boats and rigs around Hainan Island implied guarantees of security, which might well come to be provided by US naval forces. The reinforcement of Chinese air bases on Hainan Island as well as those close to the border with Vietnam and the publication in January 1980 of an official document seeking to establish the historical basis for Chinese sovereignty over the disputed islands were simply the latest moves in a protracted war of nerves.

The increasingly bitter feud between the two countries tended to confirm Vietnamese fears of a second Chinese punitive action, which might take the form of a raid on Haiphong or the destruction of coal mines along the Vietnamese coast close to China. In addition, Hanoi was feeling the effects of diplomatic isolation and economic sanctions imposed by China in concert with several western governments. Confronted with this situation, the Vietnamese had little option but to cement their links with the Soviet Union. Apart from supplying Vietnam with enormous quantities of sophisticated military hardware – including MiG 23s, tanks fitted with rapid-firing guns and radar-guided anti-tank weapons – the Soviet Union was also stationing 'combat-ready fishing trawlers' in the Gulf of Tonkin.

The Vietnamese were equally determined to remain in Kampuchea so long as China did not accept the legitimacy of the Vietnamese intervention and continued to support the Pol Pot regime. In their first joint communiqué since 1975, the foreign ministers of Vietnam, Laos and Kampuchea reaffirmed Hanoi's position that in Kampuchea there was no room for Pol Pot, Ieng Sary, Khieu Samphan or 'other reactionaries including Sihanouk'. So long as China, the United States and 'other reactionary forces' continued their opposition to the three Indochinese countries, the Vietnamese troop presence in Laos and Kampuchea was described as 'very necessary'. While the concept of an Indochina federation was not a matter of deeply entrenched Vietnamese policy – equally there was no territorial ambition as such – there could be little doubt that Hanoi wanted Indochina to be within its sphere of influence.

China for her part was adamant that no negotiations over the Kampuchea question should take place until Vietnamese troops had ceased to occupy the country. Clearly, the Chinese objective was to widen the conflict in Kampuchea, thereby further weakening Vietnam by over-extending its supplies. To this end Peking maintained its support for the Pol Pot forces and other non-communist elements opposing the Heng Samrin regime. In order to improve the international standing of the Khmer Rouge, China attempted to moderate their ultra-leftist tendencies and was partly instrumental in securing the replacement of Pol Pot by Khieu Samphan as Premier. The leadership switch, however, was little more than a cosmetic exercise since Pol Pot still appeared in effective command of whatever armed resistance remained against the Vietnamese-backed regime. Although Peking may have preferred more substantial organizational and leadership changes, the realities of the military situation dictated otherwise.

The apparent softening of ASEAN's position towards Vietnam, indicated in the communiqué issued by the ASEAN foreign ministers' meeting in December 1979, was obliquely criticised by China as implying a 'weakening of support for Democratic Kampuchea'. In a bid to counter any possible thaw in Vietnamese–ASEAN relations, Peking actively sought closer links with Bangkok and openly endorsed Thailand's open-door refugee policy which enabled the Khmer Rouge to use Thai soil as a sanctuary and a supply base for their guerrilla war against the Heng Samrin regime. From China's point of view, the massive exodus of Khmer refugees into Thailand was a decided advantage in so far as it highlighted Kampuchea's internal difficulties. The sheer number of Khmers located in Thai camps provided a powerful base for anti-Vietnamese politics and a useful lever in any future negotiation about the future of Kampuchea. Several high-level Chinese delegations visited Thailand in late 1979 and early 1980 and made a point of offering China's assistance in the event of a military conflict with Vietnam. Thailand had thus assumed a major role in the Chinese strategy of bleeding Vietnam through multi-pronged pressure around its borders. Chinese tacit support for the reactivation of the Manila Pact and for more effective strategic coordination with the United States pointed in the same direction.

There were several constraints, however, acting on China's anti-Vietnamese strategy. Apart from the Soviet–Vietnamese connection, China had to take account of the fact that an intransigent policy towards Vietnam could seriously tarnish her image as a non-expansionist power. The invasion of Vietnam had already created serious misgivings in Southeast Asian minds. Any further attempts to exploit the leverage afforded by the presence of the Chinese minority in Vietnam could easily magnify the fears of other similarly placed Southeast Asian governments. However responsive the ASEAN countries might be to China's anti-Vietnamese propaganda campaign, an excessively assertive policy towards Hanoi might eventually breed widespread suspicions that China was out to create in Southeast Asia a sphere of influence in which the degree and form of national independence are ultimately determined by Peking.

In addition to these external considerations and the rapidly shifting balance of power, both globally and regionally, China's new ties with the capitalist west will inevitably have to grapple with the limitations imposed by international economic relationships. Domestic factors, notably the vastness of China's population and its predominantly agrarian character, are also likely to restrict China's diplomatic freedom of action. The physical constraints arising from demographic and economic factors are, in any case, likely to be reinforced by the countervailing cultural and ideological sensitivities which, though currently dormant, are bound to re-emerge in the years ahead. The dislocation likely to result from the large-scale introduction of foreign capital-intensive technology and the ensuing economic and political instability might in due course compel a further reassessment of present domestic priorities. There is little reason to believe that the future development of China's political economy will be any less turbulent than it has been in the last three decades. This factor will no doubt combine with the rapid transformation of international relations to produce in the years ahead new and dramatic shifts in China's diplomatic and strategic behaviour. Confronted with a rapidly disintegrating world order the Chinese leadership may be inclined to concentrate on old jealousies and conflicts and rely on traditional concepts of power, status and national interest. It is also possible, on the other hand, that the new China, while striving to achieve a more convivial and dignified existence for her citizens, will make a positive contribution to a restructured yet more peaceful, egalitarian and ecologically viable word system. Such a possibility, however, will depend as much on the actions and attitudes of other national and transnational actors as on her own responses to structural innovation both at home and abroad.

Notes

Chapter 1

1. For an account of the establishment of western spheres of influence, see P. H. Kent, *Railway Enterprises in China* (London: E. Arnold, 1907); T. W. Overlack, *Foreign Financial Control in China* (New York: Macmillan, 1919); W. W. Willoughby and C. G. Fenwick, *Types of Restricted Sovereignty and of Colonial Autonomy* (Washington D.C.: US Government Printing Office, 1919).
2. Sun Yat-sen, Chiang Kai-shek, Mao Zedong and many other Chinese nationalists of varying political persuasions are largely in agreement about the territories China lost to the West. See Sun Yat-sen, *San Min Chu I: The Three Principles of the People*, p. 35 (Shanghai: The Commercial Press, 1928); Chiang Kai-shek, *China's Destiny*, p. 34 (New York: Macmillan, 1947).
3. Sun Yat-sen, *San Min Chu I*, p. 12.
4. Mao, 'Cast away illusions, prepare for struggle', 14 August 1949, in *Selected Works* vol. 4, p. 426 (Peking: Foreign Language Press, 1969).
5. John K. Fairbank, 'A preliminary framework', in *The Chinese World Order: Traditional China's Foreign Relations*, p. 3 (Cambridge, Mass.: Harvard University Press, 1968).
6. *Ibid.* pp. 10–11.
7. Reproduced in *Mao Tse-Tung and Lin Piao: Post Revolutionary Writings*, ed. K. Fan, pp. 91–2 (Garden City, N.Y.: Anchor Books, 1972).
8. See John Gittings, 'China's foreign policy: continuity or change?' *Journal of Contemporary Asia 2*, no. 1, 1972, pp. 20–1.
9. Mao Tse-tung, 'The Chinese Revolution and the Chinese Communist Party' December 1939, in *Selected Works* vol. 2, p. 313.
10. *Ibid.*
11. Mao Tse-tung, 'Farewell, Leighton Stuart!', in *Selected Works*, vol. 4, p. 434.
12. *Ibid.* pp. 436–7.
13. *Ibid.* p. 435.
14. See interview given by Mao Zedong to John S. Service, adviser to the US military headquarters in China, in *Lost Chance in China: The World War II Despatches of John S. Service*, ed. Joseph W. Esherick, p. 306 (New York, Vintage Books, 1975).
15. Mao Tse-tung, 'Why it is necessary to discuss the White Paper' 28 August 1949, in *Selected Works*, vol. 4, p. 443.
16. *Ibid.*
17. Mao Tse-tung, 'Farewell, Leighton Stuart!' p. 433.
18. 'A proposal concerning the general line of the international communist movement', *Peking Review*, 21 June 1963, p. 9.
19. Kuo Wen, 'Imperialist plunder – biggest obstacle to the economic growth of underdeveloped countries', *Peking Review*, 18 June 1965, p. 19.
20. Mao Tse-tung, 'On the correct handling of contradictions', 27 February 1957. Published under the theme 'On "imperialism and all reactionaries are paper tigers"' by *People's Daily* 27 October 1958. Reproduced in *Mao Tse-tung and Lin Piao: Post-Revolutionary Writings*, p. 242.

21. Mao Tse-tung, 'The present situation and our tasks' 25 December 1947, in *Selected Works*, vol. 4, p. 172.
22. See Chalmers Johnson, *Autopsy on People's War*, pp. 10–19 (Berkeley: University of California Press, 1973).
23. Lin Piao, 'Long live the victory of people's war!' 3 September 1965. Reproduced in *Mao Tse-tung and Lin Piao: Post-Revolutionary Writings*, p. 401.
24. *Ibid.* p. 402.
25. See *The Polemic on the General Line of the International Communist Movement*, Chinese Communist Party (CCP) Central Committee (CC) letter of 14 June 1963 to the Central Committee (CC) of the Communist Party of the Soviet Union (CPSU), pp. 6–7 (Peking: Foreign Language Press, 1965).
26. *Ibid.* p. 13.
27. Lin Piao, 'Long live the victory of people's war!' p. 401.
28. 'Long live Leninism!' *Red Flag*, 16 April 1960. From text in G. F. Hudson, R. Lowenthal and R. Macfarquhar (eds) *The Sino-Soviet Dispute*, p. 99 (New York: Praeger, 1961).
29. See the official report made by Lin Biao on 1 April 1969 at the Ninth Congress of the CCP, in *Peking Review*, Special Issue, 28 April 1969, p. 26.
30. *Ibid.* p. 29.
31. Mao Tse-tung, 'Cast away illusions, prepare for struggle', in *Selected Works* vol. 4, p. 426.
32. *Mao Tse-tung and Lin Piao: Post-Revolutionary Writings*, p. 240.
33. Reproduced from *Red Flag* in *Peking Review*, 22 September 1959, p. 10.
34. John Gittings, 'China's foreign policy: continuity or change?' p. 26.
35. See Lin Biao's report to the Ninth Congress of the CCP, p. 25.
36. Richard H. Solomon, *Mao's Revolution and the Chinese Political Culture*, p. 513 (Berkeley: University of California Press, 1971).
37. See Mao's speech at the opening of the Party School in Yenan on 1 February 1942. Reproduced in *The Political Thought of Mao Tse-tung*, Stuart R. Schram, pp. 179–80 (Harmondsworth: Penguin Books, 1971).
38. Mao Tse-tung, 'Analysis of the classes in Chinese society' March 1926, in *Selected Works* vol. 1, p. 13.
39. *Ibid.* p. 19.
40. See Mao Tse-tung, 'The bankruptcy of the idealist conception of history', 16 September 1949, in *Selected Works* vol. 4.
41. See Lu Ting-Yi, 'The world significance of the Chinese revolution', *People's China 4*, no. 1, July 1951, pp. 10–12.
42. These options are discussed by Peter Van Ness, *Revolution and Chinese Foreign Policy: Peking's Support For Wars of National Liberation*, pp. 50–2 (Berkeley: University of California Press, 1970).
43. Lin Piao, 'Long live the victory of people's war!' p. 400.
44. *Ibid.* p. 403.
45. *Ibid.* p. 387.
46. Edgar Snow, 'Interview with Mao', *The New Republic*, 27 February 1965, p. 22.
47. See Peter Van Ness, *Revolution and Chinese Foreign Policy*, pp. 70–2.
48. Transcript of an interview with the Australian film director John Dixon. Cited in Arthur Huck, *The Security of China: Chinese Approaches to Problems of War and Strategy*, pp. 51–2 (London: Chatto & Windus for the Institute for Strategic Studies, 1970).
49. Lin Piao, 'Long live the victory of people's war!' p. 403.
50. For one of the most penetrating studies of Mao's thought, particularly in relation to his notion of 'permanent revolution' and the stages of historical development,

see Frederick Wakeman Jr, *History and Will: Philosophical Perspectives of Mao Tse-tung Thought*, pp. 302–27 (Berkeley: University of California Press, 1973).

51. Lin Piao, 'Long live the victory of people's war', pp. 392–3.
52. Mao Tse-tung, 'People of the world, unite and defeat the U.S. aggressors and all their running dogs!', 20 May 1970, in *Peking Review*, Special Issue, 23 May 1970, p. 9.
53. See Jay Tao, 'Mao's world outlook: Vietnam and the revolution in China', *Asian Survey 8* no. 5, May 1968.
54. Mao Tse-tung, 'Chinese people firmly support Panamanian people's just patriotic struggle', *Peking Review*, 17 January 1964, p. 5.
55. For a balanced and stimulating discussion of the role of ideology in Chinese foreign policy, see Wayne Bert, 'Revolutionary ideology and Chinese foreign policy: the case of South and Southeast Asia', *International Relations 4* no. 6, November 1974. For an analysis of the complex interaction between ideological goals, the pursuit of power and the preservation of interests, see Benjamin Schwartz, *Communism and China: Ideology in Flux* (New York: Atheneum, 1970).
56. See John K. Fairbank, 'A preliminary framework' in *The Chinese World Order*.
57. Norton Ginsburg, 'On the Chinese perception of a world order' in *China in Crisis* ed. Tang Tsou, vol. 2 (Chicago: University of Chicago Press, 1968); see also Leo Yueh-yun Liu, *China as a Nuclear Power in World Politics*, pp. 12–16 (London: Macmillan, 1972).
58. Zhou Enlai, speech before the full conference of Afro-Asian countries at Bandung, 19 April 1955, in Supplement to *People's China*, 16 May 1955, p. 11.
59. *New York Times*, 25 April 1955.
60. Translated with abridgements by F. Schurrman from the Japanese journal *Sekai Stiuto*, 11 August 1964. Cited in *Communist China: China Readings, 3*, p. 368 (Harmondsworth: Penguin Books, 1967).
61. Edgar Snow, 'Interview with Mao', p. 18.
62. Editorial from *People's Daily*, 21 January 1964, in *Peking Review*, 24 January 1964, p. 7.
63. *L'Humanité*, 21 February 1964.
64. 'Vice Premier Chen Yi's Press Conference', 29 September 1965, in *Peking Review*, 8 October 1965, p. 12.
65. John King Fairbank, Testimony before the Senate Foreign Relations Committee. Cited in *Communist China: China Readings, 3*, p. 522.
66. Among these one would include A. Doak Barnett, *Communist China and Asia* (New York: Vintage Books, 1960); R. G. Boyd, *Communist China's Foreign Policy* (New York: Praeger, 1962).
67. *New York Times*, 25 April 1955.
68. Lin Piao, 'Long live the victory of people's war!' pp. 406–7.
69. 'A proposal concerning the general line of the international communist movement', p. 14.
70. 'The differences between Comrade Togliatti and us', *People's Daily*, 31 December 1962, in *Peking Review*, 4 January 1963, p. 13.
71. Mao Zedong, Speech at the meeting of the Supreme Soviet of the USSR in celebration of the 40th anniversary of the October Revolution, 6 November 1951, in *Mao Tse-tung and Lin Piao: Revolutionary Writings*, p. 215.
72. See statement that originally appeared in *Red Flag* 8 November 1960, and was cited again in 'Statement by the spokesman of the Chinese government – a comment on the Soviet government's statement of August 21', *Peking Review*, 6 September 1963.

73. Mao Tse-tung and Lin Piao, p. 239.
74. 'Vice-Premier Chen Yi's Press Conference', 29 September 1965, p. 13.

Chapter 2

1. Speech of People's Republic of China (PRC) delegate at Security Council, 28 November 1950. UN, *Security Council Official Records*, 5th Year, 527 meetings, no. 69.
2. Secretary of State Dean Acheson's 'Letter of transmittal' with China White Paper, 30 July 1949, in *The China White Paper, August 1949*, p. xv (Stanford, Calif.: Stanford University Press, 1967).
3. *Ibid.* p. xvi.
4. *Ibid.* p. xvii.
5. Memoirs by Harry S. Truman, vol. 2, *Years of Trial and Hope*, p. 400 (Garden City, N.Y.: Doubleday, 1956).
6. *New China News Agency*, 3 October 1950.
7. *Department of State Bulletin*, 11 December 1950, p. 925.
8. *The New York Times*, 8, 9 March 1955.
9. *Department of State Bulletin*, 20 October 1958, p. 602.
10. US Information Service, London, *Press Release*, 7 January 1964.
11. For one of the most lucid analyses of this psychological inversion in America's relations with China see Edward Friedman, 'Problems in dealing with an irrational power: America declares war on China', in *America's Asia: Dissenting Essays on Asian–American Relations* ed. Edward Friedman and Mark Selden (New York: Vintage Books, 1971).
12. *American Foreign Policy, 1950–1955*, vol. 2 pp. 2448–9 (Washington, DC: Department of State, 1957).
13. *Ibid.* p. 2451.
14. *Ibid.* p. 2316.
15. *Ibid.* p. 2457.
16. See D. F. Fleming, *The Cold War and its Origins 1917–1960*, vol. 2, pp. 593–4 (London: Allen and Unwin, 1961).
17. *American Foreign Policy 1950–1955*, p. 2468.
18. *New China News Agency*, 29 June 1950.
19. *Security Council Official Records*, 5th Year, 527 meeting, no. 69, pp. 2–25.
20. Reported interview with Zhou Enlai in Edgar Snow, *The Other Side of the River*, p. 88 (New York: Random House, 1961).
21. *American Foreign Policy, 1950–1955*, p. 2475.
22. *Ibid.* pp. 2468–7.
23. Cited in George McTurnan Kahin, *The Asian–African Conference: Bandung, Indonesia, April 1955*, pp. 28–9 (Ithaca, NY: Cornell University Press, 1956).
24. Supplement to *People's China*, no. 24, 16 December 1954, pp. 6–8.
25. Cited in Kenneth T. Young, *Negotiating with the Chinese Communists: The United States Experience 1953–1967*, p. 98 (New York: McGraw-Hill, published for the Council on Foreign Relations, 1968).
26. *New China News Agency*, 30 January 1956.
27. *New York Times*, 29 June 1956.
28. See D. F. Fleming, *The Cold War and its Origins, 1917–1960*, pp. 930–1.
29. See *Documents on International Affairs 1957*, pp. 112–13 Published under the auspices of the Royal Institute of International Affairs (London: Oxford University Press, 1960).

30. *American Foreign Policy, 1958*, pp. 1146–7 (Washington, DC: Department of State, 1959).
31. Cited in Allen S. Whiting, 'New light on Mao: Quemoy 1958: Mao's miscalculations', *The China Quarterly*, no. 62, June 1975, p. 265.
32. *Ibid.*
33. Although presented in a light highly favourable to Peking's point of view, the analysis of China's strategy offered by Anna Lousie Strong is nevertheless accurate in its essentials. See A. L. Strong, 'Chinese strategy in the Taiwan Strait', *New Times* (Moscow), no. 46, November 1958, pp. 8–11.
34. *New China News Agency*, 23 June 1962.
35. Edgar Snow, *The Other Side of the River*, p. 92.
36. Observer, 'Old tune, new plot', *Peking Review*, 1 April 1966, p. 15.
37. *Department of State Bulletin*, 22 May 1950, p. 821.
38. For a fuller account of the early origins of American intervention in Indochina and its bearing on Sino–American relations see John Gittings, 'The great Asian conspiracy' in *America's Asia: Dissenting Essays on Asian–American Relations*.
39. *The Far Eastern Commission: A Study in International Cooperation 1945–1952*, p. 66 (Washington, DC: US Department of State, Publication 5138, Far Eastern Series 60, 1953).
40. Speech of PRC delegate at Security Council, *Security Council Official Records*, 5th Year, 527 meeting.
41. See Allen S. Whiting, *China Crosses the Yalu: The Decision to Enter the Korean War*, pp. 156–7 (Stanford, Calif.: Stanford University Press, 1960).
42. Harry S. Truman, *Years of Trial and Hope*, p. 333.
43. Cited in Glenn D. Paige, *The Korean Decision*, p. 68 (New York: The Free Press, 1968).
44. *Ibid.* pp. 71–2.
45. See I. F. Stone, *The Hidden History of the Korean War* (New York: Monthly Review Press, 1952); David Horowitz, *From Yalta to Vietnam: American Foreign Policy in the Cold War*, pp. 110–37 (Harmondsworth: Penguin Books, 1967).
46. *China Digest*, 20 April 1948, p. 6.
47. For a more detailed account of the Chinese response in the early stages of the Korean war see Allen Whiting, *China Crosses the Yalu*, pp. 129–31.
48. Cited in *Korea: Cold War and Limited War*, ed. Allen Guttman, p. 14 (Lexington, Mass.: D. C. Heath, 2nd ed., 1972).
49. This analysis is developed in some depth by Joyce and Gabriel Kolko, *The Limits of Power: The World and United States Foreign Policy, 1945–1954*, pp. 595–9 (New York: Harper & Row, 1972).
50. Speech of PRC delegate at UN Security Council, 28 November 1950.
51. Douglas MacArthur, *Reminiscences*, p. 431 (Greenwich, Conn.: Fawcett Publications, 1964).
52. US Senate, *The Military Situation in the Far East: Hearings before the Committee on Armed Services and the Committee on Foreign Relations*, p. 3350 (82nd Congress, 1st Session, 1951).
53. Observer, 'With whom is the Soviet leadership taking united action?' *People's Daily*, 2 February 1966, in *Peking Review*, 4 February 1966, p. 12.
54. Vice Premier Chen Yi's Report on 'The international situation and our foreign policy' to the CCP's Eighth Congress, 25 September 1956. Reproduced in *Current Background*, no. 414, 6 October 1956, p. 8.
55. *New China News Agency*, 2 August 1963.
56. *New York Times*, 31 December 1964.
57. US Information Service (American Embassy, London) 26 October 1964.

58. William P. Bundy, 'The United States and Communist China', address before the Associated Students of Pomona (California) College, 12 February 1966 (Washington, DC: US Government Printing Office, 1966).

59. 'Refuting Bundy', *People's Daily*, 20 February 1966, in *Peking Review* 25 February 1966, p. 8.

60. Observer, 'Old tune, new plot'.

61. Dean Rusk, 'United States policy towards Communist China', Statement before the House Sub-Committee on Far Eastern Affairs, *New York Times*, 17 April 1966.

62. Speech by Guo Mojo reported in the *New York Times*, 27 September 1966.

63. Observer, *People's Daily*, 11 January 1965, in *Peking Review*, 15 January 1965, p. 16.

64. See *Strategic Survey 1970*, pp. 32–4 (London: Institute for Strategic Studies, 1971).

65. *People's Daily*, 7 October 1951, in *Survey of the China Mainland Press* (hereafter referred to as *SCMP*) no. 190, 7–9 October 1951, p. 2.

66. 'Statement by the spokesman of the Chinese government – a comment on the Soviet government's statement of August 3', 15 August 1963, in *Peking Review*, 16 August 1963, p. 15.

67. Jen Ko-ping, 'US imperialists' "grand strategy"', *Peking Review*, 10 August 1962, p. 15.

68. *Peking Review*, 2 August 1963, p. 8.

69. Zhou Enlai's four-point statement on China's policy toward the United States, 10 April 1966, in *Peking Review*, 13 May 1966, p. 5.

70. 'The war threat of US imperialism must be taken seriously', *Peking Review*, 8 April 1966, p. 8.

71. Editorial department of *People's Daily*, 'The historical experience of the war against fascism', in *Peking Review*, 14 May 1965, pp. 21–2.

72. *New China News Agency*, 24 March 1962.

73. *New York Herald Tribune*, 21 July 1962.

74. *New China News Agency*, 20 July 1963.

75. *New China News Agency*, 4 March 1964.

76. *New China News Agency*, 6 August 1964.

77. *New China News Agency*, 13 January 1965.

78. *Peking Review*, 13 August 1965, p. 8.

79. *People's Daily*, 5 July 1966, in *Peking Review*, 8 July 1966, p. 21.

80. *People's Daily*, 10 July 1966. See also Ch'ang Kung, 'The bankruptcy of the US "special war" in South Vietnam', *World Culture*, no. 12, 25 June 1965, in *Selections from China Mainland Magazines* (hereafter referred to as *SCMM*) no. 481, 26 July 1965, pp. 1–4.

81. 'Expose the big conspiracy of "inducement to peace talks by a suspension of bombings"', *Peking Review*, 14 October 1966, pp. 28–30.

Chapter 3

1. For an illuminating analysis of the uneasy relationship between the Russian and Chinese communist movements during this period see Robert C. North, *Moscow and the Chinese Communists* (Stanford, Calif.: Stanford University Press, 1953).

2. Vladimir Dedijer, *Tito*, p. 322 (New York: Arno Press, 1953).

3. 'More on the historical experience of proletarian dictatorship', translated in *Supplement to People's China*, no. 2, 16 January 1957, p. 10.

4. Cited in Mao Tse-tung, 'Ssu-hiang Wan-sui' (Long live Mao Tse-tung's thought)

1967, 1969. Translated by the Joint Publications Research Service under the title *Miscellany of Mao Tse-tung Thought (1949–1968)* parts I & II, JPRS no. 61269, 1974, p. 256.

5. The full text of the declaration appears as Appendix B in *Survey of the Sino–Soviet Dispute: A Commentary and Extracts from the Recent Polemics 1963–1967*, ed. John Gittings, pp. 289–90 (London: Oxford University Press, 1968).

6. Wu Yu-chang, 'Sino–Soviet friendship and unity among the socialist countries', *People's China*, no. 2, 16 January 1957, pp. 4–5.

7. *People's China*, no. 23, 1 December 1957, p. 8.

8. The full text of the communiqué was published in *Peking Review*, 12 August 1958, pp. 6–7.

9. 'China and the Soviet Union forever stand together', *Peking Review*, 2 June 1959, p. 7.

10. *Peking Review*, 10 November 1959, p. 13.

11. *Peking Review*, 2 February 1960, p. 8.

12. 'A great day of friendship', *Peking Review*, 16 February 1962, p. 6.

13. See Alice Langley Hsieh, *Communist China's Strategy in the Nuclear Era*, pp. 40 ff. (Englewood Cliffs, NJ: Prentice-Hall, 1962).

14. Donald Zagoria, *The Sino–Soviet Conflict 1956–1961*, p. 168 (Princeton, NJ: Princeton University Press, 1962).

15. In 1958, at the height of the second Jinmen crisis, the Seventh Fleet's force in the Taiwan Strait area was enlarged to 70,000 men and about 50 combat ships, including 3 heavy cruisers, 6 aircraft carriers and 40 destroyers.

16. Mikhail Suslov, Secretary of the CPSU CC, 'The struggle of the Communist Party of the Soviet Union for the unity of the international communist movement', report to plenary meeting of the Central Committee, 14 February 1964. Cited in *Survey of the Sino–Soviet Dispute*, p. 57.

17. *Ibid.* p. 135.

18. *Ibid.*

19. See Letter of CCP CC to CPSU CC, 29 February 1964, *People's Daily*, 9 May 1964, in *Peking Review*, 8 May 1964, pp. 12–18.

20. *Ibid.* p. 13.

21. *Ibid.* p. 14.

22. Allen S. Whiting, '"Contradictions" in the Moscow–Peking axis', *The Journal of Politics 20*, no. 1, February 1958, p. 133.

23. Oleg Hoeffding, 'Sino–Soviet economic relations in recent years', in *Unity and Contradiction: Major Aspects of Sino–Soviet Relations*, ed. Kurt London, p. 303 (New York: Praeger, 1962).

24. Allen S. Whiting, '"Contradictions" in the Moscow–Peking axis', pp. 134–5.

25. Letter of CCP CC to CPSU CC, 29 February 1964, p. 14.

26. See Raymond L. Garthoff, 'Sino–Soviet military relations', *Annals of the American Academy of Political and Social Sciences*, September 1963, pp. 84–85. See also Lt Colonel Robert Rigg, 'Red Army in retreat', *Current History 32*, no. 185, January 1957; and Harold C. Hinton, 'Communist China's military posture', *Current History*, vol. 43, no. 253, September 1962.

27. Cited in A. S. Whiting, '"Contradictions" in the Moscow–Peking Axis', p. 130.

28. Letter of CCP CC to CPSU CC, 29 February 1964, p. 14.

29. Cited by Harold P. Ford, 'Modern weapons and the Sino–Soviet estrangement', *The China Quarterly*, no. 18, April–June 1964, p. 161.

30. 'New training programme promulgated by general department of supervision of training', *Liberation Army Daily*, 16 January 1958, in *SCMP*, no. 1786, 6 June 1958, pp. 6–9.

31. 'Statement by the spokesman of the Chinese government – A comment on the Soviet government statement of August 3', p. 14.
32. See statement by Marshal Ho Lung in *People's Daily*, 1 August 1958, translated in *Current Background*, no. 514, 6 August 1958, pp. 5–6.
33. 'Origin and development of the differences between the leadership of the CPSU and ourselves', editorial departments of *People's Daily* and *Red Flag*, 6 September 1963, in *Peking Review*, 13 September 1963, p. 12.
34. *SCMP*, no. 1831, 13 August 1958, pp. 7–8.
35. 'China's first hydrogen bomb successfully exploded', *New China News Agency*, 17 June 1967.
36. *Die Welt*, 12 May 1958.
37. 'Statement by spokesman of Chinese government – a comment on the Soviet government's statement of August 21', *People's Daily*, 1 September 1963, in *Peking Review*, 6 September 1963, p. 9.
38. *Ibid.*
39. For a complete text of Khrushchev's message to President Eisenhower, see *New York Times*, 20 September 1958, p. 2. See also *Current Digest of the Soviet Press* (hereafter referred to as *CDSP*) *10*, no. 38, pp. 17–18.
40. Chinese statement, 1 September 1963, in *Peking Review*, 6 September 1963, p. 13.
41. Cited in Harold P. Ford, 'Modern weapons and the Sino–Soviet estrangement', p. 169.
42. *SCMP*, no. 1907, 4 December 1958, p. 6.
43. Chinese statement, *Peking Review*, 6 September 1963, p. 13.
44. Soviet government statement, 21 August 1963, in *Soviet News*, 21 August 1963.
45. Cited in *Survey of the Sino–Soviet Dispute*, p. 44.
46. Speech at reception in Peking to mark 15th anniversary of Sino–Soviet Treaty, 14 February 1965, in *Peking Review*, 19 February 1965, p. 12.
47. Cited in 'Communist China and the Ferment in Eastern Europe', *Far Eastern Economic Review 22*, no. 2, 10 January 1957, p. 36.
48. See 'The declaration of the USSR government on the foundation for the development and further strengthening of friendship and co-operation between the Soviet Union and other socialist states', 3 October 1956, *New Times* (Moscow), no. 45, 1956.
49. 'Statement by the government of the People's Republic of China on the declaration by the government of the Soviet Union on October 30, 1956', 1 November 1956, in supplement to *People's China*, no. 22, 1956.
50. For a detailed account of the Chinese analysis of the Hungarian issue, see the editorial in the *People's Daily*, 14 November 1956. Slightly abridged in *People's China*, 1 December 1956, pp. 5–8.
51. See 'More on the historical experience of proletarian dictatorship', supplement to *People's China*, no. 2, 16 January 1957.
52. *Ibid.*
53. Zhou Enlai, 'Report on visit to eleven countries in Asia and Europe' to the third session of the Second National Committee of the Chinese People's Political Consultative Conference, 5 March 1957, in supplement to *People's China*, 1 April 1957, p. 8.
54. *Pravda*, 27 December 1957.
55. 'Chairman Mao Tse-tung's speech at Moscow celebration meeting', *People's China*, 1 December 1957, pp. 4–8.
56. *Survey of the Sino–Soviet Dispute*, p. 313.
57. *Ibid.* p. 312.
58. *Ibid.* p. 316.
59. The text of this memorandum was not officially released until the open phase of

the Sino–Soviet polemics in September 1963. It appeared as Appendix 1 to the *People's Daily* article 'The origin and development of the differences between the leadership of the CPSU and ourselves', pp. 21–2.

60. *Peking Review*, 12 August 1958, p. 7.
61. *Peking Review*, 6 October 1959, p. 9.
62. Feng Ping-fu, 'Post-war movement for national independence', *International Affairs* (Moscow), no. 3, March 1959, pp. 64–86.
63. See *CDSP, 12* no. 35, 28 September 1960, pp. 8–10.
64. See supplement to *New Times*, no. 50, December 1960.
65. *The Road to Communism: Documents of the 22nd Congress of the Communist Party of the Soviet Union*, pp. 334–40 (Moscow: Foreign Languages Publishing House, 1961).
66. Contrast Mao's speech to the Ninth Plenum in January 1961 (cited in *Miscellany of Mao Tse-tung Thought*, Part II, pp. 237–45) with his '7,000 cadres speech' to the Enlarged Central Work Conference on 30 January 1962 (reproduced in *Mao Tse-tung Unrehearsed Talks and Letters: 1956–71*, ed. and introduced by Stuart Schram, Harmondsworth: Penguin Books, 1974, pp. 158–87).
67. 'The origin and development of differences . . .', p. 18.
68. *People's Daily*, 15 November 1962, in *SCMP*, no. 2862, 19 November 1962, p. 28.
69. *Red Flag*, 15 November 1962, in *SCMP*, no. 2863, 20 November 1962, p. 24.
70. *People's Daily*, 15 December 1962, in *Peking Review*, 21 December 1962, p. 6.
71. *Ibid.* p. 7.
72. *People's Daily*, 21 January 1964, in *Peking Review*, 24 January 1964, p. 7.
73. Translated with abridgements by F. Schurmann from the Japanese journal *Sekai Shuho*, 11 August 1964, in *Communist China, China Readings, 3*, pp. 368–9.
74. *Peking Review*, 12 November 1965, pp. 10–21.
75. 'With whom is the Soviet leadership taking united action?' *People's Daily*, 2 February 1966, in *Peking Review*, 4 February 1966, p. 10.
76. *People's Daily*, 2 August 1963, in *Peking Review*, 9 August 1963, p. 8.
77. *People's Daily*, 3 August 1963, in *Peking Review*, 9 August 1963, pp. 10–11.
78. Editorial, *People's Daily*, 22 October 1964, in *Peking Review*, 30 October 1964, p. 5.
79. Peter A. Toma, 'Sociometric measurements of the Sino–Soviet conflict: peaceful and non-peaceful revolutions', *Journal of Politics 30*, no. 3, August 1968, pp. 732–48. The analysis is based on a survey of the following studies: Harold Hinton, *Communist China in World Politics* (Boston: Houghton Mifflin, 1965); Thomas W. Robinson, 'A National Interest Analysis of Sino–Soviet Relations' (unpublished paper presented at Western Political Science Association held in Reno, Nevada, 25 March 1966); Donald Zagoria, *The Sino–Soviet Conflict 1956–61* (Princeton, NJ: Princeton University Press, 1962); Alexander Dallin (ed.) *Diversity in International Communism* (New York: Columbia University Press for the Research Institute on Communist Affairs, Columbia University, 1963); David Floyd, *Mao Against Khrushchev* (New York: Praeger, 1963); William E. Griffith, *The Sino–Soviet Rift* (Cambridge, Mass.: MIT, 1964).
80. Publisher's preface to *Statements by Khrushchev*, vol. 5 (Peking: World Culture Press, 1965). Reproduced in *Peking Review*, 30 April 1965, p. 16.
81. 'On the historical experience of the dictatorship of the proletariat' (written by the editorial department of the *People's Daily* on the basis of the discussion that took place at an enlarged meeting of the Political Bureau of the Central Committee of the CCP), *People's Daily*, 5 April 1956, in *People's China*, 16 April 1956, p. 4.
82. *Ibid.* pp. 6–7.
83. *Ibid.* p. 7.
84. *Miscellany of Mao Tse-Tung Thought*, p. 57.

85. *Ibid.* pp. 191–200; 247–313.
86. Editorial departments of *People's Daily* and *Red Flag*, 'On the question of Stalin – comment on the open letter of the Central Committee of the CPSU (2)', *People's Daily*, 13 September 1963, in *Peking Review*, 20 September 1963, pp. 8–15.
87. For a useful summary of the Maoist critique, see John Gittings, 'New light on Mao: his view of the world', *The China Quarterly*, no. 60, December 1974, pp. 750–66.
88. 'On the historical experience of the dictatorship of the proletariat', p. 8.
89. See 'More on the historical experience of proletarian dictatorship', supplement to People's China, 16 January 1957, p. 3.
90. *People's China*, 1 December 1957, p. 7.
91. The Central Committee of the Communist Party of the Soviet Union – Moscow Letter, published in the *New York Times*, 24 March 1966.
92. Report by M. A. Suslov, 'On the struggle of the CPSU for the solidarity of the international communist movement', 14 February 1964. Published in *Pravda*, 3 April 1964, pp. 1–8.
93. Editorial departments of *People's Daily* and *Red Flag*, 'The proletarian revolution and Khrushchev's revisionism: comment on the open letter of the Central Committee of the CPSU (8)', 31 March 1964, in *Peking Review*, 3 April 1964, p. 8.
94. Lo Jui-ching, 'Commemorate the victory over German fascism! Carry the struggle against US imperialism through to the end!' *Red Flag*, no. 5, May 1965, in *SCMM*, no. 469, 17 May 1965, p. 19.
95. 'What's behind Khrushchev group's opposition to "personality cult"?' (based on an article that appeared in *Zeri i Popullit*, organ of the Albanian Party of Labour, 12, 13, 14 June 1964), in *Peking Review*, 24 July 1964, p. 17.
96. 'Comrade Chou En-lai's speech at Peking mass rally', *Peking Review*, 6 May 1966, p. 24.
97. 'Refutation of the new leaders of the CPSU on united action', 11 November 1965, in *Peking Review*, 12 November 1965, pp. 12, 13.
98. *Ibid.* p. 16.
99. See *Pravda* editorial, 'The internationalist duty of the communists of all countries', 28 November 1965, in *CDSP 17*, no. 47, pp. 3–5.
100. The central Committee of the CPSU – Moscow Letter, *New York Times*, 24 March 1966.
101. *People's Daily*, 6 March 1966, in *Peking Review*, 11 March 1966, p. 7.
102. 'Whom is the Soviet leadership taking united action with?' p. 11.
103. 'What right have Soviet leaders to issue orders to Asian and African countries?' *Peking Review*, 5 June 1964, p. 9.
104. See *Pravda*, 14 August 1964, in *CDSP 16*, no. 33, p. 18.
105. *Peking Review*, 13 September 1963, p. 18.
106. Cited in Dennis J. Doolin, *Territorial Claims in the Sino–Soviet Conflict: Documents & Analysis*, pp. 42–4 (Stanford, Calif.: The Hoover Institution, 1965).
107. Academician V. M. Khvostov, 'The Chinese "account" and historical truth', *Mezhdunarodnaya Zhizn*, no. 10, October 1964. From excerpts reproduced in *Survey of the Sino–Soviet Dispute*, pp. 164–6.

Chapter 4

1. *New China News Agency*, 2 November 1951.
2. 'For a lasting peace, for a people's democracy', *Comminform Journal* (Bucharest), January 1950.

3. Liu Shaoqi's speech at the mass meeting in celebration of the 30th anniversary of the Chinese Communist Party, *New China News Agency*, 30 June 1951.
4. See Lin Wu-Sun, 'China and Cambodia: Friends', *People's China*, 1 March 1956, p. 17.
5. Lin Wu-Sun, 'Another example of good neighbourly relations', *People's China*, 1 November 1956, pp. 13–15.
6. Chu Jung-fu, 'Foreign relations of new China during the past five years', *World Culture*, 5 October 1954, in *Current Background*, no. 307, 6 December 1954, pp. 1–9.
7. For a more detailed analysis of this strategy, see A. M. Halpern, 'The Chinese Communist line on neutralism', *China Quarterly 5*, 1961, pp. 90–115.
8. *People's Daily*, 25 November 1957, in *SCMP*, no. 1660, 27 November 1957, pp. 28–9.
9. *People's Daily*, 26 June 1958, in *SCMP*, no. 1803, 2 July 1958, p. 17.
10. *People's Daily*, 18 March 1959, in *Peking Review*, 24 March 1959, p. 10.
11. See Yu Chao-li, 'The forces of the new are bound to defeat the forces of decay', *Red Flag*, 16 August 1958, in *SCMP*, no. 1837, 21 August 1958, pp. 42–7.
12. Zhou Enlai, 'Report on government work', First Session of the Second National People's Congress, 18 April 1959, in *Peking Review*, 21 April 1959, p. 24.
13. 'Joint statement of Chairman Liu Shao-chi and President Ho Chi Minh', *Peking Review*, 24 May 1963, p. 11.
14. *Red Flag*, 16 May 1960, in *Peking Review*, 24 May 1960, p. 32.
15. Chen Yi, 'Ten years of struggle for world peace and human progress', in *Ten Glorious Years* (Peking: Foreign Language Press, 1960).
16. See Vice-Premier Chen Yi's television interview with Mr Karlsson, correspondent of the Swedish Broadcasting Corporation, 17 February 1963, in *The Sino–Indian Boundary Question, II*, pp. 1–12 (Peking: Foreign Language Press, 1965).
17. *Ibid.*
18. *Peking Review*, 15 March 1963, p. 66.
19. *Peking Review*, 15 September 1965, p. 10.
20. *Peking Review*, 8 October 1965, p. 22.
21. See joint communiqué issued by Chairman Liu Shaoqi and Prince Norodom Sihanouk, 27 February 1963, in *Peking Review*, 15 March 1963, pp. 70–1.
22. See *Peking Review*, 8 October 1965, p. 17.
23. See *People's Daily*, 29 September 1963, in *Peking Review*, 4 October 1963, pp. 23–4.
24. *Peking Review*, 22 January 1965, pp. 17–18.
25. See *Peking Review*, 13 January 1961, p. 8: *Far Eastern Economic Review 43*, no. 7, 13 February 1964, p. 350.
26. See W. F. Choa, 'China's economic aid to developing countries', *The China Mainland Review I*, no. 1, June 1965, p. 17.
27. See 'Sino–Mali joint communiqué', 21 January 1964, in *Peking Review*, 31 January 1964, p. 9.
28. Ai Ching-chu, 'China's economic and technical aid to other countries', *Peking Review*, 21 August 1964, pp. 14–15.
29. *People's Daily*, 16 June 1950, in *People's China*, 1 July 1950, p. 13.
30. *Peking Review*, 17 September 1965, p. 9.
31. For a much fuller account of this early period in Chinese–African relations, see William Zartman, 'Tiger in the jungle', *Current Scene 2*, no. 2, 6 August 1962.
32. See Bruce D. Larkin, *China and Africa 1949–1970*, p. 45 (Berkeley: University of California Press, 1971).

33. See address by Chinese delegate to second Afro–Asian People's Solidarity Conference in Conakry, April 1960, in *SCMP*, no. 2242, 14 April 1960, p. 26.
34. Reproduced in *Peking Review*, 25 October 1963, pp. 7–14.
35. See text of Sino–Algerian joint communiqué in *Peking Review*, 3 January 1964, p. 32.
36. *Peking Review*, 14 February 1964, p. 6
37. *Peking Review*, 1 May 1964, p. 10.
38. For a more detailed account of Sino–Soviet rivalry within the Asian communist movement in the early 1960s, see Robert A. Scalapino, 'Moscow, Peking and the communist parties of Asia', *Foreign Affairs 41*, no. 2, January 1963, pp. 323–43.
39. *Peking Review*, 28 May 1965, p. 6.
40. *Peking Review*, 28 June 1963, p. 12.
41. *Peking Review*, 24 May 1963, p. 12.
42. *Peking Review*, 15 March 1963, p. 74.
43. *Peking Review*, 24 May 1963, p. 13.
44. According to the United States, North Vietnamese torpedo boats had launched an unprovoked attack upon the American destroyer *Maddox* while carrying out a routine patrol. According to the American interpretation, a second attack was launched against both the *Maddox* and another destroyer, the *Turner Joy*, on 4 August. The North Vietnamese account was substantially different. It admitted the North Vietnamese attack but claimed that it was in reprisal for the bombardment of North Vietnamese islands. As to the second attack, Hanoi insisted that it had in fact never occurred. For a full account see *Le Monde*, 5–8 August 1964.
45. *Peking Review*, Special Supplement, 14 August 1964, p. iii.
46. Much of this information is drawn from Allen Whiting who was Director of the Office of Research and Analysis for the Far East in the State Department from 1962 to 1966. See 'The use of force in foreign policy by the People's Republic of China', *The Annals 402*, July 1972, pp. 55–66.

Chapter 5

1. For a detailed account of the violent attack against the British mission in Peking, see the *Guardian*, 23 August 1967, p. 1. For the Chinese interpretation of the incident in Portland Place described as 'a new and grave political provocation engineered by British imperialism against the great Chinese people', see *Peking Review*, 14 July 1967.
2. See I. Jadoul, 'Les relations sino–Birmanes et la Révolution Culturelle', *Revue de l'Asie du Sud-Est et de l'Extréme-Orient*, 1968/2, pp. 248–72.
3. *Peking Review*, 20 October 1967, p. 27.
4. *Peking Review*, 26 December 1969, p. 41.
5. *Peking Review*, 8 December 1967, p. 21.
6. *Current Background*, no. 882, 16 June 1969, p. 31.
7. *Ibid.* p. 49.
8. *Ibid.* p. 35.
9. For a more detailed presentation of this argument see L. Vandermeersch, 'La politique extérieure chinoise à l'heure de la Révolution Culturelle', *Esprit*, no. 371, May 1968, pp. 776–89.
10. In a statistical analysis of the coverage given by the *Peking Review* to the international environment in the period 1966–69, Daniel Tretiak found that attention to the Soviet Union rose dramatically from 13.54 per cent in

July–December 1968 to 34.29 per cent in January–June 1969. See 'Is China preparing to "turn out"?: changes in Chinese levels of attention to the international environment', *Asian Survey 11*, no. 3, March 1971, p. 234.

11. *New China News Agency*, 18 June 1968.
12. *New China News Agency*, 30 September 1968.
13. For a detailed outline of China's diplomatic offensive in 1970–71, see Léon Trivière, 'L'impressionnante offensive diplomatique de la Chine', *Etudes*, October 1971, pp. 373–96.
14. Leo Tansky, 'China's foreign aid: the record', *Current Scene 10*, no. 9, September 1972, p. 2.
15. For a comprehensive survey of China's aid commitments, see Udo Weiss, 'China's aid to and trade with the developing countries of the Third World', in *China and the Current Era of Détente*, pp. 91–157 (Bruxelles: Centre d'Etude du Sud-Est Asiatique et de l'Extrême-Orient, 1974).
16. For a detailed account of the changing pattern of China's trade in 1973, see 'China's foreign trade 1973–1974', *Current Scene 12*, no. 12, December 1974, pp. 1–15.
17. *Peking Review*, 29 November 1968, p. 31.
18. See John Gittings, 'A diplomatic thaw', *Far Eastern Economic Review*, 19 December 1968, p. 664.
19. *Peking Review*, 31 January 1969, p. 8.
20. Edgar Snow, *The Long Revolution*, p. 171 (London: Hutchinson, 1973).
21. See Léon Trivière, 'Pékin à l'O.N.U., Taipei exclu', *Etudes*, January 1972, p. 72.
22. 'Don't lose your head, Nixon', by commentator in *People's Daily*, 20 February 1971, in *Peking Review*, 26 February 1971, p. 6.
23. This view is confirmed by Allen Whiting in 'Use of force in foreign policy by the People's Republic of China', in *The Annals* (China in the World Today) *402*, July 1972, p. 61.
24. 'Don't lose your head, Nixon', p. 6.
25. Stephen Fitzgerald, 'China in the next decade: an end to Isolation', *The Australian Journal of Politics of History 17*, no. 1, April 1971, p. 34.
26. For a valuable analysis of Zhou Enlai's political role, especially during the latter stages of the Cultural Revolution, see Thomas W. Robinson, 'Chou En-lai's political style: comparisons with Mao Tse-tung and Lin Piao', *Asian Survey 10*, no. 12, December 1970, pp. 1101–16.
27. More details of China's recent economic growth can be found in Gilbert Etienne, *La voie chinoise, la longue marche de l'économie, 1949–1974* (Paris, Presses Universitaires de France, coll. Tiers Monde, 1974).
28. 'The world revolution has entered a great new era', *Peking Review*, 3 January 1969, p. 17.
29. 'A great storm', *People's Daily editorial*, 27 May 1968, in *Peking Review*, 31 May 1968, p. 9.
30. *Current Background*, no. 887, 15 August 1969, p. 15.
31. *Peking Review*, 11 October 1968, p. 9.
32. *New China News Agency*, 1 August 1968, in *SCMP*, no. 4234, 8 August 1968, p. 23.
33. The proposal was given its original formulation in Brezhnev's speech of 7 June 1969 to the International Conference of Communist and Workers' Parties, translated in *CDSP*, 2 July 1969, p. 16.
34. *Peking Review*, 4 July 1969, p. 22.
35. *The Military Balance 1971–72* (London: International Institute for Strategic Studies, 1971).

36. For illustrations for this view, see Allen S. Whiting, 'The Sino–American détente: genesis and prospects', in *China and the World Community*; ed. Ian Wilson (Australian Institute of International Affairs, Sydney: Angus and Robertson); Thomas W. Robinson, 'Soviet policy in East Asia', *Problems of Communism 22*, no. 6, November–December 1973, pp. 32–50; Robert A. Scalapino, 'China and the balance of power', *Foreign Affairs 52*, no. 2, January 1974, pp. 349–85.

37. *Peking Review*, 31 January 1969, p. 7.

38. *Ibid.* p. 8.

39. *People's Daily* editorial, 15 October 1970.

40. The question of China's membership of the United Nations prior to 1971 is examined by Evan Luard, 'China and the United Nations', *International Affairs 47*, no. 4, October 1971, pp. 728–44. See also Sydney D. Bailey, 'China and the United Nations', *The World Today 27*, no. 9, September 1971, pp. 365–72.

41. *Peking Review*, 27 August 1971, p. 6.

42. Richard M. Nixon, 'Asia after Viet Nam', *Foreign Affairs 46*, no. 1, October 1967, p. 115.

43. *United States Foreign Policy 1969–1970: A Report of the Secretary of State*, pp. 396–7 (Washington, DC: Department of State, 1971).

44. *Ibid.* pp. 400–1.

45. See Robert Kleiman, 'The high road to the Great Wall', *International Herald Tribune*, 3 November 1971.

46. Cited in 'The United States and Mainland China', *Current Scene 9*, no. 3, 7 March 1971, p. 22.

47. *Ibid.* p. 23.

48. *Ibid.*

49. *Ibid.*

50. Cited in 'U.S. moves on China trade and travel', *Current Scene 9*, no. 5, 7 May 1971, p. 16.

51. *Peking Review*, 12 March 1971, p. 19.

52. Edgar Snow, *The Long Revolution*, p. 172.

53. For a text of the joint statement, see *International Herald Tribune* (Paris), 17–18 July 1971.

54. The full text of the communiqué will be found in *United States Foreign Policy 1972: A Report of the Secretary of State*, p. 643 (Washington, DC: Department of State, 1973).

55. *Ibid.* p. 642.

56. *Ibid.*

57. *Ibid.*

58. *Ibid.*

59. See statement by Marshall Green made before the Sub-committee on Asian and Pacific Affairs of the House Committee on Foreign Affairs on 2 May 1972, in *United States Foreign Policy 1972*, p. 645.

Chapter 6

1. See 'A great storm', *People's Daily*, 27 May 1968, in *Peking Review*, 31 May 1968, p. 9.

2. See 'Comrade Lin Piao's speech at National Day celebration rally', *New China News Agency*, 1 October 1968.

3. *New China News Agency*, 27 April 1969, in *Current Background*, no. 887, 15 August 1969, p. 3.

4. *Ibid.*

5. *Peking Review*, 21 May 1971, p. 5.
6. 'Commemorate August 1, Army Day', editorial by the *People's Daily, Red Flag* and the *Liberation Army Daily*, 1 August 1971, in *Peking Review*, 6 August 1971, p. 8.
7. 'Financial crisis in the West testifies to further decay of imperialism', *Peking Review*, 29 March 1968, p. 24.
8. 'Usher in the great 1970s' published on 1 January 1970 by the *People's Daily, Red Flag* and *Liberation Army Daily*, and reproduced in *Peking Review*, 2 January 1970, p. 6.
9. The document was obtained by Nationalist intelligence and translated in full in *Issues and Studies 10*, no. 9, June 1974, pp. 104–5.
10. *New China News Agency*, 24 November 1968, in *Peking Review*, 29 November 1968, p. 4.
11. 'Unite the people, defeat the enemy' (abridged translation), *Peking Review*, 27 August 1971, pp. 10–13.
12. See joint editorial of the *People's Daily, Red Flag* and the *Liberation Army Daily*, 30 November 1971, in *SCMP*, no. 5032, 13 December 1971, pp. 22–5.
13. 'Outline of education on situation for companies', in *Issues and Studies 10*, no. 9, June 1974, pp. 104–5.
14. *Peking Review*, 7 January 1972, p. 8.
15. *Peking Review*, 13 October 1972, p. 9.
16. *Peking Review*, 7 September 1973, p. 22.
17. Supplement to *Peking Review*, 12 April 1974, p. 1.
18. See, for example, 'Excellent situation: East wind prevails over the West wind', *People's Daily*, 30 September 1967, slightly abridged in *Peking Review*, 20 October 1967, pp. 26–8.
19. See Deng Xiaoping's speech to the United Nations, 10 April 1974.
20. *Peking Review*, 7 September 1973, p. 22.
21. *Peking Review*, 31 July 1970, p. 3.
22. *Current Background*, no. 913, 28 August 1970, p. 199.
23. 'Advance victoriously along Chairman Mao's revolutionary diplomatic line', editorial by the *People's Daily, Red Flag* and the *Liberation Army Daily*, in *Peking Review*, 1 January 1971, p. 8.
24. 'The world trend: medium-sized and small nations unite to oppose two superpowers' hegemony', *Peking Review*, 28 January 1972, p. 16.
25. Supplement to *Peking Review*, 1 November 1968, p. viii.
26. 'U.S. imperialism and Soviet revisionism gang up to push through Middle East "political solution" scheme', *Peking Review*, 31 January 1969, p. 23.
27. 'An explanatory note on "social-imperialism"', *New China News Agency*, 30 August 1968, in *SCMP*, no. 4252, 6 September 1968, p. 25.
28. 'Soviet revisionism is U.S. imperialism number one accomplice', *Peking Review*, 21 March 1969, p. 25.
29. *Peking Review*, 1 January 1971, p. 9.
30. For a fuller exposition of this argument see Mira Sinha, 'Strategic rediscovery of the Third World', *China Report 10*, no. 3, May–June 1974, pp. 47–8.
31. *Peking Review*, 10 November 1972.
32. *Current Background*, no. 919, 17 November 1970, p. 177.
33. *Peking Review*, 21 September 1973, p. 4.
34. *New China News Agency*, 29 June 1971, in *Peking Review*, 2 July 1971, p. 36.
35. For a masterly analysis of the operation of the triangle, see Michel Tatu, *The Great Power Triangle: Washington–Moscow–Peking* (Paris: The Atlantic Institute, 1970).

36. 'A new trick of social-fascism', *People's Daily*, 5 February 1969, in *SCMP*, no. 4357, 19 February 1969.
37. Editorial, *Pravda*, 28 August 1969, in *CDSP 21*, no. 39, 24 September 1969, p. 3.
38. The gradual but steady convergence of US and Chinese interests with respect to the Indo–Pakistani conflict is clearly presented by William J. Barnds, 'China and America: limited partners in the Indian subcontinent', in Gene T. Hsiao, *Sino–American Détente and its Policy Implications*, pp. 236–44 (New York, Praeger, 1974).
39. 'Arbatov on U.S.–China relations', *CDSP 23*, no. 32, 7 September 1971, p. 4. See also 'Nixon's coming Peking visit appraised', *Pravda*, 25 July 1971, in *CDSP 23*, no. 30, 24 August 1971, pp. 1–4.
40. 'Arbatov on U.S.–China relations', p. 4.
41. See 'How the Soviets view President Nixon's visit to Mainland China', *Issues and Studies 8*, no. 6, March 1972, pp. 4–7.
42. 'Statement of the government of the People's Republic of China', *New China News Agency*, 24 May 1969, in *Current Background*, no. 887, 15 August 1969, p. 24.
43. *Peking Review*, 10 October 1969, p. 3.
44. *Ta Kung Pao* (Hong Kong), 9 January 1970.
45. *SCMP*, no. 4714, 10 August 1970, pp. 13–16.
46. For a detailed evaluation of the military balance between the two communist giants, see Russell Spurr, 'Asia's new military balance', *Far Eastern Economic Review Asia 1976 Yearbook*, pp. 44–9 (Hong Kong, 1976).
47. *Radio Moscow*, Chinese broadcast, 16 January 1972.
48. 'Concerning certain concepts of China's Maoist leadership', *Izvestia*, 2 June 1973, in *CDSP 25*, no. 22, 27 June 1973, p. 3. See also 'On certain principles of the Chinese leadership's foreign policy course', *Pravda*, 26 August 1973, in *CDSP 25*, no. 34, 19 September 1973.
49. *SCMP*, no. 5489, 6 November 1973, p. 80.
50. *Peking Review*, 31 January 1975, pp. 16–18.
51. *Peking Review*, 28 March 1975, p. 18.
52. Shen Chin, 'Soviet–U.S. contention for hegemony will inevitably lead to world war', *Peking Review*, 31 October 1975, p. 22.
53. *Peking Review*, 5 December 1975, p. 8.
54. *Peking Review*, 7 September 1973, p. 23.
55. 'Outline of education on situation for companies', in *Issues and Studies 10*, no. 9, June 1974, p. 97.

Chapter 7

1. See Wang Hongwen's report on the constitution, *Peking Review*, 7 September 1973, p. 33.
2. For a fuller account of implications of Deng's rehabilitation, see Parris H. Chang, 'Mao's unfinished revolution', *Current Scene 14*, no. 8, August 1976, pp. 1–12.
3. Chou En-lai, 'Report on the work of the government' 13 January 1975, in *Peking Review*, 24 January 1975, p. 21.
4. 'The Great Proletarian Cultural Revolution continues and deepens', *Peking Review*, 19 March 1976, p. 9.
5. For a detailed examination of the campaign see Parris H. Chang, 'The anti-Lin Piao and Confucius campaign: its meaning and purpose', *Asian Survey 14*, no. 10, 1974, pp. 871–86.
6. 'Unfold criticism of "Water Margin"', *People's Daily* editorial, 4 September 1975, in *Peking Review*, 12 September 1975, pp. 7–8.

7. See Harry Harding, Jr, 'China after Mao', *Problems of Communism 26*, March–April 1977, pp. 1–18.
8. 'The Great Proletarian Cultural Revolution continues and deepens', *Peking Review*, 17 March 1976, p. 9.
9. *Peking Review*, 5 November 1976, p. 5. See also the *Liberation Army Daily* editorial of 22 November 1976, in *Peking Review*, 3 December 1976, pp. 8–10.
10. See Ellis Joffe and Gerald Sigal, 'The Chinese army and professionalism', *Problems of Communism 27*, November–December 1978, pp. 1–19.
11. Great play was made by the new leadership of a note that Mao is alleged to have written on 30 April 1976, 'With you in charge I am at ease'. See 'Comrade Wu Teh's speech at the celebration rally in the capital', *Peking Review*, 29 October 1976, p. 12. Two days after the purge of the 'gang of four', the Central Committee of the CCP announced that a memorial hall would be established in Peking in the honour of Mao, and that a fifth volume of his selected works would be published under Hua's direction (*Peking Review*, 15 October 1976, pp. 3–4).
12. *Peking Review*, 29 December 1978, p. 11.
13. See Ting Wang, 'Leadership realignments', *Problems of Communism 26*, July–August 1977, pp. 1–77.
14. For a more detailed survey see 'National conferences focus on economy', *Current Scene 15*, nos 4–5, April–May 1977, pp. 11–13.
15. *Peking Review*, 10 March 1978, pp. 19, 23–4.
16. *Beijing Review* (formerly *Peking Review*), 12 January 1979, p. 7; 23 March 1979, p. 9.
17. *Beijing Review*, 22 June 1977, p. 10.
18. This recommendation appeared as one of the guiding principles for China's economic reconstruction in the *People's Daily* editorial of 24 February 1979, in *Beijing Review*, 9 March 1979, p. 5.
19. 'On policy towards the national bourgoisie', *Beijing Review*, 16 February 1979, pp. 11–16, 28.
20. 'On the development of modern industry', *Beijing Review*, 23 March 1979, p. 12.
21. See reports by David Bonavia, 'A revolution in the communes', *Far Eastern Economic Review 103*, no. 13, 30 March 1979, pp. 8–9; and 'Dangers of debate', *Far Eastern Economic Review 103*, no. 14, 6 April 1979, pp. 10–15.
22. The report was translated into English and published in several instalments in *Issues and Studies*, starting in November 1977. The section dealing with war appeared in *Issues and Studies 14*, no. 1, January 1978, pp. 102–9.
23. See article by PLA unit broadcast on Peking Domestic Service, 10 April 1977, in *Foreign Broadcast Information Service, Daily Report: People's Republic of China* (Washington, DC) (hereafter referred to as *FBIS-CHI*), 15 April 1977, p. E/23; and article in *Liberation Army Daily*, 25 September 1977, in *FBIS-CHI*, 26 September 1977, p. E/12.
24. *Liberation Army Daily* editorial, 25 September 1977, in *FBIS-CHI* 26 September 1977, p. E/12.
25. *Radio Peking Broadcast*, 5 February 1977, in *FBIS-CHI*, 7 February 1977, pp. E/5–9.
26. See 'Awards for inventions', *Beijing Review*, 2 February 1979, pp. 5–6, and speech by Ulanhu, 'On policy towards the national bourgeoisie', pp. 11–16, 28.
27. This trend is incisively analysed in Charles Bettelheim, 'The great leap backward', *Monthly Review 30*, no. 3, July–August 1978.
28. The abridged translation of the *People's Daily* editorial of 29 January 1979 appeared in *Beijing Review*, 16 February 1979, pp. 8–10.
29. See Deng Xiaoping's speech at the opening ceremony of the National Scene Conference, 18 March 1978, in *Peking Review*, 24 March 1978, pp. 9–18.

30. The policy of economic readjustment was clearly spelt out at a press conference in Tokyo by Vice-Chairman Deng Yingchao in April 1979. See 'Vice-Chairman Deng expounds China's domestic and foreign policies', *Beijing Review*, 20 April 1979, p. 20. The enormous infrastructure problems hampering the modernization programme are analysed by Miriam and Ivan D. London, 'Hurdles for China's new leap forward', *Australian Financial Review* (reproduced from *Barron's Weekly*), 16 January 1979, pp. 2–4.
31. 'Chou En-Lai's report on the international situation', *Issues and Studies 13*, no. 1, January 1977, p. 125.
32. See Liang Hsiao, 'On Lin Piao's capitulationism', *People's Daily*, 28 January 1976, in *Survey of People's Republic of China Press* (hereafter referred to as *SPRCP*, formerly *Survey of China Mainland Press*), no. 6033, 12 February 1976, pp. 135–42.
33. For a thought-provoking analysis of the radical view of foreign policy, see K. Lieberthal, 'The foreign policy debate in Peking as seen through allegorical articles 1973–76', *The China Quarterly*, no. 71, September 1977, pp. 528–54.
34. 'Huang Hua's report on the world situation', *Issues and Studies 13*, no. 12, December 1977, p. 88.
35. *Ibid.* p. 90.
36. See reports by Roger Kelly, Colin Lawason, Dinah Lee in *Far Eastern Economic Review 102*, no. 40, 6 October 1978, pp. 49–57.
37. Shannon R. Brow, 'Foreign technology and economic growth', *Problems of Communism 26*, July–August 1977, p. 35.
38. See Melinda Liu, 'China stops to rethink its development priorities', *Far Eastern Economic Review 103*, no. 11, 16 March 1979, p. 108.

Chapter 8

1. See King C. Chen, 'Peking's attitude toward Taiwan', *Asian Survey 17*, no. 10, October 1977, pp. 903–18.
2. *New York Times*, 4 August 1976, pp. 1, 3.
3. 'Peking is believed seeking the conquest of Taiwan', *New York Times*, 3 August 1976, p. 3.
4. 'Keng Piao talks on 'a turning point in the China–U.S. diplomatic relations' (speech delivered on 24 August 1976 at the graduation ceremony of the Peking Institute of Diplomacy). Reproduced in *Issues and Studies 13*, no. 1, January 1977, p. 130.
5. See 'Huang Hua's report on the world situation', 30 July 1977, in *Issues and Studies 14*, no. 1, January 1978, pp. 112–14.
6. *New York Times*, 21 May 1978, p. 8.
7. *New York Times*, 28 May 1978, p. 6.
8. *Izvestia*, 4 August 1978.
9. *Beijing Review*, 22 December 1978, p. 8.
10. See 'East Asia: U.S. normalizes relations with the People's Republic of China', *Department of State Bulletin 79*, no. 2022, January 1979, pp. 25–6.
11. 'Vice-Premier Deng Xiaoping interviewed by U.S. newsmen', 5 January 1979, in *Beijing Review*, 12 January 1979, p. 17.
12. Interview with President Carter, 19 December 1979, in *Department of State Bulletin 79*, no. 2023, February 1979, p. 5.
13. *Beijing Review*, 22 December 1978, pp. 10–11.
14. This shift in attitude was formally conveyed by Deng Xiaoping to US congressional leaders during his visit to the United States in January 1979. *Beijing Review*, 9 February 1979, p. 11.

15. 'Message to the compatriots in Taiwan', 1 January 1979, in *Beijing Review*, 5 January 1979, pp. 16–17.

16. See, for example, 'Another call to Taiwan authorities', *Beijing Review*, 9 March 1979, pp. 3–4.

17. In March 1979, Foreign Minister Huang Hua strongly objected to various bills relating to US–Taiwan relations, which were being considered by the US Senate and House of Representatives. See *Beijing Review*, 30 March 1979, p. 8.

18. Huang Lhen, 'My days in Washington', *Beijing Review*, 26 January 1979, p. 14.

19. Wang Bingnan, 'Growth of the friendship between Chinese and American people', *Beijing Review*, 26 January 1979, p. 13.

20. *FBIS–CHI*, 1 February 1979, pp. A5–6.

21. For a well-considered account of the pattern of trade relations in 1970–75, see Alexander Eckstern, 'China's trade policy and Sino–American relations', *Foreign Affairs 54*, no. 1, October 1975, pp. 134–54.

22. James Srodes, 'US firms put on the pressure', *Far Eastern Economic Review*, 7 July 1978, p. 39.

23. For a more detailed list, see Bruce Nussbaum, 'Hopes that Sino–US trade will reach US $5 billion by 1981', *Far Eastern Economic Review 103*, no. 11, 16 March 1979, p. 89.

24. See Melinda Liu, 'China stops to rethink its development priorities', *Far Eastern Economic Review 103*, no. 11, 16 March 1979, p. 108.

25. See Melinda Liu, 'US and Peking find a way', *Far Eastern Economic Review 104*, no. 21, 25 May 1979, pp. 73–4.

26. Supplement to *Peking Review*, 12 April 1974, p. ii.

27. '"European Security Conference": an analysis of its "final act"', *Peking Review*, 8 August 1975, p. 5.

28. Jen Ku-ping, 'Behind the Soviet–U.S. grain agreement', *Peking Review*, 15 November 1975, p. 16.

29. 'Sabre–Rattling behind the détente smokescreen', *Peking Review*, 28 March 1975, p. 15.

30. 'New turmoil is brewing in southern Europe', *Peking Review*, 28 August 1975, p. 16.

31. 'Social-imperialist strategy in Asia', *Beijing Review*, 19 January 1979, p. 14.

32. Hua Kuofeng, 'Political report to the 11th National Congress of the Communist Party of China', 12 August 1977. *Peking Review*, 26 August 1977, pp. 40–1.

33. 'Huang Hua's report on the world situation', p. 111. The détente myth was also strongly attacked soon after the announcement of the SALT II agreement. See 'New stage in Soviet–U.S. nuclear arms race', *Beijing Review*, 1 June 1979, pp. 21–2.

34. *FBIS–CHI*, 25 October 1977, p. A1.

35. *Beijing Review*, 9 February 1979, p. 13.

36. *The Military Balance, 1978–79*, pp. 55–6 (London: International Institute for Strategic Studies, 1978). See also Jonathan D. Pollack, 'The logic of Chinese military strategy', *The Bulletin of the Atomic Scientists*, January 1979, pp. 22–33.

37. 'Remarks before a national foreign political conference', 22 February 1979, in *Department of State Bulletin 79*, no. 2025, April 1979, p. 4.

38. The briefing was given on 15 January 1979, and reproduced in *Department of State Bulletin 79*, no. 2023, February 1979, p. 20.

39. *Ibid.*

40. 'Sino–Soviet friendship treaty will not be extended', *Beijing Review*, 6 April 1979, p. 4.

41. Alain Jacob, 'Pekin: un langage nouveau', *Le Monde* (selection hebdomadaire), 10–16 May 1979, p. 5.

42. *Beijing Review*, 18 May 1979, p. 10.

Chapter 9

1. See Chae-Jin Lee, 'The politics of Sino–Japanese trade relations, 1963–68', *Pacific Affairs 42*, no. 2, Summer 1969, pp. 132ff.

2. Observer, 'New Japanese Premier's daydream', *New China News Agency*, 25 November 1964, in *SCMP*, no. 3346, 30 November 1964, pp. 31–2.

3. 'Sato government must cancel Yoshida Letter', *New China News Agency*, 12 February 1965, in *SCMP*, no. 3399, 17 February 1965, pp. 22–3.

4. *People's Daily*, 5 December 1968, in *SCMP*, no. 4316, 11 December 1968, pp. 33–4.

5. See Sato's address to the National Press Club in New York, 21 November 1969, cited in *Issues and Studies 11*, no. 6, June 1975, p. 4. See also *The Times* (London), 22 November 1969, p. 4.

6. *People's Daily* editorial, 28 November 1969, in *Peking Review*, 5 December 1969, p. 15.

7. An outline of Japan's attitude to the China question was released by the Foreign Ministry on 5 March 1964 and included in *Basic Materials on Japanese/Chinese Relations* (Nichu Kankei Kihon Shiryoshu), Kanzakai, Tokyo, 1970.

8. Japanese war indemnities owing to China were estimated at over $50,000 million by the President of the Chinese Supreme People's Court in 1951.

9. See speech by Vice-Premier Li Xiannian, 15 October 1970, reprinted in *Current Background*, no. 924, 16 February 1971.

10. Statement of Ministry of Foreign Affairs of the People's Republic of China, 30 December 1971, in *Peking Review*, 7 January 1972.

11. See 'Opposition to summit bid on Peking ties', *Japan Times*, 18 July 1971; 'China policy under fire', *Japan Times*, 21 July 1971.

12. See joint communiqué with Japan–China Memorandum Trade Office, 21 December 1971, in *Peking Review*, 31 December 1971, p. 4.

13. John M. Lee, 'Nixon–Sato talks disappoint Japan', *New York Times*, 16 January 1972, p. 8.

14. Koji Nakamura, 'Open door for China', *Far Eastern Economic Review 77*, no. 36, 2 September 1972, p. 13.

15. *Japan Times*, 17 July 1972, p. 2.

16. *Japan Times*, 19 January 1973, p. 1.

17. *Ibid.*

18. Joint statement of the government of the People's Republic of China and the government of Japan, 29 September 1972, in *Peking Review*, 6 October 1972, p. 12.

19. For a much fuller discussion of the implications of the joint statement for the legal status of Taiwan, see Gene T. Hsiao, 'The Sino–Japanese rapprochement: a relationship of ambivalence', *The China Quarterly*, no. 57, January–March 1974, pp. 116–17.

20. See 'Foreign Minister Ohira holds press conference', *Peking Review*, 6 October 1972, p. 15.

21. *Peking Review*, 22 August 1975, p. 5.

22. For a much fuller analysis of Japan–Taiwan economic relations see Gene T. Hsiao, 'Prospects for a new Sino–Japanese relationship', *The China Quarterly*, no. 60, October–December 1974, pp. 720–49.

23. 'Taiwan economy becoming more dependent on imperialist capital', *New China News Agency*, 14 November 1973, in *SCMP*, no. 5502, 26 November 1973, pp. 17–18.

24. *Mainichi*, 6 October 1973.

25. *Far Eastern Economic Review*, 7 May 1973, p. 3.

26. See, for example, *Peking Review*, 31 January 1975, p. 21.

27. *Peking Review*, 17 October 1975, p. 22.
28. *Peking Review*, 29 August 1975, p. 11.
29. *Yomiuri Shimbun*, 25 April 1975; also *Japan Times* 25 April 1975.
30. *Aksai Shimbun*, 16 May 1975.
31. *Japan Times*, 28 January 1976.
32. The increasing friction between Moscow and Tokyo was readily exploited by Peking in numerous pronouncements on the issue. See 'Japan–Soviet talks ended in discord', *Peking Review*, 20 January 1978, pp. 27–8; 'Motive behind the draft "Soviet–Japan Good Neighbourliness and Co-operation Treaty"', *Peking Review*, 17 March 1978, pp. 44–5.
33. See Chihiro Hosoya, 'Japan's "omni-directional" course' (translated from '"Zenhōi" Nihon no shinro', in *Chūō Kōron*, October 1978), *Japan Echo 5*, no. 4, 1978, p. 84.
34. The basic Chinese position is outlined in a Foreign Ministry statement of 30 December 1971, in *Peking Review*, 7 January 1972, pp. 12–14.
35. See 'Chinese Foreign Ministry statement protesting Japanese government's infringement of China's sovereignty', 26 June 1978, in *Peking Review*, 30 June 1978. Peking's territorial claim over the East China Sea continental shelf was first formally expressed on 4 February 1974 and repeated on 14 June 1977 (see 'Statement by the Ministry of Foreign Affairs', *Peking Review*, 17 June 1977, pp. 16–17).
36. On 13 August 1978, the three major Japanese newspapers, the *Aksai Shimbun*, *Yomiuri Shimbun*, and *Mainichi Shimbun*, ran editorials strongly commending the agreement and stressing its importance not only for Sino–Japanese relations but for the peace and stability of the Asia–Pacific region.
37. *FBIS-CHI*, 14 August 1978, p. A7.
38. *Peking Review*, 18 August 1978, p. 10. The same theme dominated numerous other official and semi-official pronouncements. See, for example, Chang Hsiang-shan, 'Far-reaching significance of China–Japan Treaty of Peace and Friendship', *Peking Review*, 20 October 1978, pp. 19–22.
39. 'Vice-Premier Teng at Tokyo press conference', 25 October 1978, in *Peking Review*, 3 November 1978, p. 15.
40. Cited in Shirvanishi Shinichiro, 'The potential for economic co-operation', *Japan Quarterly 26*, no. 1, January–March 1979, p. 45.
41. Tracy Dahlby, 'Peking opens the door to Japan', *Far Eastern Economic Review 99*, no. 9, 3 March 1978, p. 41.
42. Report by Vice-Premier Yu Qiuli, in *FBIS-CHI*, 6 July 1978, pp. E1–12.
43. Tracy Dahlby, 'Japan goes for the bonanza', *Far Eastern Economic Review 103*, no. 5, 2 February 1979, p. 42.
44. For a more detailed outline of the problems associated with trade financing see 'Japan gives an extra push to its trade with China', *Far Eastern Economic Review 101*, no. 38, 22 September 1978, pp. 96–7; and 'Peking's yen for the U.S. dollar', *Far Eastern Economic Review 102*, no. 41, 13 October 1978, pp. 44–5.

Chapter 10

1. *People's Daily*, 20 February 1967, in *Peking Review*, 24 February 1967, p. 10.
2. The statement was issued on 21 January 1972 and reprinted in the *Peking Review*, 28 January 1972.
3. For a full text of the Shanghai communiqué (27 February 1972), see *United States Foreign Policy 1972: A Report of the Secretary of State*, pp. 640–3 (Washington: Department of State, 1973). The seven-point plan, which was presented by the PRG delegate, Mrs Nguyen Thi Binh, at the Paris peace talks on 1 July 1971,

called on the American government to fix a date for total withdrawal of US forces in Vietnam, to respect the South Vietnam people's right to self-determination and to cease all support for the Thieu regime. The full text of the seven-point programme was published in the *International Herald Tribune*, 2 July 1971, p. 2.

4. These agreements were renewed for 1974 following the visit to China of a North Vietnamese delegation in June 1973. For a complete list of agreements during this period see *Current Background*, no. 1014, 5 August 1974, p. 74.
5. *Far Eastern Economic Review Asia 1976 Yearbook*, p. 149.
6. See Zhou Enlai's speech of June 1973 in *Peking Review*, 8 June 1973, p. 7.
7. 'Plots cannot be concealed by lies', *People's Daily*, 13 April 1975, in *Peking Review*, 18 April 1975, p. 13.
8. 'A great historic victory', *People's Daily* editorial, 18 April 1975, in *Peking Review*, 25 April 1975, p. 18.
9. 'A great victory of world significance', *People's Daily* editorial, 1 May 1975, in *Peking Review*, 2 May 1975, pp. 13–14.
10. 'Indochina belongs to the Indochinese peoples', *People's Daily* editorial, 25 April 1975, in *Peking Review*, 2 May 1975, p. 18.
11. *The Age* (Melbourne), 6 December 1973.
12. See Jen Ku-ping, 'Repulse wolf at the gate, guard against tiger at the back door', *Peking Review*, 8 August 1975, p. 11; also 'Soviet social-imperialists covet Southeast Asia', *Peking Review*, 15 August 1975, pp. 20–1.
13. See 'Burmese people's armed struggle – a red flag for people's revolution', *Peking Review*, 12 January 1968; 'The Malayan people's revolutionary struggle has continuously scored victorious development', *Peking Review*, 8 March 1969; 'Thai people's armed forces march from victory to victory', *Peking Review*, 17 January 1969.
14. *Peking Review*, 1 August 1975, pp. 20–1.
15. *Peking Review*, 24 August 1973.
16. *Bangkok Post*, 8 September 1973.
17. *Speech by Chiao Kuan-hua at the Plenary Meeting of the 29th Session of the UN General Assembly* 2 October 1974, pp. 14–16 (Peking: Foreign Language Press, 1974).
18. *Peking Review*, 22 August 1975, p. 11.
19. For a very useful examination of this as act of Sino–Soviet relations see Dick Wilson, 'Sino–Soviet rivalry in Southeast Asia', *Problems of Communism 23*, no. 5, September–October 1974, pp. 39–51.
20. *Malaysian Digest* (Kuala Lumpur), 31 October 1973, p. 10.
21. See article in *People's Daily*, 19 March 1974, in *SCMP*, no. 5582, 28 March 1974, pp. 138–40.
22. See 'China's stand on question of rights over seas and oceans', *Peking Review*, 10 March 1972.
23. Cited in Chao Ch'ien, 'Peiping–Moscow confrontation in Indochina', *Issues and Studies 14*, no. 3, March 1978, p. 60.
24. *Peking Review*, 22 August 1975, p. 10.
25. *Peking Review*, 12 September 1975, p. 6.
26. See the analysis by a Xinhua correspondent of the South Vietnamese communist victory, 'Great victory of people's war', *Peking Review*, 23 May 1975, pp. 7–9. See also 'U.S. blocks U.N. membership for the two parts of Viet Nam', *Peking Review*, 22 August 1975, p. 15.
27. Interview published in *Le Monde*, 14 October 1978.
28. *Peking Review*, 26 September 1975, p. 13.

29. For a concise outline of the background to the Sino–Vietnamese conflict, see Gareth Porter, 'Asia's new cold war', *The Nation*, 9 September 1978.
30. 'All at sea over the deeper issue', *Far Eastern Economic Review 99*, no. 5, p. 23, 3 February 1978.
31. For one of the most accurate reports of the Vietnamese–Kampuchean conflict, see Nayan Chanda, 'Clash of steel among the comrades and anatomy of the conflict', *Far Eastern Economic Review 99*, no. 2, pp. 10–15. 13 January 1978.
32. Cited in Nayan Chanda, 'The bloody border', *Far Eastern Economic Review 100*, no. 16, 21 April 1978, p. 18.
33. Vietnam reacted angrily to these revelations, repatriating all Khmer soldiers but detaining the Chinese as hostages. Nguyen Giap lodged a vehement protest over the incident and demanded an explanation during his visit to China. When this was not forthcoming, the talks collapsed without even the release of a joint communiqué. See Yokoyame Sanshiro, 'Shadow of Sino–Soviet subversion over Indochina', *Sanku Shimbun*, 5 November 1977.
34. Vietnam's attitude to the conflict was set out in detail in a document issued at a news conference in Hanoi by the Vietnamese Foreign Ministry on 7 April 1978. Reproduced in *Journal of Contemporary Asia 8*, no. 3, 1978, pp. 399–410.
35. 'Why Vietnamese authorities provoked Vietnam–Kampuchea border conflict', by *People's Daily* commentator, 12 July 1978, in *Peking Review*, 21 July 1978, p. 8.
36. *Peking Review*, 11 August 1978, p. 3.
37. See report by Nayan Chanda, 'Cambodia: fifteen days that shook Asia', *Far Eastern Economic Review 105*, no. 3, 19 January 1979, p. 12.
38. The scenario is clearly spelt out by Wilfred Burchet in *Nation Review*, 15 March 1979.
39. *Nhan Dan*, 15 July 1978.
40. For a fuller account of the decline in Chinese aid commitments to Vietnam, see Yin Ch'ing yao, 'Peiping–Hanoi conflict: origins and development', *Issues and Studies 14*, no. 10, October 1978, pp. 19–41.
41. The official Chinese explanation for the decision to curtail diplomatic links with Vietnam is contained in Chinese Foreign Ministry's Note of 16 July 1978, which was published in *Peking Review*, 30 June 1978, p. 19.
42. *Peking Review*, 14 July 1978, p. 27.
43. See 'Time will tell the true from the false', *People's Daily*, 22 July 1978, in *Peking Review*, 28 July 1978, p. 29.
44. See Vietnamese government's 'July 6th 1978 note in reply to the Chinese government's July 3rd 1978 notes concerning the Chinese decision to cut all economic and technical aids to Vietnam', reproduced in *Vietnam Courier*, no. 75, August 1978, pp. 6–7.
45. See Nayan Chanda, 'A prophecy self-fulfilled', *Far Eastern Economic Review 104*, no. 22, 1 June 1978, pp. 19–20.
46. 'Vice-Premier Teng at Bangkok press conference', *Peking Review*, 17 November 1978, p. 24.
47. 'Statement on Viet Nam's expulsion of Chinese residents' by spokesman of the Overseas Chinese Affairs Office of the State Council, 24 May 1978, in *Peking Review*, 2 June 1978, p. 16.
48. For one of the most detailed and objective accounts of the origins, composition and political significance of the 'boat people' phenomenon, see *The Boat People*, an 'Age' investigation with Bruce Grant (Harmondsworth: Penguin Books, 1979).
49. See statement issued by the Vietnamese Foreign Ministry on 27 May 1978, and

reproduced in *Vietnam Courier*, no. 73, June 1978, pp. 4–5.

50. See 'Xisha and Nansha islands belong to China', *Beijing Review*, 25 May 1979, p. 26.
51. See Huang Hua's June 1977 'Report on the world situation', *Issues and Studies 13*, no. 12, December 1977, p. 81.
52. 'Frontier forces counterattack Vietnamese aggressors', *Beijing Review*, 23 February 1979, p. 3.
53. See Russell Spurr, 'Holding back the angry giant', *Far Eastern Economic Review 103*, no. 10, 9 March 1979, pp. 14–15. According to David Bonavia, the Chinese restricted the use of air power because their fighters would have been no match for the more modern Vietnamese MIG-21s and MIG-23s, while Vietnam, which lacked sufficient trained pilots to fly the MIG-23s, was reluctant to risk the capture of Soviet pilots ('Lessons of the 16-day battle', *Far Eastern Economic Review 104*, no. 8, 4 May 1979, pp. 11–12).
54. 'Chinese representative Chen Chu's speech', *Beijing Review*, 2 March 1979, p. 20.
55. *Beijing Review*, 23 March 1979, p. 3.
56. *Pravda*, 28 February 1979, in *CDSP 31*, no. 9, 28 March 1979, pp. 6–8.
57. See Nayan Chanda, 'Protestations of peace, undertones of war', *Far Eastern Economic Review 104*, no. 18, 4 May 1979, p. 9.
58. 'Speech by Han Nianlong, head of Chinese government delegation', *Beijing Review*, 4 May 1979, pp. 10–17.
59. Cited in Nayan Chanda, 'The agonising choice', *Far Eastern Economic Review 104*, no. 20, 18 May 1979, p. 13.
60. See 'Peking loses ground in Laos', *Far Eastern Economic Review 103*, no. 8, 23 February 1979, pp. 8–10.
61. See 'What has been happening in Laos', *Beijing Review*, 6 April 1979, pp. 22–4; 'How far will the Lao authorities go', *Beijing Review*, 22 June 1979, p. 8.
62. *Straits Times* (Kuala Lumpur), 16 January 1971.
63. *New China News Agency*, 31 May 1974.
64. For a comprehensive analysis of the ideological underpinning of this shift in strategy see Greg O'Leary, 'Recent changes in Chinese foreign policy and their implications for Southeast Asia' (unpublished paper).
65. *Japan Times*, 16 May 1973.
66. 'Focus China 1974', *Far Eastern Economic Review 86*, no. 39, 4 October 1974, p. 52.
67. *Asia Research Bulletin 3*, no. 8, 31 January 1974, p. 2404.
68. For a more detailed account of trade relations between the two countries see U. Weiss, 'China's aid and trade with the developing countries of the Third World' (Part II), *Asia Quarterly*, 1974/4, pp. 279–80.
69. For the full text of the two communiqués, see *SPRC*, no. 5878, 20 June 1975, pp. 211–13, and no. 5893, 14 July 1975, pp. 43–4.
70. *International Herald Tribune*, 14 May 1976.
71. See Justus M. Van der Kroef, 'Before the thaw: recent Indonesian attitudes toward China', *Asian Survey 13*, no. 5, May 1973.
72. *Japan Times*, 27 April 1973.
73. 'Prime Minister gives interview on foreign policy', 9 December 1977, in *News Bulletin* (Thailand Ministry of Foreign Affairs), November–December 1977, p. 23.
74. 'Vice-Premier Li visits the Philippines', *Peking Review*, 24 March 1978, p. 4.
75. See Rodney Tasker, 'A courteous rebuff for Dong's diplomacy', *Far Eastern Economic Review 101*, no. 39, 29 September 1978, pp. 8–9.
76. 'Viet Nam–Soviet treaty threatens world peace and security', *Peking Review*, 17 November 1978, p. 24.

77. *New York Times*, 14 January 1979.
78. *New York Times*, 12 January 1979.
79. 'Peking lays a snare for Kriangsak', *Far Eastern Economic Review 104*, no. 20, 18 May 1979, pp. 14–15.
80. 'Chinese Foreign Ministry statement', 16 June 1979, in *Beijing Review*, 22 June 1979, pp. 21–2.

Select Bibliography

This bibliography refers only to some of the more useful secondary material readily available in books and articles. For primary sources consult the notes for each chapter.

General

Adie, Ian W. A. C., China's oil boomerang. *Asia Quarterly*, 1976/2, pp. 83–106.
— *Chinese Strategic Thinking under Mao Tse-tung*. Canberra: Australian National University Press, 1973.
Andors, Stephen, *China's Industrial Revolution*. New York: Pantheon Books, 1977.
Boorman, H. L., Peking in world politics. *Pacific Affairs 34*, no. 3, Autumn 1961, pp. 227–41.
Boyd, R. G., *Communist China's Foreign Policy*. New York: Praeger, 1962.
Camilleri, J. and Teichman, M., *Security and Survival: A New Era in International Relations*. Melbourne: Heinemann Educational, 1975.
Chai, Winberg (ed.). *The Foreign Relations of the People's Republic of China*. New York: Putnam, 1972.
Choudhury, G. W., *Chinese Perceptions of the World*. Washington, DC: University Press of America, 1977.
Cohen, Jerome Alan (ed.), *The Dynamics of China's Foreign Relations*. Cambridge, Mass.: Harvard University Press, 1970.
Davies, Derek, China's foreign policy: idealism versus reality. *Pacific Community 1*, no. 4, July 1970, pp. 564–78.
Eckstein, Alexander, *China's Economic Revolution*. Cambridge: Cambridge University Press, 1977.
Etienne, G., *La voie chinoise: la longue marche de l'économie*. Paris: Presses Universitaires de France, 1974.
Fairbank, John King (ed.), *The Chinese World Order: Traditional China's Foreign Relations*. London: Oxford University Press, 1969.
Ginneken, Jaap van, *The Rise and Fall of Lin Piao*. New York: Avon Books, 1977.
Gittings, John, *The World and China, 1922–1972*. London: Eyre Methuen, 1974.
Guillermaz, J., Problèmes posés par la Chine dans les relations internationales. *Revue Tiers-Monde 9*, July–December 1968, pp. 643–54.
Gurley, John G., *China's Economy and the Maoist Strategy*. New York: Monthly Review Books, 1976.
Halpern, A. M. (ed.), *Policies Toward China: Views from Six Continents*. New York: McGraw–Hill, 1965.
Hinton, Harold C., *China's Turbulent Quest*. New York: Macmillan, 1972.
— *Communist China in World Politics*. Boston: Houghton Mifflin, 1965.
Hsieh, A. L., *Communist China's Strategy in the Nuclear Era*. Englewood Cliffs, NJ: Prentice–Hall, 1962.
Hsiung, James Chieh (ed.), *The Logic of 'Maoism': Critiques and Explanations*. Praeger Special Studies in International Politics and Government, New York: Praeger, 1974.
Hsüeh, Chun-tu (ed.), *Dimensions of China's Foreign Relations*. New York: Praeger, 1977.

Huck, Arthur, *The Security of·China; Chinese Approaches to Problems of War and Strategy*. London: Chatto and Windus, 1970.

Kun, Joseph C., Peking and world communism. *Problems of Communism 23*, no. 6, November–December 1974, pp. 34–43.

Lawrence, Alan, *China's Foreign Relations Since 1949*. London: Routledge and Kegan Paul, 1975.

Liu, Leo Yueh–Yun, *China as a Nuclear Power in World Politics*. London: Macmillan, 1972.

— The People's Republic of China as a nuclear power: a study of Chinese statements on global strategy. *Asian Studies 10*, no. 2, August 1972, pp. 183–95.

Marabini, Jean, *Mao et ses héritiers: ombres chinoises sur le monde*. Paris: Editions Robert Laffont, 1972.

Maxwell, Neville, The threat from China. *International Affairs 47*, no. 1, January 1971, pp. 31–44.

Moulder, Francis V., *Japan, China and the Modern World Economy*. Cambridge: Cambridge University Press, 1977.

North, R. C., *The Foreign Relations of China*. Belmont, Calif.: Dickenson, 1974.

Ojha, Ishwer C., *Chinese Foreign Policy in an Age of Transition: The Diplomacy of Cultural Despair*. Boston, Mass.: Beacon Press, 1969.

La politique étrangère de la Chine. *Civilisation 19*, 1969, pp. 146–68.

Peyrefitte, Alain, *Quand la Chine s'éveillera*. Paris: Fayard, 1973.

Pollack, Jonathan D., The logic of Chinese military strategy. *The Bulletin of the Atomic Scientists 35*, no. 1, January 1979, pp. 22–33.

Prybyla, Jan S., Some economic strengths and weaknesses of the People's Republic of China. *Asian Survey 17*, no. 12, December 1977, pp. 1119–42.

Schurmann, Franz and Schell, Orville (eds), *Communist China: China Readings*, 3 vols. Harmondsworth: Penguin Books, 1968.

Simmonds, J. D., *China's World: The Foreign Policy of a Developing State*. London: Columbia University Press, 1970–71.

Snow, Edgar, Mao and the new mandate. *The World Today*, July 1969. pp. 289–97.

— *The Other Side of the River*. New York: Random House, 1961.

Solomon, Richard H., *Mao's Revolution and the Chinese Political Culture*. Berkeley: University of California Press, 1972.

Tsou, Tang (ed.), *China in Crisis*, 2 vols. Chicago: University of Chicago Press, 1968.

Tung, William L., *China and the Foreign Powers: The Impact of and Reaction to Unequal Treaties*. Dobbs Ferry: Oceana, 1970.

Vernant, Jacques, La politique étrangère de la Chine en perspective. *Politique étrangère 39*, no. 2, 1974, pp. 165–84.

Wilson, Dick (ed.), *Mao Tse-tung in the Scales of History*. Cambridge: Cambridge University Press, 1977.

Wilson, Ian (ed.), *China and the World Community*. Australian Institute of International Affairs, Sydney: Angus and Robertson, 1973.

Young, O. R., Chinese views on the spread of nuclear weapons. *China Quarterly*, no. 26, 1966, pp. 136–70.

China and the Great Powers

Barnett, A. Doak, *China and the Major Powers in East Asia*. Washington: Brookings Institution, 1977.

Brown, Leslie H., *American Security Policy in Asia*, Adelphi Papers, no. 132. London: International Institute for Strategic Studies, 1977.

Chari, P. R., US–USSR–China interaction: the strategic plane. *China Report 12*, no. 1, January–February 1976, pp. 33–42.

. Clubb, O. E., China and the superpowers. *Current History 67*, no. 397, September 1974, pp. 97–100

Deutscher, Isaac, *Russia, China and the West: A Contemporary Chronicle – 1953–1966*. London: Oxford University Press, 1970.

Feis, Herbert, *The China Triangle*. Princeton, NJ: Princeton University Presses, 1972.

Gass, Oscar, China, Russia and the U.S. *Commentary 43*, April 1967, pp. 39–48.

Gelber, Harry C., The Sino–Soviet relationship and the U.S. *Orbis 15*, no. 1, Spring 1971, pp. 118–33.

Gittings, John, China between the superpowers. *New Society 79*, no. 3, 10 October 1974.
— The great power triangle and Chinese foreign policy. *China Quarterly*, no. 39, July–September 1969, pp. 41–54.

Glaubitz, Joachim, Moscow–Peking–Tokyo: A Triangle of Great Power Relations. *Bulletin of the Institute for the Study of the U.S.S.R. 18*, no. 6, 1971, pp. 20–33.

Griffith, William E., *Cold War and Coexistence: Russia, China and the U.S.* Englewood Cliffs, NJ: Prentice–Hall, 1971.
— Peking, Moscow and beyond: the Sino–Soviet–American triangle. *The Washington Papers*, no. 6, Georgetown University Washington, The Center for Strategic and International Studies, 1973.

Hinton, Harold C., *Three and a Half Powers: The New Power Balance in Asia*. Bloomington, Indiana: Indiana University, 1975.

Kapur, H., *The Embattled Triangle, Moscow–Peking–New Delhi*. New York: Humanities Press, 1973.

Kaur, Harmala, China in the international system. *China Report 13*, no. 2, March–April 1977, pp. 30–43.

Melby, John F., Great power rivalry in East Asia. *International Journal 26*, no. 3, Summer 1971, pp. 457–68.

Petković, Ranko, China, the U.S.A. and the U.S.S.R. *Review of International Affairs 22*, nos 512–13, August 1971, pp. 6–8.

Ravenal, Earl C., The strategic balance in Asia. *Pacific Community 3*, no. 4, July 1972.

Robinson, Thomas W., The view from Peking: China's policies toward the United States, the Soviet Union and Japan. *Pacific Affairs 45*, no. 3, Fall 1972, pp. 333–55.

Scalapino, R. A., China and the balance of power. *Foreign Affairs 52*, no. 2, June 1974, pp. 349–85.

Schwartz, Harry, The Moscow–Peking–Washington triangle. *Annals of the American Academy of Political and Social Sciences 414*, July 1974, pp. 41–54.

Tatu, Michel, *Le grand triangle: Washington–Moscou–Pékin*. Paris: Institut Atlantique, 1970.

Waller, D. J., Chinese perception of Soviet–American relations 1962–1970: a pilot study. *Political Science Review 9*, nos 3–4, July–December 1970, pp. 258–69.

Whiting, A. S., Pechino–Mosca–Washington: il triangolo che cambia (Peking–Moscow–Washington: the changing triangle). *Affari esteri 4*, no. 13, January 1972, pp. 3–18.

Wilcox, Francis (ed.), *China and the Great Powers – Relations with the United States, the Soviet Union and Japan*. New York: Praeger, 1974.

Sino–American Relations

Adie, W. A. C., 'One-world' restored? Sino–American relations on a new footing. *Asian Survey 12*, no. 5, May 1972, pp. 365–85.

Ali, Mehrunnisa, The new American attitude towards China. *Pakistan Horizon 24*, no. 4, 1971, pp. 45–59.

Armand, L., Le rapprochement sino–americain: vers de nouveaux rapports entre les puissances. *Revue de défense nationale 27*, no. 11, November 1971.

Barnett, A. Doak, *Communist China and Asia: Challenge to American Foreign Policy.* New York: Random House, Vintage Books, 1960.

— A nuclear China and U.S. arms policy. *Foreign Affairs 48*, no. 3, April 1970, pp. 426–42.

Berger, Roland, China's policy and the Nixon visit. *Journal of Contemporary Asia 2*, no. 1, March 1972, pp. 1–16.

Blum, Robert, *U.S. Policy Towards Communist China.* New York: Foreign Policy Association, 1966.

Borch, Herbert von, U.S.A.–China–High stakes in power politics. *Aussen Politik 23*, no. 1, pp. 3–13.

Brown, Roger Glenn, Chinese politics and American policy. *Foreign Policy*, no. 23, Summer 1976, pp. 3–23.

Bundy, W., Chine–U.S.A.: jusqu où ira l'ouverture. *Preuves*, no. 7, 1971, pp. 36–47.

Chen, King C., Peking's attitude toward Taiwan. *Asian Survey 17*, no. 10, October 1977, pp. 903–18.

Clubb, O. E., China and the U.S.: beyond ping-pong. *Current History 61*, no. 361, September 1971, pp. 129–34.

Cohen, Jerome Alan, Recognizing China. *Foreign Affairs 50*, no. 1, October 1971, pp. 30–58.

Cohen, Warren I., *America's Response to China: An Interpretative History of Sino–American Relations.* New York: John Wiley, 1971.

Dickinson, William B. Jr. (ed.), *China and U.S. Foreign Policy.* Washington: Congressional Quarterly Service, 2nd ed, 1973.

Eckstein, Alexander, China's trade policy and Sino–American relations. *Foreign Affairs 54*, no. 1, October 1975, pp. 134–54.

Fairbank, John K., *China Perceived: Images and Policies in Chinese American Relations.* New York: Alfred A. Knopf, 1974.

— The new China and the American connection. *Foreign Affairs 51*, no. 1, October 1972, pp. 31–43.

— *The United States and China.* Cambridge, Mass.: Harvard University Press, 1971.

Fumio, Kusano, Sino–American confrontation and communist Chinese attitudes. *Review* (Tokyo), no. 9, June 1966, pp. 18–53.

Gass, O., China and the United States. *Commentary 34*, no. 5, November 1962.

Gelber, Harry C., The United States and China: the evolution of policy. *International Affairs* (London), *46*, no. 4, October 1970, pp. 682–95.

Guhin, Michael A., The U.S. and the Chinese People's Republic: the non-recognition policy reviewed. *International Affairs* (London), *45*, no. 1, January 1969, pp. 44–63.

Hinton, Harold C., *Peking and Washington: Chinese Foreign Policy and the United States.* Beverly Hills, Calif.: Sage Publications, 1976.

Hsiao, Gene T. (ed.), *Sino–American Détente and Its Policy Implications.* New York: Praeger, 1974.

Hsiung, James C., U.S. relations with China in the post-Kissingerian era: a sensible policy for the 1980's. *Asian Survey 17*, no. 8, August 1977, pp. 691–710.

Hsüeh, Chün-tu, The Shanghai communiqué: its significance and interpretation. *Asia Quarterly*, 1973–4, pp. 279–86.

Ivkov, I., U.S.A. playing the Chinese card in Asia. *Far Eastern Affairs* (Moscow), no. 2, 1979, pp. 71–87.

Kalicki, J. H., China, America and arms control. *The World Today 26*, no. 4, April 1970, pp. 147–55.

— Sino–American relations after Cambodia. *The World Today 26*, no. 9, September 1970, pp. 383–92.

— Sino–American relations despite Indochina. *The World Today 27*, no. 11, November 1971, pp. 472–78.

MacFarquhar, R., Nixon's China pilgrimage. *The World Today 28*, no. 4, April 1972.
— *Sino–American Relations 1949–1971*. Royal Institute of International Affairs, Melbourne: Wren Publishing, 1972.
Nixon, Richard M., Asia after Viet Nam. *Foreign Affairs 46*, no. 1, October 1967, pp. 111–25.
Nizami, T. A., Richard Nixon and Peking. *Indian Journal of Politics 6*, no. 1, January–June 1972, pp. 123–7.
Ojha, Ishwer C., China's cautious American policy. *Current History 53*, no. 313, September 1967, pp. 135–40 ff.
— The Sino–American confrontation: communist Chinese perspectives. *Current History 51*, no. 301, September 1966, pp. 147–52.
Page, Glenn, *The Korean Decision*. New York: Free Press, 1968.
Pye, L. W., China and the United States: a new phase. *Annals of the American Academy of Political and Social Sciences*, no. 402, July 1972, pp. 97–106.
Quester, G. H., Some alternative explanations of Sino–American détente. *International Journal 28*, no. 2, 1973, pp. 236–50.
Rees, David, *Korea: The Limited War*. London: Macmillan, 1964.
Rhee, T. C., Implications of the Sino–American détente. *Orbis 16*, no. 2, 1972, pp. 500–19.
— Japanese–American relations and the U.S.–China détente: what balance between the two? (Part One). *Asian Quarterly*, 1978/3, pp. 173–88.
— Japanese–American relations and the U.S.–China détente . . . (Part Two). *Asia Quarterly*, 1978/4, pp. 247–62.
Solomon, Richard H., Thinking through the China problem. *Foreign Affairs 56*, no. 2, January 1978.
Sredhaar, Sino–American trade. *China Report 12*, no. 3, May–June 1976, pp. 3–6.
Stone, I. F., *The Hidden History of the Korean War*. New York: Monthly Review Press, 1952.
Tsou, Tang, *The Embroilment over Quemoy: Mao, Chiang and Dulles*. Salt Lake City: University of Utah, Institute of International Studies, International Study Paper no. 2, 1959.
— Mao's limited war in the Taiwan Straits. *Orbis 3*, Fall 1959, pp. 332–50.
The United States and Mainland China. *Current Scene 9*, no. 3, 7 March 1971, pp. 21–4.
U.S. moves on China trade and travel. *Current Scene 9*, no. 5, 7 May 1971, pp. 15–17.
Whiting, Allen S., *China Crosses The Yalu*. New York: Macmillan, 1960.
Williams, Philip Maynard, *Crisis Management: Confrontation in the Nuclear Age*. London: Martin Robertson, 1976.
Wu, Yuan-li and Ling, H. C., *As Peking Sees Us: People's War in United States and Communist China's American Policy*. Standford, Calif.: Hoover Institute Press, 1969.

Sino–Soviet Relations

Adie, W. A. C., China, Russia and the Third World. *China Quarterly*, July–September 1962, pp. 200–13.
Alexeyev, I. and Apalin, G., Peking's ideological subversion. *International Affairs* (Moscow), October 1975, pp. 42–54.
Bettati, Mario, *Le conflit sino–soviétique*. Paris: A. Colin, 1971.
Cheverney, Julien, *Les deux stratégies du communisme*. Paris: Julliard, Collections Preuves, 1965.
Ch'ien Chao, Peiping–Moscow confrontation in Indochina. *Issues and Studies 14*, no. 3, March 1978, pp. 59–72.
Ch'ing-yao, Yin, Peiping–Moscow relations: a general review. *Issues and Studies 14*, no. 3, March 1978, pp. 14–33.

Clemens, Walter C. Jr, *The Arms Race and Sino–Soviet Relations.* Stanford, Calif.: Stanford University, 1968.

Clubb, O, Edmund, *China and Russia: The 'Great Game'.* New York: Columbia University Press, 1971.

Le Conflit sino-soviétique: nouveau risque de tragédie mondiale. *Le monde diplomatique,* October 1969.

Crankshaw, Edward, *The New Cold War. Moscow vs Peking.* Harmondsworth: Penguin Books, 1963.

Fetjö, François, *Chine–U.R.S.S.: le conflit.* Paris: Plon, 1966.

Fitzgerald, C. P., The Sino–Soviet border conflict. *Pacific Community,* January 1970, pp. 27–83.

Floyd, David, *Mao Against Khrushchev.* New York: Praeger, 1963.

Garthoff, Raymond L., Sino–Soviet military relations. *Annals of the American Academy of Political and Social Sciences,* no. 349, September 1963, pp. 81–93.

Gelman, Harry, The Sino–Soviet conflict: a survey. *Problems of Communism,* March–April, 1964, pp. 3–15.

Gittings, John, *Survey of the Sino–Soviet Dispute: a commentary and extracts from the recent polemics, 1963–67.* London: Oxford University Press, 1968.

Griffith, William E., *Sino–Soviet Relations 1964–65.* Cambridge, Mass.: M.I.T. Press, 1966.

Halperin, Morton H. (ed.), *Sino–Soviet Relations and Arms Control.* Cambridge, Mass.: M.I.T. Press, 1967.

Hinton, Harold C., Sino–Soviet relations in the Brezhnev era. *Current History 61,* no. 361, September 1971, pp. 135–41.

— *The Bear at the Gate: Chinese Policy Making under Soviet Pressure.* Washington, D.C.: American Enterprise Institute for Public Policy Research, 1971.

Holloway, J. K., Jr, Sea power and the Sino–Soviet split. *Current Scene 11,* no. 12, December 1973, pp. 6–12.

Horn, Robert C., China and Russia in 1977: Màoism without Mao. *Asian Survey 17,* no. 10, October 1977, pp. 919–30.

Hsieh, A. L., The Sino–Soviet nuclear dialogue, 1963. *Bulletin of the Atomic Scientists 21,* January 1965, pp. 16–21.

Hudson, G. F., Mao, Marx and Moscow. *Foreign Affairs 37,* no. 4, July 1959, pp. 561–73.

— The Peking–Moscow axis: who is top dog? *Commentary 26,* no. 6, December 1958, pp. 492–8.

Hudson, G., Lowenthal, Richard and MacFarquhar, R.,*The Sino–Soviet Dispute.* New York: Praeger, 1961.

Lowenthal, Richard, The charged antagonist. *Encounter 16,* no. 1, January 1961, pp. 48–53.

— Shifts & rifts in Russo–Chinese alliance. *Problems of Communism 8,* no. 1, January–February 1959, pp. 14–23.

— Russia and China: controlled conflict. *Foreign Affairs 49,* no. 3, April 1971, pp. 507–18.

— The Sino–Soviet dispute, *Commentary 31,* no. 5, May 1961, pp. 379–94.

Lukacs, George, Reflections on the Sino–Soviet dispute. *Studies on the Left 4,* no. 1, Winter 1964, pp. 22–38.

MacFarquhar, Roderick, China and Russia: the first decade. *Commentary,* May 1960, pp. 399–404.

Mackintosh, Malcolm, Military aspects of the Sino–Soviet dispute. *Bulletin of the Atomic Scientists 21,* no. 10, October 1965, pp. 14–17.

Mancall, Mark, Russia and China, perennial conflict. *Problems of Communism 12,* no. 2, March–April 1963, pp. 60–8.

Maxwell, Neville, Russia and China: the irresponsible conflict. *Pacific Community*, July 1970, pp. 551–63.

Mehnert, Klaus, Soviet–Chinese relations. *International Affairs 35*, no. 4, October 1959, pp. 417–26.

Méray, Tibor, *La rupture Moscou–Pékin*. Paris: Editions R. Laffont, 1966.

Mitchell, R. Judson, The Sino–Soviet conflict and the Marxist–Leninist theory of development. *Studies in Comparative Communism*, Spring–Summer, 1974, pp. 119–45.

North, R. C., The Sino–Soviet controversy. *Current Scene 1*, no. 29, 5 April 1962.

Oton, Ambrez, *Realignment of World Power; the Russo–Chinese Schism under the Impact of Mao Tse-tung's Last Revolution*, 2 vols. New York: R. Speller, 1972.

Peking and Moscow view the issues. *Current Scene 11*, no. 5, May 1973, pp. 5–7.

Salisbury, Harrison E., *The Coming War between Russia and China*. London: Secker and Warburg, Pan Books, 1969.

Scalapino, Robert A., Moscow, Peking and the communist parties of Asia. *Foreign Affairs 41*, no. 2, January 1963, pp. 323–43.

Semyonov, Y., Beijing's policy constitutes a military threat. *International Affairs* (Moscow), April 1979, pp. 64–74.

— China: Maoist line. *International Affairs* (Moscow), July 1977, pp. 57–67.

Simmons, Robert A., The Peking–Pyongyang–Moscow triangle. *Current Scene 8*, no. 17, 7 November 1970, pp. 8–18.

Labedz, L., The Soviet Union and 'The Great Proletarian' Cultural Revolution. *Survey*, no. 63, April 1967, pp. 1–7.

Stolypine, A. and Stolypine, D., *La Mongolie entre Moscou et Pékin*. Paris: Stock, 1971.

Thomson, J. R., Sino–Soviet relations. *Current History 61*, no. 361, September 1971, pp. 210–14.

Toma, Peter A., Sociometric measurements of the Sino–Soviet conflict: peaceful and non-peaceful revolution. *The Journal of Politics 30*, no. 3, August 1968, pp. 732–48.

Whiting, Allen S., Contradictions in the Moscow–Peking axis. *The Journal of Politics 20*, February 1958, pp. 128–42.

— Dynamics of the Moscow–Peking axis. *Annals of the American Academy of Political and Social Sciences 321*, January 1959, pp. 127–61.

Zagoria, D. S., *The Sino–Soviet Conflict 1956–61*. Princeton, NJ: Princeton University Press, 1962.

China and the Third World

Adie, W. A. C., China and the Bandung genie. *Current Scene 3*, no. 19, 15 May 1965, pp. 1–14.

Blake, Alex, Peking's African adventures. *Current Scene 5*, no. 15, 15 September 1967, pp. 1–9.

Detour from Algiers: Chinese 'splittism' and Afro–Asian Solidarity. *Current Scene 3*, no. 31, 15 November 1965, pp. 2–10.

Hutchinson, Alan, *China's African Revolution*. Westview: Boulder, Co., 1976.

Ismael, T. Y., The People's Republic of China and Africa. *Journal of Modern African Studies 9*, no. 4, December 1971, pp. 507–29.

Johnson, Cecil, China and Latin America – new ties and tactics. *Problems of Communism 21*, July–August 1972, pp. 53–66.

Joyaux, François, *Chinese Policies in the Third World*. Paris: Institut National des Langues et Civilisations Orientales, 1972.

Larkin, Bruce D., *China and Africa 1949–70*. Berkeley: University of California Press, 1971.
—China and the Third World, *Current History 69*, no. 408, September 1975, pp. 75–9 ff.
London, Kurt, Communism in Africa: the role of China. *Problems of Communism 11*, no. 4, July–August 1962, pp. 22–7.
Newhauser, Charles, *Third World Politics: China and the Afro–Asian People's Solidarity Organization 1957–1967*. London: Oxford University Press, 1969.
On power polarity and national liberation movements, *Current Scene 11*, no. 3, March 1973, pp. 9–10.
Prybyla, Jan S., Foreign aid: the Chinese are coming. *Current History 61*, no. 361, September 1971, pp. 142–7.
Richer, Philipe, Doctrine chinoise pour le Tiers Monde. *Politique étrangère 1*, 1965, pp. 75–97.
— *La Chine et le Tiers Monde, 1949–1969*. Paris: Fayot, 1971.
Rubenstein, Alvin Z. (ed.), *Soviet and Chinese Influence in the Third World*. New York: Praeger, 1975.
Sinha, Mira, Strategic rediscovery of the Third World. *China Report 10*, no. 3, May–June 1974, pp. 44–55.
Staar, Richard F., Moscow–Peiping competition in the Third World. *Issues and Studies 14*, no. 10, October 1978, pp. 42–58.
Thornton, Thomas Perry, Peking, Moscow and the underdeveloped areas. *World Politics 13*, July 1961, pp. 491–504.
Tsou, Tang and Halperin, Morton H., Mao Tse-tung's revolutionary strategy and Peking's international behavour. *The American Political Science Review 59*, March 1965, pp. 80–99.
Van Ness, Peter, China and the Third World. *Current History 67*, no. 397, 1974, pp. 106–9.
—*Revolution and Chinese Foreign Policy: Peking's Support for Wars of National Liberation*. London: University of California Press, 1970.
Weinstein, Warren (ed.), *Chinese and Soviet Aid to Africa*. New York: Praeger, 1975.
Weiss, Udo, China's aid to and trade with the developing countries of the Third World. *Asia Quarterly*, 1974/3, pp. 203–13, 1974/4, pp. 263–310.
Yu, George T., *China's Africa Policy: A Study of Tanzania*. New York: Praeger, 1975.
— Peking's African diplomacy. *Problems of Communism 21*, March–April 1972, pp. 16–24.
— China and the Third World. *Asian Survey 17*, no. 11, November 1977, pp. 1036–48.
— China's impact. *Problems of Communism 27*, January–February 1978, pp. 40–50.

Asia in China's Foreign Policy

Addy, Premen, South Asia in China's foreign policy: a view from the left. *Journal of Contemporary Asia 2*, no. 4, 1972, pp. 403–14.
Bandyopadhyaya, Jayantanusa, The role of the external powers in South Asian affairs. *India Quarterly 30*, no. 4, October–December 1974.
Barnds, William J., China's relations with Pakistan: durability amidst discontinuity. *The China Quarterly*, no. 63, September 1965, pp. 436–89.
—Japan and its mainland neighbours: an end to equidistance? *International Affairs 52*, no. 1, January 1976, pp. 29–38.
Bert, Wayne, Revolutionary ideology and Chinese foreign policy – the case of South and South East Asia. *International Relations 4*, no. 6, November 1974, pp. 688–714.
Buchan, Alistair (ed.), *China and the Peace of Asia*. London: Chatto and Windus for the Institute for Strategic Studies, 1965.

Butwell, Richard, China and other Asian lands. *Current History*, September 1972, pp. 121–5 ff.

Camilleri, Joseph, *Southeast Asia in China's Foreign Policy*, Occasional Paper No. 29. Singapore: Institute of Southeast Asian Studies, April 1975.

Ch'ing-yao, Yin, Peiping–Hanoi conflict: origins and development. *Issues and Studies 14*, no. 10, October 1978.

Choudhury, Golam W., Post-Mao policy in Asia. *Problems of Communism 26*, July–August 1977, pp. 18–29.

Clark, Gregory, Sino–Japanese relations: an analysis. *Australian Outlook 25*, no. 1, April 1971, pp. 58–68.

Clubb, O. Edmund, China, Russia and East Asia. *Pacific Community*, no. 4, July 1972.

Cohen, Stephen P., Security issues in South Asia. *Asian Survey 15*, no. 3, March 1975, pp. 203–15.

Copper, John F., China and Sri Lanka: an old friendship renewed. *Asia Quarterly*, 1975/2, pp. 101–10.

Das, D. P., Soviet Union, China and the Indian Ocean. *China Report 9*, no. 1, January–February 1973, pp. 9–22.

Fall, Bernard B., Red China's aims in South Asia. *Current History 43*, no. 253, September 1962, pp. 136–41 ff.

Fitzgerald, C. P., *China and Southeast Asia Since 1945*. Melbourne: Longman, November 1972.

Fitzgerald, Stephen, *China and the Overseas Chinese*. London: Cambridge University Press, 1972.

Fontaine, J. P., Liens diplomatiques entre la Chine et les Philippines. *Asia Quarterly*, 1976/1, pp. 69–72.

Friedman, Edward, China, Pakistan, Bangladesh. *Bulletin of Concerned Asian Scholars 4*, no. 1, Winter 1972, pp. 99–108.

Fukui, Haruhiro, Japan's new relationship with China. *Current History 68*, no. 404, April 1975, pp. 163–8 ff.

Gordon, Bernard K., Japan, the United States and Southeast Asia. *Foreign Affairs 56*, no. 3, April 1978, pp. 579–600.

Gurtov, Melvin, *China and South East Asia: The Politics of Survival*. Lexington, Mass.: Heath Lexington Books, 1971.

— Sino–Soviet relations and S.E. Asia: recent developments and future possibilities. *Pacific Affairs 43*, no. 4, Winter 1970–71, pp. 491–505.

Hamel, Bernard, Aspects de la rivalité sino–soviétique en Asie du Sud-Est. *Politique étrangère*, 43c année, no. 2, 1978, pp. 199–208.

Hellman, Donald C., *China and Japan: A New Balance of Power*. Lexington, Mass.: Lexington Books, 1976.

Hensman, C. R., China: how wrong how dangerous. *Journal of Contemporary Asia*, no. 3, 1973.

Hoadley, J. S., Sino–Jananese relations 1950–1970: an application of the linkage model of international politics. *International Studies Quarterly 15*, no. 2, June 1971, pp. 131–58.

Holmes, Robert A., China–Burma relations since the rift. *Asian Survey 12*, no. 8, August 1972, pp. 686–700.

— The Sino–Burmese rift – a failure for China. *Orbis 16*, no. 1, Spring 1972, pp. 211–36.

Hsiao, Gene T. Prospects for a new Sino–Japanese relationship. *The China Quarterly*, no. 60, October–December 1974, pp. 720–49.

— *The Role of the External Powers in the Indo–China Crisis*. Edwardsville: South Illinois University, 1973.

— The Sino–Japanese rapprochement: a relationship of ambivalence. *The China Quarterly*, no. 57, January–March 1974, pp. 101–23.

Johnson, C., How China and Japan see each other. *Foreign Affairs 50*, no. 4, July 1972, pp. 711–21.

Kapur, Ashok, India and China: adversaries or potential partners. *World Today 30*, no. 3, March 1974, pp. 129–34.

Kato, Shuichi, *The Japan–China Phenomenon: Conflict or Compatibility?* (translated from the Japanese by David Chibbett). London: Paul Norbury Publications, 1974.

Kaushik, B. M., Japan–China peace pact: problems and prospects. *China Report 11*, nos 5–6, September–December 1975, pp. 17–21.

Kim, Hong N., Anti-hegemonism and the politics of the Sino–Japanese peace treaty: a study in the Miki government's China policy. *Asia Quarterly*, 1977/2, pp. 101–20.

Langer, Paul F., The Soviet Union, China, and the revolutionary movement in Laos. *Studies in Comparative Communism 6*, nos 1–2, Spring–Summer 1973, pp. 66–98.

Laurel, Salvador H., The Philippines: shaping a China policy. *Pacific Community*, no. 4, July 1972.

Lee, Chae-Jin, The politics of Sino–Japanese trade relations, 1963–68. *Pacific Affairs 42*, no. 2, Summer 1969, pp. 129–44.

Maxwell, Neville, *India's China War*. London: Jonathan Cape, 1970.

Mende, Tibor, *Soleils levants: le Japan et la Chine*. Paris: Editions du Seuil, 1975.

Mohan, Ram, *Politics of Sino–Indian Confrontation*. New Delhi: Delhi Vika Publishing House, 1973.

Mozingo, David P., China's relations with her Asian neighbours. *Current History 47*, no. 277, September 1964, pp. 156–61ff.

Mustafa, Zubeida, The 1971 crisis in Pakistan: India, the Soviet Union and China. *Pacific Community*, no. 3, April 1972.

Muthiram, T.G., China's policy in South East Asia. *Journal of Contemporary Asia*, no. 3, 1973, pp. 335–46.

Palmer, Norman D., China's relations with India and Pakistan. *Current History*, September 1971, pp. 148–53.

Pettman, Ralph, *China in Burma's Foreign Policy*, Contemporary China Papers, no. 7. Canberra: A.N.U. Press, 1973.

Ramachandran, K.N., US–USSR–China triangle: impact on Southeast Asia. *China Report 12*, no. 1, January–February 1976, pp. 50–7.

Reisky De Dubnic, Vladimir, The global realignment of forces, its impact and the Indochina question. *Asia Quarterly*, 1974/1, pp. 17–41.

Saywell, William, Japan's role in the Pacific and China's response. *International Journal 26*, no. 3, Summer 1971, pp. 507–21.

Seiichi, Tagawa, Don't forget the well-diggers. *Japan Quarterly 26*, no. 1, January–March 1979, pp. 18–34.

Seth, S. P., China as a factor in Indo–Pakistani politics. *The World Today 25*, January–December 1969, pp. 36–46.

— Sino–Indian relations: changing perspectives. *Problems of Communism 23*, March–April 1974.

Sharma, Pool Kumar, *India, Pakistan, China and the Contemporary World*. London: Books from India, 1972.

Shin'ichiro, Shiramishi, The potential for economic co-operation. *Japan Quarterly 26*, no. 1, January–March 1979, pp. 35–45.

Simon, Sheldon W., China, the Soviet Union and the subcontinental balance. *Asian Survey 13*, no. 7, July 1973, pp. 647–58.

—The Japan–China–U.S.S.R. triangle. *Pacific Affairs 47*, no. 2, Summer 1974, pp. 125–38.

— Some aspects of China's Asian policy in the Cultural Revolution and its aftermath. *Pacific Affairs 44*, no. 1, Spring 1971, pp. 18–38.

— New conflict in Indochina. *Problems of Communism 27*, September–October 1978, pp. 20–36.

Tao, Jay, Mao's world outlook: Vietnam and the revolution in China. *Asian Survey 8*, no. 5, May 1968, pp. 416–32.

Taylor, Jay, *China and South East Asia: Peking's Relations with Revolutionary Movements*, Praeger Special Studies in International Politics and Government. New York: Praeger, 1974.

Tsurutani, Taketsugu, Japan, China and East Asian security. *Asia Quarterly*, 1973/3, pp. 221–42.

Van der Kroef, Justus M., Before the thaw: recent Indonesian attitudes towards People's China. *Asian Survey 13*, no. 5, May 1973, pp. 513–30.

— The 'Malaysian formula': model for future Sino–Southeast Asian relations? *Asia Quarterly*, 1974/4, pp. 311–37.

Whiting, Allen S., *The Chinese Calculus of Deterrence: India and Indochina*. Ann Arbor: The University of Michigan Press, 1975.

Wilson, D., Sino–Soviet revalry in South-East Asia. *Problems of Communism 23*, no. 5, September–October 1974, pp. 39–51.

Zagoria, Donald S., *Vietnam Triangle: Moscow, Peking, Hanoi*, New York: Pegasus, 1967.

Contemporary Developments

Adie, W. A. C., Peking's revolutionary diplomatic line. *Pacific Community 4*, no. 3, April 1973, pp. 356–75.

Armstrong, J. D., Peking's foreign policy: perceptions and changes. *Current Scene 11*, no. 6, June 1973, pp. 1–9.

Bailey, S. D., China and the United Nations. *World Today 27*, no. 9, September 1971, pp. 365–72.

Barnds, William J., *China and America: The Search for a New Relationship*. New York: New York University Press, 1977.

Barnett, A. Doak, *China Policy—Old Problems and New Challenges*. Washington, D.C.: The Brookings Institution, 1977.

Bettelheim, Charles, The great leap backward. *Monthly Review 30*, no. 3, July–August 1978, pp. 37–130.

Beyond Normalization: Report on the U.N.A.–U.S.A. National Policy Panel to Study U.S.–China Relations. New York: United Nations Association of the U.S.A., 1979.

Boardman, Robert, Chinese diplomacy and the United Nations. *Contemporary Review 219*, no. 1268, September 1971, pp. 155–60.

Bonavia, David, The fate of the 'new born things' of China's Cultural Revolution *Pacific Affairs 51*, no. 2, Summer 1978, pp. 177–94.

Brugger, Bill, *Contemporary China*. London: Croom Helm, 1977.

Camilleri, J., The new phase in Chinese foreign policy. *World Review 13*, no. 2, July 1974. pp. 32–41.

Chang, Parris H., The passing of the Maoist era. *Asian Survey 16*, no. 11, November 1976, pp. 997–1011.

Chauvel, J., La Chine et les Nations Unies. *Politique étrangère 37*, no. 1, 1972.

Chen, King C. (ed.), *China and the Three Worlds*. New York: M.E. Sharpe, 1979.

China and the seas. *Current Scene 11*, no. 6, June 1973, pp. 10–12.

China on raw materials and development. *Current Scene 12*, no. 6, June 1974, pp. 9–12.

China's new diplomacy: a symposium, Parts 1 and 2. *Problems of Communism 20*, November–December 1971, and *21*, January–February 1972, pp. 48–70.

Chiou, C. L., Chinese communist leadership crisis and new foreign policy in the aftermath of the Cultural Revolution. *World Review 11*, no. 3, September 1972, pp. 14–27.

Chung, Tan, From great disorder to great order, The Eleventh Party Congress and the continuous revolution. *China Report 13*, no. 6, November–December 1977.

Clemens, Walter C. Jr, The impact of détente on Chinese and Soviet communism. *Journal of International Affairs 28*, no. 2, 1974, pp. 133–57.

Dernberger, Robert F., Prospects for the Chinese economy. *Problems of Communism 28*, September–December 1979, pp. 1–15.

Deshpande, G. P., China's foreign policy in the seventies. *Economic and Political Weekly 5*, no. 16, 18 April 1970, pp. 677–80.

Domes, Jürgen, The 'gang of four' – and Hua Kuo-feng: analysis of political events in 1975–76. *China Quarterly*, no. 71, September 1977, pp. 473–97.

Eiland, Michael D., Military modernization and China's economy. *Asian Survey 17*, no. 12, December 1977, pp. 1143–57.

Fitzgerald, C. P., *Changing Directions in Chinese Foreign Policy*, Roy Milne Memorial Lecture, 1971. Canberra: Australian Institute of International Affairs, 1971.

Fitzgerald, Stephen, China in the next decade: an end to isolation? *Australian Journal of Political History 17*, no. 1, April 1971, pp. 33–42.

Fraser, Angus M., Military modernization in China. *Problems of Communism 28*, September–December 1979, pp. 16–33.

Funnell, V. C., China and South East Asia: the new phase. *World Today 28*, August 1972, pp. 334–41.

Gelman, Harry, Outlook for Sino–Soviet relations. *Problems of Communism 28*, September–December 1979, pp. 50–66.

Gittings, J., China's foreign policy: continuity or change. *Journal of Contemporary Asia 2*, no. 1, 1972, pp. 17–33.

– A diplomatic thaw. *Far Eastern Economic Review*, 19 December 1968, pp. 663–5.

Goodstadt, Leo, *China's Watergate: Political and Economic Conflict in China, 1969–1977*. Atlantic Highlands, N.J.: Humanities Press, 1979.

Harrison, Selig S., *China, Oil and Asia: Conflict Ahead?* New York: Columbia University Press for the Carnegie Endowment for International Peace, 1977.

Hinton, Harold C., *China's Foreign Policy: Recent Developments*, Asian Studies Occasional Paper Series no. 8. Edwardsville: Southern Illinois University at Edwardsville, 1973.

Isenberg, Irwin (ed.), *China: New Force in World Affairs*. New York: The M. W. Wilson Company, 1972.

Jencks, Harlan W., China's 'Punitive War' on Vietnam: A military assessment. *Asian Survey 19*, no. 8, August 1979, pp. 801–15.

Kim, S. S., The People's Republic of China in the United Nations: a preliminary analysis. *World Politics 26*, no. 3, April 1974, pp. 299–331.

— *China, the United Nations and World Order*. Princeton, N.J.: Princeton University Press, 1979.

Kinter, William R. and Copper, John F., *A Matter of Two Chinas*. Philadelphia: Foreign Policy Research Institute, 1979.

Kuo-hsiung, Lin, One year after Peiping's admission to the United Nations. *Issues and Studies 9*, no. 3, December 1972, pp. 39–48.

Lieberthal, Kenneth, The foreign policy debate in Peking as seen through allegorical articles 1973–76. *China Quarterly* no. 71, September 1977, pp. 528–54.

Lim Joo-Joek, *Geo-Strategy and the South China Basin*. Singapore: Singapore University Press (for the Institute of Southeast Asian Studies), 1979.

Louis, Victor, *The Coming Decline of the Chinese Empire*. New York: Times Books, 1979.

Luard, E., China and the United Nations. *International Affairs* (London) *47*, no. 4, October 1971, pp. 729–44.

Mendl, Wolf, *Issues in Japan's China Policy*. London: Macmillan, 1978.

Middleton, Drew, *The Duel of the Giants: China and Russia in Asia*. New York: Scribner, 1978.

Moody, Peter R., Jr, The fall of the gang of four: background notes on the Chinese counter revolution. *Asian Survey 17*, no. 8, August 1977.

Morrison, Kent, Peking's foreign economic policy since Chou En-lai. *China Report 13*, no. 3, May–June 1977, pp. 30–40.

Myers, Raymond H. (ed.), *Two Chinese States: U.S. Foreign Policy and Interests*, Stanford, California: Hoover Institution Press, 1978.

Nguyen Mark Hung, The Sino–Vietnamese conflict: Power play among Communist neighbours, *Asian Survey 19*, no. 11, November 1979, pp. 1037–52.

Ojha, I.C., Recent trends in Chinese foreign policy. *Social Science* (Winfield) *47*, no. 3, July 1972, pp. 134–45.

Okita Saburo, Japan, China and the United States: Economic relations and prospects, *Foreign Affairs 57*, no. 5, Summer 1979, pp. 1090–110.

Oksenberg, Michel, The strategies of Peking. *Foreign Affairs 50*, no. 1, October 1971, pp. 15–29.

Oksenberg, Michel and Oxnam, Robert B. (eds.), *Dragon and Eagle: United States–China Relations: Past and Future*. New York: Basic Books, 1978.

Peking and the territorial waters issue. *Current Scene 10*, no. 4, 10 April 1972, pp. 18–19.

Pye, Lucian W., The puzzles of Chinese pragmatism. *Foreign Policy*, no. 31, Summer 1978, pp. 119–36.

Scalapino, Robert A., The policies of the post-Mao era: an examination of the 11th Party Congress, *Asian Survey 17*, no. 11, November 1977, pp. 1049–60.

Seth, S. P., China's foreign policy – post Cultural Revolution. *Asia Quarterly*, 1976 %2, pp. 137–55.

Simon, Sheldon W., China, Vietnam, and ASEAN: The politics of polarization. *Asian Survey 19*, no. 12, December 1979, pp. 1171–88.

Starr, John Bryan, China in 1974: 'weeding through the old to bring forth the new. *Asian Survey 15*, no. 1, January 1975, pp. 1–19.

— From the 10th Party Congress to the premiership of Hua Kuo-feng: the significance of the colour of the cat. *The China Quarterly*, no. 67, September 1976, pp. 457–88.

Sutter, Robert G., *China Watch: Toward Sino–American Reconciliation*. Baltimore, Md.: Johns Hopkins University Press, 1978.

Terrill, Ross, *The Future of China*. Adelaide: Rigby Limited, 1978.

— China and the world: self-reliance or interdependence, *Foreign Affairs 55*, no. 2, January 1977, pp. 295–305.

The United States, China and Japan: A Report to the Senate Committee on Foreign Relations. Washington: Government Printing Office, 1979.

Tretiak, Daniel, Is China preparing to 'turn out'? Changes in Chinese levels of attention to the international environment, *Asian Survey 11*, no. 3, March 1971, pp. 219–37.

Trivière, Leon, L'impressionnate offensive diplomatique de la Chine. *Etudes*, October 1971, pp. 373–96.

— Pekin à l'O.N.U.: Taipei exclu. *Etudes*, January 1972, pp. 61–73.

Vasconi, L., Cina 1971 (China 1971). *Affari esteri 3*, no. 11, July 1971, pp. 23–39.

Vernant, Jacques, La Chine dans le nouveau contexte international. *Politique étrangère 34*, 1969, pp. 397–403.

Watts, Williams, Packard, George R., Clough, Ralph N. and Oxnam, Robert B., *Japan, Korea and China: American Perceptions and Policies*, Lexington, Mass.: Lexington Books, 1979.

Whiting, Allen S., China after Mao. *Asian Survey 17*, no. 11, November 1977, pp. 1028–35.

— and Dernberger, Robert F., *China's Future: Foreign Policy and Economic Development in the Post–Mao Era*. New York: McGraw–Hill, 1977.

Yahuda, Michael B., China's new era of international relations. *Political Quarterly 43*, September 1972, pp. 295–307.

— China's new foreign policy. *The World Today 28*, no. 1, January 1972, pp. 14–22.

— *China's Role in World Affairs*. London: Croom Helm, 1978.

— China's new outlook: the end of isolationism. *The World Today 35*, no. 5, May 1979, pp. 180–8.

Yeh, K. C., Foreign trade under the Hua regime: policy, performance and prospects. *Issues and Studies 14*, no. 8, August 1978, pp. 12–43.

Index